LIBERTY ROADS

The American logistics in France and in Germany, 1944-45

by Nicolas AUBIN

Maps by Antonin Collet and Clémence Barbereau, Schemes by J.B and J.M. Mongin, colors profiles by Nicholas Gohin

Translated from the French by Lawrence Brown

Histoire & Collections

*"In memory of my Father
Who on to transmittedme the passion of the History
dnd an enjoyment in the idea was made
To see me published."*

Work published with the cooperation of
Conseil général de la Manche

Histoire & Collections 2014

ROADS OF EUROPE	4
ABOLISHING THE TYRANNY OF DISTANCE	6
REVOLUTION IN WASHINGTON	8
1940, a fragmented logistical system	8
Mac Narney, le great organizer of Washington	8
Somervell and the great clear up of July 1942	10
WORLD WAR, GLOBAL WAR	12
Theory of distribution	12
Flow Mechanism	17
THE ART OF PLANNING	23
LOGISTIC AND STRATEGY, THE MASTER PLAN	24
The Master plan	24
The logistical implication of *Overlord*	25
THE BATTLE OF NORMANDY, THE ORDEAL BY FIRE	34
D-Day	34
The Highs and lows of the Engineer Special Brigades	44
Cherbourg	56
The impact on operations	61
BRONTOSAUR AND LEVIATHAN	66
FROM EUPHORIA TO DESILLUSION	68
THE BREAKOUT	68
At the river Seine 11 days ahead the schedule	68
How could they keep the motorised spearheads supplied?	72
The Master Plan is wound up	78
THE RED BALL EXPRESS (AUGUST-SEPTEMBER 1944)	92
At the heart of the Red Ball Express	92
A Human adventure	104
Supplying the Combat Zone	110
THE DRIVERS WERE NOT ALONE	114
The Air Force to the Rescue	114
the little known achievement of the railroad engineers	115
Pipes to win the war?	119
GROUND TO A HALT	122
Four Month of crisis	122
240 ships at anchor!	129
When were the crisis overcome?	139
THE INQUEST	141
A GAMBLE THAT DID NOT PAY OFF	142

Piecemeal solutions that broke up the logistical chain	142
The Black Market	146
An extravagant Army	147
A Muddled Strategy	148
The miracle of the Wehrmacht	148
A LACK OF HEAVY TRUCKS	150
the GMC, a stop-gap solution	150
Why so few heavy trucks?	151
The spare parts Nightmare	156
MUDDLED STRUCTURES THAT FAVOURED CONFRONTATIONS	164
The difficult integration of the ASF	164
ComZ, a failing administration?	169
THE FAULT IN THE DOCTRIN	174
What was the doctrin of the US Army?	174
The impossible return of the depth operational, the regulation of 1941	175
Logistic principles in agrement with the doctrin	178
REVOLUTION?	183
AT THE SCHOOL OF WAR	184
Learn the shortage	184
The innovation by the example, the Ordnance Corps	185
On the road again	186
1945, PROGRESS CONSIDERABLE	188
The inventors of the operational logistics	189
Road supplant Railroads	190
A Revolution?	191
ALONE IN THE WORLD	194
The Blitzkrieg, negation of the logistics	194
Soviet logistics and operational art of War	200
A spendthrift Germany	204
The Soviet doctrine without means	206
General informations	208
CONCLUSION	210
APPENDIX	212
A revealing case study, the Jerrycan	212
The workhorses	216
Profiles	218
Bibliography	222

ROADS OF EUROPE

In 1950, the military historian S.L.A. The Marshall noticed that *"the soldiers of the American Expeditionary Force of 1918 had used several million tons less than the surplus supplies left behind by the GIs in 1944-1945, from the Normandy beaches to the river Elbe"*.

This observation, but also Roosevelt's declaration of the United States being the arsenal of democracy, the war correspondent photos showing thousands of ships anchored in the Bay of the Seine, or never ending GMC convoys rolling along the *Red Ball Express Highway*, the memories of French kids discovering chewing gum that was so generously given away, would be the overwhelming proof that the GI lacked nothing and was able to crush a fly with a bulldozer, or more concretely, any small suspicious copse with a salvo of 155mm shells. Today, if there was ever a cliché associated with the US Army, it would be that of its abundant and well-oiled logistics. To say that it led to the birth of a logistical revolution is stating the obvious.

However, how many people are aware that from mid-June 1944 up to December, the artillery units were rationed to such an extent that by October, 80% of shells fired by XX Corps were German shells ? How many people know that the GMC was a vehicle ill-suited for long distance transport? Who knows that when the American army landed in France it had a logistical doctrine that was based on that of the First World War and which was largely dependent on rail and, therefore, ill suited to motorised warfare ? If there was a logistical revolution it was during the course of the campaign that it took place and not beforehand. It is true to say that the lack of interest, or the fact that it is looked down upon, has largely contributed to it remaining an unknown subject. Although most D-Day authors are quick to underline the vital character of logistics, they quickly leave behind the dry statistics of the Transportation Corps and dissect each phase of fighting instead. However, in the United States a historical study of military logistics has bloomed. As an extension of the US Army's historical branch that has published, since 1945, thousands of pages concerning the behind the lines service branches, researchers like James A. Huston[1], Henry Eccles[2] or more recently Charles Shrader[3], have dedicated their research to this domain.

In France, the only historian to have acquired any real recognition is the Israeli Martin van Creveld who, in his Supplying War, Logistics from Wallenstein to Patton, defends the iconoclast thesis that accuses the US Army of having become, in 1944, an army swollen with accountants that kept a tight rein on its generals and thus prolonging the end of the war. This book has never been translated into French and the torch of American logistics in Europe has been held aloft by only a few passionate and knowledgeable people who have focused on various aspects such as the port of Cherbourg, the jerrycan or the GMC[4], all of which are merely accounts or technical publications that never look at logistics from every angle. This book looks at last at only logistics, agreeing on the meaning given

---

1. James A Huston, *The sinews of war*, CMH, 1966.
2. Henry E. Eccles, *Logistics in the National defence*, Stackpole Press, 1959
3. Charles R. Shrader, *United States military Logistics, 1607-1991: A research Guide*, Greenwood Press, 1992.
4. ess, 1992.
4 Robert Lerouvillois, *Et la liberté vint de Cherbourg*, Ed Charles Corlet, 1991, Philippe Léger, *Jerrycan*, Heimdal, 2008, Jean Michel Boniface & Jean Gabriel Jeudy, *GMC, un camion universel*, EPA, 1978 and *Véhicules de l'US Army 1939-1945*, EPA, 1987.

to this word, as it is polysemous, and is almost anachronistic for the American army during World War II, which preferred at the time to use terms such as *"Administration"* or *"Administrative Support"*.

Literally, the word logistics has a double Greek origin: Logistikos, *"skilled in calculus"* and *Logisteuo*, *"administrate"*. In the shape of *"logista"*, the word enters into the Roman and Byzantine military vocabulary in order to designate officers tasked with the movement of legions, organizing night camps and supply dumps in conquered towns. Theorist Antoine Henri de Jomini, in his 1838 Art of War, found the origin of the word in the former rank of *"major-général des logis, a sort of officer who used to billet troops or set up camps, lead columns, or position them in the field"*[5]. Jomini conferred logistics a certain nobility, as he called it *"the practical art of moving armies"*. This ambitious definition can be found in the 1926 Fort Leavenworth General Service Schools manual concerning the *"art of planning and undertaking movement, evacuation and supplies"*. However, in the meantime the prism of *"logistics"* had widened. Under the impetus of Colonel Charles C. Thorpe in 1917 it transformed into *"a science that provided the means to wage war"*.

On a strategic level it integrated all of the design and manufacturing tasks linked with the civilian world and which led Thorpe's historian Stanley Falk to write that logistics is *"more than distribution, it is a war economy, including industrial mobilisation, research and development, raising funds, but also the recruitment of troops and their training."*[6] Logistics in a global war extends beyond a purely military context and encompasses the mobilisation of the whole nation united in the war effort. However, this definition was not unanimously agreed on. In 1949, a manual for the use of American forces envisaged logistics as being the *"the means of getting the right person and the right supplies to the right place at the right time and in good condition"*[7]. Historian James A. Huston sums up the idea that logistics is the *"application to war of the factors of time and space and takes into account the three Ms : Materiel, Movement and Maintenance"*[8].

This restrictive definition is used today by NATO[9]. As for civilians, they see it as mastering physical flows between a point of origin and a point of consumption with the objective of making corresponding resources available according to needs. Placing this in the military domain, it groups together all types of transportation and supply indispensable to military operations at a strategic, operational and tactical level. It is this definition -that remains the most widely used by the wider public- that were have retained. In American vocabulary it is closer to the terms *"Distribution"* or *"Logistical Support"*. All conclusions made in this book are, therefore, only valid in light of this initial definition. This publication is based on the hypothesis that, between 1944 and 1945, the United States improved (revolutionised?), often empirically, logistics that made it the only nation capable of overcoming the challenges of a world war that was industrial and mobile; a world war as it had built a previously unheard of transoceanic chain capable of placing and supplying millions of personnel in European and Pacific theatres of operations, five thousand kilometres from New York and ten thousand from Los Angeles. It was an industrial war in that it dealt with large flows that had nothing in common with those seen beforehand, even during the First World War. It was a mobile war as by 1945 it was the only country capable of undertaking sustained supply mechanised armies on the move. However, to reach such a point, the United States suffered.

Contrary to commonly held beliefs, on the eve of D Day, although they had moved armies across the oceans, they did not yet have the doctrine or the means to supply a motorised war of movement. It was far from being a well-oiled precision machine, the quartermasters had to improvise, overcome personal quarrels and administrative sluggishness, modify equipment and its skills in order to finally empirically invent a new operational logistics chain that was not fully functioning until the spring of 1945.

It was on the German plains and across the French countryside that the ground component of American logistics blossomed for the first time, a component marked by the primacy of the road over rail and by its integration into an operational doctrine. We therefore invite you to take with us the winding roads of a deep transformation of supply routes. It begins in 1942 in New York, a place where each day thousands of tons of equipment was loaded before heading to United Kingdom, and which ends in 1945 on the banks of the river Elbe where two million GIs camped out reading comics, drinking soda and smoking Lucky Strikes that the constant flow of trucks brought every day.

A Sperry Corporation advertisement published in July 1944. This company made navigation equipment before becoming a precision equipment holding company. Started during the First World War, it was really in the Second World War that the military-industrial complex was forged, allowing the GI to be the "best fed, best clothed, best equipped and best looked-after soldier in history".
(NARA)

5 Antoine-Henri Jomini, Précis de l'art de la guerre, Bruxelles, 1841 pp 182-190, volume 2.
6 George C. Thorpe's, Pure Logistics: The Science of War Preparation, introduction by Stanley L. Falk, National Defense University Press, 1986, p.XI.
7 War Department. Field Service Regulations. Field Manual 100-5 Operations, 1949. Government Printing Office, 1949.
8 James A Huston, op. cit., p.VII.
9 "Logistics consist of the planning and execution of movement of armed forces and their maintenance".
10 JC Becour and H Bouquin, L'audit Opérationnel, Efficacité, Efficience et Sécurité, Economica, 1996.

Liberty Roads, 1944-1945

PART ONE

ABOLISHING THE TYRANNY OF DISTANCE

Above.
Sunset over a convoy. A balloon is on the look-out for any sign of enemy submarines. The tipping point of the Battle of the Atlantic was in 1943, the U-Boot were no longer a threat to the Bolero build-up (Bolero was the name for the assembling of the American army in Great Britain.
(LC-USW33-034618-ZC)

Cleveland is a major port on the Lake Erie situated between New York and Chicago in the heart of the American Manufacturing Belt. This photo of an inland cargo ship and the impressive "Hulett" gantries illustrates the industrial power of the New World.
(LC-DIG-fsac-1a34828)

Moving armies over the seas is not a new thing....it can be traced back to the beginnings of western military mythology with the expedition of Troy.

However, industrialisation made it more complex as it was no longer just a case of transporting an army but also keeping it regularly supplied. This meant putting into place a complex logistical system : stocktaking and ordering resources, making them converge at a loading point, assembling the means of transportation, securing the supply routes and carrying out unloading and distribution. The French and British attempted this in Crimea in 1854 with the results we know - troops decimated by typhus and cholera and field hospitals where men died like flies. Ardant du Picq wrote at the time that *"our soldiers have no blankets or straw mattresses, in the field ambulances there are is no spare clothing...."* This war finally convinced the authorities that supplies could no longer be tendered out to private companies as it had been previously the practice, or to forage in the field.

During the First World War, the US Army had foreseen the need to supply a million men in Europe but at that time there was only one front and the American troops landed in allied territory. They were able to count on French assistance and infrastructure.

The novelty that emerged in 1942 was process of globalisation. Supplying was now on a worldwide scale. In 1944, the United States had to coordinate the moving of large volumes of supplies to seven different theatres (Europe, Italy, Middle East, Russia, China, South Pacific, Central Pacific). Most of these areas were often without operational superstructure. On 6 June 1944, with the biggest landings in history taking place in Normandy, the other side of the world saw the Americans deploy in the Mariannes archipelago the largest fleet air arm force ever seen. There were 12,000 km between the two, with the first being 5,500 km from the United States and the second, 10,000 km. No army before or since has been confronted with such a challenge , certainly not Germany, a purely European based power (Cherbourg and Stalingrad were *"only"* 3,500 km apart), not even Great Britain whose participation on the Asian-Pacific zone was not comparable to the American war effort and which was able to use its Indian base. Although globalisation is of course a procedure that weaves a network throughout the world and which abolishes the tyranny of distance, the US Army was during the Second World War, indisputably, the first to experience a global war. For this it had to take up a double challenge; first that concerning materials as it needed sufficient infrastructure and means of transport; then an operational challenge where it had to create a logistics chain capable of dealing with a flow of millions of tons whilst at the same time remaining relatively flexible in order to meet demand within an acceptable timeframe. This organisational challenge was overcome from the outset of the war.

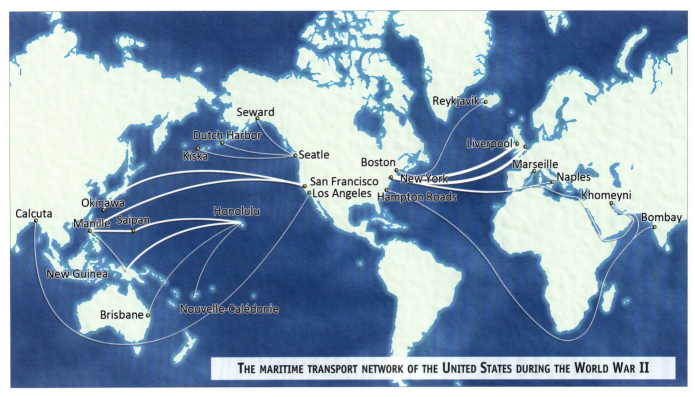

THE MARITIME TRANSPORT NETWORK OF THE UNITED STATES DURING THE WORLD WAR II

CHAPTER 1

REVOLUTION IN WASHINGTON
1940, a fragmented logistical system

A modern-day cathedral. The winter sun fills the repair workshops of the Northwestern Railroad Company in Chicago.
(LC-DIG-fsac-1a34653)

The first obstacle to overcome lay in the anarchy of the services involved in the logistical chain. As is the case with all complex human organisations, the US Army in 1941 was the result of a gradual construction. An improvisation during the War of Independence, its structure was next modified in successive layers without any rational thought being applied to how it functioned.

The first meeting of the Production Executive Committee under the presidency of Charles E. Wilson, President of the General Electric Company. From left to right: Rear-Admiral Vickery, vice-president of the U.S. Maritime Commission; Lt General Somervell, commander of the Services of Supply; Rear-Admiral Robinson, Director of Material and Procurement for the U.S. Navy; and Major General Echols, Commander of the Material Command HQ of the Army Air Force. The fact that civilian and military personnel worked together was an important factor in the synergy of the war effort.
(LC-USE6-D-006487)

Thus, at the end of the 19th century, the quartermaster services of the War Department were split up between ten bureaux placed under a double authority, that of the Secretary of War and that of the Commanding General of the Army[1]. All of the services signed contracts with civilian suppliers. There was no standardisation but a lot of inconsistencies, such as with the Ordnance that equipped the infantry with blankets but which could not purchase any for its own personnel. It was only routine and the small number of personnel that prevented it from falling into chaos.

The misfortune of the US Army was also the huge contrast between its peacetime role and means to carry it out, and those of wartime. In peacetime it was kept at a strength of less than 100,000 men. The American way of doing things and its reticence concerning centralisation, the spreading out of its strength over the entire state-continent all encouraged a decentralised quartermaster service. The purchase of food, maintenance and every day needs was negotiated locally by representatives of each technical service for some garrison units. However, in wartime, strength grew to a mass army for overseas service which, on the contrary, required an extreme centralisation and very detailed planning. The Americans had undergone the difficult experience during the Civil War and, above all, the First World War when the initial sending of the expeditionary corps to France in 1917 was a disaster and required a year before they mastered the logistics necessary for a million soldiers deployed 6,000 km from New York. The Americans hoped to retain such skills via several units that could be reactivated, such as the Supply Division, a War Department service.

Hopes were dashed. By the end of 1941, the Army was a veritable galaxy. 40 major commands and 350 smaller ones had turned into small fiefdoms whose commanders acted like nabobs. All of the latter had direct access to the Commander-in-Chief and overwhelmed him with requests. Some schemed with politicians to defend their privileges. Inter-service overlapping was rife. One example was the *"Transportation Service"* of the Quartermaster Corps which was tasked with the general distribution of supplies, but the other services retained their own distribution service. The QMC had control of the purchase of work vehicles, whereas combat vehicles came under the control of the Ordnance Corps. With mechanisation becoming generalised it was obvious that this duality had to be changed. Was an artillery tractor a straightforward truck or a vehicle that came under Ordnance Corps control as it replaced the former caissons and horse drawn equipment? Any attempt to carry out reforms came up against services that were set in their way and inter-service Byzantine quarrels. The Supply Division and its skeleton crew personnel was treated with contempt and systematically circumvented. In other words, logistics was totally fragmented.

MAC NARNEY, THE GREAT ORGANISER OF WASHINGTON

In 1940, Roosevelt sped up rearmament with the objective of having 1,686,000 men in uniform by December 1941. Each service was a hive of activity in order to absorb, equip, maintain and

The least well-known but not least important American of the war, General Brehon B. Somervell (1892-1955) was the big logistics boss at the head of the Army Service Forces. Authoritarian, career-driven and often obstinate to the extreme but indisputably competent, he played a major role in the implementation of war on a world-wide scale. His influence grew to such an extent that other generals joined forces in order for the ASF to be broken up in 1945.
(NARA)

---

1. Found here, amongst other things are the Commissary-General who purchased food, the Surgeon-General who ordered medical equipment, the Ordnance Department which equipped troops with arms and materiel, the Paymaster-General for pay and finally the Quartermaster-General which purchased textile, managed the depots and which dealt with transport in general.

Liberty Roads, 1944-1945

Lt General Somervell (right) talking with Brigadier General Hoag, commander of the Air Transport Command. Throughout the war, air transportation remained minor, even though it rendered a few precious services at Bastogne or during the offensive into the heart of the Reich in 1945.
(NARA)

Two Liberty Ships in the final phase of construction in the huge Bethlehem-Fairfield shipyards in Baltimore. Aircraft-carriers and battleships were also built here.
(LC-DIG-fsa-8e10842)

prepare such numbers. The duplication of efforts and inter service friction became more intense as each day passed. Civil agencies that had

President Roosevelt's ear made the most of the opportunity to gnaw away at Army prerogatives. For Chief of Staff George C. Marshall, it had become obvious that what was required was a central supply department capable of defending its interests in the face of civil administrators. Such a reform would only be possible by carrying out sweeping changes to the administrative structure. However, the forces of inertia were formidable. It was not, therefore, until the USA entered into the war that Marshall took the bull by the horns…..albeit discretely. He tasked a man he could trust, General Joseph Mc Narney, to come up with a new more efficient and centralised structure without consulting those concerned. Rapidly and efficiently, Mc Narney submitted a proposition that Marshall put to the President without any amendments made to it. Thanks to the executive powers that Congress had given him, Roosevelt made it official with a stroke of his pen. The 9 March 1942 decree grouped the various services into three families : Army Ground Forces, Army Air Forces and Service of Supply (SOS) – later named the Army Service Forces (ASF). All of the logistical components - Engineers, Medical, Chemical, Ordnance, Quartermaster and Signal Corps, but also the nine territorial commands and port commanders - were at last gathered together under one sole command, that of Lieutenant General Brehon B. Somervell, the former Supply Division commander. Somervell was a member

---
2. Jim Lacey, *Keep From All Thoughtful Men: How U.S. Economists Won World War II*, Naval Institute Press, 2011 pp 76-82.
3. Brehon Somervell, "Management", Public Administration Review, n°4, autumn 1944.
4. JK Ohl, *Supplying the troops,* Northern Illinois University Press, 1994, pp 55-71.

of the old Tennessee protestant aristocracy, the values of which he had retained - work, elegance, culture, stubbornness, faith but also paternalism and authority - something that had up to that point stalled his career. His was also a talented officer, a former West Point cadet who had joined the Engineer Corps and who had proved his worth as a logistics expert and manager of military posts linked to the quartermaster services of the AEF in France in 1918, as well as in 1939-1940 in the construction of thousands of items of infrastructure, including the Pentagon. He also came to the fore in civilian posts. He was tasked with setting up the hydro-electric systems of the Potomac basin, then an ambitious canal project cutting Florida from east to west, before being named by Roosevelt at the head of the Work Progress Administration (WPA) for New York. The objective of the WPA was to provide work and income for the unemployed victims of the Great Depression via a policy of great construction projects and redistribution. Used to civilian and military domains, supervising civilian employees and managing astronomical budgets, negotiating with politicians, industry leaders and trade unions, he had managed to weave a network that took him as far as the White House. Somervell in 1942 appeared as the *"right man in the right place"*. He found himself on an equal footing with the commanders of ground and air forces and was answerable only to Marshall and Robert Patterson, the Assistant Secretary of War. He oversaw entire corps : Engineers, Signals, Quartermaster, Ordnance the commanders of which were both older and of higher rank. His lack of diplomacy and the fact that all of the corps commanders felt that they were overseen by a careerist explained the gnashing of teeth, however the atmosphere after Pearl Harbor was one of unity and pulling together[2].

SOMERVELL AND THE GREAT CLEAR UP OF JULY 1942

Somervell was faced with a huge task. He had to harmonise the work of these services that were in competition with each other, reorganise them then improve efficiency. He summed up his philosophy in the following way in 1944 : *"Good management depends on five criteria. The first is a thorough knowledge of the work to be carried out. The second depends on the quality of the men placed in key posts. The third is an efficient organisation adapted to the work due to be carried out. The fourth is a straightforward and direct system of functioning that aids the execution of the activities caused by the work. The fifth is a sure method to control results. If you respect three of the five criteria the work will be carried out with reasonable success. Four will permit better than average results. Five however, are vital for the best management possible"*[3].

He began by surrounding himself with trusted men. Willhem Styer, his deputy at the Construction Division remained at his side. Charles Gross, a good friend with whom Somervell had gone through West Point, was named at the head of the new Transportation Corps. Lucius Clay, newly in charge of purchasing, had all worked closely with Somervell since 1934 and he held them in high esteem. Only Colonel LeRoy Lutes had not previously worked with him and it was on the basis of recommendations that he Somervell obtained his transfer to the post of assistant tasked with the supervision of overseas supplies. With his knowledge of the corridors of power he even managed to sideline a man put forward by Roosevelt, placing instead one of his friends, Levin Campbell, for the position of head of the Ordnance Corps[4]. This type of selection looks much like favouritism but history has proved the competence of these men and if they were perhaps not the best, they were not, and by a long stroke, the worst. As for the older service commanders and whose roles had never been challenged, Somervell chose strong arm tactics. He obtained the dismissal of five territorial commanders, the head of the Signal Corps and managed to impose deep structural reforms. Indeed, the Mac Narney reform was no more than a first step to make sure that Marshall did not have to deal with dozens of different people, but in order for the ASF not to become another simple echelon in the US Army organizational tables, Somervell had to put some order to it. In July 1942 he totally overhauled the organisation :

• The Quartermaster Corps lost its Transportation Service as well as the role of acquiring work vehicles.
• The Ordnance Corps that was already tasked with the purchase

Each theater was supplied from a single port. New York was chosen for Europe. This choice can be explained by the presence of the largest and most modern military terminal in the world. This was that of the US Army situated between 48th and 64th Street, built during the Great War. Contrary to what the official caption claims, the photo appears to be post-war.
(LC, HAER NY, 24-BROK, 53 - 1)

Loading a coal-ship in the docks of the Pennsylvania Railroad in Sandusky, Ohio. River transport remained the main means of transporting bulky loads in the United States.
(LC-DIG-fsac-1a34820)

and maintenance of combat vehicles saw its role widened to that of all vehicles.

• The key point of his reforms, however, was the transformation of the Transportation Service into an independent corps. Its activities were widened to include all not tactical personnel and equipment movement by rail, water or road whether in the US or exterior theatres. It was allowed to purchase, rent or requisition transportation and ships and to manage embarkation points, ports and railroad signal control centres.

The service which initially integrated 60,000 military and civilian personnel had to immediately get down to business that was much bigger than the calculations made in 1917. Instead of sending 122,000 soldiers and 287,000 tonnes of goods to a single theatre of operations within six months, the objective now was to send 390,000 soldiers and 1.9 million tonnes to seven theatres. The TC (Transportation Corps) progressively grew and reached 200,000 soldiers.

Somervell injected a strong dose of civilian style management. Thus, the ASF was the only military administration to increase in productivity. Somervell also led a thorough modernisation of logistics by relying on thousands of mobilised civilian logistics professionals. By sharing their skills within the various departments, they contributed to a rapid modernisation. An increasing effort was made concerning packing in lighter, easier to use, solid and weather and mould proof packaging. Easier to store, handle and transport, packaging was one of the keys to victory. Work in depots changed. The Quartermaster Corps or Ordnance made a great effort to mechanise handling. Muscle power was replaced by mobile cranes and productivity was increased. Transportation was also modernised. Ships gained in autonomy thanks to the construction of Liberty Ships equipped with loading masts. The 2,600 tonne Landing Ship Tanks were capable of transporting twenty tanks at sea then take them to a beach where they were unloaded onto the sand thanks to a twin bow door that would be used on post war roll-on-roll off ships. The only thing missing was the container ship. Somervell then placed the onus on rationalising the logistical chain in order to give it more clarity, rapidity and linking factories to depots, depots to ports, ports to relay bases, relay bases to consumers, creating a trans-oceanic network over the Pacific and Atlantic that allowed the United States to wage its first veritable world war.

CHAPTER II

WORLD WAR, GLOBAL WAR
Theory of distribution

Expediting supplies overseas over a distance of more than 5,000 km was something that had already been carried out in the First World War, but twenty years further on the loads had increased considerably.

Above.
A general view of the marshaling yards of the Northwestern Railroad Company in Chicago in December 1942.
In 1917-1918, an icy winter had brought most of the traffic to a halt. This would not be the case during the Second World War.
(LC-DIG-fsac-1a34647)

This increase was initially explained by the increase in volume, variety and complexity of equipment. Whereas the 1918 infantry division had 86 guns, 260 machine-guns, 804 motor vehicles and 1,080 carts, that of 1941 had 136 guns, 461 machine-guns and 1,474 motor vehicles whilst its manpower was divided by two. This equipment diversified and became more complex with the appearance of, for example, radios. Better performing weaponry used more ammunition. The divisional artillery of the Second World War fired two and half times more shells in the same amount of time, not to mention the amount of ammunition used by automatic weapons, or fuel consumption. Maintenance required more spare parts and superior skills. Automatically, technological advances required a larger, better trained and better equipped quartermaster service equipped to deal with larger volumes,

Above.
A merchant ship fills with fuel. In order to fulfill the need for fuels, Roosevelt convinced the big oil companies to be patriotic. Making the most of the available government funding, they opened new oil fields, building two hundred new refineries and importing massively from neighboring countries.
Thus, production went from 180 million tonnes to 244 (60% of world production).
(LC-USW4-029552)

COMPARISON OF LOADS CONCERNING THE BEHIND THE LINES SERVICES BETWEEN THE 1ST AND 2ND WORLD WAR.		
	1st World War	2nd World War
Average volume taken by a tonne of equipment	1,8 m³	2,8 m³
Initial average equipment tonnage accompanying a man	2,7 t	5 t
Daily supply needs for a man	7 kg 2	30 kg
Daily fuel consumption per man	0,5 kg (including aviation fuel)	5,5 kg (excluding aviation fuel)
Weight of daily rations	2,2 kg	3,5 kg

A locomotive takes on coal in the Chicago railroad station, December 1942. The good management of stocks, essential to the functioning of transportation, was a major component of logistics.
(LC-DIG-fsac-1a34645)

Our previous pages
The marshaling yards of the Northwestern Railroad Company in Chicago, December 1942. Avoiding jams was the main challenge to overcome when it came to coordinating the dispatching of thousands of trains towards the embarkation ports. As well as enlarging goods yards, the solution lay in the opening of points control centers.
(LC-DIG-fsac-1a34637)

---

1. After the war of 1812', the Secretary of War John C Calhoun noted that, *"our people, even the poorest, is accustomed to a luxurious way of life which protects their health and which must be continued during wars. An American will be starving in circumstances where a tartar would feel as if he was living in luxury"*. A German solider of WW2 carried on his back half of what an American soldier carried. Michael G. Dana, *"The legacy of mass Logistics"*, 19 Sept. 2000 which can be seen at www.almc.army.mil.
2. Carl T. Schmidt, *"The Division slice in two world wars"*, Military Review, N°31, Oct. 1951.
3. James A Huston, op. cit., pp.493-504.
4. Roland G. Ruppenthal, Logistical support of the armies, CMH, 1959, vol. 2, p.237.

variety and more complex supplies.

This increase is also explained by the change in the strategic situation. It was no longer possible to rely on the French to bear some of the weight of the logistical chain, this time everything had to be sent from the United States, pass via ports and a rail network that had to be built and used.

Finally, the standard of living of American citizens had considerably increased in the inter war period and a consumer society was now a reality. The needs, deemed as being vital to a middle class New Yorker now had nothing in common with those of an Oklahoma farmer twenty years previously and historically the US Army had always tried to give the best living conditions to its 'boys', convinced that its citizen soldiers had fragile morale and needed to be looked after[1]. Items such as aftershave, patriotic letter paper, comics and soda drinks became everyday supplies that made the quartermaster services job[2] harder and more complicated. To this was added the packaging which, although it helped storage, increased the overall weight.

The projection of such volumes required detailed planning and the most efficient way was to think in straightforward terms, such as what were the daily requirements of a given unit ? A day's supplies varied according to its type (strength, equipment), where it was and the season. It included not only the consumable goods (rations, fuel) but also replacement supplies (weapons, vehicles, uniforms) needed to replace losses.

On the European front, for example, it was calculated that a division accompanied by its support units (40,000 men) and two Air Wings (5,000 men each) required 1,600 tonnes per day - 1,100 tonnes of freight, 475 tonnes of fuel and 25 tonnes of vehicles. Distribution was as follows : 595 tonnes to the front, 65 to the Air Force and 365 to rear echelon units[3]. By using this data the technical services automatically released the supplies to each theatre of operations.

However, the automatic method did not allow for the response to circumstances. It was not uncommon, therefore, to supply useless items when other supplies were needed in other domains. Bradley complained about this in Normandy when he saw his stocks of mortar rounds melt away during the hedgerow fighting. In order to prevent these shortcomings, the automatic system was replaced by a semi-automatic system a few months after the opening of a new theatre of operations.

1. Each theatre sent reports concerning the state of its stocks and information on the evolution of its consumption.

2. Depending on this consumption, the General Staff revised the composition of the *"day's supplies"* and sent the maximum amount capable of being stored by each theatre according to strategic priorities. It also sent in reinforcement units.

3. By using this data, an Army Service Forces bureau- the Overseas Supply Division – subtracted the supplies already stored by the theatre and those on their way to it, what was left over corresponded to the stores needed to be sent. It of course took into account the reinforcements already on their way. These requirements were placed in order of priority as there were not enough ships to immediately send all of the planned supplies. The bureau published a request every month (every ten days for munitions).

4. The order was sent to the technical services which released the equipment and to the Transportation Corps which organised the transfer. Each order makes you dizzy. Thus, in May 1944, two million tonnes and 200,000 different items were sent to the European theatre[4].

This method was more flexible but it easily became jammed, something that was often the case as the Overseas Supply Division was not able to obtain reliable and up to date data. Also, it was incapable of anticipating certain needs. It was for these reasons that dispensations existed and the theatre commanders could always put forward requests to the War Department for particular supplies. However, given the distances involved it was not possible to react quickly to requests. It required nearly four months for a particular request to be honoured. Eisenhower, therefore, had to order materiel for September operations before his first soldier had even set foot on the continent. This delay was the reason for a lack of supplies such as winter clothing; the advance into the mountainous region of the Vosges had not been

anticipated. Operations were therefore carried out essentially with the means that had been planned for and this explains why the General Staff planned for a wide range of supplies. To keep an armoured force of 4,000 tanks up to strength, the General Staff estimated that it would be ground down by 11% each month, a hypothesis that proved to be very optimistic in Europe, and that it would require a further 2,000 tanks to be supplied. The American global war made it necessary therefore, to have the best possible coordination between the strategists and the logisticians so that the right product would be at the right place at the right time, but it also demanded that American industry be present in order to provide supplies as well as the means to transport them.

FLOW MECHANISM

Once it had left the factory, each item of supply was transported by rail to a service depot responsible for its supply, the Quartermaster Corps for uniforms, rations, fuel, the Ordnance Corps for vehicles and spare parts, the Signal Corps for radios… (see the vade mecum). There were hundreds of depots, for the most part specialised (tanks, clothing, armament, construction materials…). These were called key depots.

Others, known as distribution depots, managed various supplies for units stationed locally.

Interior zone

In 1944, there were 125 major depots and two million people loaded and unloaded up to 4 million tonnes every month. All of these technical services, but also other services in the distribution process - territorial commands in the United States and embarkation ports - were placed under the authority of the Army Service Forces.

Supplies remained in storage for a few days, or a few weeks at most, until the Transportation Corps came to transport them to New York where they left for the European front. They were packed up and listed (table of supplies classification). 90% of transport in the USA was by rail. Contrary to the First World War, the state was not forced to place private companies under its control.

Grouped together in the Association of American Railroads and the Interstate Commerce Commission, the companies dealt with two entities, a political partner in the Office of Defense Transportation (ODT) – and a military client, the Army Service Forces. The ODT, led by Joseph B. Eastsman, a man close to Roosevelt, specialised in questions of transport and was tasked with improving productivity by offering railroad companies solutions to reduce the amount of time that trains were immobilised by building repair workshops, enlarging goods stations and building new railroads. In December 1941, the park comprised of 41,000 locomotives and 2 million goods wagons. This was a third less than in 1917 but, as it was more modern, in all represented a superior transportable volume. Circulation was more fluid as since 1927 there had been a Centralized Traffic Control that grouped together in a centre the control of switches and signals for a given region. Thus, a wagon did not remain unused for more than ten days. Consolidation Stations were opened at strategic points where incomplete rail convoys were gathered together. Even if it only concerned 10% of volume transported, this system nevertheless freed up rolling stock[5]. Thus, 340 million tonnes of freight were transported during the war, 105 of which was just for 1944, a figure to be compared with the 12 million tonnes transported in 1919, the record for the 1st World War[6]. Rail traffic was also eased by the bringing into service in 1943 of two huge pipelines between Texas and Pennsylvania some 2,000 km in length : Big Inch for the transportation of crude oil and Little Big Inch for refined fuel. The flow of these pipelines that supplied factories, towns and ports on the east coast, soared from 50,000 to 754,000 barrels per day. Over one year, this represented a saving of 45,000 railroad tankers or a hundred ship tankers.

Across the Atlantic

When the rail convoy arrived in New York it entered into a

SYSTEM OF SUPPLIES CLASSIFICATION ADOPTED BY THE US ARMY

CLASSIFICATION	TYPE
I	Food
II	Clothing, weapons and other supplies planned for by the unit allocation tables
III	Fuel, lubricants, oils (POL)
IV	Construction and fortification materials
V	Munitions, explosives, chemical products

Left.
The dispersal of services became a constraint that was too heavy in order to undertake war on a global scale and in 1941 it was decided to gather them all together in a single building : the Pentagon. An irony of history, it was the future head of the ASF, Somervell, who launched the construction as head of the Construction Division. In two years, the largest office building in the world was opened (40,000 people).
(NARA)

Below.
the beginning of the German submarine offensive on the Atlantic coast paralyzed the exportations of the production areas of the Caribbean and Gulf of Mexico towards the high consummation areas of the north-east. At this time, Roosevelt named Harold Ickes as his Secretary of the Interior - . His first decision was to ration fuel. He then financed the 95 million dollars which were indispensable for the construction of two pipelines between Texas and Pennsylvania some 2,000 km in length and opened in 1943.
(LC-USW4-029616)

---

5. This rationalisation allowed railway operators in 1944 to cover the military needs whilst at the same time beating its record for passengers (1 billion). Civilians restricted by fuel rationing used public transport instead.
6. Don DeNevi, *America's fighting railroads*, Pictorial Histories Publishing, 1996, pp.73-78.

Liberty Roads, 1944-1945

"LIBERTY SHIP"

Without this shipyard, the United-States would have played a secondary role in the war. With it, they could supply thousands of men in action 6,000 km away from home. The Baltimore Bethlehem-Fairfield Shipyards Inc is an example of these huge mazes filled with gantries and giant mobile cranes which allowed for sub-contracting to be carried out. Built a few kilometers away, such as these propellers, or sent by barge from factories in the heart of the country, the parts, weighing tens of tonnes were then carried by crane to the dry docks. Riveting took over from welding as it was more rapid. Thus, ships were built in several weeks, a performance which is unique in the annals of history.
(All photos, Library of Congress)

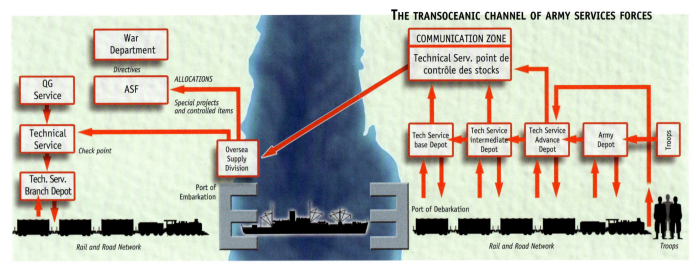

THE TRANSOCEANIC CHANNEL OF ARMY SERVICES FORCES

A Buick being loaded. The Liberty Ship had its cargo booms, essential items of equipment for operations in the Pacific and during landings, which were also used on quaysides as a complement to cranes..
(Région Basse-Normandie/NARA, P012996)

7. Units often received their full complement of equipment late. The fields allowed them to keep fit or familiarize themselves with their equipment when embarkation was delayed by a few days.

huge hive of activity. As far as the eye could see stretched goods yards, temporary storage zones, but also camps to house some 80,000 soldiers (Camp Kilmer, Camp Shanks, Fort Hamilton) and even training grounds[7]. At the end of all this one could make out the quays. This city within a city was directly administered by the Army Service Forces. It was here that the men and materiel of the US Army embarked. Other port zones were attributed to the Navy and Allies for Lend Lease, something that the Chief of Transportation regretted in 1945 when he admitted that this dividing had led to waste. Initially, all of the men working here were civilians under army contract. However, as the work was hard and badly paid, many left. In 1944, sixty docker companies had to be raised and 11,000 Italian prisoners were brought in to make up for shortfalls. The work could also be dangerous, especially when dealing with munitions. During the First World War it was decided to load shells only on ships anchored far off shore in order to reduce damage in the event of an explosion. This solution was no longer possible in 1944 given the huge amounts to deal with and ships were loaded at the quaysides but directly from the wagons to prevent them being handled twice.

A bigger worry than handling supplies was the lack of shipping. The Royal Navy had, since 1940, been crossing swords with the U-Boote in the Atlantic and the Americans were well-placed to see for themselves the heavy losses inflicted by a handful of submarines. Winning the Battle of the Atlantic was an indispensable requisite to D-Day. In order to win it was necessary to find a way of dealing with the submarines, something which was achieved with a combination of technological innovation (long-range aircraft, improved sonar, escort aircraft carriers, code breaking), as well as on a tactical level (reorganisation of convoys, anti submarine packs) which began to bear fruit in 1943. It was also necessary to build enough freighters to make good the losses and grow in strength, this would be the *"Liberty Ship"* project[8].

Launched in mid-1941, the specifications of the program were

The inter-allied War Shipping Administration centralized the management of the entire allied fleet. It attributed ships and set the loading regulations.
The Army Service Forces always complained about a lack of means, even when half of the amount of ships was attached to it.
(LC-USW33-034629-ZC)

8. The French reference concerning the Battle of the Atlantic remains Guy Malbosc, *La bataille de l'Atlantique*, Economica, 1995.
9. The question of Liberty Ships has been dealt with in French by Jean-Yves Brouard, *Les Liberty Ships*, Glénat 1993 and by Gérald Guétat, *Liberty Ship, l'épopée*, ETAI, 2001 but the best publications are in English, beginning with Peter Elphick, *Liberty, the Ships that won the war*, Naval institute Press, 2001 and the very interesting oral history on the Savannah shipyards written by Tony Cope, *On the Swing Swift : building Liberty Ships in Savannah*, Naval Institute Press, 2009. In French there is also Laurent Péricone's excellent essay "Liberty Ships : la victoire à fond de cale", Guerres & Histoire, n°10, December 2012, pp. 90-94.
10. JK Ohl, *Supplying the troops*, Northern Illinois University Press, 1994, pp. 189 & sq

ambitious : a rudimentary freighter, slow (eleven knots) but easy to build and with a large carrying capacity : 10,800 tonnes of freight, 2,804 jeeps or 260 Sherman tanks. This was no easy task especially as in January 1942, America's joining the war led to an increase in demand. It was now no longer a case of tens of ships leaving the shipyards each year, but hundreds…each month ! Roosevelt had already turned to Henry John Kaiser, an entrepreneur who had already been noticed due to his involvement in the large public projects of the New Deal. As early as 1941 he had taken the workforce of the Grand Coulee dam near Canada and put them to work on a huge shipyard at Richmond in San Francisco bay.

The first dry dock was opened within three months and eleven others followed, employing 30,000 workers. The engineers developed here new methods of modular construction. The 250,000 parts of a freighter were pre-assembled in peripheral zones around the shipyard to form 120 modules that were then towed, raised by crane and assembled in the dry dock. This was the case of the bow, stern, castle and main deck divided into seven parts. The internal parts such as the engine were subcontracted to 500 inland companies. Kaiser copied the scientific division of the work designed by the engineer Taylor for the automobile industry. The work was broken down and each worker only had a very simple task to carry out. Taylorism made up for a shortfall of qualified workers within the black and female workforce that made up the bulk of the latter. Apprenticeship workshops were created on the ferry-boats that carried the workers over San Francisco bay. Finally, the last innovation concerned welding which replaced riveting, something that was more rapid and used less metal. Added to this was the competitive spirit that existed between shipyards to see who could build ships the fastest, as well as patriotism that was encouraged by Kaiser. These methods allowed for great gains in productivity. Pre-war it took a year to build a freighter, it took 244 days to build the first production Liberty Ship, the Patrick Henry, and the average production time in 1943 fell to….42 days. The record was the Robert E. Peary, launched in four days and fifteen hours and finished off in less than fifteen days[9].

From 1942 onwards, six other sites were opened by Kaiser and three existing shipyards came under his control. Veritable movements of population took place. New towns appeared, such as Vanport City with its population of 40,000, built in Oregon in four months. In all, 18 shipyards took part in the program day and night, meeting an incredible challenge : the construction of, between September 1941 and September 1945, 2,709 Liberty and 534 Victory Ships. At the end of 1943, 1,843 ships had already been delivered, enough to supply all theatres of operations. What remained was to use them in a rational way.

This was the work of the War Shipping Administration which centralised the management of the entire allied merchant fleet. It allocated ships according to needs, availability and where they were. It set the rules concerning loading. Of course, the Army Service Forces still complained of a lack of transportation means, even in 1945 when the WSA attached to it 1,706 ships for a total of 17.3 million tonnes, 48% of its pool.

Putting together a convoy, loading the goods as quickly and as rationally as possible, meeting the escort and crossing the Atlantic revealed itself to be one of the most complex logistical tasks of the war, as the Americans found out in 1917 and 1942. In 1917, the chaos was such that the port of New York was paralysed for almost a year *(see insert)*. In November 1942, the landings in North Africa were almost cancelled due to the problems encountered in loading the materiel. However, progress was rapid and as early as the beginning of 1943, the ASF assembled within a few weeks twenty freighters destined for Algiers, loaded with 5,400 trucks, 2,000 trailers and 100 locomotives[10]. In 1944 operations had become an efficient routine, the embarkation ports had been enlarged, skills improved and it was almost 400 ships loaded with four million tonnes of goods that left American ports on a monthly basis.

Finally, the convoy loaded with goods arrived in Europe. After several days of waiting due to busy quaysides, the holds of the Liberty Ships were emptied by British civilian dock workers, too slowly in the eyes of the American military personnel who moaned in frustration at seeing their precious ships thus immobilised. At this point, the supplies had travelled over 6,000 km, an odyssey that had lasted three months.

Small vade mecum of the technical services attached to the Army Service Forces following the 1942 reform

SERVICES	MISSION
Quartermaster Service	Service tasked with supplies (purchasing, storage) of food, uniforms, fuel, various equipment. It also integrated funereal services.
Ordnance Service	Service tasked with development, purchasing and maintenance of motor vehicles, weapons and munitions.
Transportation Service	Service tasked with transport and distribution from behind the lines to the frontline (including using amphibious trucks).
Engineers Service	Service tasked with the maintenance of the transport network and pipelines, rail transport in army zones, repairs to ports and beach administration.
Chemical Warfare Service	Service tasked with the supply of chemical weapons and anti-chemical warfare measures (not used), but above all, flamethrowers, incendiary munitions and smoke devices.
Signals,	the setting up, operating of and maintenance of radio equipment, telephones and cables.
Medical Service	Service tasked with the supply of medical products, evacuation and treatment of wounded. .

Liberty Roads, 1944-1945

On 1919, Doughboys returns home aboard militarized liners. During both World Wars, it is aboard these giants that the troops crossed the Atlantic Ocean safed by their speed. Their crossed was never concern unlike that of the slow cargo boats.
(LOC, 33076u)

THE FIRST WORLD WAR : LEARNING TO FORECAST

When America declared war in April 1917, General Pershing proposed the creation of an expeditionary corps — the American Expeditionary Force — consisting of 30 divisions. Putting together, transporting and maintaining such a force was a task much bigger than the United States had ever had to previously face.

Seven months after, in the midst of a particularly harsh winter, American logistics almost collapsed. In the United States, two million tonnes of goods lay dormant in 40,000 wagons parked up in sidings, two hundred ships awaited along the quaysides of New York whereas in France, only 16,000 tonnes of goods were unloaded instead of the hoped for hundreds of thousands, a tiny amount that was entirely insufficient to render the AEF operational. The rival railroad companies gathered together within the Railway War Board were incapable of cooperating and sharing equipment and resources was a pipedream. Within the US Army, the various services placed the blame on a multitude of superfluous and useless orders. All services were in competition with each other and defended their own territory....The big question was : who is in command ? Everyone, therefore no-one ! It was chaos.

Putting things in order carried on until the spring. The civilian railroad companies were placed under the supervision of the United States Railroad Administration. This policy, although it did not obtain remarkable results, was a form of progress and noticeably increased productivity. To rationalise maritime traffic, a Shipping Control Committee was formed and which exercised total control over the entire American merchant fleet. British sailors were brought in to improve the synergy between the two fleets. Within the Army, an effort was made to rationalise the logistical chain.

In September 1917, the Quartermaster Corps created the Purchase, Storage & Traffic Division in order to centralise its purchasing and to deal with their transportation to France. In April 1918, the Division became a superstructure integrating the supplies of each service and which answered only to the Chief of Staff for military affairs and to the Assistant Secretary of War, the businessman Benedict Crowell, for everything concerning the civilian sector. This seemingly odd choice signified that the political authorities had, in fact, lost all confidence in the capacity of the military to manage quartermaster affairs and were attempting to manage them via a civilian professional.

Thus, the transportation of the AEF and its supplies was progressively improved. Every month, the PS & T Division organised a big inter-service meeting between all the civilian and military protagonists. These meetings served to set the embarkations for the following month by reconciling the requirements with the available means of transport. One the procedure was started, the Embarkation Service coordinated putting it into practice. To end the clogging up of ports, a local port administration was set up with civilian and military personnel, administrators and sailors, placed under the authority of a superintendent. It managed the arrival of trains, temporary storage and embarkations.

The trans-Atlantic logistical chain was also eased by the purchasing of a large part of the weaponry from the Allies. 100% of tanks, 88% of artillery, 81% of aircraft, 68% of mortars and 33% of the Doughboys' automatic weapons were of British or French origin. In all, 49% of the tonnage received by the AEF did not cross the Atlantic but was supplied by the European Allies.

This process of centralisation and coercion was unique in American history, but all of these measures led to a clear improvement in productivity. The 16,000 tonnes of July 1917 had reached 750,000 tonnes by October 1918. Despite this, the War Department was never able to achieve the hoped for 90 days of reserves in France and had to make do with 45 days of stock. Of course, all was not perfect, there was still inter-service tension as well as unforeseen events such as storms, torpedo attacks and accidents that could upset this precision machinery. Also, there was a lack of transport ships up to the very end of the war and only 470 were launched before the Armistice out of the 2,851 ordered[1].

1. Théodore Antonelli, *"American Industrial mobilization during WWI"*, Defense Management Journal, n°12, juillet 1976 & James A Huston, op. cit. pp 340-355.

During one year, the AEF logistics did not function properly in France. The ports were saturated, there were insufficient means and friction between the different services. It was not until the fall of 1918, and the creation of a Service of Supply and the introduction of an interface between the front and rear echelon for the regulating officer, that the situation improved. Each division had its own station and the final distribution to brigades and regiments was ensured by the organic units of the supply train. At the end of the war, 28,000 engineer troops maintained roads and 700 km of narrow-gauge railroads had been laid; rail was very useful even near the frontline. The number of trucks had swelled from 3,500 to 30,000.
(LOC, 33069u)

SECOND PART

THE ART OF PLANNING

T he secret to efficient logistics lays in good planning as it concerns bringing the means of transportation, goods and consumers to a meeting point at a given time. The Prussians compared their quartermaster general to a station master. Logistics is an art of administration and anticipation and Overlord could be considered as being one of its masterpieces.

A "Red Cross" Jeep of the 5th ESB drives onto a LCT prior to D-Day. The medics would pay a high price at Omaha Beach on 6 June.
(Région Basse-Normandie/NARA, P013195)

Never before had a military operation been so prepared and fine-tuned as Overlord, to such an extent that the Israeli military historian Martin Van Creveld, reproaches the Allies for having done too much. And why not ? *"Better too much than too little"*. Except that Van Creveld compares this example to others such as the Russian campaign of 1812 or the Schlieffen Plan of 1914 in order to reach the conclusion that rigorous planning never guarantees success. Worst still, according to Van Creveld, it paralyses command and traps it inside a precision machinery which, at the slightest upset, will transform into an infernal machine. It remains to be seen whether these accusations against an *'over-planning'* of Overlord are justified.

CHAPTER 3

LOGISTICS AND STRATEGY
The Master Plan

Since 1942, an inter-allied organisation, COSSAC (Chief of Staff to Supreme Allied Commander) led by British general Morgan, had been preparing for the landings. Not since the Schlieffen Plan for the invasion of France in 1914, which had been fine-tuned two decades beforehand, had a General Staff been given so much time - two and a half years - neither such means for a military operation.

Above.
A Liberty Ship unloads its trucks onto a Rhinoferry off Omaha. The operation, carried out with cargo booms was slow and impossible in heavy seas.
(Région Basse-Normandie/NARA, P012832)

It is true that during the planning phase for Overlord the Allies had in mind the disaster of Gallipoli in 1915. Also, the last example they had was an amphibious assault that had come up against fierce resistance that had almost caused its failure : Tarawa, in the Pacific, 20 November 1943. However, in Normandy the enemy would be more formidable than in the Pacific due to the coastal defences, but also ability to launch strong counter-attacks. The fear of failure was enormous and such an eventuality would have incalculable consequences, notably for the United Kingdom already weary from years of war. Planning was, therefore, carried out to its utmost.

In January 1944, Eisenhower was named as the man in charge to implement the landings. COSSAC was replaced by SHAEF (Supreme Headquarter of Allied expeditionnary Force). Upon its arrival it found a memo from the Combined Chiefs of Staff and piles of dossiers left by Morgan. The contrast could not have been sharper, on one hand a mission order consisting of a few lines and on the other, thousands of pages.

"You will enter the continent of Europe and, in conjunction with the other United Nations, undertake operations aimed at the heart of Germany and the destruction of her armed forces. The date for entering the Continent is the month of May, 1944. After adequate Channel Ports have been secured, exploitation will be directed towards securing an area that will facilitate both ground and air operations against the enemy"[1].

This strategic concept left an immense freedom of action and it was made more precise by Montgomery's staff as he was named as being in charge of all ground forces until the arrival of Eisenhower on French soil. In fact, Monty resumed the main parts of Morgan's project that had been established in mid-1943. On 7 April 1944, he explained with much ceremony his master plan in front of a high ranking audience at Saint Paul's School, the place where he had established his headquarters and had also been a pupil.

The master plan, an accountant's plan ?

The master plan boiled down to a three-stage offensive with each one allowing for the capture of ports necessary for achieving the next stage. The first phase covering a few weeks consisted of establishing a solid beachhead in lower Normandy with the capture of the port of Cherbourg. Whilst awaiting repairs to the port, supplies would have to transit via two American beaches, a few small fishing ports (Isigny, St Vaast, Carentan, Barfleur, Port en Bessin) and an artificial port. This phase was the most dangerous. Priority of course was given to landing fighting troops in order to secure and hold the beachhead. Lower Normandy was chosen, amongst other areas, as it combined several logistical advantages : proximity to English ports, the quality of its beaches for unloading (wide and sandy) and an easy access to the land beyond, presence of deep water ports (Cherbourg), proximity of English airfields for air cover.

The second phase was for July/August with the establishing of a solid base between the Seine and Loire rivers. Whilst the British forces pinned down the bulk of the Wehrmacht, the Americans would liberate Brittany. The capture of Breton ports was essential to the continuation of operations. It was planned that they would become the disembarkation points for American troops and that *Omaha* Beach and Cherbourg would be left for the British, but the time to get them up and running would impose a lull in operations during the month of September. This lull would be used to re-establish the rail network and the installation of pipelines linking the ports with a large depot between Rennes and Laval, as well as secondary depots in Le Mans and Chartres.

In was only when these conditions had been met and from D +120 onwards that the third phase of the offensive would take the Allies from the Seine to the heart of Germany. A twin offensive from one side of the Ardennes to the other would break the back of the German economy by enveloping the Ruhr. The right American pincer was to pin down the maximum number of forces whilst facilitating the advance of the left British pincer whose objectives were deemed as vital : capture of V1 and V2 launch sites, channel ports and Ant-

---
1. Directive from CCS to Eisenhower, 12 February 1944.

werp, liberation of Holland. Based on the idea that the Germans would try and hold each river line, strategists thought that the advance would systematically slow down, allowing enough time to re-establish railways and supply stores behind the lines. An offensive towards Berlin would, if necessary, take place in the spring of 1945. By this date, logistical constraints would have disappeared with the bringing into service of the ports of Le Havre, Rouen, Antwerp and Rotterdam, thanks to the excellent rail networks of north-east Europe.

The plan was not, in fact, very innovative. It was content in using an idea dear to General Grant : the application against the enemy of a crushing power to force an outcome[2]. It also had similarities with the strategy of 1918 that had allowed the Allies to break out of trench warfare[3]. It was prudent, sure and methodical, unlike the Blitzkrieg. Morgan had been influenced in his planning by a lack of means in 1943, Monty was loyal to it by choice and the Americans had validated it by doctrinal conviction.

THE LOGISTICAL IMPLICATIONS OF *OVERLORD*

The tyranny of logistics

Such an operation involved very detailed planning and the most subtle logistical balancing act. In order to avoid being thrown back into the sea, the Allies needed to land more fighting men and materiel than the Germans were capable of sending in.

In this race against time, the Allies had one advantage, they could try and paralyse the enemy lines of communication thanks to their air superiority and the French resistance, however, they had a handicap as they had to bring in everything by sea.

What were the requirements ? As well as reinforcements they could not overlook the daily supplies and the rear echelon equipment needs (loading equipment, transport, port repair, Air Force equipment), whilst at the same time stockpiling (vital in the event of a break in the supply lines, caused by a storm for example). Experts established several scenarios according to the number of divisions and when they were due to go into action. For example, fifteen divisions operating on the continent on D+41 demanded on a daily basis 12,000 tonnes + 6,000 tonnes of stock, by adding the landing of reinforcements and various unloading, the total reached was 26,500 tonnes/day[4].

They also estimated the available port capacities by forecasting a date of liberation for each port and the time necessary for repairs (calculations based on the experience gained in the Mediterranean). The results were compiled in the chart[5] on page 33.

These figures were made definitive in April 1944 but had been revised several times (for example, Cherbourg had seen its maximum capacity boosted from 5,000 to 8,000 tonnes), as were the anticipated dates of capture and time required for repairs (ten to three days on average) in order to adhere to requirements. This could be due to two things, either the first estimations were very prudent, or the logistics experts had bent to the demands of the strategists and gave them the figures they wanted to hear. The strategists also had to compromise and lower the projected strength of the forces involved. There was even an argument between rear echelon and front line generals over the composition of units that were to be landed. Of course, on one side we have those who wanted to give priority to the fighting men, arguing that they were, 1)indispensable to securing the beachhead, 2) indispensable to the rapid capture of ports. Others defended the idea that, 1) without large rear echelon services, the fighting men would not have the means to fight, 2) without port repair units their capture would be useless, 3) the work load of rear echelon services would be exceptionally heavy as

Following pages.
The British ports are a hive of activity. Whilst the GMC and Dukw of the 1st US ID drive onto two LST, the jeeps in the foreground have to make do with the small LCT.
(NARA)

---

2. Russel F Weigley, *Eisenhower's lieutenants*, Indiana University Press, 1981, p.32
3. Michel Goya, *La chair et l'acier*, Tallandier, 2004.
4. Ruppenthal, *op. cit.*, 1955, vol 1, p. 307. These are each time figures concerning the supplying of American armies. To have a global vision of Overlord logistics one must add that of the British.
5. Ruppenthal, op. cit., vol. 1, p. 297.

Liberty Roads, 1944-1945

Liberty Roads, 1944-1945

Liberty Roads, 1944-1945

Date	Divs	Field Forces	Air Forces	COMZ	Total	Replacements
D +5	9	172 900	8 500	41 200	222 600	6 700
15	11	297 200	21 900	83 500	402 600	43 600
25	a11	353 100	42 600	142 300	538 000	60 200
40	15	453 800	79 900	235 100	768 800	95 100
60	16	532 400	104 500	286 600	926 500	138 800
90	21	666 400	123 900	343 600	1 133 900	204 800

a Two airborne divisions withdrawn.

A quarter of the GMC were equipped with a ring-mount for the heavy machine-gun 0.50 (12.7 mm). Three types of mount were added, the M32 and M36 on the short chassis respectively with metal and canvas cabin roof, the M37 in various versions on the long chassis CCKW 353, one of which is seen here reversing onto a LST the eve of D-Day. Note the personnel's personal items piled up on the cover.
(NARA)

added to the task of daily supplies was the re-establishment of lines of communication (port, railways, roads and bridges). To sum up, the army needed everybody straight away. The chart below distinguishes the forecast strength. It shows a clear priority given to fighting units in the first days, then a balancing out with rear echelon units (ComZ) (from 2 ComZ personnel for ten with the Field Forces, the number at D+90 is one for two). However, there is an important aspect, this chart counts certain service units in the Field Forces that were organically attached to them, such as the regimental supply columns.

The compromise was not well received by ComZ however, and it deemed that left as it was, it would be incapable of honouring all of their missions[6].

Very well planned logistics

This planning left no room for a safety margin. This explains the extreme precision placed in planning unloading on the beaches, the preparation of repairing each Normandy port, even the small ones, the requests sent to MTOUSA (Mediterranean Theatre of Operation USA) for information concerning experience gained in the reconstruction of the port of Anzio and the interest shown by the Americans for an apparently crazy British idea... bringing the ports with them. We will not cover the artificial ports (Mulberry) here as the subject has been covered in a host of publications[7], but we can take note that another British idea was taken up again by the Americans : turning the Gulf of Morbihan into the hub of the American supply chain.

Experts estimated that the Breton ports would not suffice. That of Brest in particular suffered from being too distant and the probable destruction of the Morlaix viaduct cutting the Brest-Paris railway line. Anticipating the possible difficulties, the British then had the idea of using the Auray estuary, a coastal river that flowed into the Gulf of Morbihan. This site had the advantage of being protected by the western currents by the Quiberon peninsula and having a sufficiently deep channel for Liberty Ships; it was also close to the Lorient-Rennes railway.

Codenamed *Operation Chastity*, it *"only"* required the installation along the Auray channel of landing stages linked to the coast by Mulberry type pontoons. Five ships had to be able to come alongside whilst thirty mooring points would also need to be opened up. After a month of work, the experts hoped to be able to offer a daily unloading capacity of 7,000 tonnes[8]. The question of beach organisation was the centre of all attention as it would have to support the bulk of the battle for weeks. Documents detailing the unloading operations during the first seven days show the mooring points for Liberty Ships, organising fleets, detailing the unloading procedures, evacuation and constitution of first dumps. Timing was controlled down to the minute. These huge files do not leave, in theory, any room for improvisation. From D+7 up to D+90, the planning no longer reaches this level of precision but it nevertheless details how the troops will be landed, where, when and in which order. They show the dates where a given item of unloading equipment needed to be replaced by another (the switching over from landing ships and coasters to deep water freighters from Great Britain on D+22, then those arriving directly from the USA on D+42), where a type of stocking or packaging would be changed for another (fuel jerrycans replaced by pipelines from the tank-

---

6. Ruppenthal, *op. cit.*, vol. 1, p. 300.
7. The interested reader can always consult Olivier Wievorka, *Histoire de la bataille de Normandie*, Seuil, 2007, pp 127-130 & Guy Hartcup, *Code Name Mulberry: The planning, building and operation of the Normandy harbours*, David & Charles (Publishers) Ltd, 1977.
8. Ruppenthal, *op. cit.*, vol 1, p. 294.
9. O. Wievorka, *op. cit.*, p.118-126
10. Although the US Navy had at its disposal in May 1944 some 409 LST, 687 LCT and 478 LCI, it only sent 188, 279 and 124 to Overlord. Chester Wilmot, *The struggle for Europe*, Presse de la Cité, 1964, p.232
11. The American engineers had been gathering together all there was to be known about Normandy bridges for two years. They had also estimated the flow of each road. One just does not know what to think about such a level of planning. RG Ruppenthal, *op. cit.*, vol 1, p.314.
12. RG Ruppenthal, *op. cit.*, vol1, p. 315.

---

ers to the coast on D+15). In order to deal with unforeseen circumstances two emergency supply services were set up. The first, named *Red Ball Express* would allow the transportation of 100 tonnes of urgent supplies per day. All crates were stamped with a red ball indicating their extreme priority and were loaded onto a dedicated ship. The second, *Greenlight*, consisted of sending within six days, 600 tonnes of munitions or engineers' materiel in place of less urgent supplies. Compared to the thousands of tonnes unloaded every day, these urgent supplies were a drop in the ocean. It could only be hoped that the plan would go ahead without any hitches.

The question of the number of landing craft, something that would be decisive to the landings, was also at the forefront of planners' minds. Olivier Wievorka has detailed the perilous juggling necessary to assemble the allied armada[9]. The Americans had the utmost difficulty in honouring their side of the deal as they had pushed back the building of landing craft from second place in the table of priorities to twelfth in January 1943 and were forced to call upon companies that had no experience in ship building -the shipyards being full to the brim- and having dispersed their available landing craft in the Pacific and Mediterranean[10]. At the Tehran conference, General Marshall recognised that the lack of landing craft and ships had become particularly serious. There was a drawn out arbitration in order to increase production, although this did not change the fact that the number of landing craft remained insufficient.

The experts and strategists played therefore on three parameters. The first was to delay the landings by a month in order to gain a month's production. The second was to lower the amount required. They lowered the percentages of projected losses. Indeed, the landing craft would not be used only once, some were already in use in the Mediterranean and on D-Day and the following days they would have to go back and forth to bring in reinforcements. Therefore, the less that were destroyed the more they could be used for transportation and less would be required. From the initial 50%, the viability of ships was progressively increased, reaching 75% for the LCA and 95% for the LST. Thus, with the same amount, the carrying capacity for the first wave increased from 156,000 men to 189,000 and 17,800 to 21,000 vehicles. Rotation time was also reduced and Ike's deputy, Beddell Smith, put forward the idea of reducing the number of vehicles per division from 3,000 to 1,450. The third parameter involved scraping the bottom of the barrel and to take back to Britain as much equipment as possible, even if it meant cancelling an operation in the Indian Ocean against the Andaman Islands, a measure that, as once can imagine, led to strong protestation on the part of the Navy.

In comparison, the question of trucks appeared to be less urgent. However, they were just as important as without them the tens of thousands of tonnes of supplies would never get off the beaches. Five Engineer General Service Regiments would be used to repair and maintain the roads and bridges[11] used by the Transportation Corps trucks. The latter estimated its needs at 240 Trucks companies (40 vehicle road companies plus eight others in reserve) two thirds of which were heavy trucks, as well as two drivers who could work in shifts. SHAEF deemed this request as being very excessive and only attributed 160 companies, the bulk of which were Light Companies equipped with 2.5 t GMC, the landing of which would be spread out between D-Day and D+90. This led to howls of protest from the Transportation Corps claiming the probable break down in the logistics chain, but these protestations only had a limited effect on the high command[12].

This was no doubt due to the fact that from D+41 onwards, the experts counted on rail to ease the road borne requirements, at least in the Cotentin peninsula. Planned by the staff of the 2nd Military Railway Service commanded by Brigadier General Clarence L. Burpee, the re-opening of railway lines was to be undertaken as soon as possible and five Engineer General Service Regiments and a heavy bridging battalion were to accompany the troops to get the lines immediately back into service. Although the engineers were

Barrage balloons are inflated in the port of Weymouth, these protected the fleet from the Luftwaffe.
In the background we can see two LCI (L) and a LCH (on the left) whereas on the quayside are parked an International IH 4x4 truck, a Navy 6x6, three Dodge WC, a GMC, a Diamond T model 972 dump and two trailer with compressed hydrogen bottles for inflating the balloons. It required between 90 and 105 bottles for the large barrage balloons (1500-1300m altitude), and 13 to 16 for the smaller types (600m altitude).
(Région Basse-Normandie/NARA, P013180)

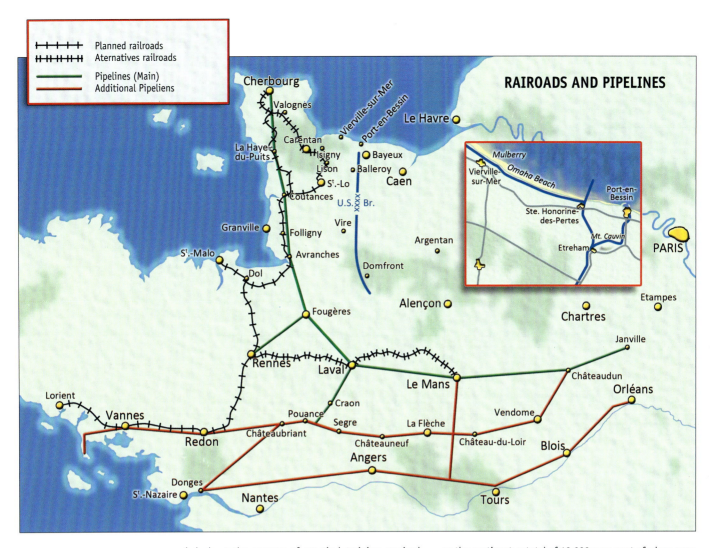

RAIROADS AND PIPELINES

13. RG Ruppenthal, *op. cit.*, vol 1, p. 318.
14. Joseph Bykofsky and Harold Larson, *The Tranportation Corps*, CMH, 1957, vol. 3, p. 243.
15. Irwin Ross, *"Trucks & Trains in battle"*, Harper's magazine, janvier 1945.
16. Maurice Matloff, *Strategic planning for coalition warfare 1943-1944*, CMH, 1959, p.422.

worried about the amount of practical training received, they had plenty of time to write detailed reports, thanks to intelligence received from the French Resistance, concerning each railway line going as far as Rennes, showing the flow of traffic, infrastructure, the type of bridges and size of marshalling yards. It estimated its material needs based on a 75% destruction rate based on experience gained in Italy, making a colossal total of 47,500 tonnes to unload in three months on a beach like *Utah*. Ideally, the Rennes railway station would be open on D+90. Two headquarters for the Railway Grand Divisions (regulation), two Railway Shop Battalions (maintenance) and two Railway Operating Battalions would await in England before becoming operational on the continent, a total of 12,000 men most of whom were mobilised railway professionals[13]. On D+90, the Transportation Corps hoped to disembark 354 locomotives and more than 5,000 wagons, not counting captured materiel[14]. In all, 20,000 wagons had been especially made and sent in kit form to Great Britain for the landings. These were specially made as the European lines were designed for light four-wheeled wagons and not eight as was the case in the United States[15].

As we can see, the task was not straightforward : *"You can not imagine the difficulties we encountered in the planning. When you have to sit down and look at the distribution of divisions, the loading charts and this type of thing, and you do not know what sort of ships you are going to load, or if you will have enough, it is enough to send you to the mad house"*[16].

When billeting decides wars

The importance of logistics was felt as far as the choice of billets in Great Britain The allocation of theatres of operation between the British and Americans was not the result of a thought process but due to a straightforward observation. The American troops were concentrated in south-east England, the British in the east. There was no question of mixing the armies and it was decided that the American troops would embark in western ports and land on western beaches. The Americans were satisfied with this as it would later simplify the arrival of troops direct from the United States who would touch French soil in the American zone (Brittany). This choice pleased the British whose armies were to advance along the Channel coast and this would ease supply lines from the UK (and if needed, their re-embarkation) as was the case in

1914-1918 and 1939-1940. This undeniably logical choice, dictated by logistics, did not take into account the operational capacities of the two armies and had two consequences, one on short term, the other long term. On the short term, the Americans, with a plethora of armoured vehicles at their disposal, would be confronted by the most problematic terrain -the bocage hedgerows- whereas the British

Port or Beach	Opening Date	At Opening	Discharge Capacity (in Long Tons) :			
			D plus 10	D plus 30	D plus 60	D plus 90
Total			14700	27200	36940	45950
Omaha Beach	D Day	3400	9000	6000	5000	5000
Utah Beach	D Day	1800	4500	4500	4000	4000
Quinéville Beach	D +3	1100	1200	1200	1000	1000
Isigny	D +11	100	0	500	500	500
Cherbourg	D +11	1620	0	6000	7000	8000
Mulberry A	D +12	4000	0	5000	5000	5000
Grandcamp	D +15	100	0	300	300	300
St. Vaast	D +16	600	0	1100	1100	1100
Barfleur	D +20	500	0	1000	1000	1000
Granville	D +26	700	0	700	1500	2500
St. Mâlo	D +27	900	0	900	2500	3000
Brest & Rade de Brest	D +53	3240	0	0	3240	5300
Quiberon Bay	D +54	4000	0	0	4000	7000
Lorient	D +57	800	0	0	800	2250

Liberty Roads, 1944-1945

Still in Weymouth, two LCT (Mark 6). The trailer seen on board is a Trailer Athey Track Laying 6-Ton BT898-4 loaded with fascines to prevent vehicles from becoming bogged down in sand. On the quaysides we can make out several mobile caterpillar cranes, jeeps and trailers belonging to the 1st US ID.
(Région Basse-Normandie/NARA, P013176)

would lack capacity -in equipment and doctrine- to exploit a more open terrain. Long term the paradox would worsen, the less mobile British army would find itself in the most favourable and decisive part of the front. It would be the British that were tasked with mopping up the Channel coast and capturing Antwerp, the cornerstone of allied logistics, then push into the Belgian-German plains and envelop the Ruhr from the north. The American army would be dependent on the success of its neighbour for its logistics and would be confronted with a more difficult terrain in the Vosges mountains, the Ardennes and the Eiffel hills. This small detail of billeting would have massive consequences in the coming days and months. The strategists, obsessed by the logistical planning, had neglected the operational planning[17].

This might seem repetitive, however, it is essential to distinguish the planning and logistics. It cannot be denied that the Allies had planned like never before, however, the logistics experts asked to give their opinion were not always listened to. As we can see, on the eve of the landings the deficit in materiel remained high enough to warrant fears of a catastrophe. This did not prevent the planners from giving the green light to Eisenhower, either by remaining deaf to requests or by playing with figures so that what had previously been impossible was rendered possible. Although logistics had dictated the choices made by strategists it finally concerned a point that has never been debated, that of the allocation of theatres of operations.

On the eve of 6 June 1944, it is easy to imagine that everybody was holding their breath, the long awaited moment of reckoning had arrived.

---

17. Russel F. Weigley, *"Normandy to Falaise, a critique of allied Operational planning in 1944"*, in Michael D Krause & R Cody Phillips (dir.), Historical perspective of operational art, CMH, 2005.

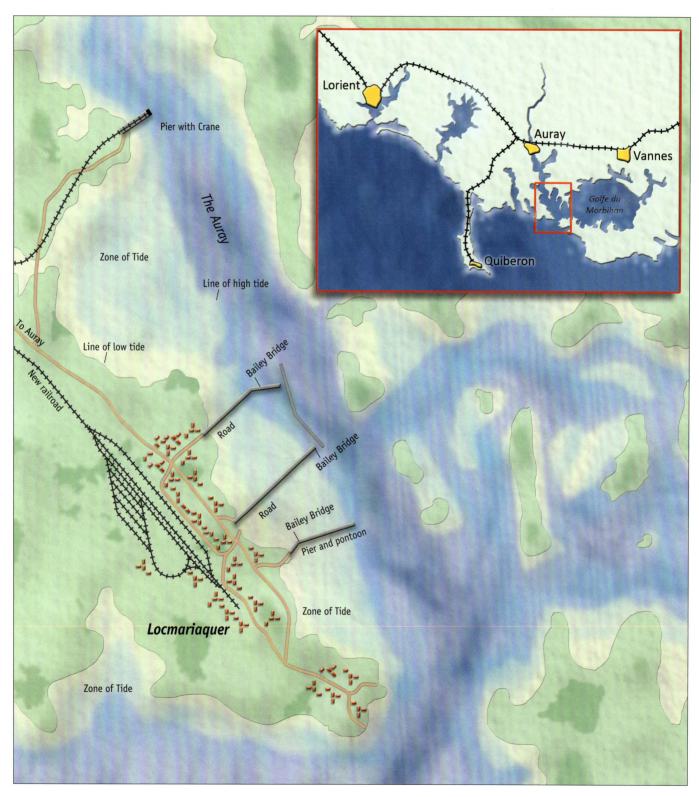

CHAPTER 4
THE BATTLE OF NORMANDY, THE ORDEAL BY FIRE

D-Day

The Americans landed on two beaches : Omaha (1st and 29th ID) east of Isigny and Utah (4th ID) at base of the Cotentin peninsula in a marshy area at the far western end of the landing area. Opposite Utah, two Airborne Divisions (82nd and 101st) were dropped to secure the inland zones and give depth to the landings.

It was planned for the first engineer units tasked with beach clearing to land one hour after the first assault wave. This hour was to leave enough time for the infantry, demolition squads and DD[1] tanks to secure the beaches. Responsibility for each beach was placed in the hands of Engineer Special Brigades. One — the 4th — was tasked with *Utah* Beach whereas two others — the 5th and 6th — shared *Omaha*. As well as the task

The cruiser USS Augusta, the flagship of the Western Naval Task Force with General Bradley on board has just completed its bombardment and the LCVP of USS Anne Arundel head towards the shore carrying part of the 2/18 Inf. Regt. which landed at 09h30 on Easy Red. They had a rendez-vous with hell.
(Région Basse-Normandie/NARA, P012688)

THE PROVISIONAL ENGINEER SPECIAL BRIGADE GROUP

- Headquarters and HQ Co.
- Signal Platoon
- Det A, 255th Sig Const Co.
- Co C, 783rd MP Bn.
- 302nd MP Escort Guard Co.
- 2nd Bn., 358th GenService Regt Det A, CIC team
- 440th Eng Dep Co. (- 3 sec.)

5TH ENGINEER SPECIAL BRIGADE
- 5th Engineer Special Brigade
- Hq & Hq Co.
- 37th Engineer C Bn.
- 336th Engineer C Bn.
- 348th Engineer C Bn.
- 61st Med Bn.
- 210th MP Co.
- 30th Chemical Decon Co.
- 294th Joint Assault Sig Co.
- 251st Ord Bn.
- 616th Ord Ammo Co.
- 3466th Ord MAM Co.
- 533rd QM Service Bn.
- 4141st QM Serv Co.
- 4142nd QM Serv Co.
- 4143rd QM Serv Co.

- 619th QM Bn.
- 97th QM Rhd Co.
- 559th QM Rhd Co.
- Co. A, 203rd Gas Supply Bn.
- 131st QM Mobile Bn.
- 453rd Amphib Trk Co.
- 458th Amphib Trk Co.
- 459th Amphib Trk Co.

ATTACHED UNITS
- 4042nd QM Truck Co.
- 6th Naval Beach Bn.
- 26th Bomb Disposal Squad
- 3rd Aux Surgical Grp (6 teams)
- S&I Sect.
- Det 1215th Sig Dep Co.
- Det, 175th Sig Repair Co.
- 467th Eng Maint Co.,one plat
- 440th Eng Dep Co., one Plat
- 607th Graves Reg Co., 2nd Plat
- 1219th Fire Fighting Plat
- 1st Med Supply Depot Sec
- Det P 165th Sig Photo Co.
- British VHF Signal Det
- Civil Affairs Det

UNITÉS ATTACHÉES À C/DU 6 JUIN
- 487th Port Bn.
- 184th Port Co.
- 185th Port Co.
- 186th Port Co.
- 187th Port Co.
- 282nd Port Co.
- 283rd Port Co
- 502nd Port Bn.
- 270th Port Co.
- 271st Port Co.
- 272nd Port Co.
- 272rd Port Co.

6TH ENGINEER SPECIAL BRIGADE
- 6th Engineer Special Brigade Hq&Hq Co.
- 147th Eng C Bn.
- 149th Eng C Bn.
- 203rd Eng C Bn.
- 60th Med Bn.
- 453rd Col Co.
- 499th Col Co.
- 500th Col Co.
- 634th Clearing Co.
- 214th MP Co.

- 31st Chem Decon Co.
- 293rd Joint Asault Sig Co.
- 74th Ord Bn.
- 618th Ord Ammo Co.
- 3565th Ord MAM Co.
- 538th QM Bn.
- 3204th QM Serv Co.
- 3205th QM Serv Co.
- 967th QM Serv Co.
- 95th QM Bn.
- 88th QM Rhd Co.
- 555th QM Rhd Co.
- 3820th QM Gas Sup Co.
- 280th QM Bn.
- 460th Amphib Truck Co.
- 461st Amphib Truck Co.
- 463rd Amphib Truck Co.

ATTACHED UNITS
- 3704th QM Truck Co.
- 7th Naval Beach Bn.
- 27th Ord Bomb Disposal Squad
- 3rd Aux Surg Group (4 teams)
- Det S&I
- Sec 3 215th Sig Dep Co.
- Det I&O 175th Sig Rep Co.

- 440th Eng Dep Co., 3rd Plat
- 467 Eng Maint Co.
- 607th Graves Reg Co., 3rd Plat
- 1220th Eng Fire Fighting Plat
- 1st Med Depot, one Squad
- Det Q 165th Sig Photo Co.
- Det C CIC Team
- Civil Affairs Det
- Det B AF Intransit Depot Gp
- 1602nd Engr Map Depot Grp

ATTACHED UNITS FROM 6th JUNE
- 494th Port Bn.
- 238th Port Co.
- 239th Port Co.
- 240th Port Co.
- 241st Port Co.
- 517th Port Bn.
- 284th Port Co.
- 285th Port Co.
- 797th Port Co.
- 799th Port Co.
- 800th Port Co.

In Jonathan Gawne, Spareheadind D-Day, Histoire & Collections, 1995, pp. 248-250.

US Coast Guards high-speed boat tows a Dukw. Many ran out of fuel on D-Day after having waiting for several hours off Omaha Beach. They had to keep their engines running in order for the bilge pumps to work, or were incapable of reaching ships too far away from Utah Beach. *(Région Basse-Normandie/NARA, P012539)*

LCI(L)-85 crammed full of ESB soldiers, manœuvres for the assault. At 08.30 hrs, the moment it tried a second landing on the flank of Easy Red at Omaha, it hit a mine and was hit by approximately 25 shells, killing fifteen men and wounding 30. The vessel caught fire and eventually sank at 14.30 hrs.
(Région Basse-Normandie/NARA, p012533)

of unloading ships they also had to clear the beaches, receive the reinforcement waves, then construct, maintain and control the exits, set up the first dumps, receive and evacuate the wounded and prisoners of war. Its personnel — fifteen to twenty thousand men — were specially trained for this role that they had already fulfilled in the Mediterranean and Pacific. Although they were built around one or two engineer battalions - which explains their nomenclature -, they were in fact an inter-arm administrative unit completed with, when required, transport companies, port units, signals, police, repairs, as well as a Naval Beach Battalion. In total, the two beaches had the in operation : 340 GMC, 950 Dukws, 16 tugs, 7 sea mules, 66 barges[2].

All the meticulous planning went to pieces in the very first hours of 6 June. At *Omaha*, most of the landing craft did not arrive at the right beach and as soon as the ramps came down all hell broke out. The first sixteen engineer teams were wiped out before they even touched the beach, 40% of their strength was rapidly knocked out as well as ten of their sixteen bulldozers. Their Beachmasters, supposed to guide the landing craft were either dead or in the wrong place. The survivors could not communicate with the command as 80% of their radios had been lost. Brave-

---

1. Duplex Drive, modified tanks rendered amphibious.
2. Ruppenthal, *op. cit.*, vol 1, p. 283.

THE ROLE OF VARIOUS UNITS

Engineer Combat Battalions & Engineer Shore Regiment	An assault unit tasked with all engineer roles on the beach (minesweeping, opening gaps, road construction…)	**Ordnance Bn**	Vehicle maintenance (MAM), maintenance of materiel and the management of ammunition dumps (V class) (Ammo)	**Medical Bn**	Medical service
Engineer General Service Regiment	A multitask engineer unit tasked with building roads and dumps inland.	**QM Mobile Bn**	Coordination of transport units and transfer of supplies	**Military Police Co**	Military Police unit
Port Bn	Port handling and unloading	**Amphibian Trucks Co**	An amphibious transport unit equipped with DUKW vehicles	**Chemical decontamination Co**	Chemical decontamination unit
Harbor craft service company	Support unit equipped with motor launches	**Trucks Co**	Transport unit (GMC).	**Signal**	Transmissions
Naval Beach Bn	Naval unit (see insert)	**Graves reg. Co**	tasked with recording war graves and burials	**Joint Assaut Signal Companies**	Signals service for air support, naval fire support and internal ESB transmissions
Ordnance Bomb Disposal Squad	Bomb diposal Unit	**Quartermaster Service Bn**	Loading and unloading, supply dump management		
Fire fighting Platoon	Fire fighters	**QM Railhead Co**	Installation and management of class I and II dumps		
Civil Affairs Det.	Relations with civilians	**QM Gas Supply Bn**	Management of class III dumps (POL)		

Opposite and previous page. **Omaha Beach between six in the morning and the beginning of the afternoon. From the hell experienced by the first waves and immortalized by Robert Capa, up to the arrival of the first reinforcements of the 5th ESB who landed at the end of the morning (center) when the beach became jammed when new waves of infantry crossed paths with supply Dukw and half-tracks trying to get off the beach (below). It was not until the end of the afternoon that the first non-tracked vehicles were able to leave Omaha. The first dumps were opened the following day.** *(chbg164, NARA © Coriello, Bibliothèque municipale de Cherbourg pr la photo de gauche, les autres NARA).*

ly, the teams attempted anyway to work under enemy fire, without materiel or protection. In these conditions they were only able to clear a narrow corridor. The beach was nothing more than a hellish landscape swept by automatic weapons and where 25,000 men were trying to survive. It was at this time that the first landing craft carrying soldiers of the 37th Engineer Combat Battalion arrived, four other battalions followed. They only added to the chaos. Those who managed to cross the beach were put to work by officers and fired back at the enemy. From 8.30 onwards, some teams cleared mines and destroyed a few obstacles. The anti-tank ditch was filled to the west of the beach. Upon the recommendations of the Beachmasters, Bradley ordered the delay of the second wave so as not to add to the confusion and hundreds of landing craft sailed around in circles. Dozens of Dukw ran out of fuel and sank.

After four long hours, the first German strong points were neutralised and an exit secured. The engineers worked where they had landed. They unblocked the ramps of damaged landing craft, swept for mines, moved obstacles and barbed wire, laid wire mats on the beach and opened up routes inland. At midday, the Naval Beach Battalions had established communications between the ships and themselves. By 14.00 hrs, the first tanks rolled off the beach by exit D1. Exit F1 was cleared but vehicles could not manage to get through. In the centre, where most of the first wave had concentrated, it was not until the end of the afternoon that a first exit, E1, was opened allowing access to the coast road. The personnel spent a lot of time looking after the hundreds of wounded men. Enemy fire slackened with each passing hour. By the evening, all of the NBB were operational to coordinate the hordes of landing craft and at around 23.00 hrs, three exits were open. The beaches emptied. Finally, the balance sheet at the end of the day was remarkable given what the fighting men had been through : 34,000 men out of the planned for 56,000 had landed, as well as a third of the vehicles[3]. Naturally, no supply dump had been opened and there remained a lot of minefield clearing and cleaning up to be done before the first crates could be stored.

The landings were going better at *Utah*. Whereas the men fighting at *Omaha* accumulated bad luck, those at *Utah* made

ESB STRENGTH			
	Men	Vehicles	Trailers
HQ Prov. ESB Group	1393	172	11
5th ESB	8722	916	304
6th ESB	8708	919	304
11th Port	8631	597	15

[3]. Ruppenthal, *op. cit.*, vol 1, pp.380-384.

THE 1st ENGINEER SPECIAL BRIGADE

The small units attached to the ESB often changed during the period from June to December 1944. The list below shows the brigade composition at its maximum strength.

- 1st Engineer Special Brigade, Hq & Hq Co.
- 531st Eng Shore Regt, 3 Shore Bns
- 24th Amphib Trk Bn.
- 462nd Amphib Trk Co.
- 478th Amphib Trk Co.
- 479th Amphib Trk Co.
- 306th QM Bn.
- 556th QM Railhead Co.
- 562nd QM Railhead Co.
- 3939th QM Gas Supply Co.
- 191st Ord Bn.
- 3497th Ord MAM Co.
- 625th Ord Amm Co.
- 161st Ord Plat.
- 577th QM Bn.
- 363rd QM Serv Co.
- 3207th QM Serv Co.
- 4144th QM Serv Co.

- 261th Med Bn.
- 449th MP Co.
- 286th JASCO
- 33rd Chem Decon Co.
- 3206th QM Service Co. (1 section)

ADAPTED UNITS
- 2nd Naval Beach Battalion
- 23rd Ord Bomb Disposal Sec
- 38th Eng Gen Serv Regt, 2 Eng GS Bns
- 467th Eng Maint Co.,
- 1st plat 440th Eng Depot Co.
- 1 plat 1605th Eng Map Sect
- 1217th Eng Fire Fighting Plat
- 1218th Eng Fire Fighting Plat
- 262nd QM Bn.
- 4061st QM Serv Co.
- 4083rd QM Serv Co.

- 4088th QM Serv Co.
- 4090th QM Serv Co.
- 4092nd QM Serv Co.
- 4190th QM Serv Co.
- 244th QM Bn.
- 552nd QM Railhead Co.
- 3877th QM Gas Supply Co.
- 3878th QM Gas Supply Co.
- 308th QM Railhead Co. *(attachée au 306th QM Bn.)*
- 3877th QM Gas Supply Co. *(attachée au 306th QM Bn.)*
- 4132nd QM Serv Co. *(attachée au 577th QM Bn.)*
- 607th QM Graves Reg Co., 4th — Plat *(attachée au 577th QM Bn.)*
- 537th QM Bn.
- 3692nd QM Truck Co.
- 3683rd QM truck Co.
- 3684th QM Truck Co.
- 4002nd QM Truck Co.
- 4041st QM Truck Co.
- 815th Amphib Truck Co.
- 816th Amphib Truck Co.
- 817th Amphib Truck Co.
- 818th Amphib Truck Co.
- 3615th Ord MAM Co. *(attached to 191st Ord Bn.)*
- 175th Sig Repair Co.
- Det 215th Sig Depot Co.
- Det 999th Sig Serv Co.
- Det 980th Sig Serv Co.
- Det 3111th Sig Serv Co.
- Det 165th Sig Photo Co.
- Det E 1st Med Co., 2 Sec
- 6th Surgical Group (12 équipes)
- 3rd Aux Surgical Group
- 301st MP Escort Guard Co.
- 595th MP Escort Guard Co.
- Company D, 383rd MP Bn.
- 52nd Finance Disbursing Section

- Det, 8th AF Intransit Depot Grp
- Det A, 11th Port
- 490th Port Bn.
- 226th Port Co.
- 227th Port Co.
- 228th Port Co.
- 229th Port Co.
- 518th Port Bn.
- 278th Port Co.
- 281th Port Co.
- 298th Port Co.
- 299th Port Co.
- 300th Port Co.
- 301st port Co.
- 519th Port Bn.
- 280th Port Co.
- 279th Port Co.
- 302nd Port Co.
- 303rd Port Co.
- 304th Port Co.
- 305th Port Co.

In Jonathan Gawne, Spareheadind D-Day, Histoire & Collections, 1995, pp. 248-250.

These C ration boxes have been loaded onto a Dukw with the help of a net. The absence of containers – which would not appear until the 1950s – was a real handicap.
(chbg062, NARA © Coriello, Bibliothèque municipale de Cherbourg)

A filled to the brim heads towards the coast; the latter was sometimes up to ten kilometres away. Without the Rhinoferries and these valiant little amphibious vehicles, the landings would not have been possible. (Région Basse-Normandie/NARA, p013242)

the most of being under a lucky star. Firstly, they landed a kilometre south of the right beach. This mistake turned out to be a stroke of luck as the defences there were much less dense. At *Omaha* errors in the timing had led to disastrous consequences, but at *Omaha* the early arrival of demolition squads allowed them to find all of the non-water obstacles. One good surprise was that their work was rendered easier and when the tide began to rise, not only were routes

LANDING AN ENTIRE ARMY, THE ROLE OF THE NBB

Whereas the operations in the Pacific were limited to landing a few units, the landings in Europe involved entire army corps. The chaotic landings of *Operation Torch* confirmed the need to have a naval unit on the shore in order to coordinate the final approach of landing craft and the actions of the navy and army on the coast.

It was for this role that the Naval Beach Battalions (NBB) were created in 1942. They were trained under by the Engineer Special Brigade to which each NBB was attached (2nd NBB with the 1st ESB, 6th NBB with the 5th ESB and the 7th NBB with the 6th ESB).

The role of the NBB was to ensure signals between the coast and the ships, clear and mark channels for the landing craft, carry out urgent repairs, aid and evacuate the wounded.

For this, each NBB had four platoons, one for signals, medical services, hydrography to destroy obstacles and one for repairing ships. Each NBB was commanded by a Beachmaster who held authority over all movement as far as the high tide mark.

Given the length of the beaches (8 kilometres for *Omaha*), the Beachmaster delegated his authority to subordinates, the Battalion Beach Groups who managed an area large enough for an assault by an infantry regiment.

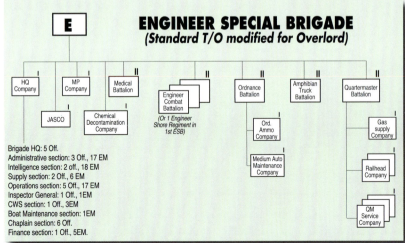

opened but all of the beach was cleared. Four breaches in the wall were rapidly opened, avoiding congestion on the beach and the engineers got to work setting up the first temporary dumps on the shore. However, by the end of the day the results of the operations were mixed. Fearful of the relatively active German artillery, the ship captains had dropped an-

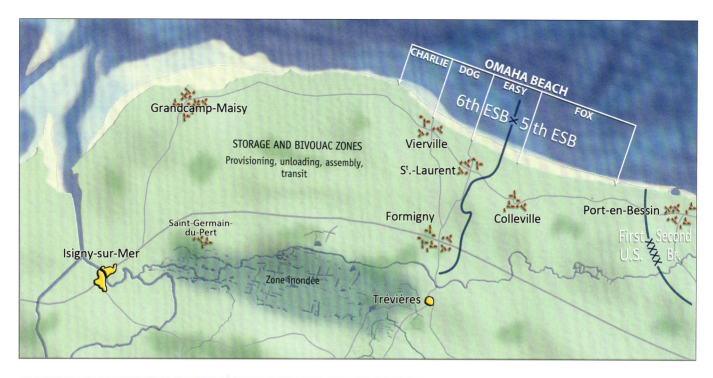

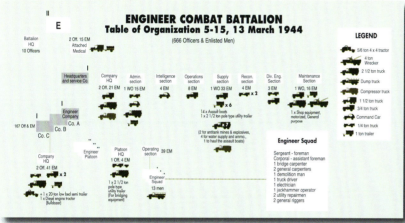

One of the advantages of the Dukw was of course its ability to transport its load beyond the shore and towards the forward dumps. However, although it frequently did this, it was advised against being used on the road as it took it away from its initial amphibious role. *(NARA)*

chor kilometres away from the beaches, forcing the landing craft to sail more than ten kilometres and therefore slowing down and disorganising operations. Also, the lack of good communications did not aid the Beachmasters in their task. Landing craft had dropped their ramps or opened their doors too far from the shore and the vehicles, despite their water-proof kit, had their engines flooded or just got stranded in the sands and given the fact that the tide was rising, their fate was sealed. Most of the engineers' equipment and vehicles was also missing as only 6 out of the 12 LST loaded with their equipment reached the shore on 6 June and even then, one was immediately destroyed by a direct hit. Many fields that had been planned for use as storage and bivouac zones were not captured until nightfall. The opening of partially flooded coastal roads was slower than planned and caused traffic jams back on the beaches. Finally, by the evening,

Omaha, 8 June 1944. Whilst the ESB clear the beach (6), barges (8), Rhinoferries (4 & 5) and Dukw (9) ensure the trips between the freighters which have sailed as close as possible to the shore (8). The LST have been beached despite the reticence of the Navy (1). The chaos was progressively cleared and replaced by an efficient routine. Sign posts sprang up everywhere. Fascines have been laid allowing for the circulation of the GMC and Dodge trucks (7, 9 & 10) following the white tapes denoting areas cleared of mines (3).
(Région Basse-Normandie/NARA sf 1, chbg116, NARA © Coriello, Bibliothèque municipale de Cherbourg)

Liberty Roads, 1944-1945

3

4

5

7

8

10

Liberty Roads, 1944-1945

With Weymouth Pavilion as a backdrop, the Rangers are checked a final time by EMBARCO (Embarcation Control). At the same time they were given donuts and coffee by the Red Cross. In England, several structures overlapped and un-necessarily complicated embarkation on procedures.
(NARA)

Liberty Roads, 1944-1945

Liberty Roads, 1944-1945

	THE THEORETICAL ROTATION OF DUKW AT UTAH BEACH		NOTICED ROTATION
	Tramp steamer	Liberty Ship	
Distance from shore	800 m	5 km	10 km
Distance between the shore and unloading point	800 m	800 m	2 km
Average speed at sea	5 km/h	5 km/h	4 km/h
Average speed on land	10 km/h	10 km/h	10 km/h
Loading times	10 min	15 min	15 min
Unloading times	10 min	10 min	30 min
Trip	30 min	130 min	320 min
Theoretical rotation	50 min	155 min	365 min

Source: Jonathan Gawne, Jour-J à l'aube, histoire & Collections, 1995, p. 280.

4. The Communication Zone (ComZ) was the administration which dealt with the rear echelon areas. It took over from the Service of Supply which existed in the United Kingdom from 1942 to D-Day. It was commanded by General Lee who came under the dual authority of Somervell on an administrative level and Eisenhower on an operational level. ComZ was itself sub-divided into sections including an Advance Section (ADSEC) which was placed just behind the Combat Zone.

23,000 out of the planned 32,000 men had landed, but only a handful of vehicles. It was clear, therefore, that the laborious planning had in no way avoided chaos. The following days would confirm the gulf between theory and reality.

THE HIGHS AND LOWS OF THE ENGINEER SPECIAL BRIGADES

The situation was difficult on the beaches but there was also chaos in the English ports. Never ending road and rail convoys arrived constantly in the embarkation zones. Once they were in the marshalling areas they had to be dealt with as they could not be sent back. Camps became overcrowded and the chaotic situation reached its worst point on 12 June. The marshalling areas were saturated and units were no longer recorded upon their arrival and simply lost. This led to V Corps commander, Major-General Gerow, to personally travel across to England to prove that a unit was still stationed there whereas the rear echelon ComZ were adamant that it had already been sent to Normandy. Several services overlapped. Whilst the BUCO supervised the process of listing the units and materiel to activate in cooperation with Bradley and Eisenhower, it was carried out in practical terms by its subdivision MOVCO (Movement Control). Except that MOVCO did not have control over the interior movement of port zones, this was the domain of EMBARCO (Embarkation Control). Whilst BUCO and MOVCO depended directly on the supreme command, EMBARCO was a substitute of ComZ[4].

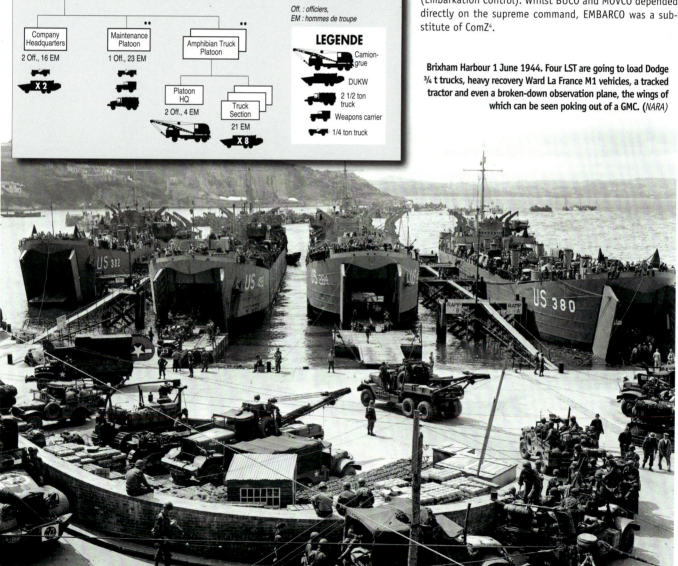

Brixham Harbour 1 June 1944. Four LST are going to load Dodge ¾ t trucks, heavy recovery Ward La France M1 vehicles, a tracked tractor and even a broken-down observation plane, the wings of which can be seen poking out of a GMC. (NARA)

Although EMBARCO had a lesser legitimacy, BUCO did not have control over the various billet organisations, supply dumps and movement which were all attached to ComZ. Added to this were the delays concerning the rotation of ships. Immobilised off the beaches for longer periods of time, there was a lack of tramp ships. When they returned it was rarely recorded and the port authorities had no reliable document to allow them to plan the day's embarkations. Working round the clock, several officers collapsed with exhaustion. Finally, these blocked ports were only cleared by a measure that was as straightforward as it was radical; the materiel and units were embarked according to the return of ships and no longer worrying about any sort of planning. The storm of 19 June, by preventing the rotation of ships, gave a four day respite that proved to be a Godsend[5].

In Normandy, the unloading procedures did not work. All of the transport manifests indicating which unit, with which equipment and strength, was on board a certain ship, was sent by mistake to the British sector. It was planned for EMBARCO to next send to the First Army the names of ships and their loads so that it could, according to requirements, establish debarkation lists and send them to the brigades. However, in reality the ships arrived at any time, dropped anchor wherever they wanted and often kilometres away from the beaches - due to a fear of German artillery - forcing the Dukw and the Rhino ferries[6] to make return trips of more than ten kilometres in rough seas, six hour rotations for these small vehicles that could only carry three tonnes, a drop in the ocean given the volume of supplies at stake.

Too often overloaded, the DUKW ran out of fuel and sank. For a while, all trace of the 30th ID was lost off the coast of Normandy. Before commencing unloading, the First Army insisted on planning it. What followed next was a drawn out wait while representatives climbed on board, checked the load and then sent the list to their superior officers in order to determine priority. The mediocre cooperation between the Army and the Navy did nothing to help the smooth running of operations[7].

To make all of this even more complex, it was planned to, in the shortest possible time, for the Beachmasters to hand over to a new authority, the NOIC, Naval Of-

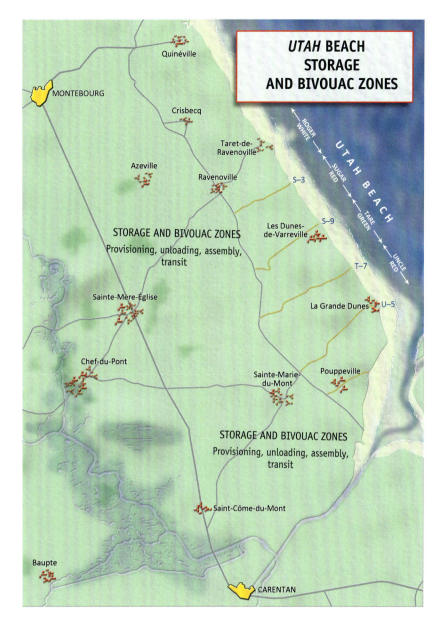

Little-known and un-glamorous, the mobile cranes played an essential role in the success of Overlord. The mechanical assistance in handling supplies was a real advantage that the German znd Soviet armies did not enjoy.
(Région Basse-Normandie/NARA)

ficer in Charge. At *Omaha*, this officer declared himself incapable of carrying out his role due to having lost all of his papers and the brigades ended up working without having recourse to his services. These difficulties revealed an insufficient preparation made worse by an excessively complicated chain of command. Each beach had its own difficulties : *Omaha* suffered from the chaos engendered by D-Day and *Utah* was hindered by a too slow advance which prevented the beaches from being placed out of the range of German artillery and the marshy character of the region.

On land, the Dukw were forced to accompany the troops as there was a lack of trucks, something that also lengthened the rotation times. It is true that one of the main problems facing the engineers was the lack of vehicles. The trucks had been, at times, destroyed by enemy fire or stuck in the sands, but more often than not they were still on board ships, or had their engines drowned as the waterproof kits were rarely effective. In the 5th Brigade,

---

5. Ruppenthal, *op. cit.*, vol 1, pp.422-426.
6. Large motorised pontoons were made by the Seebees on the beaches and used to transport up to 18 trucks or 10 tanks up to the beaches.
7. It was true at the top as well as at the bottom, the civilian sailors under contract refused for example to supply the Dukw that moored alongside with fresh water.

Liberty Roads, 1944-1945

All of the American logistics in action. Protected by a swarm of barrage balloons, four LST are ready to empty their holds whilst more and more coasters and Liberty Ships arrive. This photo was taken on 9 or 10 June at Omaha.
(Région Basse-Normandie/NARA, p012621)

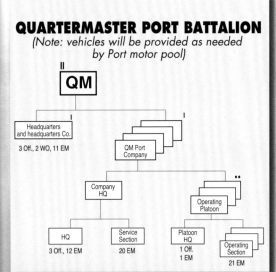

Photo 1 was taken before the landings in Selsey harbour in southern England. It is interesting because it shows the inside of the Dukw and the control panel, but mostly because it shows an unusual angle of the Mulberry elements. One can see a floating causeway (Whale) with at base the Phoenix breakwaters and Loebnitz pier heads. The other photos were taken when the St Laurent Mulberry was opened on 16 June. Within ten days, a causeway had been assembled *(2)* and connected to the impressive pier heads *(3)* to which a first LST has moored, helped by a tig *(4)*. Within two hours, it will be emptied and first M8 armored cars and 345 of the Half Tracks belonging to the 702nd Tank Destroyer Bn landed *(5)*. On the right one can see a semi-forward cabin GMC (AFKWX 353). The great storm would soon break-up this huge Lego kit.
(Région Basse-Normandie/NARA)

QUARTERMASTER PORT BATTALION
(Note: vehicles will be provided as needed by Port motor pool)

Liberty Roads, 1944-1945

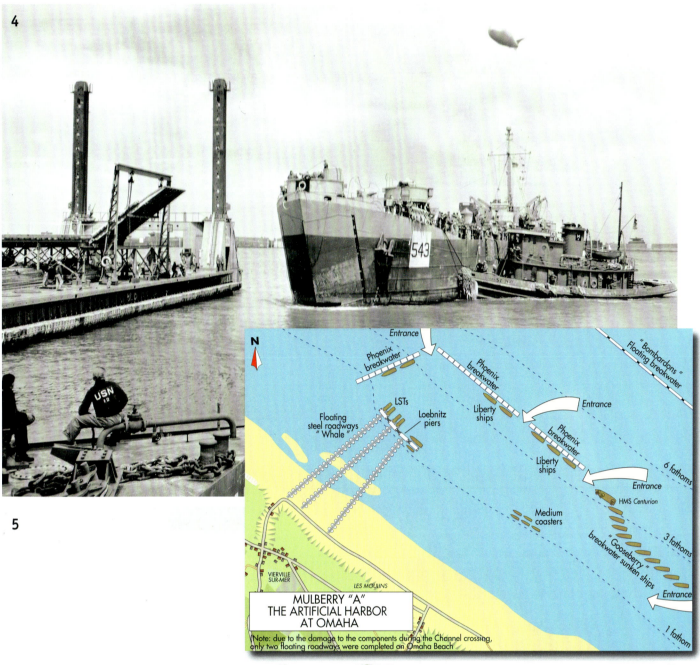

Liberty Roads, 1944-1945

1

2

3

Liberty Roads, 1944-1945

THE STORM

Of 19 to 22 June hit the coast of Normandy with high winds which, joined with the tide, created a two to three meter swell. The Gooseberry breakwater of scuttled ships should have provided protection but the ships had not been sunk correctly, either too deeply or with too much space between them such as *HMS Centurion* here which is literally submerged *(1)*. The waves entered into the Mulberry and broke up the fragile causeways *(2)* and *(5)*. Some pier heads lost their four pillars as we can see in the background *(5)*. Worst of all, more than one hundred barges broke their moorings and crashed into things such as these LCI and LCT *(3 & 4)* and even a large LST visible in the background I. Most were re-floated in July. 19 precious Rhinoferries and the only Seebees repair barge also sank *(6)*. On 22 June, *Omaha* was a scene of desolation.

(Région Basse-Normandie/NARA)

VESSELS DRIVEN AGAINST THE COAST BY THE STORM OF 19-22 JUNE	
Utah	**Omaha**
1 LCI	2 LST
45 LCT	78 LCT
45 LCVP	12 LCI
10 Rhino ferries[1]	1 LCF
11 Rhino tugs[2]	83 LCM
3 LCF	19 Rhino ferries
64 LCM	22 Rhino tugs
25 LBV	1 Workshop Rhino
1 Fuel barge	39 LCVP
5 Liberty Ships	3 Liberty Ship
	17 LBV
	2 LSC
	1 Fuel barge
	1 Workshop barge
	1 Food barge

1. Motorized pontoons.
2. Push tug boats.
In Jonathan Gawne, *Spearheading D-Day*, Histoire & Collections, 1995, p. 278.

Liberty Roads, 1944-1945

44 trucks were under water. Generally speaking, the lack of space due to the slow advance disrupted the opening of planned supply dumps and created a great deal of congestion.

By 16 June, the Navy Construction Battalions had made enough headway with Mulberry A for the first LST to berth. It took two hours to unload it, a time that was brought down to 40 minutes for those that followed. This was a great improvement on the 12 to 14 hours that the ship was immobilised when it was on the beaches. However, the weather combined with German resistance in order to upset the plans. Planning had taken into account seven days of bad weather but in reality it was three weeks of wind and rain that hindered operations, including gales between 19 and 22 June. Described as having been an event of biblical proportions, it was really nothing exceptional. The force 6 to 7 winds, blew at speeds of only 45 to 60km/h, but created a swell of two to three metres and this was much too rough for the small barges and Dukw. Operations were stopped. Before long, damage was extensive : the breakwaters anchored in deep water and far too dispersed to help the circulation of shipping proved useless and the waves poured into the port, breaking jetties and sweeping over the road sections that they carried. Phoenix caissons and boats that had broken free drifted wildly inside the moorings, adding to the destruction already wreaked. Mulberry A did not survive and losses in landing craft and barges were high.

The beached ships were stripped to save their loads. All men were used to clear the beaches of debris and the Dukw that had remained sheltered on land got back to work on the 22nd.

Given these events, Operation Overlord could have ended in disaster, but what had not been taken into account was the ability of the men on the ground to improvise. As early as 8 June, the Navy allowed its precious LST to beach, despite the risk of tearing their hulls. In this way they could rapidly unload at low tide then sail away at high tide. In the space of fifteen days, 200 LST beached at *Omaha*. After the storm the barges were also beached. It was decided on the 10th to no longer adhere to the rules of priority and to unload in the order of arrival. The NOIC headquarters, which had been inefficient up to that point, was reorganised. On 12 June, the First Army lifted the black out that had forbidden, for safety reasons, work at night. The general chaos was overcome by common sense and sweat. Each quartermaster soldier moved seven tonnes on a daily basis. Thus, the beach teams broke records. At the end of June, the daily disembarkation reached 115% of forecasts at *Omaha* and 124% at *Utah*. The deficit in vehicles began to be absorbed and by the second week, the first supply dumps on dry land were opened. The beach, which had up to that time been used as a temporary dump, became an immense redistribution hub where goods arrived by barge, Dukw or pontoons, transferred by the help of cranes onto the GMC trucks which then left for the dumps. In order to cope with the daily passage of thousands of vehicles, the engineers widened the narrow coast roads and maintained them with broken stones, pebbles and even used batteries as bedrock on 400 metres of new roads. Some control points counted one vehicle every five seconds and traffic jams were common. Dust became a veritable problem for the men and machines. The ESB then set its decontamination units spreading oil over the roads. The confused agitation of the first days had been transformed into an efficient routine. The American generals could breath a sigh of relief, but a new source of worry was already on the horizon...there was a problem at Cherbourg !

CHERBOURG

As far as the planners were concerned the story of Cherbourg was already written : liberated on D+11 and open three days later, it was due to reach its cruising speed by the beginning of July with 6,000 tonnes per day. The only problem was that Cherbourg was not liberated until 26 June (J+20) and it was an apocalyptic vision that met the two men due to play a decisive role in the following days : Commodore Sullivan and Colonel Sibley. Sibley was no less than the commander of the 4th Major Port and was tasked with the reconstruc-

THE 11th PORT

The composition of the 11th Port evolved throughout the campaign. The following list shows the main components when it reached its maximum strength.

11th Port Hq & Hq Co (Colonel Whitcomb)

1594 Eng Utility Plat.
334th Harbor Craft Co.
990th Port Signal Serv Co.
1st Bn, 358th Eng GS Regt

302nd MP Escort Guard Co.
3531 Ord MAM Co.
40th Sig Const Co.
516th Port Bn.
534th Port Co.
535rd Port Co.
536th Port Co.
537th Port Co.
509th Port Bn
306th Port Co.
307th Port Co.
308th Port Co.
309th Port Co.
514th Port Bn.

526th Port Co.
527th Port Co.
528th Port Co.
529th Port Co.
688th QM Bn.
91st QM Serv Co.
145th QM Serv Co.
4058th QM Serv Co.
556th QM Service Bn.
4183rd QM Service Co.
4182nd QM Service Co.
4093rd QM Service Co.
3263rd QM Service Co.
554th QM Service Bn
4058th QM Service Co.

4145th QM Service Co.
4191st QM Service Co.
4146th QM Service Co.
512th QM Bn.
4009th QM Trk Co.
3582 QM Trk Co.
3583 QM Trk Co.
512th QM Group
467th Amph Trk Co.
468th Amph Trk Co.
469th Amph Trk Co.
174th QM Bn.
470th Amph Trk Co.
821st Amph Trk Co.
819th Amph Trk Co.

The task of the 80 British deep-sea divers in the port of Cherbourg was considerable: sweep the port of mines, help in the removal of sunken vessels, carry out indispensable topographical readings for the circulation of ships in the port. One of the great difficulties was that they had to undertake these tasks in murky waters, meaning that there was the risk of falling victim to a mine or coming across a network of Katy mines that were linked up and booby trapped. For their work under water, the divers were had aquatic welding apparatus as well as blow torches for cutting metal. The somewhat cumbersome looking suits and equipment were in fact reliable and efficient and allowed the wearer to work for one hour submerged. *(chbg014, NARA © Coriello, Bibliothèque municipale de Cherbourg)*

A causeway at Utah Beach. It is made from assembling metal caissons approximately two meters in length. Its minimum width was two caissons, but was sometimes increased up to four as seen here. The causeway floated at high tide and allowed for easy mooring for the Rhinoferries, LCT and LCM. In the background we can make out the anti-tank wall. *(Région Basse-Normandie/NARA, p013022)*

An overall view of the routine put into place at Omaha after a few days of trial and error. Whereas the LST were beached, the Dukw were emptied directly on the beach with the help of cranes. GMC trucks equipped with cranes carried the supplies to the forward dumps opened in the surrounding fields.
(Région Basse-Normandie/NARA, p012158)

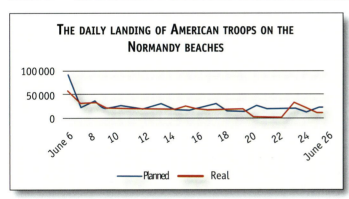

THE DAILY LANDING OF AMERICAN TROOPS ON THE NORMANDY BEACHES

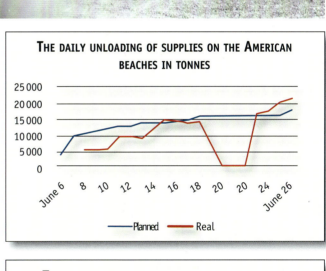

THE DAILY UNLOADING OF SUPPLIES ON THE AMERICAN BEACHES IN TONNES

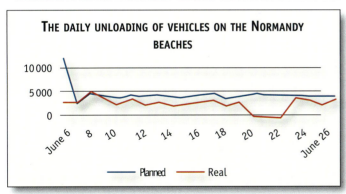

THE DAILY UNLOADING OF VEHICLES ON THE NORMANDY BEACHES

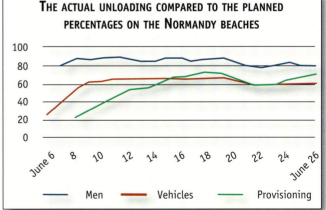

THE ACTUAL UNLOADING COMPARED TO THE PLANNED PERCENTAGES ON THE NORMANDY BEACHES

This 105mm howitzer of the 32nd Field Artillery is ready to be landed. The breech and main parts have been waterproofed with a magnetic paste which would be cleared away once the gun began firing. The artilleryman perched on the gun wears the insignia of the 1st US ID on his helmet.
(Région Basse-Normandie/NARA, p013202)

The tables above list the gross performances of the American beaches during the first twenty days of Overlord by making the distinction between the unloading of men, vehicles, supplies and, finally, a table which recaps the state of advancement of the various unloading compared to the accumulated forecasts. We note that :
1. The Americans suffered big delays by the evening of 6 June, delays that were never really rectified throughout this same month.
2. That the landing of troops was globally as planned for D+1.
3. That the unloading of vehicles after the encouraging start of D+1 to D+3 then stabilized below what had been forecast, making a daily deficit of around one thousand vehicles. By having landed around 60% of what had been forecast, the Americans in Normandy were lacking almost 37,000 vehicles at the end of June.
That the supply chain paid a high price for the difficulties of 6 June. On the two beaches, only 796 of the 14,550 tonnes of supplies had been landed during the first two days (5% of what had been forecast). By D+5 half of the supplies were still missing and still 30% by D+10, whereas the initial delay started to be made good. This was not the priority of the operators before the beginning of the second week.
5. The impact of the storm of 20-21 June can be clearly seen, something which almost totally paralyzed port activity. For three days, less than 10% of the planned traffic was dealt with. However, activity began again immediately once the wind had dropped and the loss of Mulberry A is not visible on the chart, proof that the beach had been able to increase its productivity and achieving more than just compensating for the lost days. For the Americans, the sacrifices made in order to design the artificial ports would have been of more use elsewhere.
6. In all, on 20 June, 60% of vehicles, 70% of supplies and 78% of the forecast personnel had been landed on the Normandy beaches.

Liberty Roads, 1944-1945

tion and opening of the port. Sullivan was the world specialist in re-floating. He had been in charge of the re-floating of the liner Normandie and the bringing back into use of the port of Salerno in 1943. The spectacle that met them was that of endless destroyed quays, half sunk ships blocking access, twisted masses of rails, a sabotaged lock gate and collapsed cranes...and this was just the tip of the iceberg....thousands of mines lay hidden under the murky waters of the docks. The task of opening the port within fifteen days appeared to be unachievable, impossible....in some ways this was not a bad thing as the motto of the

333rd Engineer General Service Regiment present in Cherbourg was *"difficult things we can deal with straight away, the impossible will take a little longer"*.

An exemplary reconstruction

Cherbourg based historian Robert Lerouvillois wrote a romanticized account of the first meeting of 4th Major Port on 27 June[8]:

"These were very odd soldiers. Dressed in fatigues like the others, but whose favourite weapons were the slide rule and the telephone. Bureaucrats ? Not really, with these men, we could move mountains....In any case we would soon find out, if there was ever a word that they did not understand it was the word "impossible".

It did not take much time to get down to work as that very afternoon....

"- Sir, a radio call ! Its the headquarters in Portsmouth." Sibley took the phone. On the other end of the line was a voice as calm and resolved as his own.

"Sibley ? Right, I'll explain the problem. We have four merchant ships here, all loaded. They were due to go to Mulberry A, you know the rest. These are supplies for the frontline : in two weeks we will have four army corps in the Cotentin. It is impossible to unload on the beaches, Cherbourg will have to take them. There you are, you have fifteen days ahead of you".

Sibley was not the type to lose his temper, not even swear. He simply replied :

"- We'll see what we can do. I'll call you back as soon as I have found a solution."

[...] Sibley asked *"Langstroth, can you see a useable quay anywhere?"*

"-No", answered Colonel Guy Langstroth, commanding the 333rd Engineers, *"at least not at the harbor station or the arsenal. Given the state of the port don't even think about it. By working day and night I hope to clear the Homet sea wall in a month, but no way in fifteen days"*.

Siverson intervened, he was the lieutenant-colonel of the Water Division that would be tasked with unloading.

"- At a push with a Liberty Ship we could do without a quay and even cranes : their unloading masts were designed to do that job. The problem is the mooring of merchant ships. The British have told me that they can make a channel as far as the middle of the great harbor, but that's all. The Liberty Ships won't be able to go any further, there are too many mines all over the place to let large ships through".

Everybody thought things over. How could they bring the ships' loads onto land ? If there was a beach...

"- There is a beach", said Stevenson, *"the artificial beach in front of the Napoleon statue. I've thought it through, it would be possible with amphibious trucks, but a Dukw, especially in the great breakwater won't take more than two and half tonnes due to the swell and a Liberty holds eight or ten thousand tonnes"*. Sibley looked at a map of the great harbor and drew a first line from the western fort to the great harbor.

"- Ok, let's say that the merchant ships moor in this sector".

A second line as far as the Homet jetty, running around it, then going across all of the great harbor as far as the beach.

"- Whoa ! That's at least three kilometres ! The minesweepers are going to have their work cut out opening a passage for the Dukw, even with a narrow channel marked

---

8. Robert Lerouvillois, *32 trains pour Le Mans*, Isoète, 1994, pp.106-108.

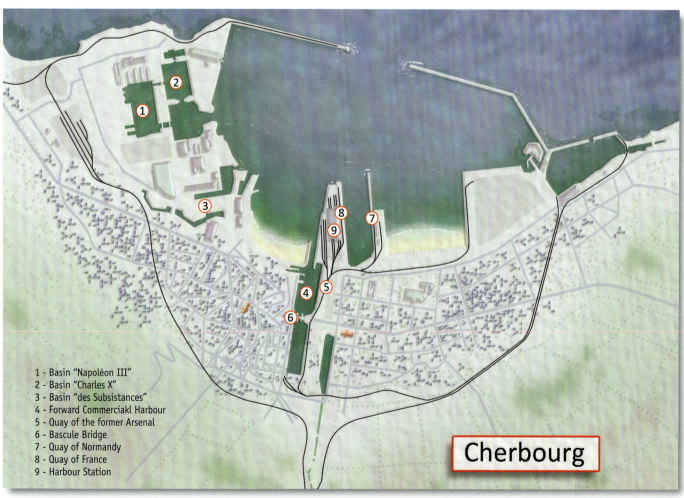

1 - Basin "Napoléon III"
2 - Basin "Charles X"
3 - Basin "des Subsistances"
4 - Forward Commerciakl Harbour
5 - Quay of the former Arsenal
6 - Bascule Bridge
7 - Quay of Normandy
8 - Quay of France
9 - Harbour Station

At Right, from top to bottom.
The GMC CCKW 353 Le Roi D 318 air compressors were indispensable to the teams at Cherbourg. The compressor had its own 34hp engine which supplied air to the pneumatic tools (jackhammers, cutters...) stored in the side lockers.
(13573_8, NARA © Coriello, Bibliothèque municipale de Cherbourg)

In the port, a jib crane on a floating platform lifts wrecks. The planners had foreseen the need for heavy lifting and construction equipment. The German hopes to see the port blocked for months on end were dashed.
(Région Basse-Normandie/NARA, p012768)

out with buoys". Slide rules were taken out. Let's see, two tonnes five per trip, that makes between three and five thousand trips with a return trip of six kilometres and just for one merchant ship !

"- What do you think Silverson ?"

"- One can't say that it would be impossible but it will be devilishly long ! I've aready talked about with the Navy guys and they looked at me as if I was crazy".

"- Right," interjected Sibley, *"The beach is the responsibility of the 342nd Engineers".*

He turned to his colleague.

"- What remains to be done in your sector ?"

"- The anti-tank wall has been blown up. We are using the broken down debris to make ballast, we are getting the beach ready. If we are going to use that many Dukw on a daily basis we will need concrete ramps, otherwise they will get bogged down. We are also going to have to cobble together a system of light signalling so that the amphibious trucks can find the emplacement of the ramps at night. The last thing is wrecks in front of the beach. Sullivan says that they are probably not mined as the Jerries no doubt did not have time to do it. He's going to take care of it".

Of course this account comes across as being hagiographical with its apocryphal quotations, but is has the dual merit of placing the reader in the atmosphere of the time and displaying the problems faced by the Americans. In a few lines the American projects were outlined and the most urgent of them was started on 1 July :

• 1 July, the start of mine-clearing operations in the great harbour thanks to the minesweepers of the Royal

Cherbourg, a crane on a pontoon unloads a Caterpillar D7 angleDozer equipped with a LaPlant-Choate hydraulic system on a trailer towed by a Case tractor equipped with a dozer. The bulldozer was probably the most useful vehicle for the engineers. It is incredible when one thinks that only a few years previously, the US Army did not want anything to do with them as they considered that men equipped with shovels and picks could do the same job.
(Région Basse-Normandie/NARA, p001132)

Liberty Roads, 1944-1945

The Germans had scuttled dozens of vessels and equipment: ships, barges, tugs, railcars and even cars. To bring them back up to the surface required using very powerful cranes, most often positioned on floating platforms. However, before they could be used the port had to be swept of mines and an access channel cleared. This titanic task lasted for three months. *(Région Basse-Normandie/NARA, P001070)*

Navy 9th Flotilla, the Royal Canadian Navy 35th Flotilla and Y2 Squadron of the US Navy Yard Motor Minesweepers. By the next day, two minesweepers had already been sunk by mines.

• 3 July, the deep sea diving team of the Royal Navy led by Commander Landon began to explore under water obstacles in order to made safe any booby traps so that they could be re-floated.

• 6 July, Sullivan and his team began re-floating wrecks.

• 8 July: the start of minesweeping in the small harbour.

• 16 July, the first four Liberty Ships were moored. Barges and Dukw began going back and forth. Arrival of eleven pontoon cranes to lift wrecks.

However, a beach did not make a port and during this time the engineers were busy putting the Homet seawall back into service. This wall had been torn apart along a length of 120 metres and in its entire width. In some areas it had lost fourteen metres of its height! To do a good job it would require moving the debris and totally rebuilding. The engineers dealt with the most urgent aspects. Debris clearing was reduced to its most basic. To fill in the breach, hundreds of tonnes of rubble were brought in, something that was not lacking. To render it solid, pine trunks and railway sleepers were pushed down using steam hammers then a sort of basket was built with long steel bars positioned horizontally and bound together with a netting made from steel cables. All that remained then was to pour in the rubble. The only protection against hulls hitting the structure was straightforward poles that protruded more than others, bunched together in twos or threes and crowned with old tires. All that was then needed was a bulldozer and a steam roller and the new roadway was ready to hold railway lines and cranes....whilst awaiting the first ships. On the Mielles sea wall, the engineers built wooden landing stages for Rhino ferries and LCT. At Querqueville, the Americans discovered the first good news, the oil terminal was almost intact, only the mooring installations had been destroyed and the mined underwater obstacles prevented it from being opened immediately. Since 11 July, the French railway workers and the Americans of the 729th Railway Operating Battalion put the Cherbourg depot lines back into service, as well as those going to Carentan.

Robert Lerouvillois runs out of superlatives for this *"remarkable"*, *"prodigious"*, *"mad undertaking"* and *"cra-*

Liberty Roads, 1944-1945

zy challenge". He heaps praise on the courage of the deep sea divers who worked in the murky waters in order to make safe German booby traps, the mine clearing personnel armed only with their detectors. He praises the genius of the American engineers, their sense of improvisation, reactivity and determination. One could compare these men on the ground with the bureaucrats in London and their hare-brained planning. But this would be forgetting the that if the 4th Major Port was able to be so efficient, it was thanks to the planning that had been undertaken well before D-Day, assembling troops and materiel indispensable to the reconstruction of the port.

Within a week most of the units were already at work. The personnel were almost all experienced veterans of the Mediterranean campaigns. The existence of Port Construction & Repair Groups was an especially good idea. Like the Engineers Special Brigades, these units had a changeable composition but all had a basic core of a headquarters and construction battalions. It was impossible to estimate beforehand the needs of the large supply depots ready to use in the UK. Unlike other armies, the US Army could, therefore, count on heavy equipment. The end of July saw the arrival of eleven pontoon cranes, a 30 tonne floating crane and another weighing 60. The Americans owed these units mainly to one man, Ben Moreell. A former pupil of the Parisian Ecole nationale des Ponts et Chaussées, this Chief of Civil Engineers of the Navy was the man who had personally advised Roosevelt concerning the creation of the Construction Battalions, the famous ,CB or Seebees - that recruited men from the construction profession and which was commanded by officers who were all qualified in civil engineering. The first recruits were former New Deal construction site workers : the Hoover dam, Boulder dam, freeways and New York skyscrapers. There were more than sixty professions represented. Already present in Britain on the Mulberry construction sites, they were then assembled in Normandy before getting to grips with their biggest European challenge at Cherbourg[9].

A more laborious exploitation

On 24 July, a month after the liberation, the port of Cherbourg was almost ready to start working again. The first oil tanker was due in the next day and the Sea Trains for the 29th with the Twickenham Ferry. As for the LCT and Liberty Ships, the first would berth respectively on 31 July and 9 August, some 19 days late. The engineers had not been able to follow the timescales which were, it has to be said, far too optimistic. The 4th Major Port immediately started the second phase, increasing tonnage from 8,000 to 28,300 with enough berths on the quays and breakwater to simultaneously deal with 28 Liberty Ships, 14 LST, 75 barges, 13 tramp steamers, 2 Sea-Trains and a tanker; this phase was to be completed by mid-September. To achieve this new quays had to be put back into service, particularly in the commercial port, the arsenal and transatlantic inner harbour.

In his analysis of the archives, Robert Lerouvillois has omitted a few failings in the American system. This mostly concerned the handling of supplies. First of all, the dock workers complained of a long-lasting lack of equipment. There were not enough tugs, cranes or barges. Also, the

9. Paul Kennedy, *Le grand tournant*, Perrin, 2012, p. 356

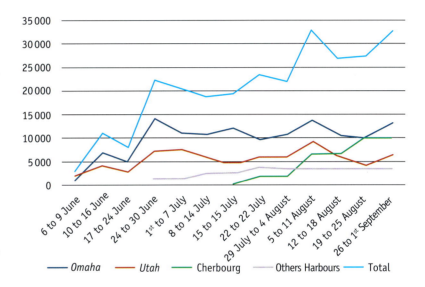

UNLOADED DAILY AVERAGE FROM D-DAY TO SEPTEMBER 1 (LONG TONS)

4TH MAJOR PORT UNITS AT CHERBOURG

DATE OF ARRIVAL	UNIT
27 June	28th Bomb Disposal Unit
30 June	I/333 Engineer Special Service Regiment Headquarters of the 4th Major Port and 1056th Port Construction & Repair Group The 4th Major Port comprised of the following for unloading : 6 Port Battalions HQ, 20 Port Companies, 2 Harbor Craft Maintenance Company, one Port Marine Maintenance Company and 4 Amphibian Trucks Companies, equipped with 200 Dukws, 176 barges, 38 tugs, 11 sea mules Three minesweeper flotillas
1er July	III/333 Engineer Special Service Regiment II/332 Engineer General Service Regiment 342nd Engineer General Service Regiment 416th Engineer Dump Truck Company
3 July	417th Engineer Dump Truck Company
6 July	29th Bomb Disposal Squad
8 July	434th Engineer Dump Truck Company
9 July	483rd Port Battalion
13 July	I/332 Engineer General Service Regiment II/333 Engineer Special Service Regiment 197th Engineer Dump Truck Company
18 July	328th and 335th Harbor Craft Company
25 July	12th Major Port HQ (as administrative support to the 4th.)
5 August	398th Engineer General Service Regiment
11 August	1071st Port Repair Ships Group 982nd Minesweeping Company (British)
20 August	1075th Port Repair Ships Group
25 August	1055th & 1053rd Port Repair Ships Group

The swing bridge linking east and west Cherbourg , but above all it controlled the maneuvering of the gates to the commercial port. Despite the efforts by the French Resistance to prevent it, the Germans were able to blow up the bridge, leaving the deck twisted but intact. The deck was cut away with blow torches and was rapidly replaced with a sliding Bailey Bridge to allow ships to pass through.
(Région Basse-Normandie/NARA)

Liberty Roads, 1944-1945

THE CONTRIBUTION MADE BY SMALL NORMANDY PORTS						
Port or beach	Opening date		Unloading capacity daily average (in long tons)			
			D + 30 (6 July)		D +60 (6 August)	
	Planned	Actual	Planned	Actual	Planned	Actual
Port en Bessin (minor system for tankers)	D + 10	D +19	700 (split in two between British and Americans)	2 000	700	8 000
Isigny	D + 11	D + 18	500	740	500	740
Grandcamp	D + 15	D + 11	300	675	300	675
St Vaast	D + 16	D + 33	1 100	1 172	1 100	1 172
Carentan		D + 49	0	0	0	0 (300 tonnes/day from 25 to 31 July)
Barfleur	D + 20	D + 50	1 000	0	1 000	803
Granville	D + 26	D +101	700	0	1 500	0
TOTAL			3 600	2 587	4 400	3 390

The port of Barfleur on the eastern tip of the Cotentin peninsula was liberated on 21 June. However, it was only opened a month later. The presence of mines and debris, the lack of personnel and the modest infrastructure available explains this delay.
(Région Basse-Normandie/NARA, P011636)

---

10. Ruppenthal, *op. cit.* vol II , p.80.

twelve ships that had brought across the materiel of the 4th Major Port were initially due to berth at Cherbourg, something that was of course impossible and the convoy was forced to sail to *Utah* instead where the materiel was badly stored and it took weeks to find it. The personnel were still trying to find their straps, nets and lifting straps. Also, Sibley did not have enough qualified crane operators and two experienced sergeants had to be sent from Britain in order to give the men a much needed training course. This did not prevent half of the cranes breaking down due to human error. As was the case on the beaches with communication between the Navy and Army, that between the Ports Battalions and ships was difficult and led to confusion and delays[10].

The table opposite compares the daily unloading on the two beaches, Cherbourg and the other Normandy ports. It clearly shows that in July, it was still on the beaches that the logistical effort depended. These managed to beat records with peaks of more than 13,500 tonnes at *Omaha* Beach compared with the hoped for 6,000 and 9,300 tonnes at *Utah* instead of the planned 5,700. These exploits partially made up for the delays at Cherbourg whose output was very low until the beginning of August. In July only 31,000 tonnes of freight were unloaded instead of the hoped for 150,000 (21%). The effort made to use the small Normandy ports should also be noted. All of these had the drawback of being small fishing ports that were dry at low tide, which meant that supplies had to unloaded quickly at high tide. They were not equipped with heavy unloading machinery and were only accessible to small tramp steamers due to their shallow waters and small quays. Also, those of Carentan and Isigny were at the end of narrow channels several kilometres in length.

All of the ports were found in good condition, despite the presence of mines, booby traps and other obstacles. Liberated later than planned, they opened with a delay of between one week and one month (apart from Grandcamp). Quickly, the ADSEC ordered the engineers to improve output to make up for the initial delays. At the beginning of August, it imposed a new total objective of 17,000 tonnes (four times more than the initial plan). To achieve this it would require dredging. The French dredger *Divette*, found intact in the British zone, was brought across. However, the hopes placed in her were soon dashed and the operation was finally cancelled.

The sign that the Americans made use of whatever they could was seen in the opening of the port of Carentan. The planners had rejected this port due to its very enclosed position, but the lack of supplies led the ADSEC to order its opening. Operational on 25 July, it was rapidly blocked by the running aground of three tramps steamers. The access channel was obviously too narrow and by

the end of the week the port was closed with a daily traffic that did not exceed 300 tonnes. Finally, the fishing ports showed themselves to be incredibly difficult to use. They used large amounts of engineer materiel that could have been of use elsewhere. Only capable of allowing in small tramp steamers, they rendered the planning and embarkation work in England more complex, even rendering it necessary to lighten their loads with Dukw vehicles before they entered the ports. Was it really worth all the effort ? In July no doubt yes, when the situation was especially precarious, but this was not the case once Cherbourg had been opened. What was learned from this experience weighed heavily in the balance in the choice of abandoning the reestablishment of Breton ports in August-September. Opened until mid-October, their activity did not reach 10% of the total volume of supplies unloaded in Normandy on this date.

The situation in the American zone deteriorated in July. The US Army only received 61% of the projected supplies (compared to 70% in June).

THE IMPACT ON OPERATIONS

However, the tactical impact was low. Firstly, the logistical services fulfilled their primary mission, that of bringing in more fighting men into Normandy than their German counterparts. The balance of power was never unfavourable. Better still, the rate of landings was higher than what had been planned for with a surplus of 100,000 fighting men at the end of June. The 83rd Infantry Division landed nine days ahead of schedule.

The supply chain suffered from delays. With a 40% deficit, one might think that this would halt operations. However, this was not the case. Within the first days, the Americans had simply emptied six ammunition barges that had run aground on the evening of 6 June and who were due to, in any case, be used to make up for unforeseen needs. From 15 June onwards, the First Army rationed mortar ammunition, the reserves of which had run low due to the violence of the hedgerow fighting and by the odd habit of the artillery personnel in forming ammo dumps wherever they wanted. In the second half of June, munitions were attributed in priority to the VII Corps commanded by Collins that was advancing towards Cherbourg; Middleton, commanding VIII Corps, delayed his attack towards the south of the Cotentin by fifteen days, allowing the Germans to strengthen their defences.

Bradley, in his memoirs[11] said *"We never had enough ammunition to fire what we should have"*. The storm made the crisis worse and each gun was rationed to fire on a daily basis only a third of its normal allocation of ammunition. Aircraft were needed to bring in an

---
11. Omar Bradley, *A soldier's story*, Gallimard, 1952, pp292-294.

emergency supply of 500 tonnes of shells whilst Bradley requested that five preloaded Liberty Ships anchored in English waters holding emergency ammunition supplies, be sent as a matter of urgency. Such measures made by the planners were of huge help. The constraints on ammunition consumption were eased in July and Bradley authorised the firing of a day's shell allocation on the first day of an offensive, half the following days and a third in so-called "quiet" parts of the front.

In fact, many units did not follow these orders and shell consumption during the hedgerow fighting again reached a worrying point, to such an extent that on 16 July, strict rationing was reinstated with the aim of preparing *Operation Cobra*. The deficit was not as big for other supplies. The slow advance meant that less fuel was used, especially as the Tombola system opened in Port en Bessin was much more efficient than had been foreseen (see insert). Spare parts were plentiful

The Terre-Plein des Mielles area that had only just been begun before war broke out. The teams of the 1056th Ports Repairs and Construction Group and those of the 333rd and 342nd Engineer Regiments are making a berthing area for the mooring of barges and LCT. The framework was made up of wood floated across from England and salvaged railway tracks. In the background we can make out the lifting winches for moving the beams. The latter were pushed down with the help of the crane in the foreground which held the *"sheep"* : a steam-hammer which slid along a guiding track.

Liberty Roads, 1944-1945

PORT OR BEACH	OPENING DATE		DAILY AVERAGE UNLOADING CAPACITY (IN TONNES)							
			D + 10		D + 30		D + 60		D + 90	
	Planned	Actual	Planned	Actual	Planned	Actual	Planned	Actual	Planned	Actual
1. *Utah* and Quinéville beach	D Day	D Day	5 700	5 931	5 700	7 000	5 000	6 060	5 000	3 314
2. *Omaha*	D Day	D Day	9 000	8 535	6 000	13 500	5 000	13 630	5 000	9 230
3. *Gold*	D Day	D Day								
4. *Juno*	D Day	D Day			British beaches					
5. *Sword*	D Day	D Day								
E. Port-en-Bessin (minor system for tankers)	D + 10	D +19			700 (shared by British and Americans)	2 000	700	8 000	700	8 000
C. Isigny	D + 11	D + 18			500	740	500	740	500	740
2. Mulberry "A" (Saint-Laurent)	D + 12	D + 8 then abandoned			5 000	0	5 000	0	5 000	0
3. Mulberry "B" (Arromanche)	D + 12	D + 8	Port British artificial port with the theoretical rate of 5000 tonnes but which reached 8 900 tonnes by D+60							
Cherbourg	D + 15	D + 40			1 600	0	6 000	6 500	7 000	13 500
D. Grandcamp	D + 15	D + 11			300	675	300	675	300	675
B. Saint-Vaast	D + 16	D + 33			1 100	1 172	1 100	1 172	1 100	1 172
PLUTO (major system, underwater petrol pipelines) Bambi route	D + 20	D + 68 (closed three days later)			3 000	0	3 000	0	3 000	0
A. Barfleur	D + 20	D + 50			1 000	0	1 000	803	1 000	803
F. Granville	D + 26	D + 101			700	0	1 500	0	2 500	0
Saint-Malo	D + 27	Never			900	0	2 500	0	3 000	0
Brest	D + 53	Never					3 240	0	5 300	0
Baie de Quiberon	D + 54	Abandoned					4 000	0	7 000	0
Lorient	D + 57	Never					800	0	2 250	0
TOTAL			14 700	14 466	26 150	24 387	39 290	33 580	48 300	33 434

A tramp steamer berthing at Barfleur. The small fishing port never reached the hoped-for 1,000 daily tonnes, less than one-tenth of Omaha Beach.
(Région Basse-Normandie/NARA, P001139)

Next page, top.
Each beach had a Rhinoferry that had been turned into a workshop barge. The one seen here operated at *Utah* Beach. With their two five-tonne cranes that could be used when afloat, they rendered inestimable services by carrying out repairs on barges and other landing equipment which would have been impossible on land.
(Région Basse-Normandie/NARA, p012778)

Next page, bottom.
24 July 1944. The Empire Traveller tanker berths at the Querqueville oil facility. By luck, these installations were found intact. The only obstacles which took three weeks to clear were mines, a few wrecks and sabotaged berthing equipment. It was via Querqueville that the bulk of the fuel used in the pursuit of August-September 1944 passed through.
(Région Basse-Normandie/NARA, p001131)

Liberty Roads, 1944-1945

as most of the vehicles that landed were new. Captured enemy stocks were also used, such as telephone wire or construction materials. By the end of July the situation for the 1st Army was deemed as being satisfactory with 16 days of fuel and 9 days of ammunition.

The secondary mission of the ADSEC was the forming of a solid logistical base for the continuation of operations. Concerning this point, the situation was not as good. Lacking depth, its supply depots were saturated. Luckily the Luftwaffe was not present in the skies. Also, it was unable to repair railway lines that stubbornly remained in enemy hands. On 25 July (D+49), instead of being in Lorient, Nantes and Le Mans, the Allies occupied territory that had been foreseen for D+15 and were bogged down in the bocage south of Saint-Lô. Not having the Brittany ports also meant that it became increasingly difficult to supply an army that was growing in size with the arrival of Patton's first divisions. To top everything off, the rear

echelon troops were the main victims of the cuts that were made. At the end of July, only 94 of the 130 ADSEC Truck Companies had been landed (it was, therefore, lacking 1,728 trucks). Its services were reduced to 63,000 men instead of the planned 235,000 and the *"division slice"* was now only 31,000 instead of the usual 40,000. Even if, compared to British troops, the American army retained a larger logistical base, it was obvious that it would have to make sacrifices at the beginning of the campaign. To sum up, the ADSEC was going through a difficult time and feared for the future. It managed to support static warfare such as the hedgerow fighting that was taking place a few kilometres away from the beaches, but if operations ever speeded up, it considered itself incapable of moving forward.

Road maintenance was essential to logistics as added to the damage caused by the fighting, there was also the wear and tear caused by the passage of thousands of vehicles, not mentioning the need to widen certain pathways, or even build new ones from scratch. This maintenance was the domain of the ESB. The Engineer Light Equipment Coys opened small stone quarries near the exit of the D1 road at Virile *(seen here)* and at Carentan. A steam-shovel fed a stone-breaker and the gravel thus obtained was removed on a belt. It was used notably for filling in bomb craters west of Saint-Lô. The Engineers were also well-equipped Caterpillar tractors, seen here is a D7 with an angle dozer and CK7 LeTourneau equipment. Although the registration plate has been censored, the vehicle belongs to the 49th Engineer Combat Battalion, attached to the 1106th Engineer Group. In the background is an immobilized convoy of the 30th ID. *(Région Basse-Normandie/NARA, p013323 & p011449)*

FUEL...THE ALLIES LOSE PLUTO BUT WIN WITH TOMBOLA

At SHAEF the question of fuel supplies was at the heart of all thinking well before the invasion. In February 1944, POL staff officers (Petrol Oil, Lubricants) estimated fuel requirements at 7,000 tonnes per day at D+14, 9,000 at D+41 and 14,000 at D+90, making up a quarter of all supplies. The first weeks were to see supplies being brought in via the beaches in jerrycans and by the network of Port en Bessin (the minor system). This system consisted of mooring tankers near the beaches and linking them to the shore via a pipeline that was held afloat with buoys. On-shore pumping stations would then feed tanks (Etreham, Sainte Honorine des Pertes, Colleville, then later Balleroy) whose total volume was to reach 8,000 tonnes. The fuel would then be moved in tanker trucks and jerry cans, then pipes towards the front line. This was the TOMBOLA program. Once Cherbourg was liberated, as well as the Querqueville oil terminal, the Americans were convinced to use one of the odd ideas that they had come to expect from the British : bring across fuel via the first underwater pipeline in history, PLUTO (*Pipe Line Underwater Transport of Oil*).

The operation began well and each vehicle landed with a load of jerrycans that were sufficient for six days of operations. From 7 June onwards, tramp steamers loaded with new jerrycans appeared off the beaches. When Port en Bessin was liberated by 47th RM Commando, the experts saw that the moles were directly accessible to tankers with a displacement of under 1,300 tonnes. This allowed the daily flow to increase from the planned 700 tonnes to 2,000. The problems encountered in berthing the tankers were alleviated by the assistance of French fishermen who transported the petrol barrels on their small boats. Progressively, the pipeline network was enlarged. At the end of July, instead of the planned 45 km of pipes, there were 115. More tanks were set up to store the 24,000 tonnes of fuel. Apart from during the storm, the Army never used more fuel than what was brought in and stocks increased - by mid-July 142,000 tonnes had been brought ashore - meaning that they could calmly wait for the port of Cherbourg to be repaired and the installation of PLUTO.

The British had been working on this project since 1942. Mountbatten had had the idea when he learnt that flexible pipes had been placed under the sea in order to set fire to an eventual invasion fleet and he put forward the idea of adopting the system in order to build a pipeline linking England with France. On 15 April 1942, Clifford Hartley, chief engineer with the Anglo-Iranian Oil Company, suggested using telephone cable with its copper inner removed, retaining the four lead and steel outer covers. He put forward the idea of working with the famous transatlantic cable maker...Siemens. This system would consist of a very heavy hollow tube in which fuel could be pumped at very high pressure (1,500 PSI) offering a flow of 25,000 jerrycans per day. His fear was that sea currents might break the cable when it was placed by a cable-laying ship.

It would have to be laid, therefore, when the sea was totally calm and in one go. This project led to the creation of the Hais[1] cable, a lead tube strengthened with flexible steel wire but with a lower flow capability (6,000 jerrycans/day). To play safe, the War Office decided to develop another system, the Hamel[2], which comprised of a special flexible steel tube, welded at each end and rolled around an enormous floating drum, ironically named *HMS Conundrum*. This may have been lighter but it took up more space. The drum weighed 1,600 tonnes and was towed by three tugs. In order to deal with any eventuality, 550 km of tubes were made and 6 drums, each one with a capacity of 112 km of tube, making it possible to cross the Channel without having to join up the tubes.

Laying the pipelines was fraught with difficulties. On 12 August, the first Hais cable was cut by the anchor of its cable-laying ship, the Latimer. A second, then third cable were laid at the end of September. The Hamel drum turned out to be unusable as it was covered in barnacles. Finally, when the system was put into service, only two underwater pipelines out of the four initially planned worked between Sandown on the Isle of Wight and Querqueville. However, problems accumulated and after only 12 days, the "*Bambi Route*" was closed and on 4 October, after having carried 3,500 tonnes of fuel, that is to say hardly nothing. PLUTO appears, therefore, to have been a military fiasco, even though it paved the way for modern underwater pipelines.

Given the low storage capacity of the Querqueville terminal and the fact that it could not be used during storms, most fuel still came in via the Minor System. At the end of August, the TOMBOLA system had allowed 175,000 tonnes of fuel to be unloaded (88,000 for the British and 87,000 for the Americans) making up almost half of the total. Thanks to the work carried out by the Royal Engineers, six tankers could simultaneously discharge 8,000 tonnes of fuel per day. However, the arrival of autumn meant that other areas for unloading had to be found. On shore reserves were also starting to seriously decrease, going from 14 days to 2.5 at the beginning of October.

The British then authorised the Americans to discharge 1,000 tonnes of fuel per day at Ostend, but the improvement came from the re-opening of infrastructure in the lower-Seine area - Petit-Couronne refinery near Rouen and the tanks at Le Havre - and the opening of the port of Antwerp[3]. The first tanker berthed at Le Havre on 31 October and at Antwerp on 3 December. Finally, the American army never lacked fuel on the continent, despite the delays in capturing Cherbourg, the failure of PLUTO or the late opening of the ports north of the river Seine.

1.This name was formed with the following initials : H for Hartley, the name of the engineer who invented the tube ; AI for the Anglo-Iranian oil company and S for Siemens, the company which made the tube.
2. Combination of the first syllable of the two names of the inventors : engineers Hammick, of the Irak Petroleum Company and Ellis of the Burma Oil Company.
3 The British also used another Pluto, the "*Dumbo Route*", laid in October between Dungeness and Boulogne. Up to 17 lines were laid, eleven of which comprised of a Hamel-Hais composite, they proved to be satisfactory as they covered 8% of the total amount of fuel sent to the continent with the highest quantities reaching at times 4,250 tonnes per day.

A storage area for the terminus of the Tombola pipeline was set up at Mont Cauvin near Etreham.
(Région Basse-Normandie/NARA, P000973)

CHAPTER 5
BRONTOSAUR AND LEVIATHAN

Was the Master Plan the Infernal Machine as stated by Martin Van Creveld in Supplying War ? Without going as far as that, it is obvious that this logistical Leviathan with its tentacle like infrastructure and carefully planned timing that Overlord had become, fell apart when it came into contact with reality and that it could have suffocated under its own weight if the men on the ground, at the embarkation ports or on the beaches, had not used their initiative in turning their backs on procedure, then cooperating together to find the best solution to clearing blockages.

In terms of paperwork, Overlord exceeded the Schlieffen Plan of 1914 that had been carefully planned for thirty years by the German Imperial Staff. The planners were thousands of officers from various services and authorities. All worked along the lines of the American administrative system : the answer to each new project (or problem) resided in the creation of an inter-service committee. Due to the complexity of the landings, there were more than a hundred committees, specialised in the preparation of the transportation of men and supplies towards the embarkation ports (BUCO), or embarkation (EMBARCO), or the management of the artificial ports (Task Force 127.1). Each committee integrated representatives from the corps concerned. Together they made an inventory, set objectives and allocated tasks. After a conference, each committee transferred the carrying out of the task to its services. Cooperation was rendered difficult by their geographical dispersion in a 100 km radius around London which made it necessary to form an express courrier service[1]. As projects multiplied there were more participants to integrate, to such an extent that a special committee was formed to control the correct functioning of inter-service cooperation. Added to this was the extra difficulty of working within the framework of a coalition. All personnel were overcome by a bureaucratic fervour. Thousands of manuals of procedures, reports and minutes, therefore, climbed up the chain of command, becoming even more burdened as they went with the additions of each intermediary.

At committee level, then the top, they were managed by secretaries and deputies who compared them and summarized the major points in memo form which were finally given to general officers. Having noticed this fervour, Martin Van Creveld compares SHAEF to an inverted brontosaur, that is to say an organisation with a brain that is far too oversized compared to the body[2]. This description is reminiscent of that made by Frederick Brook in a book about IBM where the author shows that, faced with the complexity of modern computer development, the company increased its manpower. However, contrary to what they hoped for, allocating more people to a project did not speed it up and only led to an increase in the amount of interaction. Most of the time spent on a project was spent in formal or informal meetings and various forms of communication and so on, to the detriment of directly useful work. The areas of friction, but also the grey areas left by each team convinced them that they were the domain of another team and led to lower efficiency. Brook came to an iconoclast conclusion, in order to improve the performance

1. Martin Van Creveld, *op. cit.*, p.205.
2. *Ditto*

TORCH, 1942

The counterexample of the feverish planning for Overlord can be found in the first landings of the war in North Africa, November 1942.

The least that can be said about Torch is that it was improvised. It was only on 5 September 1942 that Marshall informed Somervell of the impending operation. Thus he had only two months in which to prepare landings of a rare logistical complexity as it would require converging two fleets, one having sailed 2,800 nautical miles, the other 4,800, towards five different areas spread out over 1,000 km. Indeed, the landings on the Algerian coast was to be carried out by American troops already deployed in Great Britain, whereas a corps arriving directly from the United States would land in Morocco. Also, the operation would be carried out thousands of kilometres from the embarkation ports, something that rendered necessary a solid supply planning due to the distances involved and the rotation times of shipping.

The organisation of Torch soon became a difficult task. Instead of comprising of a third of personnel as had been the case in 1918, the ASF was now only 12% of personnel and was overwhelmed by the amount of work. In Great Britain, the situation went downhill so quickly that Eisenhower was forced to employ civilian personnel and demanded Somervell to send more men, never mind if they had not all been trained. It was no surprise that depots in Great Britain descended into chaos. There was no harmonisation in cataloguing and at times not even an inventory, to such an extent that it was decided not to take materiel necessary for Torch from these depots. This made it necessary, therefore, to resend 260,000 tonnes of equipment directly from the United States within a ridiculous timeframe. Somervell calculated that in order to respect the deadlines, the equipment would have to arrive in Great Britain by 26 September and, therefore, to have left the USA by the 12th, making a week in which everything had to be gathered and loaded. This was an impossible task and only 131,000 tonnes reached the British ports when the first soldiers left on 20 October. Some of the supplies joined the convoys off Portugal. The loading for the Moroccan expeditionary force was no easier given that its composition fluctuated daily, making it necessary to re-jig the planning[6]. Embarkation in the US was carried out on an alphabetical basis and not by ship, something which caused great confusion and foreshadowed a lot of problems when it would come to trying to rapidly unload the materiel. Above all, Patton left half of his vehicles on the quaysides as the lack of escort ships had led to modifying the format of convoys. In the English docks, 20% of stores was stolen, training ammunition was loaded to make up for the lack of combat munitions and the fatty lamb meat rations did not agree with the GI stomachs[7].

The landings themselves were a huge mess. In Casablanca, Patton was slowed down by the impossibility to efficiently unload the ships. It was necessary in fact to empty all the holds and re-classify everything before distributing supplies. It took more than a week to render some units operational and others often began operations without all of their equipment. Patton said that it was lucky for them that they were faced by French armed forces.

Although it was not a fiasco, the landings were nevertheless successful, but Torch left a deep impression on the Americans, especially Eisenhower who was definitively convinced of the necessity of perfectly planned landings. The command also came to the conclusion that better adapted landing craft were required, specially trained troops to control the beaches - the future Engineer Special Brigades – and that it was necessary to make its chain of command more fluid. All lessons learned would prove to be essential to the success of *Overlord*.

OPERATION *TORCH*

of a think tank, such as a military staff for example, it had to be made smaller[3].

This planning fervour is not only explained by the complexity of the project, it was also the consequence of superfluous infrastructure (COSSAC, SHAEF, ComZ, ETOUSA, each unit's headquarters staff) which were progressively aggregated and which was finally the expression of American culture and its military doctrine. Culturally, the planners were thousands of officers who often hailed from the business world. They were all part of a progressive, rationalist and optimistic society concerning man's capacity to master his environment. With them it was a cultural trait to believe that problems could always be solved by technical solutions.

Doctrinally, the manual emphasised the importance of making an administrative plan before any operation. This plan was supposed to give the staff all of the elements and logistical options necessary to draw up a battle plan. Moreover, Eisenhower made it a point of honour to *"calmly weigh up all the risks before making a rock solid decision[4]"* and in doing so he was following the tradition of the great union generals or General Pershing. If the landings were to be a success, its logistical base had to be perfect. He had become convinced that as his army was mostly made up of civilians in uniform that they especially needed to be guided. This conviction was all the more solid due to the decisive character of the operation. His conviction had become unshakeable since he had seen with his own eyes, two years earlier, the dangers of improvised landings in North Africa.

It cannot be contested that this extremely detailed planning did not stand up to events and that the first weeks revealed great flaws, most of which originated from administration. More than the storm, more than damage caused by the Germans, it was the lack of cooperation between the Army-Navy, ComZ-SHAEF and the useless complexity in the chain of command that slowed down the unloading of supplies. We realise that inter-service training and working together were neglected before the invasion, preventing the services from ironing out any problems concerning procedures, leading to too much trial and error, misunderstandings and even resistance on D-Day.

One might come to the conclusion that improvisation is superior to planning. It is true that on several occasions, the situation was saved by the teams of the Engineer Special Brigades and the port engineers who proved to

Equipment being landed from a LCT. A D7 bulldozer with an angle dozer and CK7 LeTourneau equipment comes to the assistance of jeeps that are in danger of being swamped by the rising tide.
(Région Basse-Normandie/NARA, P001205)

be reactive and practically minded. However, this would be forgetting that these teams were only there because, thanks to experience gained in Africa, the need for them had been anticipated.

With all due respect to Martin Van Creveld, the detailed planning also rendered great assistance by activating welcome safety nets and supplying adequate equipment, in particular the Dukw and barges that were so essential in the first weeks.

Overlord, therefore, invites us to rethink the nature of useful planning. After the war, the military historian Ruppenthal came to the conclusion that the real challenge facing modern planners is not putting themselves in the place of the men on the ground by detailing each stage, but rather resides in the setting up of a flexible infrastructure with well trained personnel and the right equipment that will allow the troops to carry out their mission. Another military historian, Clayton Newell, wrote that logistics was an art form not a science as it involved the capability of dealing with the unforeseen[5]. The abandoning of thousands of pages of procedures supposed to facilitate unloading on the beaches for a much more efficient improvisation by the well trained men of the Engineer Special Brigades goes in this direction, as does the rapid and unforeseen reconstruction of the port of Cherbourg which contrasts with its more laborious exploitation, despite it being planned down to the last detail. Up to this point in time the planners overrode the generals but this was reversed in spectacular fashion thanks to the success of Operation *Cobra*.

Whilst the 531st Engineer Shore Rgt de-fuses a mine in the background, an Engineer's GMC heads inland from Utah Beach along a sandy track covered with metal mats. With four divisions in combat as early as 7 June, the risk of creating a logjam in this marshy area was a real source of worry for the planners.
(Région Basse-Normandie/NARA, P012695)

3. Frederick Brook, *The Mythical Man-Month: Essays on Software Engineering* (1975), cited by Michel Goya on his Blog, *La voie de l'épée*, 13 Sept. 2012
4. Dwight Eisenhower, *Crusade in Europe*, Doubleday, 1948, p.185
5. Clayton Newell, *"Logistical Art"*, Parameters, mars 1989, p.38.
6. JK Ohl, *op. cit.*, pp. 189 & sq.
7. RO Atkinson, *An army at Dawn*, Henry Holt, 2002, p.22.

THIRD PART

FROM EUPHORIA TO DISILLUSION
The breakout

Worn out by six weeks of fighting, the German VII. Armee fell apart under the attack of 26 July. Bradley ordered the commanders of the VII and VIII Corps to push towards Avranches. The town was captured in the 30th and the undamaged bridges over the rivers Sée and Sélune opened the door to Brittany.

On 13 August south of Vire, a Half-Track M3A1 passes in front of a Stug III of the Sturmgeschütz-Brigade 394. With the speeding up of operations, the Germans left behind more and more equipment that was either damaged or simply out of fuel.
(Région Basse-Normandie/NARA, p. 130-131)

On 1 August, the 12th Army Group became operational. Bradley took command of it and had under his command the First Army with Hodges who was tasked with pivoting towards the east and covering Patton's Third Army as it captured the Breton peninsula. The six divisions of the *VIII Corps* pushed through the gap at Avranches within 72 hours with the objectives of capturing Rennes and Saint Malo. Having anticipated hard fighting for the ports that had been transformed into fortresses, the Master Plan had planned for other units of the Third Army, XV, XX and XII *Corps* to follow up for the capture of Quiberon and Brest. Patton, however, did not see things in the same way. This hot-headed and rash cavalryman also had an oversized ego and had been sitting impatiently in England for the last two months and was not prepared to let the glory slip from his hands. He had little time for logistical questions and indeed only met his G-4 (officer in charge of his army's logistics) on two occasions, the first when he took command and second in April 1945. As early as 1 August, he focused not on the west, but towards the east where the decisive battle would no doubt take place. Seeing the frontline crumbling in front of him and the heavy resistance put up by the Germans against the First US Army and the 21st British Army Group, he saw an incredible opportunity: by driving hard toward the east it would be possible to encircle the German army south of the river Seine and then cross the latter before the enemy could dig in along it. The conquest of the Brittany ports, a central objective of the Master Plan, was now

of secondary importance. Montgomery came to the same conclusion and went even further. He considered that the Brittany ports were no longer of importance and that once the German armies had been destroyed, it would be easy to take the ports in upper Normandy that were of much greater strategic use[1]. This was partially agreed upon by Eisenhower on 2 August to the great displeasure of the logistics experts.

AT THE RIVER SEINE ELEVEN DAYS AHEAD OF SCHEDULE

The logistical planners immediately warned Eisenhower of a serious problem. They were lacking the equivalent of 127 road companies in order to maintain contact with the armoured spearhead[2]. On 11 August, the planning branch of SHAEF announced that only four to six divisions would be able to be supplied on the Seine on 20 August and even then only if they immobilised divisions near the ports, used British transport units, flew in 1,000 tonnes of supplies per day and by-passed Paris in order to avoid feeding its population. It is probable that Patton did not hear these warnings, in any case he would have ignored them. Whilst the VIII Corps received the order to liberate Brittany, the rest of the Third Army was turned around to face the east[3].

In order to take the Germans by surprise in Brittany, Patton counted on his cavalrymen: Wood (4th Armoured Division) and Grow (6th AD). He by-passed Middleton, the commander of the VIII Corps, who he deemed too cautious[4]. The 4th AD drove towards Quiberon via Rennes,

---

1. Nigel Hamilton, *Master of the Battlefield: Monty's war years, 1942-44*, Mac Graw Hill, 1983, pp. 778-779.
2. Faced with the sudden increase in distances between the dumps and the frontline that had been envisaged on the Seine, Colonel Whipple, the SHAEF G-4, estimated that the requirements at 426 road companies. 227 were available and it was thought that railways could replace 108, something which left a deficit of 127.

GMC HI dumpster of the 164th Engineer Bn. working in the rue de Bretagne in Cherbourg. Its oversize dumpster placed great strain on the chassis. The Engineers played a decisive role in the pursuit when crossing water obstacles, clearing lines and rubble. *(Région Basse-Normandie/NARA, p000384)*

the 6th Armoured advanced on Brest, whilst a temporary force[5] was tasked with capturing the Rennes-Brest railway and its bridges before the Germans could destroy them. They were accompanied by only two infantry divisions: the 83rd and the 8th.

At the same time in the east, the 79th ID liberated Fougères on 3 August and Laval on the 7th. The 90th ID covered the fifty kilometres to Mayenne in half a day on 5 August. The bridges over the river were captured intact. This advance confirmed that Haislip's XV Corps was only faced by a reduced enemy force. An infantry regiment of the German 708. ID and a 9. Panzer reconnaissance battalion, both recently arrived, attempted, unsuccessfully, to halt Haislip. On the 8th, the Americans were at Le Mans. The previous day saw the Wehrmacht attempt a desperate offensive at Mortain in an attempt to recapture Avranches and cut off the Third Army. The failure of this attack opened up a window of opportunity for the Allies. The best units of the Panzerwaffe were now caught in a trap that appeared to be easy to close. For Bradley it was no longer necessary to advance as far as the Seine as the encirclement could be carried out with less effort south of Falaise. He ordered Patton to pivot the XV Corps, reinforced with the 5th AD and the French 2e DB commanded by Leclerc, with the objective of driving towards Argentan 100 kilometres north of Le Mans and which was reached five days later. It was at this point that Bradley ordered Haislip to halt his advance towards the north and wait for the Canadians to close the pocket. It took the latter six days to cover the remaining 40 kilometres, six days that the Germans used in order to save what they could. Patton did not remain inactive during this time and gave himself new objectives. The first of these, which was in the spirit of the Master Plan, consisted of capturing the

3. For Russel F. Weigley, this choice of launching the VIII Corps and its two armored divisions into Brittany was an error which weakened the 3rd Army for an operation that turned out to be without interest for the rest of the campaign. It is easy to see mistakes 70 years after the events and this line of thought would not have been accepted by Eisenhower, a prudent strategist whose mind was muddled by the alarming reports of his G-4. On 2 August, the hope of rapidly capturing the Brittany ports was still alive. Rather than pointing out this corps diverted to Brittany, one should rather retain the three corps launched into the enemy's rear. Russel F. Weigley, *"Normandy to Falaise, a critique of allied Operational planning in 1944"*, in Michael D Krause & R Cody Phillips (dir.), Historical perspective of operational art, CMH, 2005, p. 402.

4. Two factors contributed to the sidelining of Middleton. First, the rapid advance brought about a rupture in communications with the spearhead troops. It took up to 36 hours for a message to receive an answer, something which encouraged his subordinates to use their initiative. Later, Patton turned the 6th Cavalry Group into a unit for the gathering of information that drove all over the place for the exclusive use of the Third Army headquarters, meaning that it was very often better informed than Middleton.

5. Centred on the 6th ATk Group and the 15th Cavalry Group, commanded by Brigadier-General Earnest.

A GMC HI dumpster of the 164th Engineer Bn working in the rue de Bretagne in Cherbourg. Its big dumpster was a real burden for the chassis. The Engineers played a decisive role in the pursuit phase, crossing water obstacles, mine clearance and clearing obstacles. *(Région Basse-Normandie/NARA, p011451)*

Liberty Roads, 1944-1945

LOGISTICS IN AN EXTERIOR THEATRE OF OPERATIONS

By landing in France, the supplies landed in what the Americans call an exterior theatre of operations. All of the logistical procedures involved were written down in the Field Service Regulations Administration 100-10 which was updated on 15 November 1943. It listed all those involved, how they interacted, the general organization and supply procedures.

Pages 8-11 thus show the main areas of the logistical chain:

"In view of decentralized control, a theatre of operations is usually divided into a Combat Zone, the zone pf active operations under the authority of the combatant units, and a Communication Zone (ComZ), grouping together the rear echelon zones and administrating the theatre in its entirety [...] In the initial phase of a campaign, the theatre of operations can only comprise of the Combat Zone.

The Combat Zone comprises of the forward zone of a theatre of operations. Its depth depends on the amount of combatant units, the type of operations and the type of communications network and enemy attitude. The Combat Zone is sub-divided into Army, Corps and Divisions Areas, each being under the authority of the combatant unit concerned. [...] In the event of an advance, the frontal area of the Combat Zone will itself be pushed forward as much as possible in order to relieve commanders from the administration of as much territory as possible."

he Communication Zone included all of the territory situated between the rear border of the Combat Zone (decided by the theatre commander) and the border of the theatre of operations (decided by the War Department). In this zone were concentrated the main quartermaster installations, transport and medical evacuation and other administrations required to support the forces present in the theatre. It was the link between the Combat Zone and the Zone of the Interior. This Communication Zone was entirely independent of the of the Combat Zone commands which were only its clients and was autonomous in its management of supply flows. It only answered to the SHAEF Supreme Commander, Dwight Eisenhower, whilst the ASF, as supplier to the Zone of the Interior was the third party involved.

In concrete terms, in the narrow bridgehead of June and July, the responsibility fell directly to the supply bureau of Bradley's 1st Army (G-4). However, with the arrival of the 3rd Army and the frontline becoming more distant, the 1st Army handed over the management of the ports and dumps to General Lee's Communication Zone. As the advance progressed, ComZ decentralized its work by opening sections: an Advance Section for forward dumps just behind the Combat Zone, intermediate sections in charge of specialized dumps and Base Sections managing ports. Each section had at its disposal units of each technical service, Transportation Corps, Ordnance, and Quartermaster. Thus, the supplies passed from hand to hand and descended the supply chain from dump to dump depending on what was required. Theoretically, they were moved by train – pipelines for gasoline – along the lines of the Great War model, either by requisitioning the French SNCF, or by using trains of the Military Railways Service.

Once arrived in the Combat Zone, they were taken by army supply train units which supplied the divisions to which they belonged. Since 1943, Washington recommended to armies to keep their dumps as close as possible to the frontline. The Army Supply Point was therefore broken up with satellite dumps. These forward dumps were called railheads when supplies were brought up by train, and truckheads when by road. One was generally found behind each army corps. For the theoreticians, it was only from this point on that the road became the mode of transportation and it was said at this point that the supplies were tactical. In theory, distance was not to exceed 150 km and to be as often as possible reduced to short distances of fifty kilometres.

The final kilometres were in theory covered by divisional quartermaster companies tasked with stockpiling reserves and by regimental or battalion quartermaster companies tasked with keeping combatant troops supplied on a daily basis. This choice of short-circuiting the divisional and army corps dumps on a daily basis was made in order to limit and breaks in the chain and economize means. Thus, the divisional supply train saw its strength reduced to a small company for the infantry divisions and to nothing at all for the armored divisions. However, this complicated the task of the Army Supply Points which had to deal with a multitude of small requisitions rather than ten large ones.

Such coordination was only possible thanks to a regulating authority and precise procedures. For example, a Regulating Station was opened to the immediate rear of each army in order to coordinate transportation between the Advance Section and the various Army Supply Points.

General Marshall, the Army Chief-of-Staff, his naval counterpart Admiral King and Eisenhower, Supreme Commander of the Allied Expeditionary Force, visit the Normandy front in June 1944. It was the question of logistics which occupied most of their time.
(NARA)

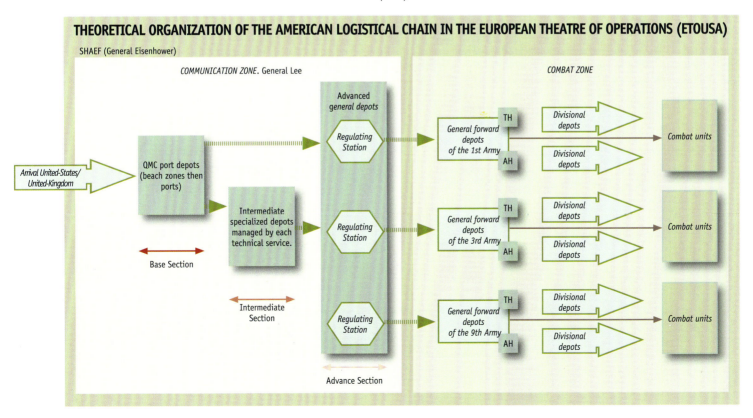

Liberty Roads, 1944-1945

space left between the rivers Seine and Loire. On 15 August, he engaged two new corps, the XII (35th ID and 4th AD freed up from Brittany) with the objective of taking Orléans, and the XX (5th ID and 7th AD) towards Chartres. The following day, the XII Corps entered Orléans after an advance of 200 kilometres in 24 hours. Two days later, 2,000 Germans were taken prisoner at Chartres and Paris was now only 80 kilometres away. Patton then removed two of the XV Corps divisions (the 5th AD and the 79th ID) halted south of Argentan and launched them towards Dreux, then Mantes. They met with hardly any opposition and the advance was rapid, covering 100 kilometres on 16 August. On the 20th, the 79th ID established a bridgehead north of the Seine, whilst the 5th AD began to advance down the river in order to encircle the Germans. It took five days of hard fighting to advance 30 km and it was finally beaten in reaching Louviers by the XIX Corps that had advanced from Evreux. The operation was a failure; the attack carried out by the

First Canadian Army and the First US Army had the effect of squeezing a toothpaste tube: instead of encircling the enemy, the latter had been pushed towards the opening in the Rouen area from where it was able to escape.

Generally speaking, this phase of the campaign was badly handled by the Allies who let a decisive victory slip through their fingers.

At this time, the lodgement zone was cleared. After having counted up to a delay thirty-five days, the Allies finally reached the Seine eleven days ahead of schedule. Contrary to the prophets of doom in London, it was not four infantry divisions that were on the right bank of the Seine but the bulk of the First and Third Army. For the second time since June, the ingenuity of the men on the ground had prevented the logistical system from falling apart.

HOW COULD THEY KEEP THE MOTORISED SPEARHEADS SUPPLIED?

The ADSEC naturally first sought to put back into service the railway network. This was the most economical and efficient mode of transportation over long distances. As early as 3 August, two engineer regiments were busy putting back into service the

Saint-Lô/Rennes/Le Mans railway, but the damage suf-

Rivers have always been a major factor in the slowing down of an advance. One allied bombing or German sabotage would suffice to immobilise an entire division in front of a collapsed bridge. However, the US Army had bridging equipment, either the Bailey Bridge (bottom, near Carentan), M1 or M2 Steel Treadway (pontoon) Bridge (top and middle), as well as a whole range of lifting and clearing machinery like the Caterpillar D4 bulldozer and GMC Leroi seen below.
(NARA, via Région Haute-Normandie p013055 & p011608 and via Arch. dép. de la Manche, 13-Num 1289 & 1322)

Liberty Roads, 1944-1945

did not prevent the Third Army on 12 August from demanding 25,000 tonnes of ammunition to be delivered within three days to the Le Mans rail station. It was then decided to fall back on a one-way secondary track passing via St Hilaire du Harcouët. Elements of the eleven engineer regiments were busy night and day and under sniper fire in order for the first convoy of 22 trains to cross no less than 97 Bailey bridges five days later. However, this exploit was not exploited further as the Le Mans station was far too damaged to cope with such a large amount. Also, as the line was one-way, the trains could not return to Saint-Lô where wagons were soon in short supply.

Whilst awaiting for the rail network to be repaired, supplies were transported by road. At the end of July, the Transportation Corps were using 94 Truck Companies. Fleets of trucks were organised between the dumps near the beaches and the areas furthest forward, although this was not achieved without a certain confusion and total improvisation. Given the speed of the advance, it was sometimes difficult to locate fighting units. On 4 August, General Grow asked Patton for a delivery of 40 tonnes of fuel the following day at Pontivy... that is to say 40 km beyond his frontline at that time. Stop-gap measures were taken such as temporarily removing trucks form combatant units giving an extra ten GMC to the Truck Companies, and the loan of three companies of British lorries. On 10 August, two companies of tank transporters were converted into HGVs capable of carrying 45 tonnes. 1,400 extra trucks were found by combing out the depots in Britain. The GMC were loaded with hundreds of jerry cans, thus allowing answer the most urgent needs.

AT THE HEART OF THE BATTLE
The Regulating Stations

Something that played an essential role but which re-

This small waterway is not an obstacle for tracked vehicles, but the same cannot be said for the truck convoys.
(270, NARA © Coriello, Bibliothèque municipale de Cherbourg)

In theory it was up to the railroads to provide supplies to the armies. However, this required materiel, but the bulk of the French rail equipment had been destroyed. Also, by the end of July, only one line had been opened, one way, linking Cherbourg with.... Lison, north of St Lo.
(Région Basse-Normandie/NARA, p013079)

Liberty Roads, 1944-1945

A GMC on a medical mission speeds towards Vire, passing by a destroyed Das Reich Panzer IV near Pont-Farcy. The pursuit phase was speeding up.
(Région Basse-Normandie/NARA, p013049)

mains relatively unknown are the ADSEC Regulating Stations. These consisted of a small team led by a Field Service Regulation Officer. They were tasked with organising and controlling road and rail traffic between the army and the dumps in the rear. There was one station per army, the 24th followed the Third Army and the 25th accompanied the First Army, both had been activated at the end of July when the bridgehead was sufficiently large to necessitate their intervention. However, in total contradiction to the importance of their mission, these men had not undergone thorough training. They had received hardly any training as to the procedures in vigour within the ADSEC and the novice officers did not even no what their exact role was.

All they had as a sort of manual was a small brochure that summed up the methods used in....1918. They had to, therefore, improvise. The station head office was a hive of activity where the personnel had to juggle with a multitude of information: on one hand it had to keep constantly up to date with the locality of fighting units and current operations, something which explains why it shared the G-4 *"offices"* of each army, on the other hand it received a multitude of information as to the amounts of supplies allocated by

the ComZ, where they were to be found in the depots and the availability of transport. Using all of this, it formed convoys, established their priorities, worked out itineraries and chose the rail and road terminus from where the fighting units would re-supply. The fluctuating situation led to frequent modifications to itineraries and priorities. Administrative red tape was abandoned in order to gain time. A verbal suggestion from the G-4 was enough to modify the destination of convoys, much to the regret of the ADSEC which felt it was losing control of operations. Detachments of two or three men on a jeep, or on motorbikes, were tasked with opening new routes. The station also sent detachments to various strategic points (crossroads, train station) to assist the Military Police, guide lost convoys or give instructions to others that sometimes left without knowing their destination. Sometimes a motorbike led the way for a convoy to prevent it from getting lost. Signposts were rare and often obsolete. Despatch riders assured liaison between these detachments and the regulating station as radio communications were either insufficient or deficient. Of course, this continual improvisation led to a serious amount of waste. Convoys found themselves immobilised without instructions, goods were lost and army corps stated having received materiel that they had not asked for whilst waiting for items they had requested. Despite this, up to the end of August there was nothing serious lacking and the advance was able to continue.

Full speed ahead no going back

This confusion was aggravated by the multiplication of overlapping services and which were, on the whole, autonomous. The generals had to request their supplies without always knowing who they should ask. Should they ask Eisenhower, Lt. General John Lee, commanding the ComZ, his subordinate Maj. General Ewart Plank, head of the ADSEC, or directly the regulating station officers? Bradley and Patton did not have words strong enough to describe what they thought of Lee who they accused of abusing his authority and of favouritism. The ostentatious luxury in which he set himself up in Valognes on 7 August led to even more resentment.

The other problem was the increasing distances that had to be covered. The ADSEC, to which it had been planned to attribute a strip one hundred kilometres in depth to cover behind the lines, found itself with distances of three to four hundred kilometres to cover when it did not have sufficient manpower. It was also thought that there would be enough time to set up forward dumps. On 13 August, the ADSEC opened a dump in Laval. It was there that the Third Army quartermaster services was is-

Three photos that symbolize the Liberation with American columns passing by burnt out SS Pz IV and other vehicle. At the top, a 4th Arm. Div. M8 armored car, in the middle, a column of Shermans, including a 76 mm of the 67th Armored Regiment of the 2nd Arm. Div., and below, a M4 of the 3rd Arm. Div. at St Fromond. For the tank crews, the breakthrough heralded six euphoric weeks.
(Région Basse-Normandie/NARA, p013388, p013129 & p013015)

Liberty Roads, 1944-1945

In the afternoon of 26 July, two light "Stuart" tanks of the 33rd Armored Rgt speed south towards Marigny. The front tank is equipped with a hedgerow cutter.
A few days later, a Tank Destroyer M10 (camouflaged under branches) of the 702nd T.D. Bn still partially equipped with its "fording kit", passes by a M4 of the 743rd Tank Bn. near Lonlay l'Abbaye. *(Région Basse-Normandie/NARA, p012462 & p011236)*

Whilst two M8 armored cars of the 82nd Armored Reconnaissance Bn, 2nd Armored Division US patrol the streets of Saint-Sever on 4 August, a few streets away a 76 mm M4 picks its way through the wreckage.
(Région Basse-Normandie/NARA, p012094 & p012093)

Three American M5A1 Stuart light tanks of the 25th Cavalry Recon Sq of the 4th Arm. Div. drive through Coutances on 29 July 44. Since the landings, this outdated tank has proved to be ill-suited in close-quarter combat, as well as in a reconnaissance role. It remained, however, in service, draining away its share of fuel that was becoming increasingly rare on the frontline. *(Région Basse-Normandie/NARA, p011768)*

sued with its supplies. However, this dump was inefficient as the requirements were such that no stocks could be constituted. As soon as they arrived the goods left again without even having been unloaded. Planning was no longer possible and the only rule was that of first come first served. Also, this dump was immediately rendered distant by the advance of the fighting units and was replaced by the Le Mans dump which was itself 200 km from the frontline. As for the great dump that was to be opened between Rennes and Laval, it never saw the day. To sum up, there were no longer any forward dumps and supplies passed directly from the Normandy dumps to army dumps, not by rail as had been planned, but by road. Troubles were not over even when the supplies arrived at the army dumps as the latter were also dangerously far away from the frontline. The manual planned for their setting up ideally between 75 and 150 km from the frontline which implied that during the advance having to move the dump every two days which was of course impossible. With the First Army, the dump opened near Vire on 12 August was abandoned before it even became operational. It successor at Loupe (200 km east of Vire) only functioned for a few days before it was moved again. Finally, a 200 to 300 km logistical no mans' land formed between the units on the Seine and the closest dumps, a distance that the army trains found increasingly difficult to travel. It was also impossible to build vehicle spare parts dumps, something which explains the large amount of breakdowns that wore down the road companies.

The situation worsened from 15 August onwards when Patton was forced to halt the XII Corps at Orléans and leave the VIII Corps in Brittany. The lack of medical and signalling supplies reached a critical point: ten tonnes of medical materiel were discovered in Orleans, 15 tonnes at Dreux and 20 tonnes at Fontainebleau, to which was added 500 kilometres of telephone cable in Chartres. It was only thanks to the capture of seven railway tankers in Sens that operations east of the Seine were able to start. The ADSEC decided to ration divisions. It only supplied 162 tonnes per day to an infantry division and 247 tonnes for an armoured division, figures that should be compared with the theoretical amount of 650 tonnes per day. On 15 August, SHAEF authorised the CATOR (Combined Air Transport Operation Room[6]) to mobilise the planes of the IX Troop Carrier Command to bring in rations. Even so, this required airstrips for the planes and only that of Le Mans was operational but it was already far away from the armoured spearheads. It was only on the 19th that the first planes were able to land. By the end of a week 4,200 tonnes of rations had been unloaded, but this was still a long way from the 14,000 tonnes that had been planned for. 22 August saw 383 loaded Dakotas immobilised in England as the airfields on the continent were saturated. In the long term, the reports sent to the supreme command set off alarm bells concerning the running out of reserves on the continent. Contrary to the plan, no port in Brittany was useable yet[7]. With

---
6. CATOR was tasked with coordinating and regulating all transport aircraft traffic apart from those used in airborne missions.
7. Saint Malo fell on 17 August but the port was in ruins. Brest was besieged up to 19 August, whereas Lorient and St Nazaire held out until the end of the war.

Liberty Roads, 1944-1945

The Sherman was equipped with a 425hp Chrysler Multibank A57 aircraft engine which ensured maneuverability and responsiveness but which consumed 452 litres per one hundred kilometres for a capacity of 727 litres. With a range slightly higher than 150 km it required frequent refuelling, contrary to the T34. *(NARA)*

How to get round an obstacle whilst waiting for the engineers to finish their job.
(13-Num 1286, NARA © Archives départementales de la Manche)

Two Sherman M4A1 (76) and a M4 of the 32nd Armored Regt, 3rd Arm. Div., 26 July 1944, at St Jean de Daye, being fitted with their hedgerow cutters. Note the black camouflage stripes on the side of the Sherman, replacing the too-visible white stars. *(NARA)*

At right.
As far as the river Seine, the Americans accompanied their divisions with a multitude of support units: chemical warfare, anti-aircraft and heavy artillery, such as the gun seen here, thus wasting precious fuel and immobilizing means of transport.
(195, NARA © Coriello, Bibliothèque municipale de Cherbourg)

the impending arrival of autumn, landing supplies on the beaches ran the risk of slowing down due to weather. The same report stated its worry concerning the disappearance of precious jerrycans. It could not be said whether the Allies would be halted first by the lack of fuel or by their incapability to transport it to the frontline.

However, all that people remember for 17 August is that the Allies came very close to encircling two German armies near Falaise. The Third Army liberated Dreux and Orléans and found itself faced with hardly any enemy opposition. This was a success that had not been foreseen a month previously. Despite the warnings of the quartermaster services based in London, Eisenhower had gambled and won by allowing his generals a free rein. Finally, despite walking a tight rope and hindered by a complex organisation, an obsolete doctrine of employment and partially ill-suited equipment, the ComZ had always managed to supply Patton's spearheads. Although on paper Overlord was a campaign led by accountants, the reality on the ground meant that it was in fact led by strategists. The quartermaster services went back to their initial role, that of making operations possible and not dictating the speed of the campaign.

THE *MASTER PLAN* IS WOUND UP

Following this success, Ike, Patton, Montgomery and others wanted to advance as far as the Rhine with the aim of achieving victory before Christmas. As far as Eisenhower was concerned the thrashing meted out to the Germans would allow the Allies to push on beyond the river Seine. The only problem was that nothing had been planned. There was a flurry of activity in all services and four new plans were put to Eisenhower.

A new situation, four new plans

The first plan was put forward by the strategists at SHAEF. Their report was clear; it was out of the question

Liberty Roads, 1944-1945

12TH US ARMY GROUP ORDER OF BATTLE AT THE BEGINNING OF SEPTEMBER

1st US ARMY (LT-GENERAL COURTNEY H. HODGES)		3rd US ARMY (LT-GENERAL GEORGES S. PATTON)		9th US ARMY (LT. GENERAL WILLIAM H. SIMPSON) Operational on 5 September and deployed in Brittany.	
XIX CORPS (MAJOR-GENERAL CHARLES H. CORLETT)	30th ID 79th ID 2nd Arm. Div.	XX CORPS (MAJOR-GENERAL WALTON H. WALKER)	5th ID 90th ID 7th Arm. Div.	VIII CORPS (MAJOR-GENERAL TROY H. MIDDLETON) W	2nd ID 8th ID 29th ID 83rd ID
V CORPS (MAJOR-GENERAL LEONARD T. GEROW)	4th ID 28th ID 5th Arm. Div.	XII CORPS (MAJOR-GENERAL MANTON S. EDDY)	35th ID 80th ID 4th Arm. Div.	III CORPS (MAJOR-GENERAL JOHN MILIKEN)	94th ID 104th ID
VII CORPS (MAJOR-GENERAL J. LAWTON COLLINS)	1st ID 9th ID 3rd Arm. Div.	XV CORPS (MAJOR-GEN. WADE H HAISLIP)	2ᵉ DB (Leclerc)		6th Arm Div.

Transmissions, Regulating, Decisions, the three keys to the pursuit phase. Photo 1 (posed for the camera) still manages to portray the keys to the success of motorized operations: the mastering of telecommunications, a solid skill in the use of cartographic tools and a heightened sense of decision making. The photo, like 2 and 3 were taken in a telephone exchange in the château de Chiffrevast near Valognes, the ComZ HQ of General Lee in September. The other photos highlight the tools at the disposal of the linchpins of American logistics, the Regulating Stations. Nothing would have been possible without these small headquarters placed at the interface between ADSEC and the fighting units. They coordinated, planned, regulated and made decisions. Their weapons were telecommunications: firstly radios (5), then teleprinters (3), but also the telephone (6) that the Signal Corps worked hard at putting back into service (4). Photo 5 shows the precarious conditions in which the Regulating Stations worked, always on the side of the roads, here in a cowshed with a "rest room" at the foot of the BD71 field telephone switchboard. Photo 6 shows a BE70 tester which controls the correct functioning of the lines. Whilst the stations were hard at work, the generals were clashing over the strategy to adopt once the Seine was crossed: Lt Gen Omar Nelson Bradley, 1st Army and future head of the XII US Army Group, Maj-Gen Leonard Townsend Gerow, V Corps who would replace Bradley at the 1st Army, Gen Dwight David Eisenhower, the Supreme Commander, Maj-Gen Lawton Joseph "Lightning Joe" Collins, VII Corps. Following photo, Ike is seen here talking with Maj. Gen. Ira T. Wyche, commander of the 79th ID. (All pictures from Rég. Basse-Normandie/NARA)

Liberty Roads, 1944-1945

Liberty Roads, 1944-1945

Liberty Roads, 1944-1945

Previous pages.
A Jeep and a GMC driving through the ruins of St. Lô. They carry extra jerrycans as fuel dumps were sparse.
(Région Basse-Normandie/NARA, p012890)

Montgomery (left) was in favour of an offensive on a narrow front along the channel coast. Eisenhower (right) was not against the idea but had to also deal with political imperatives and a certain reserve concerning Monty.
(Région Basse-Normandie/NARA, p013042

to halt the advance. Militarily it would be stupid to allow a broken enemy to reorganise. It would also be politically dangerous at a time where a race against time had been engaged with the Soviets[8]. However, although they threw the time frame of the Master Plan away, they retained the strategic principles: a pincer movement operation towards the Ruhr by advancing around the Ardennes. On the left, the British would follow the Rouen-Amiens-Brussels-Düsseldorf axis (Montgomery's 21st British Army Group), whilst on the right the Americans would advance via Metz and the Sarre in order to reach Cologne (Bradley's 12th US Army Group). This twin advance also prevented any problems concerning national sensitivities. It spread out the enemy forces whilst at the same time leaving the possibility of putting more onus on one part of the pincer depending on how the situation evolved. Finally, it also allowed for the encirclement of German units withdrawing along the river Rhône following the landings in Provence. However, the flip side of the coin was that this choice would dilute the advance and totally ignored logistical constraints.

This was the reason why one man spoke out, Colonel Whipple, the head of SHAEF (G-4) quartermaster services. He estimated that only eleven divisions, four of which were armoured, could cross the Seine, and even then would have to leave behind all heavy artillery, mobilise all transport aircraft and take away vehicles from other divisions in order to form extra transport units. The objec-

---
8. On 22 June 1944, the Soviet armies launched Operation Bagration and tore to pieces Heeresgruppe Mitte, advancing 600 km in two months.

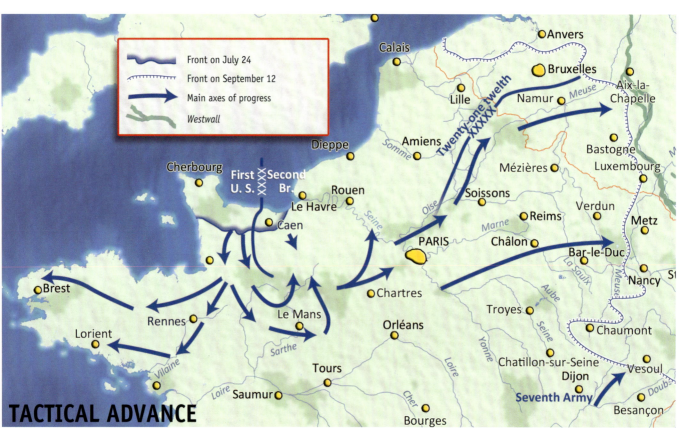

TACTICAL ADVANCE

A succession of ruined towns and villages, this was the scene in lower – Normandy. Luckily, the speeding up of operations led to less destruction. The Half-Track is towing a 57 mm anti-tank gun, a weapon currently encountered even though it was obsolete in 1944. *(NARA)*

A few hours after the liberation of Pré en Pail, men of the local Resistance begin their savage cleansing of collaborators. After the wildy celebrating crowds, this was what the GIs who liberated France would see next. Those perched on their Sherman are obviously watching with amusement, unaware of the unfloding drama.
(Région Basse-Normandie/NARA, p013437)

Liberty Roads, 1944-1945

A Dozer tank opens up a gap for the infantry. One of the keys to logistics was maintaining a homogeneous vehicle park in order to render maintenance easier, without going without specialized equipment. The multi-task Sherman which was easy to modify, was a trump card in the American pack compared to the heterogeneity of the German vehicle park. *(Région Basse-Normandie/ NARA, p013436)*

RATIONS K, C AND 10 IN 1, ALL OF AMERICA IN A BOX!

As with all armies, the American army had to feed its men on a daily basis using field kitchens using fresh foods (A rations) or those in tins (B rations). However, this formula did not allow for the feeding of single fighting men and its logistics were complex (B rations comprised of 110 different items that all came from the United States and which were stored in various places in the New York docks) compared to rations that were prepared, packed and easy to consume, transport, store and keep a count of. It was only for the sole reason of logistics and with disregard for nutritional practices that in 1907, the US Army tried out a first individual ration, known as "*iron rations*" as it came in a tin. It comprised of a 85g piece of cake, 28g of sugared chocolate, salt and pepper. An improved version became the "reserve ration" that became well known to the Doughboys of 1918, which was then followed by the C rations in 1938. It was the latter that would form the basis of the GIs food. Designed by the QMC laboratories in Chicago, these rations were of improved nutritional value and could be kept for longer. It came in a kit comprising of accessories and six 340g circular tins, three M tins and three B tins. The M tins contained marinated meat with onions starter and a hot meal (meat-beans, meat-mashed potato, stew-vegetables) and the B tin contained bread, dessert (crackers, candy, toffees) and a powdered drink (coffee, orange juice or cocoa). As for the kit, it was well stocked with water purification tablets, chewing gum, cigarettes, writing paper, toilet paper, knives and forks and even a wooden tray. The full C ration had drawbacks: its taste, being always the same food, its weight and its not impractical circular shape.

The B part of C rations.

The Army then looked at rationalising its packaging, something which led to the 10 in 1 and K rations. In 1943, the QMC took a look at the British rations and came up with pre-cooked collective rations for five, then ten men. Its specifications imposed rations comprising of "*elements of B rations (modified to reduce the volume and weight) packed in boxes of five full ration packs… the packaging had to be water, mould and chemical proof. Collective rations had to be in a size and shape that men and animals could carry and sufficiently robust to cope with normal conditions of handling and transport*". Transported in accompanying vehicles, the 10 and 1 rations could follow the fighting men and at the same time offer a slightly larger choice of menu (five versus the three in the C rations). As for the most famous rations, the K, it was in theory reserved for emergencies. It was designed by the special advisor to the Secretary of War, Ancel Keys, a researcher at the University of Minnesota. Its success, however, was due more to its exceptionally compact size its rectangular packaging the idea of which came from the Cracker Jack manufacturer. Like the C rations, the K rations held three breakfasts, dinners and suppers along with their accessories. The composition varied, but a typical breakfast held, for example, scrambled eggs with ham, dry biscuits, a bar of dried fruit, a cereal bar, instant coffee and sugar. It provided 3,000 kcal per day, an amount that was far too low for a combatant (3,600 kcal), but in any case the US Army deemed that it was sufficient given that these rations were not to be used for an extended length of time: two or three days. However, K rations were so practical that they became the standard rations for units on the move and this led to problems of malnutrition.

Thus, from June to mid-July, the GIs had to make do with pre-cooked C, K or 10 in 1 rations and the situation worsened during the pursuit phase. However, apart from a few days at the beginning of the September, the GI never had to loot in order to survive and this is one of the big differences with the other armies of the Second World War. German food stores captured during the pursuit were welcomed as they offered a change in diet rather than because the men were going hungry. They even swapped rations with civilians. The more popular B and A rations became more common in November after the first refrigerated wagons and trucks landed and a cold chain was set up.

The invention of combat ration packaging was one of the major American inventions of the conflict and bears witness to the constraints in transportation, storage and distribution that were unknown within the other armies. But this was only made possible by the existence of a food processing industry that at te time was unique in the world and the 300 million K rations, and as many again C rations, bear witness to the scale of the effort.

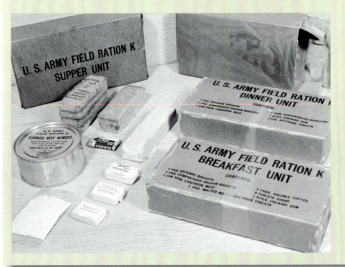

Liberty Roads, 1944-1945

A Kettenkrad has been put into use by the Military Police in charge of traffic control in Cherbourg. The convoy is made of the star American vehicles: GMC 2 ½ Ton, Dodge ¾ Ton and Jeeps.
(Région Basse-Normandie/NARA, p00957)

A column of 2nd ID jeeps has just crossed a Bailey Bridge. The vertical metal post attached to the hood is to protect the men in the jeep from decapitating wires strung across the roads.
(Région Basse-Normandie/NARA, p011256)

Liberty Roads, 1944-1945

GIVE ME FIVE!
THE OPTIONS OPEN TO EISENHOWER FOR THE PURSUIT

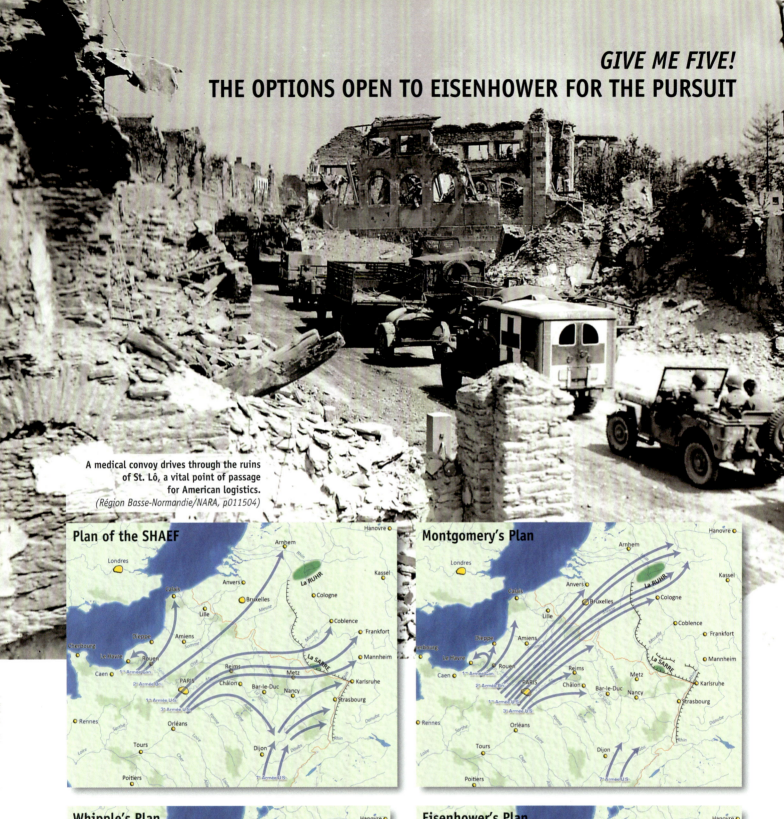

A medical convoy drives through the ruins of St. Lô, a vital point of passage for American logistics.
(Région Basse-Normandie/NARA, p011504)

Plan of the SHAEF

Montgomery's Plan

Whipple's Plan

Eisenhower's Plan

Liberty Roads, 1944-1945

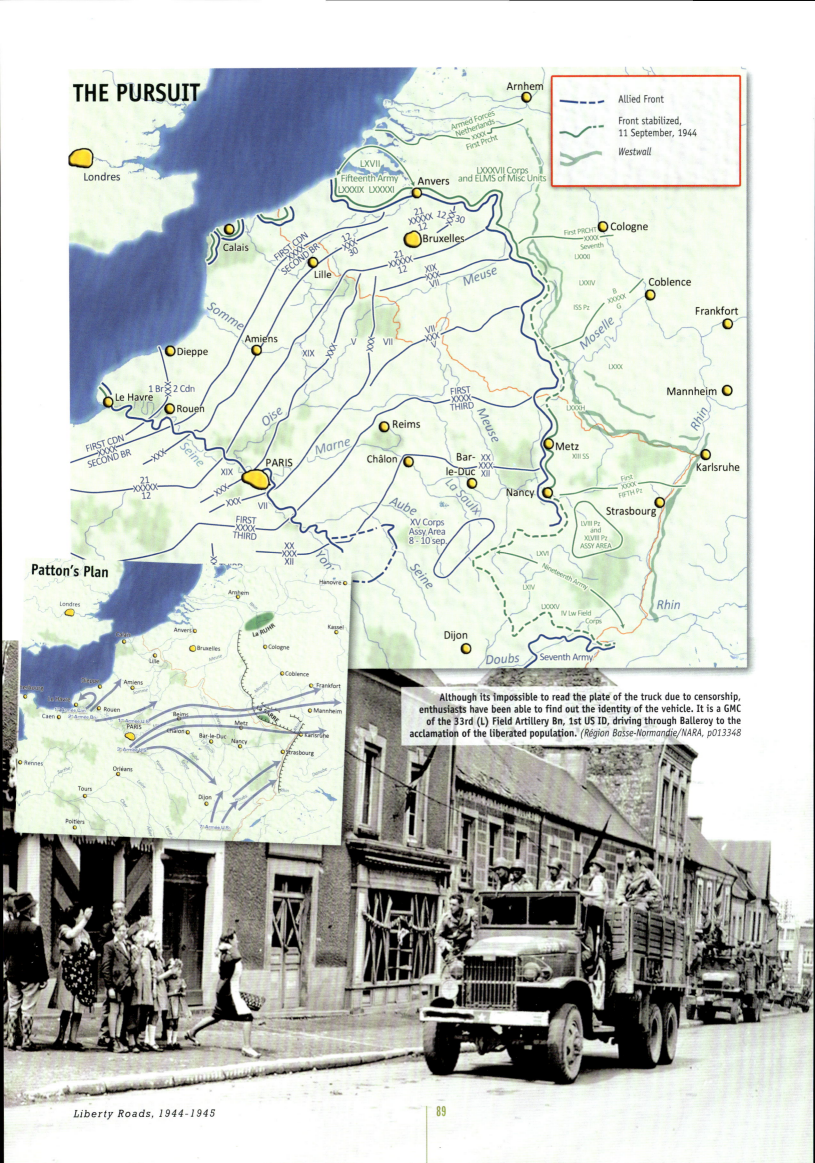

Although its impossible to read the plate of the truck due to censorship, enthusiasts have been able to find out the identity of the vehicle. It is a GMC of the 33rd (L) Field Artillery Bn, 1st US ID, driving through Balleroy to the acclamation of the liberated population. *(Région Basse-Normandie/NARA, p013348)*

Liberty Roads, 1944-1945

SIMPLIFIED ORGANIZATION OF THE AMERICAN LOGISTICAL CHAIN AT THE END OF AUGUST

Normandy Base Section (COM Z) → Port zone and beach zone → Main depots/dumps in the rear echelon zone (Normandy)

Advance Section (COM Z) → Army depots/dumps → Truckheads

Army Zones → Truckheads → Combat Unit

- **Utah Beach:** *1st Engineer Special Brigade*
- **Omaha Beach:** *5th* and *6th Engineer Special Brigade*
A brigade comprised of fifteen to twenty thousand men. It was an administrative unit with engineer units, road transport companies, port units, road signals, police, and repairs.
- **Cherbourg:** *4th Major Port* with 9 port battalions and 8 engineer battalions.

COM-Z
Motor Transport Brigade with more than a hundred Quartermaster Truck Companies (5 Dodge ¾ Ton, 48 1.5 Ton to 5 To trucks and semi-articulated). 5,000 vehicles.

Army supply train
A pool of 30 to 45 Quartermaster Truck Companies (5 Dodge ¾ Ton, 48 GMC) but with only 4 to 8 at the 3rd Army (200 to 400 vehicles) and 11 to 16 (550 to 800 vehicles) with the 1st Army were attached to supplies, the others were reserved for tactical missions (troop transportation, supporting the Ordnance Corps...).

Divisional supply train
Inf. Div.: 1 *Quartermaster Truck Company* (5 Dodge ¾ Ton, 48 GMC)
Arm. Div: no organic divisional supply train but two Quartermaster Truck Companies which were attached to each division by the army to complete the battalion supply trains.

Keys
→ Oil pipeline
→ Roads
→ Red Ball Express
→ Railroads

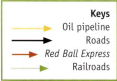

The front page of a 1984 edition of American Legion Magazine. This veterans' publication pays tribute the African-American soldiers. The illustrator offers an idealized and naïve portrayal of the Red Ball Express which he compares to thrust through enemy-held territory, as seen by the explosions and, the corpse by the roadside and the two armed soldiers sat on the load. The Red Ball has joined the Far West pioneers in popular memory.
(Charles Waterhouse, "Gangway"©US Army Transportation Museum)

---

9. Letter from Montgomery to Alanbrooke, 20 August 1944.
10. Cf Patton, *War as I knew*, Houghton Mifflin Coy, 1975, p. 114 and Bradley, Soldier's story, p. 398.
11. Letter from Eisenhower to Marshall dated 24 August following a meeting with Montgomery the previous day.
12. It comprised at this time of the 82nd and 101st US Airborne Divisions, the 1st British Airborne Division and the 1st Polish Airborne Brigade.
13. It finally began on 25 August but had to be slowed down after three days and up to 7 September due to a lack of ammunition. The ruined port only fell on 19 September.

---

tives would be the river Somme on 20 September with Sedan and Nancy following on 20 October. However, Whipple had been discredited over the last few weeks and his pessimistic forecasts had been regularly proved wrong by the reality on the ground. He persisted in saying that a Trucks Company could only cover 200 km per day whereas in fact they often drove a third more than this distance. He calculated that a division needed 650 tonnes of supplies per day whereas in a pursuit phase with little actual fighting, this amount was reduced to 350 tonnes and consisted mostly of fuel.

On the continent, Montgomery was in favour of a third project. Together, the Allied armies would constitute *"a mass of forty divisions that would fear nothing"* with one single push along the Channel coast[9]. This idea was attractive for several reasons. Apart from conforming to the doctrine of concentrating forces it would also allow the Allies to reach the Ruhr via the shortest route whilst at the same time destroying all of the V1 and V2 launch sites in the Pas de Calais that had become a priority for the British government. It would also slip around the Siegfried Line, the strength of which was an unknown quantity. This was also a careful plan as it avoided the dispersion of logistical means and ensured the rapid liberation of the Channel ports that would shorten the supply lines. This would also make the capture of the Brittany ports less urgent. Militarily speaking, the weak point in this plan was the risk of a counter attack against the right flank of the armies and it was for this reason that Monty put forward the idea of using the Third Army as flank guard along the Troyes-Sedan axis. Although Bradley did not voice any disagreement at the time, he mostly foresaw political problems that this attack on a narrow front would create.

This plan was unacceptable for the Americans who were advancing ten times faster than the British. The slowness with which Montgomery closed the Falaise Pocket had really annoyed them. Patton and Bradley were now convinced that only the Americans had the know-how to carry out a pursuit. Leaving it in the hands of Monty would guarantee a slow advance, allowing the Germans the time to regroup. It would also mean losing the victory laurels and make the British the great liberators of Europe.

Patton and Bradley saw the 12th US Army Group pushing eastwards towards Berlin in the hope of causing the political collapse of the Third Reich. Officially they were preparing to send the V, XII and XX Corps towards the Rhine and Karlsruhe, Mannheim and Wiesbaden without worrying about a threat to their flanks[10]. Ten divisions could cross the Rhine as long as all the others were immobilised on the Seine. However, this would require Eisenhower giving the green light and it was up to him to decide which of the four plans would be followed.

The art of compromise

Monty was dismayed when he found out that Ike was thinking of following the SHAEF plan and came back to latter with his own plan. Ike listened carefully to what he had to say and even amended the plan. *"For a long time I had though that we could undertake the operations in the north and at the same time advance in the east, however, I later found, given the huge importance of the objectives in the north, that we should first concentrate on this movement"*[11]. There was no longer any question of spreading out allied forces on either side of the Ardennes, Hodge's 1st US Army with the bulk of the 12th US Army Group's fuel stores would accompany Montgomery by following the Paris-Liège-Cologne axis. The 1st Airborne Army[12], ready to land to the rear of the Wehrmacht lines, was also placed under the command of the 21st Br. Army Group. Patton's 3rd US Army would have to content itself with an attack that was just a straightforward diversion with the aim of reaching the river Meuse.

Eisenhower was guided in his choice by logistical considerations. On 24 August, he wrote to Marshall: *"I don't have the slightest doubt that we can rapidly reach what was before the French-German border, but it won't be of any use reaching it before we are able to exploit it"*. The American advance in the east was conditioned by the need to improve the supply system and he saw the SHAEF plan as being too optimistic. He was also worried because Patton had abandoned his VIII Corps in Brittany to such an extent that Brest, which it had been hoped to capture by 12 August, was not attacked until ten days later[13]. Also, Paris had been liberated on the 25th, something that had not been planned for. This meant that the population had to be fed and provided with coal and medical supplies. There was the risk of precious convoys being diverted away from the armies. In these conditions it was clear that the offensive along the Channel coast was the priority. The choice of retaining a secondary attack towards the east was important for two reasons: militarily it would force the Germans to disperse their forces whilst at the same time leaving Ike an alternative in the event of Monty failing in the north; secondly on a political level it would not leave Patton in a strictly defensive posture.

Finally, the plan adopted on 23 August, satisfying both the Americans and the British, created formidable hurdles. On an administrative level, the operation became complex as the main offensive in the north would be carried out under the joint command of Monty and Bradley. However, as events had shown in Falaise, it was difficult to coordinate inter-allied operations. What was even more damaging in this plan was the fact that the separation between the 12th and 21st Army Group ran right along the best and shortest

CHAPTER 7

RED BALL EXPRESS (AUGUST-SEPTEMBER 1944)

On 23 August, the ADSEC services were informed of the decision to pursue the advance beyond the Seine. As stipulated by the manual, they decided to open a large supply dump just behind the armies: Dreux for the First Army and Chartres for the Third. The aim was to gather 100,000 tonnes of supplies before 1 September. However, given the limitations of the rail network, 82% had to brought up via road. The challenge was daunting. *"It won't be said that the ADSEC stopped the Allies when the Germans didn't manage to"*.

The 3886th Truck Company sets off. The convoy commander's Jeep will bring up the rear of the convoy led by the GMC with the blue pennant. The latter has been fitted with an in-unit made holder for an extra twelve jerrycans (240 liters) over the driver's cabin. Each truck had to carry enough gasoline for a return trip. *(13-Num 1085, NARA © Archives départementales de la Manche)*

It was with these words that the head of the ADSEC, Brigadier-General Ewart G Plank, opened his daily staff meeting on 23 August 1944. Two Communication Zone officers, Lt Col. Loren A Ayers and Major Gordon K Gravelle put forward the idea of copying the emergency transport carried out in southern England in June. A one-way loop had been opened to link the depots with the embarkation port. Why not do the same by increasing the manpower and length of time? On paper the operation looked straightforward, a route would be used continually in the manner of a belt. The trucks would be loaded with priority supplies (fuel, rations and ammunition) and converge on Saint-Lô. Here the convoys would be formed as well as the start of a one-way itinerary. One route was reserved for vehicles going and another for those returning. The Red Ball Express Highway was born.

AT THE HEART OF THE RED BALL EXPRESS
Red Ball on the road

Thirty-six hours later, the first trucks were rolling along a route that was not yet totally defined. Traffic controllers were sent to Verneuil sur Avre and for three days remained there looking out for the convoys, only to learn that the itinerary had been modified at the last moment. The first drivers navigated using a stylised map of the front that had been published in the last edition of the *Stars & Stripes*. There had been no time to distribute procedures and the truck teams drove along the Highway as if they were on a racing circuit. One third of trucks broke formation, came to sudden halts, then drove headlong to catch up their position. The Highway was also still being used by a multitude of vehicles that were not part of this service.

From the outset the operation was monumental. Out of

GMC decorated with .30 caliber cases and a pin-up. Personalizing equipment was a practice that was encouraged in the US armed forces. *(13-Num 1095, NARA © Archives départementales de la Manche)*

Liberty Roads, 1944-1945

the ADSEC's 82 Truck Companies, only five escaped mobilisation as they were essential to the unloading of rail convoys. The other 77 were placed under the command of the Advance Section Motor Transport Brigade (MTB). The next day, 41 other companies were taken away the Normandy Base Section. This was a real gamble as these trucks were needed for unloading supplies on the beaches and train stations. After these trucks were taken away there were only 23 companies left, reducing port activity by 50%. Stores in Normandy soon began to melt away. Two companies were loaned by the British (one with 3-Ton trucks, the other with 6-Ton[1]). Finally, two M20 tank transporter companies were added. Due to the density of traffic on the narrow Lower-Normandy roads, the ADSEC decided to reserve access to Red Ball convoys that were recognisable by a red circle on a white background. On 29 August, the Red Ball comprised of 132 companies with a total of 5,958 vehicles. 25,000 direction signs were placed along the route, stating both in French and English that the road was reserved for priority military traffic. Advertisements were placed in the press and radio messages informed civilians:

"At the frontline, soldiers are awaiting weapons, gasoline, shells, bullets and a multitude of other indispensable supplies. The Red Ball convoys are transporting these supplies along the Red Ball Express Highway. This is why they need to drive fast. Thousands of lives could be needlessly lost because of a few lost seconds. A single civilian vehicle can hold up an entire convoy and cause the loss of countless seconds as well as lives. In the name of the fighting men, we ask civilians not to interfere in any way with military traffic. We know that you are inconvenienced by having to use small roads, but nothing else is as important as victory".

Loading

The operation was complex on an administrative level. The ADSEC set the composition of convoys, timetables and loading, whereas the Normandy dumps were managed by another authority, the Normandy Base Section. The ADSEC, therefore, needed regular inventories. Some trucks arrived at the wrong dump, others drove around for hours in the bocage before finding the right one. Once there it was sometimes necessary to wait for the order of loading before finding the goods lost amongst the mess, verify the volume and then finally get the vehicles out of the dump that had become a mud pit after the first rains. The result of all this was that loading times soared, varying between 11 to 39 hours. As the ADSEC estimations often turned out to be wrong, some

1. They were given back on 4 September.

The crews await their orders and make the most of the break to rest, sunbathe, read or smoke. Be it at the departure point or the destina,tion patience was an essential quality when loading could take 39 hours. The vehicles, a mix of CCKW and forward cabin AFKWX, are loaded with rations and ready to leave. All have a one-ton trailer.
(13-Num 1096, NARA © Archives départementales de la Manche)

Liberty Roads, 1944-1945

An army requires mobile field hospitals. The US Army had luxurious models, delivered in kit form and which could be made operational within a few hours. However, they had to use secondary roads and were not allowed to travel on the Red Ball. (Région Basse-Normandie/NARA, p000762)

Unhook the net, lift the crates and pass them to the next man.... something that was repeated a thousand times... these men of the 6th ESB near Omaha were tiny, but nevertheless, indispensable cogs in the machine. To make up for the lack of manpower, the Army recruited civilians who were (badly) paid. Rare items of equipment in other armies, the winch-trucks and tracked Quick Way cranes, capable of lifting 5 tonnes, had become essential equipment in the American arsenal. *(Région Basse-Normandie/NARA, p013356 & 011787)*

convoys left half empty, whereas others waited for extra vehicles in order to finish loading. The ADSEC then issued the order to systematically fill in any empty space with ration crates and jerry cans, or if there was too much to leave it behind for the next convoy. In time the system improved and loading times stabilised between 4 and 19 hours.

To make up for the vehicle deficit, Washington had authorised doubling the load capacities, something that appeared to be a good choice given that these had been calculated for operations on difficult terrain and not tarmac roads. The small GMC trucks carried five tonnes of goods, but often more. This was particularly true when it came to heavy ammunition crates. "*A 155 shell weighed fifty kilos and we reached the maximum payload in two rows of crates. People laughed when they saw such a small load and officers ordered us to carry on loading and to ignore the weight restrictions*"[2]. For former mechanic Fred Reese, the drivers were "*a hell of a team. Their loads were twice as high as their cabin and the vehicles swayed dangerously. But they were not afraid. These guys were crazy*". Also, each truck carried enough jerry cans for a return trip, C rations, a breakdown kit and water. Thus, the average tonnage loaded per truck during the operation reached 7.3 tonnes.

Getting it there

In order to simplify organisation, ADSEC decided that

A column of Chevrolet 1 ½ ton tractors belonging to the 3014th Company being refuelled. The Red Ball consumed a third of the gasoline it transported.
(13-Num 4132, NARA © Archives départementales de la Manche)

---

2. Recollections of Robert Emerick, 3580th Truck Company. All the veteran accounts are taken from David P. Colley, *The Road to Victory*, Potomac Books, 2000.

A Diamond T 980 M20 drives through the ruined town of Vire, leaving in its wake an impressive cloud of dust. Note the typical Red Ball signpost, red on a white background, which recommends reducing speed, as well as the MP distracted by three civilians. Vire is 30 kilometres south of Saint-Lô, the starting point of the route. *(13-Num 1091, NARA © Archives départementales de la Manche)*

Without these cranes, the one here is a Quickway E55 on a 6X6, 6 Ton, Brockway mod 666 chassis, the quartermaster services would have been overwhelmed. These excellent vehicles, variants of construction yard vehicles, were not, however, in sufficient numbers. The muddy ground rendered the work more difficult. However, this photo is part of a series taken in Normandy during the month of June. The number 17 in a yellow circle indicates the maximum weight of the vehicle, an essential indicator for crossing bridges. *(Région Basse-Normandie, NARA, p001044)*

each convoy leaving Saint-Lô would be made up of vehicles from the same company. A jeep or truck led the way and was identifiable by a blue pennant. Each vehicle was separated by 55 metres. The convoy was subdivided into groups of at least five trucks. An interval of one minute was authorised between each group and two minutes between each convoy, the rear of which was identified by a jeep with a green pennant. The latter carried the convoy commander and a mechanic. A convoy of forty vehicles would take twenty minutes to pass by. This almost constant parade has led to deep-set and apocryphal tales. A jeep driver is said to have explained his absence of several days by stating that he had become between two trucks and had been unable to leave the road until they had reached their terminus. Some veterans have said that a civilian vehicle got onto the road and was crushed between two GMC when the convoy had to brake suddenly.

The narrow roads in the villages made the convoys slow down. The vehicles had to move slowly through junctions even though the houses had been destroyed. The speed limit of 40 km/h (24 in towns) was hardly ever adhered to. It is true that a GMC could drive easily at 80 km/h, even when loaded, and some drivers tampered with their trucks so that they could reach a speed of 110 km/h. A popular expression in the British Army stated that in order to avoid an American convoy, getting off the road was not enough; it was better to climb up a tree. Dozens of civilian families lost family members. Every two hours - 50 minutes from each even hour - the men were allowed to take a break. Every six hours the break was thirty minutes, just enough time to

Liberty Roads, 1944-1945

eat something. To avoid night time accidents, the cat's eyes were removed from the trucks and the order was given to drive along at full beam.

Broken down vehicles, or those involved in an accident, were left at the roadside for the mechanic in the rear of convoy jeep to look at. Depending on the seriousness of the breakdown, the driver was either ordered to immediately carry out repairs then join the next convoy, or wait for the towing teams who drove along the itinerary and who would then tow the vehicle to the repair workshop. Convoys, therefore, had to keep to the right-hand side of the road to allow the passage of maintenance vehicles. The Ordnance Corps had set up its workshops around Saint-Lô, Vire Alençon, Mortagne, Chartres, Nogent-le-Roi, Mayenne and Mortain. Small Piper Cub observation flew over the roads in

The MPs control the traffic whilst the Engineers continue clearing the roads with a CCKW 353 LWB dumpster (top photo). Below, CCKW 353 vehicles pass by a Dodge ¾ T. Luckily, once out of Normandy, destruction was less frequent.
(Région Basse-Normandie, NARA, p013007 & p013357)

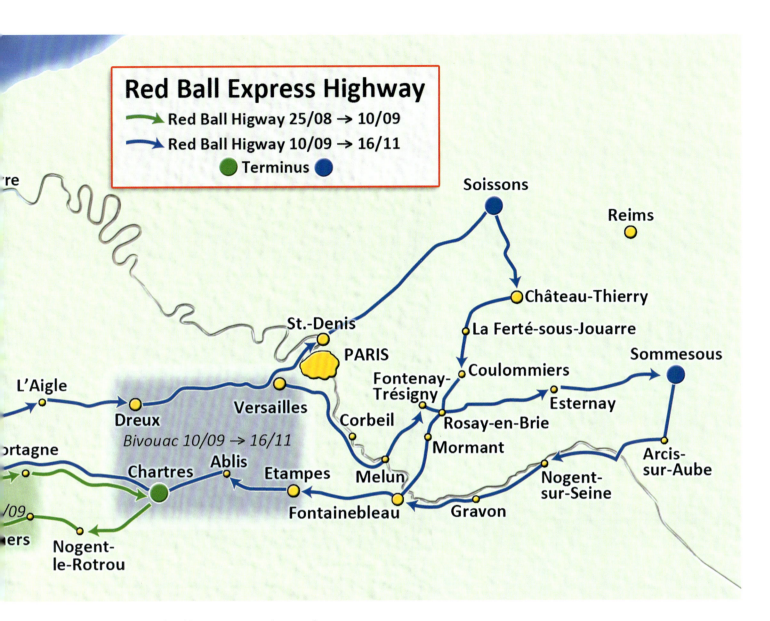

order to spot and signal accidents. However, at times, trucks remained broken down at the roadside for several days. On 15 September, the commander of the MTB complained to the ADSEC that no breakdown crew had patrolled the road between Mortagne and Chartres for five days.

The operation demanded the mobilisation of several services. Three Military Police companies, an infantry regiment and the French police were present in each town that was passed through. Along with the MTB officers, they set up Traffic-Control Points to regulate traffic, check loads, guide convoy leaders towards refuelling and water refilling points, forbidding unauthorised vehicles from using the road, find them an alternative itinerary and prevent black market activities. However, these units were very under strength. Two Engineer General Service Regiments and the French Ponts and Chaussées maintained the roads. Their job was made more difficult and dangerous because the roads were not closed during repairs. Ambulances took injured men to the field hospitals. The Signal Corps made sure that communications worked between the depots, the ADSEC offices in Saint-Lô, the Traffic-Control Points, the Regulating Stations set up at the terminuses and the mobile repair teams.

Generally speaking, the improvised administrative organisation proved to be deficient. Whereas all the convoys were managed by the MTB, the annex maintenance units, repair and police units were under the orders of the territorial commands through which the Highway passed (Normandy Base Section, Paris Base Section...). Instead of dealing directly with the Ordnance companies, the MTB had to send a request via the ComZ offices, then the Base Sections before it ended up with the chief me

Unloading

Initially, each convoy had to unload in the Chartres – Dreux – La Loupe triangle, but in the turmoil the drivers did not know exactly where they were headed. Indeed, the final destination was not decided by ADSEC but by the Regulating Stations in charge of each army's supply dump[3]. It was during a control that the convoys' leaders found out their final destination. The road was considered to be a kind of supply dump where the Regulating Stations could dip into in

The drivers caught a few hours of rest in tents that were set up in the bivouac zone. Cases of exhaustion progressively increased, but also acts of sabotage to try and stop this infernal rodeo.
(13-Num 1087, NARA © Archives départementales de la Manche)

3. The 24th followed the Third Army and the 25th accompanied the First Army.

Liberty Roads, 1944-1945

The arrival in a dump for these 4X4 Autocar or White tractors with 12 1/2-Ton lowered trailers. The third vehicle tows a British *"Queen Mary"* trailer originally designed for transporting aircraft.
(13-Num 1088, NARA © Archives départementales de la Manche)

angry and jumped out of our vehicles, threatening to report the colonel and his men, but this achieved nothing and we left with just enough gas to get back to our camp". Not all of these robbers were as understanding and went as far as siphoning off the trucks' petrol tanks, worsening the delays and disorganisation of the Highway. A more discreet, but no less illegal method was carried out by Hodges who sent reconnaissance planes to spot his neighbour's fuel dumps. In such a situation, the ADSEC was incapable of keeping its inventories up to date.

The Regulating Stations were ordered to inform their depots on the arrival of a convoy six hours in advance. Naturally, improvisation was the order of the day most of the time and some convoys were immobilized for 39 hours before being unloaded. In time, the Regulating Stations became more efficient by using the maxim of Maréchal Berthier where *"three messengers are better than one if you want to make sure information arrives"*. The trucks would then leave via a different route. Sometimes they took back with them empty jerry cans that were in short supply behind the lines, POWs or, on rarer occasions, corpses. When they arrived back at their bivouac after fifty hours of driving, the truck crews grabbed a few hours of rest before a new rotation. It was here that the Truck Companies' camps could be found, as well as field hospitals and repair workshops.

Starting again

Twelve days after the route was opened, 90,000 tonnes of goods had been unloaded in army dumps. The objective was reached with a delay of five days. Of course, all of the companies did not operate at the same time and it has been calculated that on a daily average, 83 were on the road. The overall efficiency and the lack of an alternative convinced ComZ to continue with this method but by modifying the outcome. Instead of wanting to open large supply dumps that were soon far from the frontline, the route became a sort of belt fed flow system that lengthened as the armies advanced. The route was extended to east of Paris and split in two to follow the 1st Army (terminus at Soissons) and the 3rd Army (terminus at Sommesous). The dual route was now over 1,000 km in length and a rotation took three days. On 19 September, the route was extended further and the terminuses moved to Hirson, then

In order to save gasoline, Bradley would belatedly order the immobilization of the heavy artillery south of the Seine, such as this 8-inch gun towed by a tracked High Speed M4 of the 195th FA Bn.
(Région Basse-Normandie, NARA, p000737)

Liberty Roads, 1944-1945

Colored soldiers at rest in their billets. Some are standing around the war correspondent Rodolph Dunbar. It says a lot that the journalist that is showing some interest in them is an African-American himself and a member of the ANP (*Associated Negro Press*). *(© CMH & Région Basse-Normandie, NARA, p013009)*

A MYTH AND AN ESSENTIAL PART OF REMEMBRANCE

Due to flagging morale in September, the *Stars & Stripes* and *Yank* publications opened their columns to these men who worked far from the spotlight. These articles, increasingly full of praise, helped to put the *Red Ball Express* in the public eye.

The role of these men was even made into a Broadway musical in the spring of 1945 with *'Call Me Mister'* at a time of controversy. The war was dragging on whereas the American public had thought it was all but over following the breakthrough at Avranches. The focus, therefore, had to be placed on the image of a victorious America, but also a nation that was resourceful and which had colossal industrial means at its disposal. The success of the Red Ball Express Highway thus covered up the aspects of the pursuit that had not gone as well as they should have. Finally, Hollywood contributed towards the transformation of this episode into a myth via an eponymous movie that came out in 1952. In this movie, a young lieutenant played by Jeff Chandler, is ordered to re-supply Patton's troops. The mission was hard enough but he also has to deal with a mixed group of men consisting of veterans who have seen it all, new recruits and a hateful sergeant (Alex Nicol). Well integrated archive film, the use of Major-General Frank Ross as technical advisor and the presence of French actors helps make this movie appear a little more authentic. Red Ball Express is considered as being an honest B movie that skilfully combines action, drama and humour, set against an historical backdrop, but which takes on another dimension when put back into its context. Firstly, the presence of a black corporal (Sidney Poitier), a victim of racial discrimination, evokes the fight for civil rights at the beginning of the 1950s. The movie then glorifies the individual and human adventure, in the manner of the westerns that were popular at this time. The Red Ball Express was a return to the American pioneering spirit. The GMC convoys were reminiscent of the wagon convoys that pushed deep into the huge and frightening Far West. Like the cowboy, the lieutenant proves his worth by his leadership skills and bravery. The message carried by the movie finds its meaning in the context of the time when it came out: the Cold War. Like the characters in the movie, the eclectic American population of 1952 has to pull together and identify themselves in a positive archetype in order to fight the Soviet enemy. Finally, the movie looks less at history and rather what was at stake at this time. In the United States, like in other countries, remembering the war became a tool of political struggle and the Red Ball Express had the advantage of being famous, an example of the situation of African-Americans and, therefore, symbolic of their role in defeating the Nazis. African-American politicians fought for years in order to force Congress to pass a bill honouring the *"valiant African-American war heroes who served in the Red Ball Express"*. The fact that this bill was not passed until June 2004 shows the resistance that was put up and the fear of seeing the national memory disappearing and being replaced by those focusing on ethnic communities.

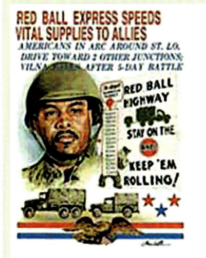

A souvenir Red Ball Express envelope from 1994, memories of the Red Ball were especially sharp within the African-American community.

Liberty Roads, 1944-1945

Liège for the 1st Army and Verdun for the 3rd Army with loops of 1,400 kilometres.

This longer route demanded even more vehicles at a time when strength was dwindling. However, on 16 September, Eisenhower ordered eight companies to be loaned to Montgomery for his own route, *the Red Lion Expres4*. This meant looking for new means of transport and forty companies were formed by taking vehicles from the 26th, 95th and 104th ID that had recently landed. Assembly workshops near Cherbourg and Isigny built a hundred vehicles daily. But, even with these reinforcements, the strength reached a ceiling. 182 companies took part in the second phase, but the average number on the road was not more than 74 companies, ten less than during phase one. Deliveries dropped by a half (4,625 tonnes per day).

Luckily for the Americans, the discovery of almost intact railway lines north-east of Paris allowed them, at the end of September, to open two axis: Aubervilliers-Soissons-Charleroi and Vincennes-Verdun. Platforms were transformed in order to load directly wagons from the Red Ball trucks. Aubervilliers and Vincennes could take respectively 225 and 400 wagons and load 20 and 115 at the same time. Apart from one crane at Vincennes, the work was carried out by hand using hundreds of French workers. This multi-modal platform was such a success that at the beginning of November, all of the loads that could be moved by hand passed via these stations, beyond Paris the Red Ball Express only carried heavy loads. Only five tractor companies were still in use (300 tonnes delivered per day).

A HUMAN ADVENTURE

African-Americans made up almost 80% of the 50,000 men[5] who took part in the Red Ball Express. Due to official segregation, blacks and whites served in separate units. They were separated to such an extent that whites never even saw black personnel during the operation, even in the bivouacs. In the "*colored*" companies, one hundred and fifty black enlisted men, NCOs were commanded by seven white officers. The military deemed that the authority of black officers would not be recognised by the troops. The even recommended that black personnel should be commanded by officers from the southern states, the former confederate territory, as they were used to the black community and giving orders. The US Army, therefore, recreated the worst type of rural American racial division. The following account by an officer who wished to remain anonymous bears witness to this paternalistic and contemptuous state of mind: "*I think that my cleverest soldier had an IQ of a hundred. The average was eighty. Most of them could not read or write. But they got by*"[6]. Since their arrival in Great Britain, the African-American personnel were banned from leaving their camps unless accompanied by a white officer; officially for their own safety. Given menial tasks within the quartermaster services, they were humiliated yet again when the journalists who came to cover the Red Ball Express ignored them and concentrated on the more uncommon white units.

Thousands of POWs were also used for loading and basic maintenance tasks (checking oil levels, cleaning windshields). Almost all veterans remember seeing acts of sabotage, the most common being adding water to fuel. Official reports were more balanced and the prisoners were described as being disciplined, docile and efficient and on several occasions, the head of a depot preferred POWs to French workers. Indeed, seven thousand French workers were taken on in Lower-Normandy, but in September and October, complaints began appearing as for the civilians, "*the Germans paid better*"[7].

The daily life of a GMC crew was monotonous. They sometimes had to spend 72 hours in an often damp and sometimes icy cold cabin. They ate their C rations cold... until they discovered that the exhaust manifolds could heat them up. Initially, each vehicle only had one driver. It was not

---
4. It linked Bayeux with Brussels and was supposed to convey 500 tonnes of supplies per day in view of Operation Market Garden.
5. The 20% of white personnel are seen in at least 75% of photographs.
6. Account given to David P. Colley, *op. cit.*, p. 84.
7. Stéphane Lamarche, *La Normandie américaine*, Larousse, 2010.

THE ORDER OF BATTLE FOR THE MOTOR TRANSPORT BRIGADE - 18 SEPTEMBER 1944
Total: 182 Trucks Companies, Source: ADSEC, 09/19/1944

Quartermaster Truck Group	Quartermaster Truck Battalion	Quartermaster Truck Company
27 (bivouac near Maintenon)	476	378
		3343
		3574
		3584
		3622
		3623
		3984
		3990
	238	644
		661
		751
		3395
		3433
		3689
	239	3870
		3987
	103	3393
		3400
		3420
		3552
		3861
		3904
		3985
		4010
	174	399
		645
		660
		3383
		3398
		3543
		3866
		3871
		4009
		4271
	519	3394
		3903
		3982
		3988
		3986
		3989
		4011
		4252
467 (bivouac near Epernon)	8	3342
		3578
		3387
		4262
		4263
		4264
	152	3582
		3595
		3627
		3629
		3882
		2885
	153	3618
	171	360?
		3617
		3632
		3886
		4265
		4266
		4267
	Coy. Attached to 467 Gp	3573

Quartermaster Truck Group	Quartermaster Truck Battalion	Quartermaster Truck Company	Quartermaster Truck Group	Quartermaster Truck Battalion	Quartermaster Truck Company
470	157	141	520 *(Continuation)*	181 *(Continuation)*	3368
		147			3872
		3418			4255
		3681		520	401
		3683			3397
		3684			3453
		3690			3992
		3889			4001
		3991			4002
		4268			4004
	467	3901			4270
		3544	26th Prov trk Regt *(formed from immobilised 26th ID)* *(bivouac near Châteauneuf en Thymerais)*	1	7100
		3594			7101
		3613			7102
		3884			7103
		4269			7104
	Coy. Attached to 470 Gp	134		2	7105
		3384			7106
		3478			7107
		3549			7108
		3593			7109
		3612		3	7110
		3631			7111
		4003			7112
		4254			7113
		3981			7114
513 *(bivouac near Rambouillet)*	163	146	95th Prov Trk Regt *(formed from immobilised 95th ID)* *(bivouac near Houdan)*	A	951
		3575			952
		3580			953
		3609			954
		3614			955
	175	3602		B	956
		3625			957
		3628			958
		3630			959
		3883			9510
		4259		C	9511
		4260			9512
		4261			9513
	466	159			9514
		3610			9515
		3611	104th Prov Trk Regt *(formed from immobilised 104th ID)* *(bivouac near Chartres)*	A	1
		3621			2
		3888			3
		4256			10
		4257			13
		4258		B	4
520 *(bivouac near Nogent le Roi)*	104	400			5
		541			6
		662			11
		3983			14
		4251		C	7
		4006			8
		4007			9
		4008			12
	137	380			
		543			
	181	3417			
		3419			
		3691			
		3862			
		3864			
		3867			

Liberty Roads, 1944-1945

A nice photo of a U 7144 T tractor with its tanker in which we can see its serial number "ASCZ 3990 TC TRK 21". "ASCZ" corresponds to the corps to which it belongs, the Advance Section Communication Zone, "3990 TC" designates the Transportation Corps company and "TRK 21" that it is the 21st truck. The civilian in the photo must have been given special permission by the Military Police to be going against the traffic on the Highway.
(Région Basse-Normandie, NARA, p013444)

The Signal Corps was responsible for re-establishing communications and for linking up the various regulating stations.
(Région Basse-Normandie, NARA, p013010

This column includes one the 169 Chevrolet G-7113 tractors to be made with a 3.5 t stake trailer and platform. All of the trucks appear to be carrying the same loads, not ammunition given the volume, but perhaps more likely ration crates.
(Région Basse-Normandie, NARA, p013457)

Alençon, 5 September, Corporal Charles H. Johnson of the 783rd MP Bn is seen here in front of a Highway signpost. On the left-hand side, the movable arrow indicates the goal to be achieved (11,000 tonnes). It should be remembered that the initial objective was under 7,000 tonnes and that the record was more than 12,000 tonnes.
(Région Basse-Normandie, NARA, p011135)

Various vehicles seen here on the Gambetta square in Isigny-sur-Mer. Whilst a crane helps load up an Engineer's GMC dumpster truck, a Caterpillar D4 angledozer is parked up to allow a convoy to pass through with a load of explosive materials.
All of this is orchestrated by a MP on board a Jeep.
(Région Basse-Normandie, NARA, p013006)

Clearing the roads and verges of mines was an essential task in rendering the roads safe. The mine-detectors also helped to find all of the metal cans with their sharp edges that ripped up the tyres.
(©NARA)

The combination of speed, fatigue, stress, alcohol, lack of training and the bad weather conditions led to numerous accidents. Diamond T 969 quickly rights a GMC in order to prevent the convoy from losing too much tme.
(13-Num 1092, NARA © Archives départementales de la Manche)

¾ of the transport companies had African-American personnel who were given the menial tasks. The press coverage given to the Red Ball Express was the occasion for them to be in the limelight.
(NARA & CMH)

surprising, therefore, that any stops were used to nap rather than maintenance for which they were planned for. Some men slumbered at the wheel. When the driver behind realised this he would wake him up by gently bumping the truck or by pressing on the horn. Some exhausted men deliberately damaged their vehicles in order to get a few hours of precious sleep. The increase in accidents proved that a second driver was indispensable. Any soldier whose mission was not essential was asked to become a driver for a period of fifteen days. These men were mostly taken from divisions that had recently arrived and not yet in combat. They were trained to drive in two or three days. A GMC was not as straightforward to drive as a normal car and, in any case, most of the men had never driven before. During the driving course, they were taught how to change a wheel, check the oil levels, deal with minor breakdowns and Highway code. They were then thrown into the rodeo. It was not uncommon for drivers to switch over when on the move, but generally speaking the presence of a second driver had a positive effect, as much on the driving as on morale.

The drivers also asked to be armed, even though the risk of coming under air attack or by a sniper was very low[8]. Despite this, the trucks were armed with Cal. .50 MG on a ring mount and were occasionally accompanied by Dodge M6 Gun Motor Carriages. Significantly, the M6 was equipped with a 37 mm anti-tank gun, a weapon that was obsolete in the event of an encounter with an enemy tank, but this shows that its presence was essentially for peace of mind. The danger posed by mines, however, was very real. Although the

---

8. Some ran into the enemy at the beginning of the operation when the trucks were sent right up to the frontline.
9. Hines William, *"History of the General Purpose Vehicles"*, Maintenance Bulletin N°11, USFET, US Army, 1945/1946, p147.

roads were checked, the verges were not and this explains why the truck crews used extra sand bag protection and drove in the middle of the road rather than to the right as stipulated by the regulations.

Following a rotation, they slept for a few hours in tents or farms in the middle of the countryside. Any rare entertainment was provided by the US Clubmobil, a GMC converted for use by the female Red Cross volunteers who served hot coffee and donuts. Shows were also put on by actors who drove around with their equipment on a jeep and trailer, which explains their "*Jeep Shows*" nickname. In these conditions it was not surprising that these young men of 18/20 years of age, "*borrowed*" a truck in order to go to a nearby town or Paris. A memo issued by the MTB commander, Colonel Richmond, shows just how bad this problem became: "*Hundreds of trucks drive around the towns and villages at night.... I have no idea how they manage to leave the bivouac without the commanders knowing... No passes are to be issued, even on an individual basis. This must stop now*"[9].

It was no surprise that by October, the medical services reported a worrying increase in venereal disease. A report from the 514th Truck Regiment stated that several trucks left the Highway to stopover at a whorehouse. Alcohol was another form of entertainment for the soldiers. This was one of the French peasant's currency of exchange. Swapping Calvados for Lucky Strikes no doubt caused many accidents. The military courts estimated that the consumption of alcohol had been at the root of half of the 169 men tried for rape.

SUPPLYING THE COMBAT ZONE

Just because the supplies were in the hands of the army supply services did not mean that they were in the hands of the combatants, far from it in fact, given that the Combat Zone had

Liberty Roads, 1944-1945

SUPPLY UNITS OF THE 1st ARMY

With the First Army, the supply units comprised of the 471st QM Group that was tasked with class I, II, III and IV supplies and the 71st Ordnance Group that was tasked with class V supplies.

471 QM GROUP
- ● **471st QM Bn** (transport) — 200 GMC
- 370st QM truck Co
- 3702nd QM truck Co
- 3703rd QM truck Co
- 3704th QM truck Co
- ● **380th QM Bn** (gas transport) — 200 tanker vehicles
- 134th MQ Tank Truck Co (2000 gal.)
- 3549th MQ Tank Truck Co (750 gal.)
- 3584th MQ Tank Truck Co (2000 gal.)
- 3981th MQ Tank Truck Co (750 gal.)
- ● **81st QM Bn** (transport) — 200 GMC
- 3705th QM truck Co
- 3706th QM truck Co
- 3707th QM truck Co
- 3708th QM truck Co
- ● **202rd Q M Bn** (equipment collection and repair)
- 216th QM Salvage Repair Co
- 224th QM Salvage Repair Co
- 294th QM Salvage Repair Co
- 233rd QM Salvage Collection Co
- 235th QM Salvage Collection Co
- 999th QM Salvage Collection Co
- 579th QM Laundry Co
- ● **158th QM Bn** (specialised handing in dumps):
- 345th QM Depot supply Co
- 348th QM Depot supply Co
- 279th QM refrigeration Co
- 581st QM sale Co
- 200th Gasoline Supply Co
- 3814th gasoline Supply Co
- 3192rd Service Co
- ● **532rd QM Bn** (general handling):
- 3168th QM service Co
- 3169th QM service Co
- 3170th QM service Co
- 3216th QM service Co
- 3217th QM service Co
- 3218th QM service Co
- 3230th QM service Co
- 3233rd QM service Co

71st ORDNANCE GROUP
- ●**Ammunition Bn** (handling in dumps)
- 6 Ammunition Co
- ●**Ammunition Bn** (Truckhead handling)
- 6 Ammunition Co
- ● **102nd QM Bn** (munitions transportation)
- 5 Co (225 GMC)

On the road, between Mamers and Alençon, a convoy passes by a Federal 94x43B or C tractor with a semi trailer 6ton/10ton gross stake body stuck in the ditch. The Federal differed from the Autocar U 7144 by the absence of the headlamp protective grill that was part of the radiator grill, and the absence of the four bolts visible on the outside of the fender. (Région Basse-Normandie, NARA, p000392)

Coffee tents were set-up in the bivouacs or in the regulating stations for the drivers.
(13-Num 5669, NARA © Archives départementales de la Manche)

considerably expanded. At the beginning of September, the army dumps were 400 km away, more than double the planned maximum distance[10]. As it was impossible for divisions to re-supply over such distances, mobile Truckheads were opened. These were not depots but meeting points between the army supply services and the fighting units of the same corps[11]. These Truckheads were redeployed every four days, moving forward over an average distance of 60 km.

Six hundred vehicles were obviously insufficient for such distances and Hodges was forced to immobilise units in order to bring them up to strength. Two Engineer General Service Regiments allowed for the formation of fourteen truck companies and a chemical battalion and four anti-aircraft regiments supplied another ten companies. The army's supply services were thus boosted by 1,300 trucks. Such a drain on transportation naturally led the armies to demand that the Red Ball convoys drive on as far as the Truckheads, meaning that the demands on their own convoys were lessened as well as avoiding an unnecessary moving of supplies from one truck to another. What they forgot though was that this would lead to the breaking up of the Red Ball chain. Colonel Mc Namara was constantly in his Piper Cub in order to spot and guide convoys that were lost between La Loupe and the Truckheads.

Once the Truckheads were reached, there remained a further 100 to 200 km before the frontline. Therefore, it was impossible for small regimental quartermaster platoons to fetch supplies, the manual stipulated that they had to accompany the advancing fighting men. They were replaced by the divisional quartermaster units. Up to distances of 60/70 km, the fifty GMC trucks of the Trucks Platoon accompanied by their Service Platoon, were easily sufficient. We have no data from the pursuit, but a report written by the 84th Inf Div in November 1944 states the daily use of 14 trucks for the transportation of rations, 4 for jerry cans, 3 for laundry and return of repaired equipment and 3 for the transportation of mines and barbed wire, making 24 vehicles out of the issued number of 48[12]. Leaving at 08.00 hrs with damaged equipment and POWs that they would hand over to the capable hands at the army depot, they were back at the divisional depot by 11.00 hrs and available for other tasks in the afternoon, such as troop transportation[13]. These trucks did not carry ammunition as this was done by the Ordnance Co. On this date, the Truckhead was only thirty kilometres away, making one hour to get there, one hour for loading and another for the return trip. At the beginning of September these same conditions were met but for distances of 150 to 200 km, meaning rotations of 6h30x2 + 1h of loading = 14h, making one sole daily rotation undertaken by 24 vehicles by alternating one day out of two for the GMC drivers. Although at the limits of operational capacity, this was nevertheless in the realm of possibility. We have also found that some vehicles covered much longer rotations, sometimes as far as Cherbourg in order to find materiel that was not in any other dump. The average total distances covered in September were between 5,000 and 9,000 kilometres. In fact, unit diaries show more of a lack of manpower than vehicles. One 49 man platoon for cataloguing, loading and unloading the supplies for an entire division was in fact insufficient. Within the 4th, 30th and 29th ID, manpower was found by using men recovering from wounds and battle fatigue, thus allowing a strength of 250 men.

The 3rd Army adopted a different strategy. Instead of reinforcing the army quartermaster supply units, Patton ordered that divisions be strengthened in order to make them totally mobile. Up to six Trucks Coys. were added to the divisions, enough to carry all of the infantry or to ensure rotations to cover supply needs of several days up to a distance of 600 km. However, with a reduced strength of less than eight companies, the army quartermaster supply units was totally incapable of opening Truckheads. Its sole depot was that of the Red Ball Express terminus: Chartres then Somessous. Thus, each divisional commander was faced with a dilemma, either advance quickly to the detriment of supplies, or to re-supply over long distances but slowing down the advance.

This certainly explains the difference between the two armies, the Third being much faster, but also the one that had the most problems in keeping its spearheads supplied.

At Right, top.
July 44, a CCKW 353, one of the 40% of GMC to be equipped with a 91 m-long winch.
(Région Basse-Normandie, NARA, p011769)

At right, bottom.
A 1939 first production run ACKWX 353 sold to the US Army 2,425 $. Its civilian origins are obvious. Note the fuel-tank on the right-hand side of the chassis between the front and rear axles.
(NARA)

---

10. William F. Ross, Charles F. Romanus, *The Quartermaster corps*, CMH, 1965, vol. 4, p. 454.
11. Typically, a Truckhead counted in its ranks a Railhead Co. for the handling of rations, and a Gasoline Co. for the handling of fuel, an Ammunition Co for munitions and more rarely, a Bakery Co and a Service Co. (for odd jobs). *The Quartermaster Corps*, vol. IV, op. cit., p.464.
12. *The Quartermaster Corps*, vol 4, p. 458 & *The Ordnance Corps*, vol 3, p. 270.
13. *The Quartermaster Corps*, vol 4, CMH, p. 472.

THE LEGENDARY GMC OF THE US ARMY

The 'Jimmy' alone incarnates the opulence of the US Army. With more than 500,000 of these vehicles made, they were omnipresent on the roads of France. However, in its design phase, nothing foreshadowed it becoming a legendary truck.

As with all equipment, the GMC was the combination of need, constraints and compromise. The need appeared in 1939 with the re-birth of the US Army. Having been reduced to an obsolete force of less than 200,000 men, it had to become a large modern army within two years. Each service then expressed the urgent need for a range of all-terrain, multi-task utility vehicles. The constraints were essentially on a legal level. The legislator in charge of the good management of the slender amount of public money, forced the Quartermaster Corps[1] to choose the cheapest option when contracts were handed out, but more seriously, these bids had to remain vague and not contain any constraint that would make the manufacturer design specific vehicles. The vehicles would have to combine *"standard road performance with sufficient off-road handling"*. Apart from a few specialised vehicles, *"they had to come from the civilian market and be easy to mass produce"*.

There was only one solution in order to avoid chaos: reduce the number of bids. The QMC would, therefore, limit its orders to five standard commercial, but all-terrain types of chassis. The Deuce &-a-Half, in reference to its 2 ½ t range, was first designed for the Quartermaster Corps and the daily supplying between the army dumps and the fighting units, as well as the for the transportation of troops when the infantry divisions had to move rapidly[2]. What was required therefore, was a basic vehicle capable of operating at the front line over difficult terrain. The basic platform of this vehicle had to be easily adaptable to make dumpers or tankers. These constraints led towards the choice of a six-wheeled vehicle; something that was not commonly encountered in manufacturers' catalogues. Indeed, the civilian market was more one of 4x4 vehicles, or a niche market for companies specialised in drilling, for example, who therefore bought giant 6-20 tonne vehicles. The Army was heading into unknown territory.

Civilian origins

Studebaker, Mack and a few other manufacturers responded to the bids. Yellow Trucks, a sister company of General Motors, came up with the best price and was awarded the first order for 2,466 vehicles under the designation of ACKWX 353. It was no surprise that this derived from the three-axle drive and stretched wheelbase of the 1 ½ ton ACK 353 4x4 that was itself developed from the civilian AC range. The design teams had been working on it since 1938 on the request of the French army. The latter had ordered 2,000 vehicles of the 4x4 version in September 1939, then another thousand of the new 6x6 version in 1940. The American rearmament program therefore benefited the French.

The ACKWX retained the engine, cabin and many internal parts of the AC type and all of the equipment that had proved itself. Visually speaking, the civilian heritage was obvious. However, the US Army soon complained about the lack of engine torque that affected its off-road performance. Luckily in July 1940, the law was amended and authorised the Quartermaster Corps to state the required specifications and to negotiate directly with the manufacturer. Thus, starting in October 1940, Yellow Truck introduced an improved version, the CCKWX 353 which curiously was numbered with the "C" code that corresponded to 1941. Its more powerful 270 model engine and increased wheelbase were better suited for military needs. Over 13,000 were made and the range included tankers.

It would be easy to believe that the situation was satisfactory, but this was far from being the case. During the entire course of this 1939-1941 period, truck production was lower than what had been planned for. One of the obstacles to overcome was the lack of special parts, in particular the drive axles made by Timken. These delays convinced GMC of the need to develop its own type of drive axle, the Banjo, which appeared at the end of February 1941. 13,186 new Jimmy vehicles, renamed

MODEL	PRODUCTION						PARTICULARITIES
	1940	1941	1942	1943	1944	1945	TOTAL	
ACKWX 353	2466						2466	Initial version of which no truck saw service outside of the United States
CCKWX 353	5707	7481					13188	Appearance of the 270 model engine. First trucks to have the standard 145 or 160 inch wheelbase and the flat engine hood
CCKW 352/353		43315	110986	130843	127978	91157	505940	Appearance of the "Banjo" axle drive. Regularly modified
AFKWX 353	3		613	1619	4000	1000	7235	Version with cabin positioned further forward
DUCKW			325	4508	11316	5088	21237	Amphibious version
CCW 6x4		558	22687	255			23500	Road version
TOTAL	8176	50796	111599	132462	131978	92157	527168	

---

1. The service tasked with the purchasing and development of utility vehicles in 1939.
2. Contrary to a deeply entrenched cliché, the US infantry divisions were not motorised units. Of course, animals had been replaced by vehicles and all of the support units such as the artillery or engineers were transported by truck, but the infantry battalions only had, organically, a few trucks, in general Dodges, for the transportation of equipment, with the men moving on foot. Truck companies were called upon at times, such as by Patton and Hodges in the summer of 1944.

GENERAL CODE						VERSION CODE	
1st letter	2nd	3rd	4th	5th	Number	Letter	Number
Year code **A:** 1939 **B:** 1940 **C:** 1941 **D:** 1942	**C** for the conventional cabin in a rearwards position **F** for the cabin placed further forward **U** for an amphibious vehicle	**K** for front wheel drive	**W** for rear engine tensioner	**X** for non-standard wheelbase, deleted in 1941	**352:** short wheelbase code **353:** long wheelbase code	**A:** platform without winch **B:** platform with winch **C:** stock rack bodywork **D:** tanker bodywork without winch **E:** tanker bodywork with winch **F:** van bodywork **G:** water bowser without winch **H:** dump truck with winch	**1:** "Split" drive axle **2:** "Banjo" drive axle

CCKW 352 or 353 depending on its wheelbase, were ordered[3]. A few months later saw a hundred vehicles leave the production lines on a daily basis.

It was at the end of 1941 that the history of GMC changed dramatically. At the time it was only a mid-range vehicle whose *"Light-Heavy"* designation showed its mongrel character. However, the War Production Board promoted the Deuce &-a-Half to the rank of the US Army's workhorse. What had been 7% of the production run in 1939 now had to reach 50% in 1944. Confronted with the obligation of streamlining its production, the Army moved away from the too complex heavies and turned instead to the 2 ½ t. This was the most versatile compromise. Its off-road capabilities satisfied the combatant units, especially the artillery, and its volume gave it a carrying capacity of 5 tonnes on the road that was deemed as being perfectly sufficient, especially as a version with a cabin placed more forward that would allow bulkier loads to be carried was being looked into. The need for these vehicles was no longer counted in thousands but in hundreds of thousands.

The constant drive towards simplicity

Contrary to a commonly held belief, the GMC trucks were far from being identical. The design plans were constantly modified in order to respond to a twin demand: improving compatibility with the rest of the US Army vehicle park on one hand, and making production easier and saving raw materials on the other. In the first category we could mention the transformations on the braking system, lighting, engine and dashboard; for the second, the most visible changes

concerned the cabin. From 1942 onwards, the ashtray, trimmings, locks and glove box disappeared. July 1943 saw the appearance of a version with a tarpaulin replacing the metal cabin. This new cabin meant that space was saved when transporting the vehicle by ship, but it also reduced the outline of the GMC, something that could be useful on the frontline. The GMC became more austere with every passing month and due to tiny modifications it became increasingly bare. Useless screws and rubber joints were got rid of. Wood replaced steel, particularly for the platform. This frugal choice also eased production by authorising a multitude of subcontractors grouped together with the Ordnance Industry Integration Committee for Wood Cargo Bodies. The steel mass was divided in two, going from 770 to 320 kg.

As small as they were, each of these modifications could lead to considerable collateral damage. Thus, the straightforward addition of a blackout drive lamp on the left-hand side could mean that its surrounding had to be redesigned: mudguards, attachments, protective cover, installation of a new button on the dashboard, cables and updating of the spare parts catalogue... all of which caused a lot of headaches.

One week later, another modification was made to the cooling system. These incessant modifications ended up causing a slightly adverse effect on the vehicle's performance. The new engine parts lacked space and their less coherent integration imposed more complex fine-tuning.

It is said, however, that this vehicle was unbreakable, but these parts were designed to last only 6 to 9 months, or 40,000 km. Indeed, the Army was aware of the short lifespan of a military vehicle. During the Sicily campaign, half of the vehicle park was destroyed within a month. There was no point, therefore, in building *'Swiss precision'* vehicles like the Germans did, whose park was designed to last thirty years. Even so, the parts last well enough to ensure that there are still thousands of GMC trucks in use 70 years after.

A motorized pontoon unloads onto a GMC 353 and a AFKWX 353. This meant that unnecessary handling and effort was avoided, especially as the trucks' platform was high due to the presence of a large engine bridge underneath.
(Région Basse-Normandie, NARA, p011366)

Liberty Roads, 1944-1945

A prolific family

The short wheelbase 352 type vehicles were normally made for the artillery. On the chassis version of the CCKW, the addition of a technical bodywork allowed it to undertake a large range of roles; radio truck, maintenance and engineering workshop, weather station, shop for combatants, canteen, command post, photographic workshop, surgical theatre.... The Engineers at first, then other arms of service, also received the dumpster GMC. Unfortunately, it was badly designed on a too large 353 chassis and the dumpster could take a load that could quickly reach ten tonnes, a weight that was too heavy for the suspension.

The AFKWX, the forward positioned cabin of which had also been taken from the civilian model, is easily recognisable. Made only from 1942 onwards, this version offered a higher load capacity thanks to its 15-foot (4.5 m) then 17-foot (5.1 m) body that was ideal for bulky loads. The CCW was a purely for road use variant and did not have a forward drive axle or lower level transfer case that were only useful on difficult terrain. The CCW was rarely deployed in overseas theatres of operations. Finally, the DUKW appeared in 1942.

By mid-1942, GMC reached its production peak -15,000 per month - following the opening of a second factory, that of Chevrolet[4] in Saint Louis. From October 1942 onwards, production stabilised at around 11 to 12,000 vehicles every month. Even this did not allow GMC to fulfil the colossal demands of the military and the latter turned to other manufacturers. Unfortunately for them, nobody accepted to build under licence a vehicle made by a competitor. Officially, this refusal was justified by the considerable difficulties that would have arose by adapting the production lines to manufacture an unknown vehicle. In fact, they were afraid that their design teams would lose their skills. The Army, therefore, was forced to accept that these manufacturers make their own 2 ½ t. Alongside the 560 000 GMC Jimmy trucks, we can find the M5-6 made by International Harvester of which 37,088 were made starting in 1942 and powered by their own 111hp engine . Studebaker also made nearly 200,000 US-6 with a 87hp Hercules JHD engine and sub-contracted 22,204 to Reo. Although they shared some common parts with the GMC, they differed sufficiently for the Army to turn them down and most of these vehicles were attributed to other arms of service or exported as part of the Lend Lease program.

The "universal" truck

The strength of the GMC was that it matched the requirements of an industrialised army. It was progressively stripped of anything fancy. Easy to mass produce and maintain, a GMC could be totally rebuilt by a team of mechanics in 72 hours. Thus, its rate of availability remained at between 70 to 90% in 1944, whereas the German truck fleet was at most 50 to 60%, and the British lost 1,500 3-Ton trucks within a few days on the roads of France. It was no doubt more robust than the others, but any breakdowns were immediately identifiable and often easily repaired and mechanically it was not beset with complex assemblies or spare parts. It had also been designed with novice personnel in mind and any parts that required particular attention were painted red for easy identification - oil level, water, gaskets - and each vehicle was delivered with its oil and anti-freeze cans. For Robert Rubino, a vehicle enthusiast and collector, "It was not a mechanical treasure, on the contrary, it was a heap of iron... but that is why it was the best"... with this in mind, the Jimmy incarnates the quintessence of what is required of a military vehicle entirely built around a philosophy: multi-role, straightforward and efficient. A veteran stated that *"There was no equivalent of the Jimmy in the arsenals of our enemies and allies"*.

Previous page, top.
A six-cylinder 104 hp GMC 270 engine is unpacked and checked over before being fitted.
(NARA)

Previous page, centre.
A 1939 ACKWX 353 1 ½ t shows off its all-terrain capabilities. This version, sold to the French army in 1940, allowed the GMC to increase in importance.
(NARA)

Previous page, bottom.
A forward-cabin AFKWX 353, ugly but liked.
(RR)

A first production run CCKW 353 with metal roofed cabin. As the months passed by, the GMC was stripped of any useless fittings made lighter in order to save steel, as seen in the photo below.
(RR)

A column of British ACKWX 353 towing laundry trailers, take part in an exercise in southern England in October 1942. This model differs from its American counterpart by a 28 cm longer wheelbase, a less powerful engine and by the mounting of two spare wheels behind the cabin.
(RR)

However, the GMC was not designed for strategic use and its legend, in particular along the Red Ball Express Highway, is mostly owed to the negligence of the Army that was not concerned with equipping itself with heavy trucks, leaving it to almost bear the burden alone in August 1944. Designed to carry 2.5 tonnes off-road, the drivers loaded between 5 to 10 tonnes on road, something that soon wore out the gear box and suspension. Precious time was lost, as contrary to the 4/5 t tractor that could un-hitch its trailer, the GMC was halted at the depot the time it took to load and unload. For the Transportation Corps, the Jimmy was a stop-gap measure. Luckily, as Ernest Larsen said, *"the GMC was a hell of a truck"* [5].

---
3. *Out of a total of 300,000 vehicles ordered in 1941.*
4. Remember that GMC and Chevrolet had been part of the same group since 1918.
5. This technical table owes a great deal to The Jimmy Ancestry articles written by Bryce J. Sunderlin in Army Motors, n°47 to 59, 1991-92.

Liberty Roads, 1944-1945

CHAPTER 8

THE DRIVERS WERE NOT ALONE
THE AIR FORCE TO THE RESCUE

The Red Ball Express odyssey has mostly overshadowed other initiatives that were taken to maintain contact with the mechanised spearheads: air supply, the repairing of the rail network and the construction of pipelines.

On 15 August, SHAEF ordered CATOR[1] to do all that it could to supply Patton with 2,000 tonnes per day. Four days later, the first rotations undertaken by C-47 Dakota aircraft loaded with urgent supplies (medical, rations) began between England and Le Mans. However, Le Mans was already too far from the frontline. By the end of the week, 600 tonnes of rations had been unloaded daily. This was far from the planned for 2,000 tonnes, especially as the liberation of Paris demanded urgent supplies amounting to 500 tonnes. But despite bringing in Dakotas from the Mediterranean front, the weekly deliveries remained too low. Starting on 25 August, General Brereton of the 1st Airborne Army demanded the return of his planes as they would be needed for airborne operations. Stopgap measures were taken by requisitioning all of the C-47 aircraft allocated to the VIIIth and IXth Air Service Force, as well as transformed B-17 and B 24 bombers. However, this experiment did not get very far as the runways in France were too short for such planes. Bradley became angry and on 4 September, demanded a daily supply of 3,000 tonnes of fuel. Half of Brereton's Dakotas were requisitioned again and the supplying of Paris was suspended. On 8 September, 200 C-47 aircraft were supplying the 21st Army Group and 400 the 12th Army Group. 220 flew from the Querqueville airfield near the Cherbourg oil terminal. The runway was lengthened in fourteen hours by the 342nd Engineer General Service Regiment. 1,200 tonnes of fuel were able to be loaded the same day and flown to Reims. However, this exploit went no further. By 16 September, the daily tonnage received by each army group did not go over 500 tonnes. The next day, the Dakotas flew over Arnhem and brought the air bridge to a temporary halt. It came back into service again in October and November, supplying 675 tonnes per day, mainly fuel.

Finally, the figures achieved appear to be modest compared to what was hoped for, something that was common with Second World War air supply. The causes are not to be found in the lack of aircraft, nor in the tensions that existed between Brereton and CATOR, but rather in the inexperience and capabilities of the aircraft at the time. In Great Britain, too many planes had to wait hours for their loads that took a long time in arriving from depots. In France, too many crews had to remove their loads themselves, thus slowing down rotations and blocking airfields. Thus, on 22 August, 383 loaded Dakotas remained in England and on 1 September, only 70 bombers were able to land out of the 200 that were available.

Patton Lacked gasoline and several thousand liters were sent to him via the Air Force. The improvised air bridge was not a big success. Capable of carrying a load of three tonnes, the C-47 Dakotas carried less than the small GMC truck. It was also difficult to find intact airfields nearby.
(NARA)

Liberty Roads, 1944-1945

The advance of the armies soon moved them far from the airfields. As for the load capabilities, they remained too low compared to the cost of such an operation. A C-47 could only carry 2 ½ tons of freight, a drop in the ocean. Despite this failure, SHAEF maintained the rotations until December which allowed for the establishment of an efficient routine that improved procedures. ComZ also rationalised its loads by creating a 270 t pack of emergency supplies with everything that a division would need. 675 tonnes were now delivered daily with less than a hundred aircraft.

THE LITTLE-KNOWN ACHIEVEMENT OF THE RAILROAD ENGINEERS

The Red Ball Express and the air bridge were only transitory measures., only the repair of the rail networks would be able to provide the long-term supplying of the American armies over such long distances. This meant not only the repair of the network but also the building up of rolling stock. In 1939, the French SNCF national railway company had a park of 11,800 locomotives, but in 1944 less than 2,800 were still operational and even then they would have to fall into allied hands undamaged. To build up the numbers, 49 steam and 25 diesel trains were landed on 12 August. This was far from the 900 that were initially planned for. On 17 August, a single line was opened as far as Le Mans, allowing the passage of thirty-two convoys, but the damage to the station and the difficulties in getting the trains back to Cherbourg brought things to a halt. However, the damage caused by the Germans was not as bad as originally thought: trains were repaired and stores of spare parts for American locomotives dating from 1918 were found with the help of French railway workers. But, it was above all the allied bombing that damaged the stations and destroyed bridges. The presence of the Falaise pocket also held up the opening of direct lines towards Paris.

At the end of August, 18,000 men and 5,000 POWs were busy on reconstruction work. Each army had a railroad engineer group at its service. Two lines were opened, one for the First Army via Vire and Dreux, one for the Third via Le Mans and Chartres. Thus, between 24 August and 2 September, 70 trains delivered 30,000 t of supplies, representing a quarter of the volume unloaded by ADSEC[2]. But a new challenge arose: crossing the Seine. Although the first train arrived in Batignolles station as early as 29 August, four days after its liberation, it could not go any further as there were not many bridges left intact and this caused a bottleneck. This meant that the lines towards Liege and Verdun, which were intact, could not be used. It was only on 15 September, as we have seen, that once the French rolling stock was back in service, ComZ brought up 4,000 tonnes per day of supplies by truck to the railway stations of northern Paris, then sent them towards the frontline. Although this formula did not simplify handling the supplies, it had the advantage of reducing the distance to be covered by road. By the end of September, the first tanker convoys made it to the Belgian frontier and the region of Verdun.

In the vicinity of Reims, a nurse helps unload fuel before taking on wounded men and flying back to England.
(NARA)

ALG A-6 airfield at La Londe near Utah beach. Return flights between the lower-Normandy airfields and Reims took place for emergency gasoline deliveries.
(Région Basse-Normandie, NARA, p012365)

1. The Combined Air Transport Operation Room was tasked with regulating the traffic of all transport aircraft apart from those used in airborne missions.
2. A standard convoy carried 400 to 450 tonnes of freight.

A great many bridges were damaged and more than eleven engineer regiments got to work in order to repair them. The Cherbourg-Le Mans line was opened on 17 August and passed over this viaduct near Coutances, the missing arch of which was filled with a Bailey Bridge. We can see a 140 US steam locomotive pulling another full train with a 141 US. A few kilometres further on, the train was halted by a zealous French stationmaster as war or no war, petty paperwork had to be filled in. This one-way line could only deal with a weak flow.
(Région Basse-Normandie, NARA, p011795)

THE RAILROAD WORKERS ARRIVE

Rails to replace, holes to fill, bridges, water tanks and coal depots to re-build, the task was huge for the Engineers and the French railroad company (SNCF) *(1)*. As 75% of the park had been destroyed, 20,000 railcars and 1,000 locomotives had to be brought over as an emergency measure, specially designed for use on the French railroads and stored in Wales *(2)*. The materiel was landed via specially designed ships. On 25 July, the Texas and Lakehurst seatrains arrived at Cherbourg. They carried with them the 728th Railway Operating Bn and all of its equipment. On the Texas: 20 vans, 26 covered cars, 20 cars, nine 50-tonne flat cars, 20 steam locomotives including six 0-6-0 types for the marshaling yard, fourteen 2-8-0 types and coal tenders for the main operations. The Lakehurst unloaded 16 diesel locomotives, 20 tankers, fifteen 50-tonne flat cars, 8 covered cars, 8 cars and 8 vans. As the quaysides were still out of use, two barges were equipped with rails *(3)*. The cars were unloaded via the ship's goods boom. The barges then moored along the quaysides parallel to the lines and cranes lifted the cars. The British loaned two train-ferries, the Twickenham and Hampton *(4)*. Built in 1936 for the

Southern Railway, these 118m-long ships carried a six-car train and locomotive which before the war ran on the London-Paris line.... the first Eurostar. The 333rd Engineer Regiment rebuilt the Homet quay for these ships in record time. Thanks to their mobile swing bridge, they could literally place a whole train onto the tracks *(5)*. A handfull of LST *(6)* were also equipped with rails on their decks. The Engineers improvised concrete ramps at the Mielles slipway equipped with mobile trolleys on which rails were fitted and which slid along the ramp depending on the tide *(7)*. Once the LST rails were fitted to those of the trolleys, the cars were shunted off by a locomotive or pulled by a winch. A few minutes later, the train would leave, loaded, towards the frontlines *(8)*. 14 LST moorings were rapidly opened, allowing 23,000 railcars to be unloaded at Cherbourg (85% of the total in western Europe).
(All pictures, NARA via Bibliothèque municipale de Cherbourg).

A welder in action. (NARA)

But then the pursuit came to an end. During the course of the first fifteen days of September, 5,000 tonnes were unloaded daily in the stations of the Beauce region and those south of Paris. This represented a superior volume to that of the Red Ball Express. It is remarkable when we think of the state of the rail network and the short time in which it took the engineers to get it working again. It is remarkable when we think of the personnel discovering the rail routes and equipment without any means of communication that could have led to terrible accidents, especially as the crews drove the trains for periods of 60 to 84 hours. However, this achievement remained unseen as, on one hand the stations were far from the army depots, the trains eased the burden on the trucks but did not replace them, and on the other hand, most of the tonnage was absorbed by the Parisians. But this help was indispensable and if the railways had not been there, many road convoys would have been diverted from their main role, that of supplying the armies. In October, the monthly traffic of Parisian stations reached 800 incoming convoys and 1,000 outgoing, a figure that was still very low[3]. In November, for the first time, the railways took over form the road as the main form of transport, 1,300 American locomotives[4] and a thousand French were in service[5].

Pipes to win the war?

Finally, there were the pipelines. This was the most straightforward way to transport fuel. The Americans had decided to open several pipelines linking the ports (Cherbourg, Donges) in the army zones. Taking into account the rapidity of the advance, the initial plans were changed completely and instead of opening more pipelines, all of the effort went into a single line that left from Cherbourg towards

Alençon, then extending towards the east. In order to gain time, the pipes were simply laid in ditches alongside the roads and passed over obstacles via ramps and bridges. 7,200 men and at least 1,500 POWs worked on the pipeline. The engineers reached Chartres on 9 September, three weeks after its liberation. But, at that time, Patton was in the Lorraine and Hodges in Belgium and there was, therefore, nearly another 500 kilometres to cover by truck. Also, the flow only reached a third of what was required and the rest had to be brought up from Saint-Lô or Cherbourg.

In September, despite the centralisation of operations in the hands of a Military Pipeline Service, the situation worsened. The engineers were lacking equipment to go further, it took 15 days to link Chartres to Coubert in the Paris suburbs and then…. nothing until February 1945. To sum up, the pipeline was late and too far from the frontline; it had been a very long term investment that had been of hardly any use during the pursuit.

The first train from Cherbourg is due to arrive at Lison station north of Saint-Lô. The train arriving is a *"Broadway Limited"*. According to French railroad worker Marcel Leveel, author of the book *"Rails and haies"*, 2004, (p.168), *"The 720th Railway Operating Battalion arrived at Lison on 16 July 1944. The Americans poured into the station courtyard in the afternoon […] It seemed to me that these were our new tenants and we realized that we would have to yet again move over and make space for them. They only left us two offices, all the rest was US territory. It would, therefore, be our American "Bahnhof" that would get the rail network up and running again by laying tracks and getting the trains moving. Good luck to them. These were American rail workers but they were dressed exactly the same as soldiers. As there were no translators, Franco-American relations were at a low-ebb."*
(Région Basse-Normandie, NARA, p014710 & p011670)

3. This number corresponds to the daily traffic of the French St.-Lazare railway station today.
4. Mostly 0-6-0 and 2-8-0 steam locomotives but also 130 powerful 650hp diesel locomotives and twenty-six 380hp locomotives which were much less visible near the front line as they did not emit smoke.
5. On the subject of railways, consult Ruppenthal, *op. cit.*, Ron De Nevi, *America's fighting railroads*, Pictorial Histories Publishing, 1996 & Ron De-Nevi & Bob Hall, *US Military Railway Service*, Stoddart, 1992.

THE RAIL WORKERS IN THE BATTLE

Extracts from an account that was published in an Irwin Ross article *"Trucks & Trains in the battle"*, Harper's Magazine, January 1945

"At midnight the train was completely loaded. Food, boxes of ammunition, gasoline, engineering equipment. The five-man crew was routed out if its pup tents.

The company commander pushed a case of K-rations into the cab. 'Where are we off to?' The engineer asked. He was still sleepy. 'Never mind', the CO said. 'Just keep going till someone stops you.' He had only the vaguest idea where they were going. Somewhere up front, that was all.

Eighty-six hours later they were finally stopped at a forward dump a few miles behind the armies. It had been a sleepless, harrowing trip. They had driven through the blackout without headlights, never knowing what loomed round the next bend. Tracks sagged dangerously when the cars passed over the newly filled-in bomb craters. Snipers fired at them as they entered a tunnel. Planes strafed them. Three times they were halted by trains stalled in front of them. Twice they were stopped for lack of coal, and once for water. For fuel they chopped up cross-ties found along the track, and for water, pressed a civilian fire pump into service.

The trains moved on the heels of Engineer gangs-as soon as a section of rail was repaired, the cars rolled. When telephone lines hadn't been strung, jeep couriers dashed between dispatch points with orders for the trains. If a courier was knocked off by a sniper, the trains were stalled for hours […] In the blackout, when lanterns hadn't been furnished, the brakemen signalled with lighted magazines, the flames of cigarette lighters, or glowing cigarette butts […] The demands on the railways were so large that sometimes trains were overloaded, which caused them to stall. This necessitated cutting the train in half and pulling each section into the first available siding. The sidings were frequently far apart, and by the time the engine returned to pick up the second section, later trains - dispatched as frequently as every thirty minutes from the station - were piling up for miles down the track."

Liberty Roads, 1944-1945

A STORY OF GAS!S

Port en Bessin *(1)*, a small fishing port in the Calvados department, was the first allied oil port. Small 1,300t tankers docked here. The pipes, which here *(2)* pass over part of the west jetty destroyed by the accidental beaching of a Landing Craft, were simply laid on the roadsides like at Escures *(3)* and headed to a large depot opened at St Honorine des Pertes *(4)*. The tanks stored 24,000 tonnes of oil *(5)*. Although this helped maintenance *(6)*, it was not surprising that some of the pipes were pierced by civilians for domestic use. On 25 July, the first tanker, the Empire Traveller *(7)*, berthed at the Querqueville terminal *(8)* managed by the men of the 87th Engineer Petroleum Distribution Co *(9)*. By 30 November, 657,000 tonnes of fuel had passed via Cherbourg. This day was a tipping point in the logistical system. Gasoline supplies went from the fragile phase of improvised bridgeheads to that of industrial exploitation via a rational system designed for intensive use. The Army would never go without gasoline in Europe, although it still needed to be brought up to the fighting men...
(Toutes photos, NARA)

Liberty Roads, 1944-1945

CHAPTER 9

GROUND TO A HALT

The Red Ball Express would remain open until mid-November and was closed down at the same time as the Normandy beaches, and depending on whether you look at things from the point of view of the quartermaster or that of the army commander, the balance sheet was not seen in the same way. ComZ deemed the operation as having been successful.

Despite being a 6x6, this CCKW 353 seems to be stuck. Torrential rains fell in the Vosges at the beginning of October.
(CMH)

1. This is of course the total declared as being delivered by ComZ whatever the mode of delivery, via Red Ball or another mode of transport.

Its initial mission was to deliver 100,000 tonnes in the Chartres region. Despite the difficulties, in barely six days the traffic reached its peak with 12,342 tonnes transported on 29 August. With 89,000 tonnes delivered by 5 September, making a daily average of 7,500 tonnes, the initial objective had almost been reached. The continuation of the operation was accompanied by a doubling of the distance to cover, something that did not prevent maintaining the rate of supply and even increasing it with 7,000 tonnes daily delivered in September and nearly 12,500 tonnes in October[1]. On this basis, it is justifiable to raise the Red Ball Express to the same supply hall of fame as the *Voie Sacrée* (Sacred Way) at Verdun, or the Berlin Airlift.

For Patton and Hodges, who estimated their needs as being 13,000 tonnes per day in September, then 20,000 in October and 30,000 in November, these amounts were, as far as they were concerned, totally inadequate, especially as over time, the bringing up of pertinent supplies had progressively worsened. Three complaints constantly came up. In the midst of the pursuit, the armies were slowed down by the lack of gasoline and maintenance, in October the attack on the Westwall was hindered by a lack of ammunition, something that reduced covering fire and which cost the infantry dearly, and finally in December, the latter shivered because the Army Service Forces had not anticipated the rigours of winter, whilst at the same time complaining about the lack of cigarettes.

FOUR MONTHS OF CRISIS

End of August, out of fuel?

It is no surprise that the first complaints came from Patton's army. It is hardly surprising as this army was rationed

Crisis concerning	Fuel	Maintenance	Munitions	Winter clothing	Cigarettes
The impact on operations	★★★★★	★★★	★★★★★	★★	★
Period	— 3rd Army. Rationing from 26 August to 5 November with supplies running out between 30 August and 4 September. — 1st Army Rationing from 4 Sept. to 15 Oct.	September — october	Mid. september — mid. December	November-january	In September then in December
Main causes	— Distance of depots	— Distance of depots — Negligence — Absence of priority — Usual wear and tear	— Break up of logistical chain — Poor port capacity	— Errors in planning — Late orders by the ETO — Inter service friction and lack of understanding between ComZ and ASF	Black market

Liberty Roads, 1944-1945

starting on 26 August, whereas it found itself at the forefront of the allied armies. It would receive no more than half of the amount of fuel that it had used over the previous days.

In his order of the day n°6, Bradley ordered Patton to *"advance as far as the Châlons-Reims line and to prepare to continue the advance rapidly in order to capture the Rhine crossing areas between Mannheim and Coblenz"*. Such a discrepancy between the immediate low-key objectives and the ambitious perspective of crossing the Rhine, highlights the ambiguity of allied orders during this period. In the short term, Bradley seemed to be bowing down to the M-520 directive that placed his army group in the role of supporting the 21st Br. Army Group. On paper, Patton was supposed to slow down as the Meuse river was not far from his forward units that had already gone past Troyes, but Bradley left him an opening to *"be ready to continue his advance"*. For the energetic general, this was a barely concealed authorisation to push on beyond the Meuse. Under the pretext of securing bridgeheads over the Meuse, his forward units -in fact his entire army - pushed on first to the Moselle river, then the Rhine. In other words, they had to continue to push forwards.

On 26 August, his two corps (XII and XX Corps[2]) each with three divisions, were deployed on the rivers Seine and Yonne from Melun to Troyes. Without waiting for the XV Corps that was stuck in the Mantes bridgehead, Patton ordered all of his forces to attack with the initial objective being Reims for the XX Corps and Châlons for the XII Corps.

Even before the start of operations, the XII Corps was concerned about running low on gasoline. The ADSEC could only supply it with 81 tonnes on 24 August and 205 the following day, whereas it required 530 to cover a hundred kilometres. It was only the capture of thirty-seven German tanker wagons at Sens that allowed the pursuit to continue. The Sherman tanks pushed aside the weak German units (48. ID, 338. ID, 708. ID and 17. SS. Pz-Gren-Div). The Marne was crossed within five days, Reims reached by XX Corps, Châlons liberated by the XII Corps and bridgeheads established on the Meuse. However, on 28 August, worrying reports began building up concerning the fuel situation, especially with the XII Corps. The armour's gasoline tanks were almost empty but dumps were captured at Châlons (400,000 litres) which provided a breathing space until 29 August and allowed the pursuit to continue up to the Meuse. The next day, XII Corps stated that it had to halt its armoured spearheads before they ran out of fuel.

The Third Army's momentum was halted by a lack of gaso-

---
2. XX Corps comprised of the 7th Arm Div and 5th and 90th ID. XII Corps the 4th arm div and the 35th and 80th ID.

The first complaints about the lack of fuel dated to the beginning of August and entire Third Army divisions were immobilized two weeks later. *(NARA)*

The US Army laundry services landed with their washing machines... and they were mobile. This trailer required a tractor, a vehicle which would not be available when needed on the Red Ball Express. *(NARA)*

Engineer Company (LE), 3rd Army, build a road with a Caterpillar D7 bulldozer equipped with a Le Tourneau "CK7" angledozer, at the rear, one can see the power control unit with its cable pulley drums. *(Région Basse-Normandie/Nara, p012275)*

Liberty Roads, 1944-1945

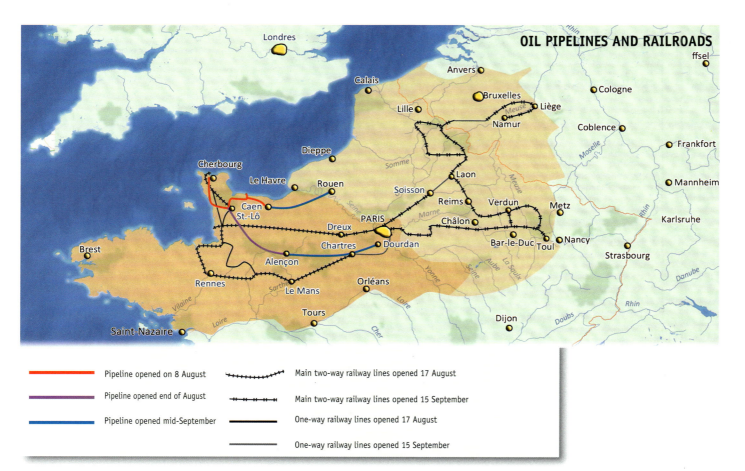

OIL PIPELINES AND RAILROADS

- ——— Pipeline opened on 8 August
- ——— Pipeline opened end of August
- ——— Pipeline opened mid-September
- ——+——+—— Main two-way railway lines opened 17 August
- ——+——+—— Main two-way railway lines opened 15 September
- ——— One-way railway lines opened 17 August
- ——— One-way railway lines opened 15 September

line. On 30 August, Patton went to see Bradley to argue his case, but he was unsuccessful as not one drop of fuel could be delivered before 3 September. Bradley stated that his was halt was a necessary evil. What was important was the advance of the First Army. Patton and his officers did not understand how the fastest advancing army could be sacrificed for others that were slower. Major-General Manton S. Eddy, commanding XII Corps, noted that *"if we had had enough gasoline the war could have been finished within a few weeks"*. When reading these accounts, the running out of fuel was sudden, total and long lasting. On 30 August, Patton thundered *"We aren't getting any more gas. I told Gaffey (Third Army Chief of Staff) that we had to roll on until our engines stopped, then continue on foot. We have to cross the Meuse and we will. In the last war (1914-18), I siphoned off three-quarters of my tanks' gas to fill the last quarter. Eddy should do the same"*. The same day, in a letter to his wife, he stated, *"If only I could steal a little gasoline, I would win this war. It's sad to say but a colored quartermaster company stole a little thanks to a carefully staged accident. I also captured around 4,000 tons of German gas. Its poor quality but its ok for a warm engine"*. The deliveries had become ridiculous:

On 30 August and 1 September, the army stocks had run out, IV Corps which was on its way to reaching the Third Army, was halted. 90% of the gasoline burned in the fuel tanks was German. A 4th Armored Division combat report stated that *"due to the lack of sufficient quantities of gasoline for offensive operations, the division was forced to maintain a defensive posture in its bridgehead to the east of the Meuse. From 1 to 10 September, the 25th Cavalry was only able to carry out patrols by siphoning off the fuel tanks of other divisional vehicles"*[3]. The Third Army was undeniably slowed down 150 km from the Rhine due to a lack of fuel.

Was this sacrifice beneficial to the 1st Army? The effort made on a logistical level is obvious.

96% of the promised amounts were delivered, covering 89% of the estimated requirements.

What did the 1st Army do with it? On 26 August, it received the order to accompany the 21st Br. Army Group heading northwards with the aiming point of Aix-la-Chapelle and the Ruhr. However, on the 26th, many divisions had not yet crossed the Seine as they held up by mopping up operations. Only VII Corps had been able to move out of the Melun bridgehead and it was not until the 29th that operations north of Mantes could begin (XIX and V Corps). Despite the favourable terrain, sporadic enemy action and enough fuel, the average advance in the first days was only forty kilometres, a rate that was twice as slow as the Third Army. XIX Corps missed the opportunity to encircle elements of two Panzer Divisionen and eight to ten Infanterie Divisionen in the region of Tournai. At Mons, 25,000 Germans were captured but 40,000 got away [4] due to the procrastination of the 3rd Armoured Division and the slowness of the 1st ID that took two days to fill the gaps left by the armoured spearheads.

When Ike took over the command on the continent on 2 September, he was aware of the delays in the north and told Bradley that he was going to go back to a wide front strategy. He authorised the sending of fuel supplies to help Patton just at the time when the First Army was beginning to run low and he ordered Gerow's V Corps to change direction in order to fill the gap left between the two armies in the Ardennes.

The First Army was then forced to halt its XIX Corps due to a lack of fuel and only had one corps left (the VII) heading towards the Ruhr. The lack of fuel hit the First Army later but was just as bad. The 3rd Arm. Div. Was halted for several hours on 4 September and for all of the 6th. The 5th Arm. Div. Was halted on 7 and 8 September for the 28th ID, the infantry using less fuel. Although Luxemburg was liberated on 9 September and the German border reached on the 11th, the American divisions came up against the Westwall.

---

3. Martin Blumenson (prés.), *Patton, carnets secrets*, Plon, 1975, p 338. It would appear that the number of 4,000 tonnes given by Patton is exaggerated as the Third Army archives 'only' 500,000 gallons (1 500 tonnes or 1.8 million de litres) captured from the enemy.
4. Belonging to 18. Feld-Div (L), 3. and 6. Fallshirm-Jäger-Divisionen, 47., 275. and 348. ID. Amongst those who escaped was SS-Obergruppenführer Bittrich.

Gasoline supplies to the 3rd Army

	28 August	29 August	30 August	1er September	2 September	3 September	4 September
Volume delivered in litres	1325000	700000	121133	?	96149	190000	900000

Liberty Roads, 1944-1945

Lacking artillery and ammunition, Hodges ordered a halt until 14 September in order to build up supplies. On this day, German resistance stiffened. Although one division managed to break through to a depth of eight kilometres, it became stuck in front of a strongly held second line. Mödel had just brought up a fresh division supported by a

Panzerbrigade and two armoured Kampfgruppen. Two more days were necessary to cross the fortified zone, but the infantry and tanks found themselves bogged down in an industrial and residential zone that was ideal for the defenders and full of minefields. The tanks were at the mercy of the Panzerfaust and on 17 September, the Americans even pulled back. Hodges had to admit that Aix la Chapelle would not be taken without a large scale offensive.

On Patton's front, 900,000 litres of gasoline were delivered on the 4th, followed by 5.2 million litres over the next three days. On the 5th, four days after the forced halt, the advance continued, but five days later the Americans became bogged down in a bloody battle along the Moselle river. The crossing of the latter south of Metz by the

11th Infantry Regiment (5th ID) on the 8th, was a fiasco. The operation was an improvised affair with few barges, no artillery or air support and was faced by a bolstered German defence[5]. Further south, the situation was better. After the French Division Leclerc had destroyed *Panzerbrigade* 112 at Dompaire, Nancy fell on the 16th. However, the advance beyond the Moselle had really slowed down. From 18 to 22 September, the 4th US Arm. Div. dislocated two other *Panzerbrigaden* near Arracourt... thirty kilometres east of Nancy. The American generals had to admit that the pursuit was over.

During these September weeks, Ike and Bradley continued their dithering and could not decide which army should be given priority. On 10 September, Bradley met his two army commanders and told them that *"the armies would be given the same priority concerning supplies, although the capture of Brest would be given the utmost priority"*. Precious fuel and transport was therefore diverted for an objective that everyone deemed as being already secondary as the day before, Bradley and Patton had agreed that *"the capture of Brest at this time was pointless as it was too far from the frontline and its port was very badly damaged"*. There was a change in tone two days later. Bradley told Patton that SHAEF had given priority to Montgomery and that the Third Army was to hold to *"hold defensively the western banks of the Moselle"*. However, Patton managed to obtain permission to freely undertake operations for a further four days. Like he had done at the end of August, Patton hoped that any success would change Eisenhower's plans. This he partially achieved on 15 September as a new Eisenhower general order, although giving priority to operations in the north, no longer mentioned Patton halting on the Moselle. Of course, it clearly stated that *"all the available central army group resources* (Bradley's) *have to be thrown into the support of the First Army in order to establish bridgeheads near Cologne and Bonn for the capture of the Ruhr. Once the northern army group* (Montgomery) *and the 1st Army have established bridgeheads on the other* side of the Rhine,

Below
A Sherman and a motorbike are towed by two recovery tanks on M3 chassis. It is unlikely that this tank was repaired at the workshops as there were so many other with less damage. Within the 3rd AD, two-thirds of the tanks were unavailable at the beginning of September.
(NARA)

5. The 1,200 American soldiers were in the positions of three battalions: the Voss battalion comprising of Russian Front veterans with stomach ailments, the SS "Berg" battalion formed with transmission school cadets and the 2. Abt. du SS Panzergrenadier Regiment 37 of the 17. SS Pzgren. Div.

Gasoline supplies to the 1st Army from 6-12 September 1944

	Estimated needs 31 August tonnes per day (t/pd)	Allocation by Com Z (t/pd)	Volumes received by the 1st Army (t/pd)
Gasoline and Oils	2200	2028	1954

Third Army infantry crossing the Meuse, mid-September 1944.
(NARA)

the 3rd Army will advance through the Sarre and cross the Rhine". Reading this, Patton would have to wait for other formations to cross the Rhine before starting to advance again, but it goes on to say that by waiting, the Third Army would constitute *"a permanent threat and prevent the enemy from strengthening his northern front by removing troops defending Metz"*. Patton was not to remain stationary therefore, but continue combat operations in order to pin down the enemy and this would involve crossing the Moselle and attacking Metz. In other words, Ike was sitting on the fence.

It was the same with Bradley who continued to share equally the supplies between Patton and Hodges (see table). Of course, on paper this was not exactly the case as in the eventuality of ADSEC delivering more than 7,000 tonnes of supplies daily, the excess would go as a priority to the 1st Army. But this was a theoretical priority given the difficulties in reaching this amount. It was only on the 21st that priority was clearly given to Hodges and even then without his being to the detriment of Patton who retained his initial allocation of 3,500 tonnes. On this date, the question of fuel had become less important. The front had stabilised at the German border and in the Lorraine.

PERIOD	ALLOCATION PER ARMY		
	1st Army	3rd Army	9th Army
27 August to 4 September	5000	2000	-
5 to 13 September	3500	3500	-
14 to 20 September	3500[1]	3500[2]	-
21 to 27 September	5000[3]	3500	900

The lack of gasoline brought the Third Army to a halt between 30 August and 4 September and slowed down many First Army units in the early days of September.

This is a long way off being the sudden, total and long lasting running out of fuel that Patton complained about. Was this not finally much a do about nothing for such a short period concerning the running out of gasoline? This is no doubt not the case as it had been at the heart of talks in general staffs and had led to the rationing of armies and changing the wide front strategy that Ike wanted. It also led to halting of several divisions, or even whole corps behind the front line. The result was that in September, the forces of the XII US Army Group engaged in the pursuit was reduced to 10 infantry divisions and five armored divisions out of the 19 infantry divisions and 7 armored divisions that had landed in Normandy. Finally, the rarity of gasoline and fear of running out led the generals to reduce and delay their activity until mid-October for the First Army, and up to November for the Third.

As well as the fuel problems that were at the forefront, there was also a veritable crisis concerning maintenance, a crisis that has more or less been forgotten today.

The lack of gasoline gave the defenders an un-hoped for breathing space and it was only after weeks of fierce fighting, symbolized by this Pak 43/41 gun, that a convoy of 95th ID Jeeps and Dodges entered Metz in November.
(NARA)

September, the maintenance crisis

At the same time as the fuel crisis *"A third of Third Army vehicles were destroyed or being repaired"* according to Patton's corps commanders, generals Eddy and Walker. With the 3rd Arm. Div. in mid-September, only 75 of the 232 tanks were still operational. Following six weeks of pursuing the enemy, the vehicles, which had not been maintained, were in a terrible condition and there was a spate of breakdowns. This was a structural constraint specific to motorised units that was encountered during German operations in the USSR and North Africa. The absence of turnover between spearhead units and units at

rest inexorably wore out vehicles. With or without fuel, the units required a 48 hour rest every six weeks, the time required to repair engines and replace worn out parts. It is no doubt possible that battalion commanders hid behind a partial lack of fuel to justify a halt that the high command refused to allow them to take[6]. Without maintenance, the vehicles broke down more frequently and overloaded the services of the Ordnance Corps. In the US Army, the maintenance and repairs were filtered via four repair echelons. Everyday and minor repairs were carried out at the frontline. Bigger repairs were undertaken by a maintenance battalion that accompanied each army corps, whereas a heavy group dealt with 4th echelon army installations. The 1st Army maintenance was coordinated by Colonel Medaris and that of the 3rd Army by Colonel Nixon, both had a great freedom of action concerning the organisation of their personnel.

Their main concern was in maintaining contact with the armoured spearheads. The workshops moved every week. Due to a lack of transport, they left behind a lot of their spare parts stores and this led to the second concern: running out of these stocks. As they were not deemed priority, these parts were not transported on the Red Ball Express and only arrived from time to time, brought up on troop or replacement equipment convoys. A tank transporter company never left Normandy without all spare space being taken up by spare parts. The tanks themselves were literally festooned with various items of equipment. But this was not enough and in September, the 1st Army only received 10% of its spare parts requirements. In October, the lack of tires and tracks became dramatic and even in December, half of the spare parts were still slumbering in Normandy whereas 46 transport ships waited to be unloaded.

In the first five months of the campaign, instead of receiving a monthly allocation of 800 trucks, Medaris only received a total of 562 of which 400 were stuck in Normandy.

In order to compensate, Nixon and Medaris looked towards civilians. Paris and Belgium were full of mechanical construction companies ready to work for the army. Unfortunately they lacked raw materials. Only *Gnome & Rhone* in Paris accepted to immediately overhaul two hundred tank engines, the other contracts were not dealt with before

The Hürtgen forest is infamous in the annals of American history. Badly led and in terrible conditions *(1)* **with insufficient supplies to provide fire-support** *(2)*, **the battle for the control of the Ruhr dams bled white several divisions in October and November. The pursuit was nothing more than a distant memory.** *(NARA)*

6. It should not be forgotten either that the Americans carried out here their first campaign of a war of movement on a large scale and that logistical considerations had been neglected during their training. Roman Jarymowycz in *Tank Tactics*, Stackplole Books, 2009, pp. 71-74, 217 reminds us that the only manoeuvres where these considerations were taken into account went back to Louisiana in 1941.
7. Constance McLaughlin Green, Harry C. Thomson and Peter C. Root, *The Ordnance Corps*, CMH, vol.3, 1968, p. 296.

Liberty Roads, 1944-1945

Siegfried Line dragons' teeth: obstacles that would have to be crossed. (NARA)

7. Constance McLaughlin Green, Harry C. Thomson and Peter C. Root, *The Ordnance Corps*, CMH, vol.3, 1968, p. 296.
8. With XX Corps, foreign-made shells represented 80% of shells fired in the last week of October.
9. Ruppenthal, *op. cit.*, vol II, p. 124.

1945. The situation was better in Belgium and a thousand contracts were signed before the end of the year[7].

September-October, the munitions crisis

After that of fuel and maintenance, another problem arose in September, that of a lack of munitions. On 12 September, Hodges delayed a first offensive against the Westwall by 48 hours due to a lack of shells and heavy artillery pieces. This was mainly due to a hardening German resistance, but was also the indirect consequence of the lack of fuel. Indeed, Hodges had halted his heavy artillery between the Seine and the Somme in order to save fuel and free up tractors that could be of use to the logistical units. He therefore needed time to move the artillery to the frontline and this lack of firepower was therefore purely temporary.

The lack of shells would, however, become longer lasting and revealed a structural crisis. It only concerned certain types of shell, but these we of strategic importance as they were either the most used (105 and 155 mm), or indispensable in certain circumstances (such as the 240 mm needed to tackle the Westwall). We have the figures for the third week of October *(see table on page 131)*.

On this date, the fighting was concentrated around Aix la Chapelle for the 1st Army and Metz for the 3rd Army. These were assaults against fortified positions that required a colossal fire support. But, for the Third Army, daily shell expenditure was only 1.1 shells per 105 mm Howitzer and 0.4 for 155 mm shells. In October, its total consumption did not exceed.... a day's operations in the Ardennes two months later. Counter-battery fire was forbidden. At the VI Corps, only one division could attack at a time in order to benefit from a reasonable artillery protection. With the 35th ID, a report stated that the lack of support was responsible for the bloody failure of two attacks. Whilst awaiting for better weapons, the Americans used tanks

(75 mm), tank destroyers (76 mm) or anti-aircraft guns (40 mm), the ammunition of which was in plentiful supply, as well as captured guns such as the 88 or 105 howitzers, but also Russian 76.2 guns and French 155 that had seen use in many armies[8]. The 1st Army was the best off with thirty rounds per 105 and fifteen for the 155. However, this was a long way from the sixty rounds fired in Normandy. At the end of October, only ten American divisions were able to operate at the same time purely due to the lack of shells.

This shell crisis can be explained at first by the non-renewal of stocks in Normandy. In Cherbourg, the priority in September was given to the disembarkation of fresh units and given the fact that the storms off the beaches slowed this down, only two Liberty Ships carrying ammunition were unloaded in the first week of October. Thirty-five were waiting off shore. The change in priority ordered by ComZ concerning ammunition arrived on 1 October, but it was not until the first second week that things were speeded up with eight ships being unloaded. This was not enough. In Paris, Lee began to use whatever he could. He ordered the unloading of

Whilst the Allies were at the Westwall, almost 1,000 km away, the town of Brest fell... a field of ruins. (NARA)

Although the pursuit ended with mixed results on 15 September, it was also due to the structural constraints inherent to motorized armies: maintenance. The Ordnance Corps mechanics were overwhelmed with work and were lacking spare parts. They are seen here changing the transmission on a Ford M8 armored car sat on jacks. A Dodge WC52 equipped with a leverage bar attached to the fender helps lift the vehicle. The tracks were not the first thing to break as is the case with this M4A1 of the 70th Tank Bn. *(Région Basse-Normandie/Nara, p013076 & p013375)*

CONSUMPTION OF AN ARMORED AND AN INFANTRY DIVISIONS
(AFTER THE FIELD MANUAL 101-10, AUGUST 1949 FROM THE DATA COLLECTED IN 1944-45)

Tonnes per day (Arm. Div./Inf. Div.)		
Mark	Attack	Pursuit
I	40/51	42/50
II & IV	137/55	46/41
III	103/44	174/136
V	375/430	66/69
Total	655/580	328/296

ships in England and the conveying of ammunition by LST as far as the beaches at Le Havre. He combed through dumps left behind in Normandy, something that turned out to be a wise decision that brought in 4,000 tonnes of shells. The sticking point was not now only in distribution, but in unloading at the ports.

240 SHIPS AT ANCHOR!

In September, only 883,500 were unloaded compared with 000 tonnes the previous month. In October, this figure fell to under 790,000 tonnes (a 16% drop in two months)[9]. 150 ships waited in the Baie de Seine on 1 September. This increased to 240 on 20 October and on this day, only 25,400 were landed, 20,000 less than planned[10]. Instead of growing in strength, the logistics were standing still, however, contrary to commonly held beliefs, this standing still did not precede the advance bogging down, but took place at the same time.

The cause is obvious, the Americans had not found any

---
10. William Whipple, *"Logistic Bottleneck"*, Infantry journal, mars 1948 in Charles R. Shrader (dir.), United States Army Logistics, An Anthology, vol.2, University Press of the Pacific, 2001.

Lee ordered the requisitioning of the surplus vehicles in Great Britain and brought them over as a stop-gap measure to replace the hundred or so GMC which were lost everyday on the Red Ball Express Highway. *(NARA)*

Liberty Roads, 1944-1945

Unloading heavy-caliber shells from a Liberty Ship. Only two ships loaded with ammunition were able to be unloaded in October due to the weather conditions. Thirty-five were anchored off the shore. *(Région Basse-Normandie/NARA, p001062)*

An interesting photo showing work in an army zone marshalling yard. Whilst one train departs empty towards the rear, the crews load 105 mm shells into the GMC trucks. A conveyor belt, something of which only the Allies had, made this task easier. *(NARA)*

Unloading a small tramp steamer in the port of Isigny directly onto a GMC. The tides and the shortness of the quayside limited the flow of supplies to 740 t for the small Normandy port. *(13-Num 1683, NARA © Archives départementales de la Manche)*

other points of entry other than the Lower Normandy beaches and the ports opened in June-July. In September, Normandy still represented 91% of the amount of supplies unloaded and 82% in October. If it was not for the remarkable work of the beach services, the American army would have quite simply ground to a halt. However, it was lucky in that it carried on breaking records thanks to the opening of Beach Transfer Points, the improvement of road transportation and unloading techniques.

The time of illusions

The rapid advance into Brittany at the beginning of August had brought with it the hope of a rapid improvement to the situation. Sadly, for the Americans, they were not able to capture the largest ports. On 25 August, ComZ looked into the possibility of using small ports such as St Malo, Cancale and St Brieuc. The report that was drawn up was not very optimistic: the scale of destruction and the lack of port equipment would make it necessary to undertake work that was beyond the means available and such an undertaking was not worth its while. The rapid liberation of Rouen (30 August), Antwerp (4 September) and Le Havre (12 September) appeared as a solution to the Brittany problem. They combined superior potential (deeper ports, length of quays, storage space, cranes....) with much better rail networks that allowed for the rapid despatch of supplies inland and a proximity to the frontline. With Le Havre alone, the Americans shortened the distance by 400 km compared with Brest, thus saving 280 GMC for every 5,000 tonnes unloaded. Antwerp could even make up for all of the other ports. Let us look at how this was possible. It could take the biggest ships in service at the time along its 50 km of quays spread out within its 18 inner harbours. Its infrastructure was the dream of any logistics expert: 625 cranes, 900 warehouses, most of which were refrigerated, 495 petrol tanks (for a volume of 124 million gallons), 1,000 km of railways at the heart of Benelux 120 kilometres from the First Army front and waterways that included the ultramodern Albert Canal. Also, Antwerp had fallen into allied hands almost undamaged and its dock workers, well organized by the Belgian resistance, were ready to start work.

This un-hoped for liberation of Antwerp started a period of euphoria, not only did victory appear to be at hand, but the thorny problem of logistics appeared to be resolved. On 3 September Whipple (SHAEF G4) recommended the abandoning of Breton ports for those of the Channel. For once, SHAEF and ComZ were in agreement and on the 7th, SHAEF cancelled the work being undertaken in southern Brittany, especially Operation Chastity. Only Brest, Morlaix, Saint Malo were to remain open. On 14 September, Lee announced to his subordinates that Le Havre and Rouen would only be used as interim ports whilst awaiting the for the opening of a large Belgian port that it was hoped would soon take place. In these conditions, it was out of the question to exhaust themselves on the lower Seine ports and Lee set modest objectives: 3,000 tonnes for Rouen and 8,500 for Le Havre. Blinded by Antwerp, the Americans had lost sight of the forest for the

Top and bottom.
American tactics depended on massive fire-support. However, the sixty shell daily allocation per gun in Normandy fell to 30 for the 1st Army 105 mm guns and 15 for the 155 mm in October. For the 3rd Army, each gun only fired on average one shell per day. All operations were consequently slowed down.
(NARA)

ARTILLERY SHELL CONSUMPTION BETWEEN 15 AND 21 OCTOBER 1944

	First Army		Third Army		Ninth Army	
	Total fired	Average amount fired per day	Total fired	Average amount fired per day	Total fired	Average amount fired per day
105 how	109 469	30	3 401	1.1	15 946	18.1
4.5 inch	2 940	12	172	0.7	401	2.4
155 how	24 341	15	553	0.4	2 171	3.6
155 self-propelled	2 001	8	315	3.8		
155 Gun	5 941	10	640	2.5	930	5.5
8-inch how	3 819	15	391	1.1	284	1.7
8-inch gun	159	2	66	1.6		
240 how	627	3.7	35	0.3		

Source: Memo from Col T.B. Hedekin, 12th Army group Artillery section for the G-3 of the 12th Army group, 19 November 1944

The port of Brest was destroyed by sabotage and fighting. In a flooded dry-dock, the wreck of a Sperrbrecher will have to be re-floated in order to clear the area. *(NARA)*

trees. Indeed, they had not taken into account that the port was situated 110 km down the Scheldt estuary and that the mouths of the latter remained Wehrmacht property and would do until mid November.

The time of disillusion

It was not until the end of September that the illusions disappeared and a first report stated a sense of urgency. In Normandy, as the road companies tasked with transporting supplies had been mobilised for the Highway, the Normandy Base Station port services could only deal with six merchant ships in Cherbourg and two that were off the beaches. Work was affected and slowed down the activity of the Dukw by 30

Liberty Roads, 1944-1945

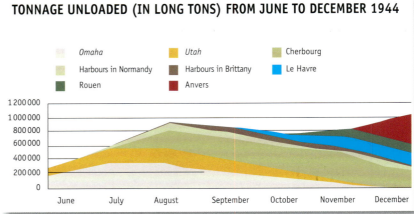

TONNAGE UNLOADED (IN LONG TONS) FROM JUNE TO DECEMBER 1944

A myriad of 16th Port Dukws approach a Liberty Ship anchored at Le Havre. It required thousands of return trips in order to empty such a 10,000 tonne ship with these small vehicles capable of carrying 2.5 tonnes. It was only in December that the first quays were opened.
(13 584_8, NARA © Coriello, Bibliothèque municipale de Cherbourg)

The Paris liner, gutted by fire that started in its bakery in April 1939. It suffered the same fate as the Normandie liner in New York. The amount of water sprayed over one side led it to tip over. It still blocked the Transatlantic quay in 1944 and would do so until 1947. *(NARA)*

to 40%. The latter were worn out by four months of incessant rotations and spent more and more time undergoing repairs. Also, as the weather conditions were deteriorating, it was becoming obvious that Omaha and Utah's days were counted. In October, the daily traffic on the beaches dropped from 11,500 to 7,000 tonnes. The substitute for this, the option of using ports in northern Brittany, was not successful.

Opened only by mid-September, they offered a daily supply flow of only 3,000 tonnes instead of the hoped for 30,000. For Ruppenthal, they did not even make up for the effort spent in making them reusable and in any case, they were soon only used to supply local garrisons and civilian needs before being closed early.

(see below)

This left Rouen and Le Havre. Le Havre had been mortally damaged by sabotage, in particular the lock opening into the inner ports that was just a heap of ruins. This allowed the tide to flow into the inner ports and further damage the quays. As well as this, the city centre had been flattened by British carpet bombing that had been as pointless as it had been bloody for the civilian population (3,000 victims) and the road and rail superstructure was damaged. Reports even suggest that Le Havre was in an even worse state than Cherbourg. On 20 September, a week after its liberation, two General Service Regiments, one of which had worked at Cherbourg (the 373rd), and two PC&R groups began work. Forecasts were barely optimistic. Of course, they hoped to make the beach accessible to LST and Dukw vehicles within two weeks, but they did not believe that it would be possible to reopen a few quays and railways before November and enlarge the port in order to reach 10,000 tonnes per day before December. As early as 2 October, the first 16th port Dukw began going back and forth to the tramp steamers anchored off the beach. On the first week 2,000 tonnes were unloaded per day, the second week saw this amount increase to 3,650 and the third 5,000 tonnes, a remarkable performance that was unfortunately let down by problems in getting the supplies transported away due to bad coordination with the British due to the fact that the Americans cut the logistical lines, as well as a lack of locomotives. Despite the opening of the first berths in December, the traffic stabilised at this level until January 1945, way below the hoped for 10,000 tonnes per day.

Rouen underwent a similar evolution. Its quaysides were intact, but the amount of wrecked ships blocking the Seine

Trucks drive out of the hold of a beached LST at St Michel en Grève. Although the Britanny beaches took some of the burden off those in Normandy, these supplies were for the VIII Corps in action at Brest, an objective which had become useless and which diverted too many precious supplies and means. (NARA)

Three LST have simply beached themselves on the shore of the beach at Le Havre in front of the Frascati hotel. In the foreground, the 373rd Engineer General Service Regiment is still busy clearing the beach. They have already partially destroyed the anti-tank wall in the background to allow vehicles to pass through. (NARA)

BRETON PORT TRAFFIC					
Port	Opening date	Closing date	Days opened	Total unloaded (Long Tons)	Daily average (Long tons)
Saint-Michel en Grève (beach for LST)	12 August	30 September	81	60 343	745
Saint-Brieuc	16 September	15 October	30	9 521	317
Morlaix-Roscoff	5 September	14 December	101	212 636	2 105
Saint-Malo	not re-opened				
Brest	not re-opened				

THE PORT BATTALIONS

"The same thing done a hundred times over: unhook the net, then lift one by one the heavy crates smothered with paraffin and pass them to the next man who would pile them up. A boring, exhausting and monotonous task that had to be repeated for twelve straight hours, for weeks and months on end with no break, whether in sunshine or storms. Endless nights lit up by arc lamps, in the rain that turned everything that was touched sticky. Battered by high winds in this port of Cherbourg which, only last summer, they would not even have been able to find on a map. On quaysides shiny with dampness, [...] on board moored barges, balanced on the large Rhinoferries that bobbed up and down in the waves; soaked by spray on board the tiny Dukws; working in the holds of the merchant ships, or with pallets of spare parts or tinned food lined up under the cargo booms... returning exhausted, [...] crashing out on a camp bed, the small of the back broken with fatigue, [...] living in tents erected by the shore where one shivered in December, grabbing a few hours sleep, a quick cup of coffee then begin it all again..."
Robert Lerouvillois, *Et la liberté vint de Cherbourg, op. cit.,* p. 203. In the photos, apart from several semi-forward cabin GMC trucks (AFKWX 353) we can see a Chevrolet G 7113 4X4 tractor that were allocated in large numbers to the Transportation Corps to compensate for the lack of heavy tractors.
(©Coriello, Bibliothèque municipale de Cherbourg)

channel and the destruction of equipment meant that extensive repair work was required. Work commenced with little conviction during September, a sign that ComZ did not really place much faith in it, and it was not until 27 September that an initial objective was set for 3,000 tonnes per day. An extra month would be required to deploy the 11th Port. Between 15-31 October, 48 ships were able to come into the port and only 1,500 tonnes per day were unloaded; the Liberty Ships were required to remove some of their load within the Le Havre breakwater before sailing up the Seine and there was a lack of lighter tramp ships.

It was, therefore, no surprise that it was a struggle to reach the pre-war output, and this port had been the main port of entry for British forces during the Great War. By the end of December the situation appeared satisfactory at last with a rate of 75% of quay occupancy (15 berths for Liberty

Liberty Roads, 1944-1945

Ships and 26 for tramp steamers) but these figures are misleading and the ships were not turned around quickly enough and the unloading stagnated at under 5,000 tonnes per day. The exploit of Cherbourg would not be repeated at Rouen and Le Havre. Instead of allowing an increase in strength, these ports only allowed to compensate, with some delay, for the loss of activity on the Normandy beaches.

In the space of a few days, the Americans went from a state of euphoria to one of panic. At the beginning of October, SHAEF looked at the possibility of transferring the British ports of Ostend and Calais to ComZ. The Americans were now forced to ask for British help, but this project did go any further. Lee then turned towards the south. Indeed, since the end of August, Marseille and Toulon had been liberated. Marseille almost immediately took in Dukw and barges and as early as 3 September as first inner port was cleared. Within a month, a major port complex was opened with 44 berths, 32 of which could be used for Liberty Ships. 13,000 tonnes were unloaded daily, more than enough for the needs of the VIIth US Army and the French 1ere Armée. Lee, therefore, suggested to Eisenhower to divert some of the traffic towards the Mediterranean, beginning with three divisions arriving from the USA. Although this looked good on paper, this option came up against administrative stumbling blocks: the Mediterranean ports were not under SHAEF control, but that of the NATOUSA (North African Theatre of Operation). Even if possible, the Marseille-Lyon line was not able to transport such a large quantity of goods. Already by October, 40,000 tonnes were lying dormant on the Marseille quaysides and the Americans were reduced to requisitioning horse-drawn wagons. This operation undertaken to relieve pressure was limited, therefore, to these three divisions and a few hundred trucks.

Whereas the months of June to August had been ones of successful improvisation, those of September to November were those of disillusion. Neither ComZ, SHAEF, or the armies found solutions to the multiple points of congestion. The supply chain became stuck and the American generals were reduced to playing a waiting game and pointing the finger at a scapegoat. As the solution resided in Antwerp and this port was not open, the blame was placed on Montgomery who was incapable of clearing the mouth of the Scheldt. Thus, in his

memo of 8 October, Colonel Whipple stated that, *"The failure to open Antwerp has endangered our entire winter campaign. Making the operation of secondary importance was justified temporarily when the northern salient required strengthen-*

Liberty Roads, 1944-1945

ANTWERP: MONTY'S FAULT!

Prudent men are often those who take the smallest gambles and Montgomery was a very prudent man. However, he was also determined to make his mark on the history books and put into motion Churchill's instructions. Already covered in glory following El Alemein, he needed a Waterloo in order to elevate himself above Wellington in the British national conscience. By the beginning of September he was convinced that the end of the war was imminent. If ever there was a time to overcome his prudent nature and forge his legend it was now!

Having failed to convince Eisenhower to totally adopt the narrow front option, Montgomery took the gamble of obtaining the same result with only the forces at his disposal. This would be Market-Garden, the crossing of several water obstacles in one single drive and opening the way to the Ruhr and the great northern plains of Germany. This choice was also justified politically, as apart from victory over Germany, it would also guarantee the most advantageous position for the British after the war. This was all about retaining the illusion of being a great imperial power, remaining an equal partner with the United States and not being relegated to the level of a junior ally. This illusion could only be preserved if the British Army retained the most important role within the coalition. It would have to remain in the spotlight. However, clearing the Antwerp area was an obscure mission which would only end up by providing the Americans with the means to shine. Crossing the Rhine would make sure that the eyes of the world remained on the British. Monty, therefore, played his own card and that of his country instead of playing the team game. Ignoring Eisenhower's instructions to first guarantee the opening of the port of Antwerp, Monty focused on Arnhem. After the war, he justified his choice by first arguing that a victory on the Rhine would have made clearing Antwerp easier by distracting the German forces; this is a questionable argument. Secondly, he thought that the Channel ports could make up for Antwerp, forgetting to mention that in the plans these ports were reserved for British supplies.

It was also impossible for his army group to prepare Market Garden and the clearing of the Antwerp area due to a lack of means. Monty only had in the sector the 2nd British Army (reduced to two corps). More than ten days after the liberation of Antwerp by XXX Corps, Monty issued an operational order that was almost entirely dedicated to Market-Garden. The 2nd Br. Army would move away from the Belgian port and the task of clearing the area was handed to the 1st Can. Army. But the latter had just liberated Le Havre (1st Br. Corps, two divisions) and was besieging Boulogne, Calais and Dunkirk (2nd Can Corps, two divisions). Only its two armoured divisions (4th Can. Arm. Div & 1st Pol. Arm. Div.) were in Belgium and had become bogged down north of Gent for two days, incapable of passing the countless canals that crisscrossed the region. Their tanks were powerless and lacked infantry and artillery support. It took the Poles eight days to reach the south bank of the Scheldt, cutting off the Germans in the Breskens pocket.

Whilst the 2nd British Army failed in crossing the Rhine, the Canadians captured Boulogne on 22 September and Calais on the 30th. As had been the case at Rouen and Le Havre a few days earlier, it was only ruins that were liberated and the ports were unusable. It had now been a month that the intact port of Antwerp was waiting to be used and that the Germans had been adding the finishing touches to the defences from one side of the mouths of the Scheldt to the other. This lack of thrust angered Eisenhower

The LCT land numerous LVT Buffaloes, indispensables for clearing the flooded Walcheren islands which controlled the Scheldt estuary. *(RR)*

who, in diplomatic terms, made his views known to Montgomery.

[...] *It is because I want to organise this final advance rapidly by capturing the Ruhr, that I insist on the importance of Antwerp. As I said to you, I am ready to provide you with what you need to capture the Antwerp approaches, including any airpower or any other means*". In his directive dated 27 September, two days after the sad end to Market-Garden, Montgomery mentioned the importance of clearing the Antwerp area, but placed operations south of the Rhine on the same level of importance. The required to gather the necessary forces and supplies for the Canadian Army meant that operations could only really speed up in the second week of September, something that Monty acknowledged with a typically British stiff upper lip which annoyed Ike.

On 29 September, the supreme commander reiterated its orders to speed up preparations. On 4 October, Ike hit the ceiling when Monty came back again

Sherman flail tanks of the 79th AD which were of great use in mine-clearing, drive off the two LCT. Simonds used the large allied arsenal to design an inventive and efficient assault. *(RR)*

Liberty Roads, 1944-1945

asking for the command of the 1st US Army in order to capture.... the left bank of the Rhine.

On 9 October, an angry Ike wrote to Monty: *"If Antwerp is not operational by mid November, all of our operations will be halted. I have to tell you that of all the operations along the entire frontline, Antwerp is the most important and I believe that it requires all of your personal attention"*. However, it would take another week and an exchange of angry letters before Monty at last accepted to gather his generals together in order to indicate to them that Antwerp was of the utmost priority over all other operations.

Clearing the mouths of the Scheldt meant that operations within three distinct areas:
• Clearing the Breskens pocket south of the sea area of the Scheldt (Operation Switchback)
• Clearing the north bank and isthmus of the Zuid Beveland (Operations Suitcase & Vitality)
• Capturing the island fortress of Walcheren controlling the entrance to the estuary (Operation Infatuate)

To achieve these objectives, the 1st Canadian Army initially only had weak means at its disposal. The terrain was either marshy or urban, but always interlaced with canals and was, therefore, unsuitable for the use

A LCT landing LVT and Weasels on Westkapelle beach, 1 November. (DR)

The sea flooded into Westkapelle via a breach made by heavy bombers. (RR)

of armoured divisions. For logistical reasons, the 51st ID was immobilised at Le Havre and Simonds had to make do with the 2nd Canadian ID and the British 49th ID that had arrived at Antwerp around 20 September. But these units, especially the Canadian, had suffered in Normandy. Some companies were down to only fifty men, others were at full strength but with a majority of new recruits that had received less than two months of training. It was, therefore, with a numerical inferiority and on terrain that favoured the defender, that operations began in the northern suburbs of Antwerp. It was no surprise that the advance was extremely slow, especially in light of the fact that some of the defenders were the paratroopers of the 6 Fs Regiment, veterans of Crete and Normandy. After having liberated Calais, the 3rd Can. ID joined the frontline and was attached to Operation Switchback which began on 6 October. It too would have to attack with inferior numbers and had to begin by crossing the Leopold Canal. The battalions that managed to cross found themselves stuck in two bridgeheads, the narrowness of which made it difficult to send in reinforcements. It was impossible to dig trenches deeper than thirty centimetres without running the risk of flooding them as the terrain was wet, but the men were under intense German artillery fire. *"The medical officer told us that since 6 October, between 250 and 300 wounded have come through the regimental aid post"*, making a third of total strength, stated the Regina Rifle Regiment diary on 12 October. *"We think that this has been the worst fighting since D-Day. [...] We have used incredible amounts of ammunition, each man fired off up to 25 grenades per night. In the space of 90 minutes, on the night of the 10th, the artillery fired up to 2,000 shells in front of our frontline and our mortar platoon fired 1,064 rounds in three hours!"*. This could be an account straight out of the First World War. Thirty-nine days had passed since the liberation of Antwerp and the German defensive line had hardly been dented.

Progressively and under Eisenhower's impetus, who lent an American division, released strategic bombing aircraft and the required landing and fire support equipment, the tide was turned. Eight divisions were engaged, including units of the 2nd British Army[1]. However, it took almost a month to clear the Breskens pocket and six weeks to clear the isthmus of Zuid Beveland. At the beginning of November, only the Walcheren

---

1. The inventory of which shows a multi-national dimension which was an additional obstacle as apart from the 2nd, 3rd and 4th Canadian Divisions, there were also the British 49th and 52nd Scottish Divisions, the 1st Polish Armoured Division and the US 104th Division, plus the support units such as the 79th Arm div (The famous Hobart's Funnies) and the commandos of the 4th Special Service Brigade.

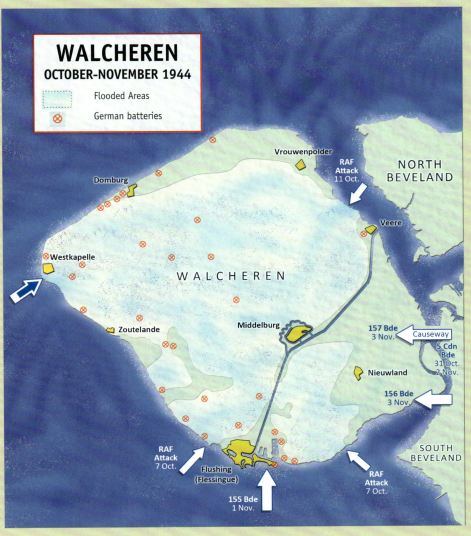

Liberty Roads, 1944-1945

fortress till defied Simonds; the Belgian dock worker had been waiting now for sixty days. Walcheren fell a week later on the 8th following an amphibious operation. A hundred minesweepers could not start clearing the waters, a task that would last twenty days before a first convoy of 19 Liberty Ships was able to sail up the Scheldt and berth at the port, 85 days after its liberation.

The responsibility of this delay can be fully blamed on Montgomery who, as early as 4 September, was not interested in clearing the Antwerp area and only focused on crossing the Rhine. He deliberately continued in this direction until 16 October, abandoning the Canadians to its fate. He used his position of being an untouchable subordinate to deliberately ignore the orders issued by SHAEF[2].

And yet, this delay could have been considerably longer:

• If, instead of systematically and uselessly counter attacking, sometimes armed just with the bayonet, the Germans had simply remained in a defensive posture within their successive defence lines. This was the reason why the 64. ID was defeated at Breskens despite outnumbering the Allies, holding very favourable terrain and several defence lines, or that Keg. Chill wore itself down by trying to push the 2nd Canadian Division back to its jumping off line. These offensive reflexes played into allied hands as they were able to batter the attackers under a hail of artillery and aircraft fire.

• If the Allies had not benefited from the progressive weakening of the Walcheren garrison that was initially given a full infantry division, the 70. ID, which was then reduced to, on the orders of Von Runstedt, four infantry battalions, two fortress, two engineer and the gunners of the Kriegsmarine batteries Ma. Art. Abt. 202 when the final attack went in.

• If the army had not been commanded by Lieutenant-General Guy Simonds, by far the best Canadian officer who replaced at the last moment General Crerar who had fallen ill on the eve of operations. Walcheren is a good example of Simonds' skill. The fortress was taken in a concentric attack whilst the Canadians of the 5th Inf Bde and the Scottish soldiers of the 157th Inf Bde undertook a diversionary attack, starting on 31 October, along the 1,200 m causeway that links Walcheren with the isthmus of Zuid Beveland. Two landings took place the following day, one in the south at Flessingue (Commando n°4 with Kieffer's French troops, 155th Br. Inf Bde),

the other in the west at Westkapelle (4th Special Service Brigade). At Westkapelle, Simonds had sent in heavy bombers beforehand in order to break the dykes and soften up the defences so that the Buffaloes could penetrate into the island and thus take the German batteries from the rear. The artillery support barges sacrificed themselves - 9 out of 27 were sunk - in order to cover the landing craft. The Germans were taken by surprise as they did not believe that the Allies would have the audacity to land at the foot of their batteries. Due to the flooding caused by the breaches in the dykes, they could no longer move around, contrary to the well-equipped attackers who had amphibious tracked vehicles. This meant that the Germans could only put up a disjointed defence on their strong points and in the towns before surrendering. Generally speaking, General Simonds put together an original plan of attack, trying to avoid frontal attacks and using all of the technical innovations at his disposal by Hobart's 79th Arm Div (Wasp flamethrower tanks, Buffalo amphibious assault vehicles, flail tanks, Churchill AVRE) and by placing the onus on combined actions as seen by the landings during Switchback and Vitality or, of course, the attack on Walcheren[3].

---

2. Officially, Montgomery was Eisenhower's subordinate, the supreme commander, but the latter had no power of coercion over him. He could not have him removed from his command as this was only possible if undertaken by the British Imperial General Staff, in reality by Churchill himself.

3. The clearing of the Scheldt has been covered by many publications, the most recent of which is by Terry Copp, *Cinderella Army*, University of Toronto Press, 2006, Whitaker, Denis & Shelagh, *Tug of war: the Allied victory that opened Antwerp*, Stoddart, 2002, Rawling Gerald, *Cinderella operations: the battle for Walcheren*, Cassel, 1980

Previous page, top.
Flessingue was the objective for N° 4 Commando which included in its ranks the French personnel led by Kieffer.
(RR)

Previous page, bottom.
Montgomery arrives. The obstinate assurance of the British field-marshal was his main quality and his worst flaw.
(NARA)

Right.
Montgomery and Patton shaking hands in 1943. It was in Sicily that a mutual dislike and contempt was born, something that would affect the entire 1944 campaign.
(CMH)

Below.
Despite its snow chains, this GMC has fallen victim to the ice and snow. The weather conditions were awful due to the torrential rains which fell as early as September, followed by a cold snap in November.
(Transportation Museum)

---

11. By mid-October, Hodges had stored enough gasoline for 6.5 days, whereas Patton only had enough for a day. A week later, Hodges stocks had risen to ten days, those of Patton remained the same until November.
12. In December 10% of wounded men were hospitalised for trench foot.

ing (the region of Nijmegen), but it cannot be justified now. The lack of supplies allocated to the 3rd and 9th Armies and the minimal support lent to the 1st Army can only be rectified by the opening of the port. Fifteen divisions are idle because this relatively modest operation is dragging on. The 21st Army Group must make the clearing of Antwerp its top priority and ensure that no time will be wasted from now on". For General Marshall, Ike had placed all of his eggs in one basket, a basket that was within range of the German V1 and V2 weapons. However, once the Scheldt was cleared and its channel swept of mines, nearly 6,000 tonnes were unloaded in three days. Two weeks later, lead by Colonel Doswell Gullatt, an engineer who had acquired a solid port experience before the war at Mobile and who had commanded the 5th Engineer at Omaha Beach, 85,000 tonnes of supplies were already sitting on the quaysides. By mid-December, Antwerp made up 48% of the tonnage landed in Europe; making 19,000 tonnes per day! By this date, the port problem was over.

WHEN WERE THE CRISES OVERCOME?

The improvement of the situation was progressive, unconventional and unequal from one army to another. The lack of gasoline was felt over a six-week period from the beginning of September to mid-October for the First Army and 12 weeks for the Third Army[11]. By mid-October, the army group received a daily quota of 5,900 tonnes of fuel (1.6 million gallons) with 800 tonnes transported by rail, 1,600 t by trucks directly from Cherbourg and 2,900 t from Coubert, the pipeline terminus. 600 t came from Ostend, a port that was shared with the British.

Maintenance was improved with the halt of the pursuit and a change in procedures. Thus, the opening of an engine repair workshop in mid-October near the 1st Army frontline allowed for the repairing of 800 engines in fifteen days. The lack of spare parts remained until January 1945 and was a considerable hindrance.

The rationing of ammunition introduced in mid-September was maintained for three months, up to the Ardennes counter-offensive. However, we can also add the obligation in August-September for the fighting men to eat only K rations that had insufficient calories and the lack of winter clothing, jackets and overshoes that continued up to January 1945, or the cigarette crisis in December. It could be said, therefore,

that the American army was handicapped by the logistical situation until mid-December 1944. ComZ did not erase the last traces of the excesses of the pursuit until the end of January 1945[12]. It is obvious now that during the course of the summer, the American logistical chain failed. Under radiant summer skies that were free of any Luftwaffe threat, thousands of GMC trucks had not been enough to supply the two American armies even though the latter only comprised of less than twenty large units. The ASF who knew how to keep armies in the field beyond the oceans had been incapable of covering the last few hundred kilometres over good French roads. Worst still, it had taken weeks and even months to set up an efficient supply chain. The price paid for this was very high. How can one explain what was perhaps not a fiasco, but at least a failure?

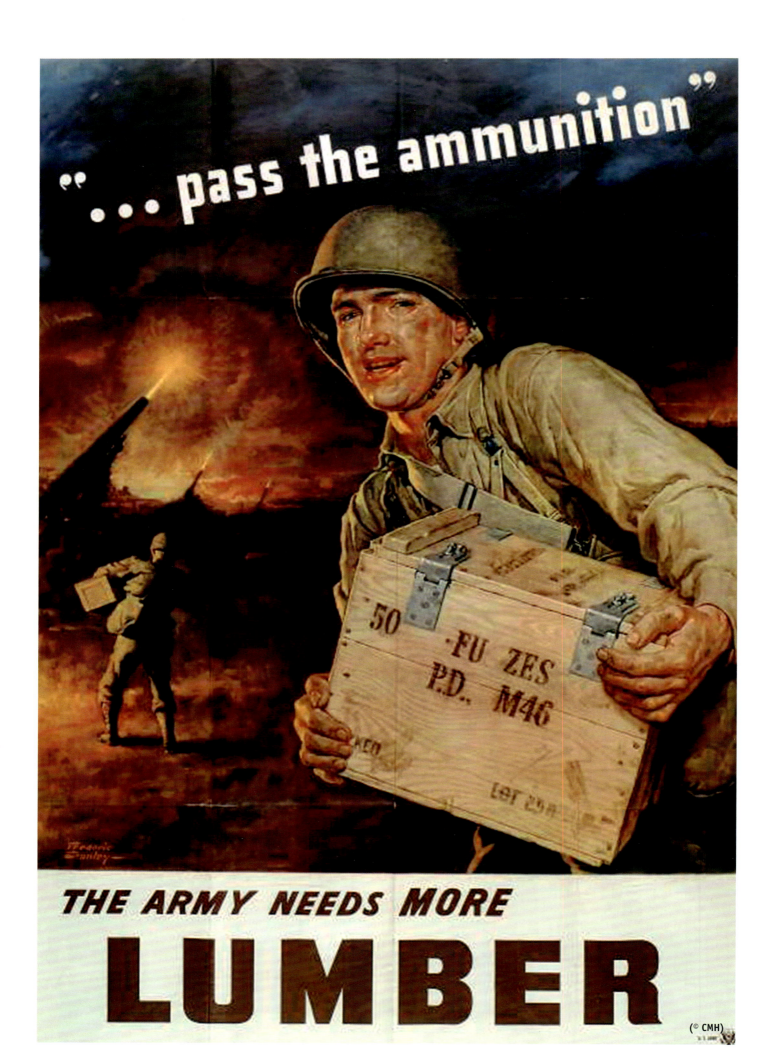

Liberty Roads, 1944-1945

FOURTH PART

The September rains turned the dumps into mud baths. (NARA)

THE INQUEST

By reading the first pages, the history of American logistics was one of a suspended fiasco. Having survived thanks to the genius and spirit of initiative shown by the men on the ground, the anarchy of the landing, the late capture of a devastated port and the sudden acceleration of operations at the end of July, the overburdened logistical chain finally broke and slowed down the Americans until the end of the year. What remains is to know why the American logistical chain suffered such a breakdown. There are many causes which are both connected to the situation at the time and structural. Above all, what was omnipresent was a doctrine which was ill-suited to mobile operations and which had not taken into consideration the projecting of motorized armies deep within enemy territory. The fumbling of 1944 was a consequence of the decisions taken in 1941.

CHAPTER 10

A GAMBLE THAT DID NOT PAY OFF

At the end of November, in the face of persistent difficulties, generals Eisenhower and Somervell, the latter commanding the Army Service Forces, decided that it would be of use to meet the chief of operations, Lt. Gen. LeRoy Lutes. On 5 December, Lutes arrived in Paris accompanied by five experts.

A Red Ball bivouac zone and 1st Army maintenance centre rapidly filled up with broken down vehicles. To gain time, the parts were replaced and not repaired. As spare parts were lacking, the mechanics took them from other vehicles. The Red Ball operation condemned the entire American logistical chain in the short term.
(13-Num 1084 & 1294, NARA © Archives départementales de la Manche)

He remained there until January and his report was so worrying that Somervell in person, in other words God, decided to see things for himself. General Lee, in charge of the quartermaster services within the entire theatre of operations, found himself in the spotlight and during his first meeting with Lutes, after having placed the blame on Montgomery the scapegoat (without Antwerp it was impossible to unload the ships indispensable for the American armies), he put forward two explanations. The first of these was that the stalling of his logistics was the inevitable consequence of the Red Ball Express. By concentrating all means on this route, the future had been deliberately sacrificed and had led to the breaking up of the supply chain. The gamble had not paid off, the war was not over and this meant that they had to accept the fact that it would take time to rebuild; much to Lee's regret. The second explanation was that Washington had remained deaf to the pleas of his services prior to D-Day concerning the lack of means given to the rear echelon services. This miserliness was now being paid for in the field. A gamble that had not paid off and a lack of means, these were the arguments put forward by Lee.

PIECEMEAL SOLUTIONS THAT BROKE UP THE LOGISTICAL CHAIN

Lee was positive in his affirmations, the piecemeal solutions used to supply the armies in August and September had quite simply led to the breaking up of the entire logistical chain.

Also its huge cost in precious fuel is enough to make one's head spin: one litre of gasoline was used in order to transport two and the Red Ball Express had worn out the means of transportation. These were requisitioned trucks that had already been worn down by a month of intensive operations. They were frequently overloaded and badly driven by inexperienced or negligent drivers, deprived of maintenance and forced to drive increasingly long distances. The tired drivers gained a reputation for being on edge. Some units ended up

with the less than flattering nickname of Truck Destroyer Battalions. Without maintenance, there was an increase in breakdowns: batteries destroyed as they were used without distilled water, overheated engines due to a lack of cooling liquid and engine oil, axles were not greased and broke, suspensions collapsed and vibrations loosened nuts and bolts. Having seen the lack of maintenance, ADSEC decided to group together all of a company's mechanics into one single crew tasked with maintaining all vehicles that arrived at the bivouac. However, they were soon overwhelmed by the 1,000 to 1,500 trucks that arrived every day. In the first fortnight of September, the Ordnance Corps undertook 2,500 heavy repairs, double the amount of the previous fortnight. On 28 September, 1,500 trucks were immobilised. Two hundred had been in accidents and the others had suffered mechanical breakdowns. Six hundred were deemed as being beyond repair. The lack of spare parts began to be felt as the bulk of these were in the Normandy dumps and this led to a daily immobilisation of a hundred trucks. The Americans, however, had two aces up their sleeve which prevented disaster. The first of these was the ease with which mechanics could work on a GMC. These trucks were of simple design and were easy to work on. The engine could be replaced in four hours, the transmission system in two. The second was the standardisation of the vehicle park which meant that parts could be taken from other vehicles. This foreshadowed the consumer society of today; the mechanics did not repair a part, they just replaced it.

The tyres posed a particular problem. In the space of a month 55,000 had been changed. Overloading, wear and tear and negligence caused punctures but two thirds were in fact caused by the sharp edges of food tins thrown onto the road by the truck crews. In one night, a company had 54 punctures. In October, a few trucks were equipped with a magnetic device to clean the roads. As they were still not equipped with a spare wheel, the drivers carried on with a punctured tyre which ended up destroying it. On 9 October, the risk of running out of tyres worried the Transportation Corps. They estimated a need for 180,000 in the next seventy-five days but there were only 2,000 tyres in the continental dumps and 46,956 in Great Britain. The 158th Ordnance Company, the only company equipped for the re-treading of tyres could not keep up with demand. The Army then turned towards Michelin who would go on to repair two hundred tyres per day. ComZ also offered to get tyres made but neither Michelin nor Goodrich had the necessary raw materials to respond immediately to this request. The Army Service Forces went through the American barracks with a fine tooth comb in the hope of finding forgotten stores of tyres. Finally, given the fact that they could not rely on a massive supply of tyres before January, ComZ was forced to change the mentality of the drivers. The latter were encouraged by the press and radio to change their way of driving in order to save tyres and the best drivers were rewarded with a week-end's furlough in Paris.

To make up for the wearing down of manpower, 68 extra companies were created by immobilising combatant units. The production line tasked with building the vehicles that arrived unassembled in Cherbourg got down to work and built 120 vehicles per day, both jeeps and trucks. French workers were taken on to fill gaps in man-

The evolution of the ComZ vehicle park

	July	Auguste	September	November	December
Number of Trucks Coys	94	146	115	?	200
Of which Heavy coys	?	?	?	20	50
Number of trucks	4512	8468	5520	?	10000
Rate of availability	?	?	70 %	60 %	75 %

power. However, these efforts did not allow to compensate for losses and in September, the MTB 'only' had 115 companies. To sum up, the Red Ball operation, as necessary as it had been, was a desperate solution that compromised the future. As early as the end of September, ComZ was struggling to carry on its mission. For the sole month of November, 15,000 trucks were destroyed across the entire theatre of operations. Mobilised by the Red Ball and faced with a frontline that was moving further forward, ComZ was unable to set up intermediate and advanced supply dumps, creating a veritable No Man's Land between Normandy and the front. As the storage, storekeeping and handling in the Normandy depots had gone down hill with the acceleration of operations and the first rains that had transformed the dumps into mud baths, any attempt throughout the weeks to rationalise became impossible and, although the volumes transported remained high, the quality had deteriorated. Moses, the G4 of the XII Army Group, complained that he was not receiving what his troops required. Indeed, ComZ replaced what it could not find in the dumps with other goods in order to make sure that space was not wasted during transportation. The absence of advanced dumps slowed down the speed of operations as each item lacking for the armies had to be found in the Normandy dumps rather than nearby, then loaded onto already overburdened convoys. Patton and Hodges lived in constant fear of having to postpone an operation. In these conditions, they

Above.
A tyre dump at Ecausseville on the site of the airship hanger. The Red Ball convoys would use up 55,000 tyres. By 15 September, there were 44,000 waiting to be repaired. Punctures were what drivers feared the most on roads littered with metal fragments.
(NARA)

Liberty Roads, 1944-1945

Two excellent series of photos which allow us to follow the return trips of the Dukw and LCT to the Liberty Ships. The LCT were particularly useful for landing the GMC, Dodge and half-tracks directly onto the causeways. For the crates, although the LCT could carry more than the Dukw, the latter could carry its load directly to the dumps. The going to and fro of the GMC AFKWX 353 and other vehicles soon wore away the beach, despite the placing of metal Sommerfeld mats. Some merchant ships came in so close to the shore that they found themselves beached at low tide. In September, the flow collapsed due to a lack of operational vehicles and the swell which frequently halted operations.
(13 Num 675, 1676, 1654, 3673, 1649, 1650, 13 824 NARA
© Archives départementales de la Manche, and others NARA)

Cherbourg dockers loading a GMC with 155 mm shells. Seven thousand Normandy workers were taken on to assist the Americans. Contrary to a widely held belief, relationships between the liberators and the liberated became fraught with conflict. The French thought that the Germans had paid better, whereas the Americans complained of thefts from the dumps, also finding French labor laws to restrictive and even fearing communist infiltration.
Région Basse Normandie/NARA, p011361)

Once the beaches were closed, Isigny returned to civilian life. Military traffic was now concentrated on the Cherbourg-Saint-Lô road.
(NARA)

believed that it was wiser to store whatever they could, just in case, and this made the situation worse by immobilising goods that could have been of use elsewhere. For ComZ, therefore, the slowing down of operations was an indispensable breathing space.

THE BLACK MARKET

The US Army of 1944 was also plagued by its inability to deal with the problem posed by the black market. Gasoline may have been priceless for the fighting men, but it certainly had one on the black market, 5,000 francs (100$) per jerrycan. Tinned food, cigarettes, tunics, boots and even trucks were also sought after by civilians.

The General Staff, therefore, placed great importance in the fight against the black market. The first in the list of suspects were the French workers on the quaysides and platforms. After four years of occupation and the continuing rationing, the discovery of American opulence was enough to tempt more than one Normandy inhabitant, and for some of them, they even saw an opportunity to make a fortune, with the reselling of American goods being a very lucrative activity. The Cherbourg newspapers mention several cases of people being sentenced for stealing from badly, or totally unguarded dumps and reveal the existence of black market networks that stretched as far as Paris. At the end of August, the *sous-préfet* of Calvados (a high ranking French state representative) called for the people he administered to be honest. In January 1945, the Normandy Base Section

1. St. Lamarche, *La Normandie américaine, op. cit.* pp.. 124-126.
2. Interview by Stéphane Lamarche in March 1999, op. cit., p. 126.
3. Interview by the author, 28 November 2012

fired all of the bakers working in the Cherbourg arsenal suspected of stealing and replaced them with "more reliable" POWs[1]. Bernard le Quéré, a young Frenchman who had worked for the Americans, remembered the huge scale of the black market and stated that trucks were abandoned by French drivers on the roadside, empty of course. Jean-Marie Aubin[2], a child at the time, who finished up at the end of the war dressed from head to toe *"made in America"* said that: *"the criminals also got rid of their GMC trucks by dumping them into the port of Le Havre"*[3]. However, the sheer amount of missing items leaves no doubt as to the fact that people within the US Army were involved and that in the great majority of cases, it was American military personnel who were at the origin of the trafficking, more often than not for alcohol.

Due to the casual racism of the time, the General Staff was not surprised that mostly black drivers or stevedores were implicated. The situation was particularly sensitive on the Red Ball Express. The officers and NCOs in charge of the convoys received very strict orders: no stops in towns, avoid as much as possible any contact with civilians, patrol along the convoy and watch out for any drivers walking away from their trucks during halts. The Military Police could only do so much. In the first days of the Red Ball Express, some drivers pretended to be broken down so that they could open up their stalls on the road side. Military Police that had been on surveillance duties for days on end and who had not been relieved were hungry and

In this spare parts depot at Ecausseville, the huge quantity of axles shows the wear and tear on vehicles.
(NARA)

easily persuaded to turn a blind eye in exchange for some rations. Some drivers claimed that their GMC had been stolen, whereas they had simply sold the vehicle along with its load. The General Staff then decided to make drivers financially responsible for their vehicle. The parks and dumps were guarded but as a veteran remembers, *"the dumps had no up to date inventory. We could go in and load what we wanted without anyone coming to check us. The Army had no trace of what the trucks had carried.*[4]*"* During the winter, the postal services noticed a large increase in the amount of money that was being sent home by soldiers, some of which was certainly the result of black market activity. 19,000 soldiers had deserted and the police suspected them of living off the proceeds of the black market in military equipment, something that was mentioned in *Yank* magazine: *"The most lucrative profits are being made from trafficking gas and not rations. French gangsters are at large in Paris, in the bars, cafes and hotels, the bordellos of Montmartre or Montparnasse, and are doing business with deserters who are supplying them with large quantities."* The only document which allows us to see the scale of the trafficking is a report made by the Normandy Base Section at the end of November 1944 and which states that the pillaging of rail and road convoys led to a 25% loss of all materiel destined for use by combatant units, making up the sum of 20,000 lost tonnes[5]! Such an amount leaves us scratching our heads, especially if we take into account the fact that civilians were not interested in ammunition. Without more precise information we can only speculate on the reliability of such a number by, for example, speculating that a decimal error was made (2.5%) or that the writer of the report was only talking about certain types of supplies such as cigarettes. It is true that the black market had led to much exaggeration, such as the number of 2,000 trucks stolen in the Paris region, or the 66 million packets of cigarettes that disappeared out of the 77 million that were landed in September[6].

AN EXTRAVAGANT ARMY

For Lee, however, the main cause of the slowing down in September 1944 was not to be found within his own team, but rather with its very negligent customers. Lee released a Quartermaster Corps report proving that ComZ had done its job.

91% of the allocations and 58% of the Army's requirements had been met during the pursuit. Better still, concerning gasoline, 89% of the required amounts had been delivered. If Hodges men had felt that they had been lacking supplies it was not ComZ's fault, but due rather to their own negligence.

But does this allow us, based on Lee's affirmations, to write that a culture of wastage had spread throughout the US Army? Some examples suggest that this may have been the case. On 28 August at Braine, the 486th Anti-aircraft Artillery Battalion brilliantly managed to halt a rail convoy of 36 rail cars, some of which were carrying Tiger tanks, but their determination in destroying the locomotive with their 37 mm guns deprived the Army of a precious locomotive. The tank crews did the same in order to boost their statistics as the destruction of trains counted for the awarding of medals. Another type of waste is mentioned by Don Hale, an observer with the 358th Field Artillery Regiment (3rd Army) who remembers that, in Septem-

SUPPLIES TO THE 1ST ARMY FROM 6 TO 12 SEPTEMBER 1944 ACCORDING TO A QUARTERMASTER CORPS REPORT			
	Estimation of requirements 31 August tons per day	Allocation by ComZ tons per day	Volumes received by the 1st Army tons per day
Ration	1150	993	553
Gasoline and oil	2200	2028	1954
Munitions	1100	64	413
Equipment/ spare parts for vehicles	150	0	49
Engineers' supplies	300	128	24
Engineers' supplies	525	286	168
Chemical warfare supplies	10	0	0
Medical supplies	30	0	0
Miscellaneous supplies	75	0	48
Total	5540	3500	3209
Source: William F. Ross, Charles F. Romanus, The Quartermaster Corps, CMH, 1965, vol. 4, p. 456.			

ber," *we received the order to use up all of our 105 mm shells between two and three o'clock in the morning so that the GMC loaded with shells would be available to go and find gas for the tanks that had to press on forward. Our observation group had to invent new targets every day.*[7]*"*

At a higher level, it was only on 31 August that the 1st Army corps commanders ordered the halting of the anti-aircraft, artillery and engineer units. The movement of these superfluous units over five days had wasted a lot of fuel and deprived the Army of precious means of transportation (1,300 trucks) that could have been better used elsewhere. The luxurious motorisation of American divisions had thus turned round and bitten them. A 6th Arm. Div. report dated 26 August shows that many so-called utility vehicles were burning up fuel that would have been more precious in the fuel tanks of armoured vehicles and trucks. *"We have too many road leeches in our division"*.

This wastage was paid for the following month. Generally speaking, the ASF reproached the combatants for not having managed their stocks, for exclaiming that they did not have enough when stocks began to diminish when ComZ was trying to put into place a hand-to-mouth supply flow. This discrepancy was at the origin of many misunderstandings. Indeed, curiously, in November when all of the generals insisted that there was a constant lack of supplies, stating that only 62% of the planned for supplies were arriving, the armies managed to reconstitute their stocks.

It is clear, therefore, that they exaggerated their requirements and adopted a martyr-like posture. These exaggerations can be firstly explained by a bureaucratic reflex on the part of the G-4 of each army that had always tried to maintain its theoretical stocks. They then shouted out that there was a dramatic lack of supplies, not when these were lacking at the frontline, but as soon as their reserves diminished. This bureaucratisation also explains why shaving kits or handkerchiefs are found in the priority requests. We can also no doubt see in this the fear of a real lack of supplies which led the G-4s to anticipate an eventual ComZ breakdown. As the latter arrogantly overestimated its supply capacities, it was not surprising that the armies expected it to accomplish the impossible. Finally, the rationing system led to a veritable competition between the armies which prof-

Above, left.
An American soldier seeking to improve his rations buys carrots from a Normandy peasant. He is paying with a 50-Franc *"flag money"* bill, a currency that was put into place by the Allied Military Government of Occupied Territories (AMGOT).
(NARA)

Above, centre and Right.
Civilians, some working unloading a barge in a port, others in the countryside on a packaging chain. They are sorting ammunition to make individual packs. Note the omnipresence of conveyor belts which help carry out the work, and the quayside activity in the background.
(© Coriello, Bibliothèque municipale de Cherbourg)

---
4. Interview by David P Colley, *op. cit.*, p. 155.
5. St. Lamarche, *op. cit.*, p. 127
6. These figures were put forward respectively by Newsweek of 8 January 1945 and Yank of 4 May 1945
7. Interview by R Goralski & RW Freeburg, *Oil and War*, Morrow, 1987, p. 260.

The worsening weather conditions had a diverse effect on the logistical chain. Some secondary roads became muddy tracks.
(13-Num 1494, NARA © Archives départementales de la Manche)

EVOLUTION OF STOCKS IN THE FORWARD DUMPS		
	Stocks of the XII AG	Stocks of the ADSEC
28 October	155 000 t	Almost nil
5 November	180 000 t	100 000 t
15 December	222 000 t	294 000 t

ited the priority First Army, with the latter continuing to demand extra supplies when its neighbouring armies were not even receiving essentials. Concerning operations, the same G-4 reports worried the generals and dissuaded them from engaging in operations. To sum up, General Moses, the quartermaster commander within the 12th Army Group appears to have been unsuccessful in moving from opulent logistics to an emergency hand-to-mouth supply flow.

Even at the top of the hierarchy, the weeks of August were ones of euphoria and blinkered vision[8]. The collapse of the German armies, the ease and rapidity of the advance led Patton and Bradley to get carried away. They ended up becoming convinced that it only required an objective to be set in order for it to be attained. All of these weeks were marked by the desire to play their own personal hand and negligence (dispersion of forces, not taking the Wehrmacht seriously which they allowed to escape several times at Falaise, the Seine, Tournai or Mons, as if it no longer constituted a threat[9]).

Why did these generals worry over austere logistical constraints? The fact remains that whilst the ADSEC services and the British Army were reactive and immediately undertook radical measures, the officers of the Third and First Army continued to carry out a *"rich man's"* campaign.

A MUDDLED STRATEGY

Lee also pointed the finger at Eisenhower's hesitant strategy. After having given priority to the north front rather than the east, Ike changed his opinion on 2 September and let Patton off the leash again. His choices may have been pertinent in July and August, but those of September were hesitant. However, what Lee forgot to mention, no doubt for the good reason that he did not know, was that Eisenhower's u-turn can be explained for political as well as logistical reasons. Politically, Eisenhower was under pressure from the Americans who did not want their victory to be snatched from them by Monty. But, at the beginning of September, the 2nd Br. Army after having lagged behind, advanced further than the 1st US Army and entered Belgium. The speed of its advance meant that Monty was right, something which annoyed the Americans who were convinced that they were being sacrificed for the British. Logistically, the SHAEF G-4, Colonel Whipple, who as we know was very cautious, also began to worry Eisenhower. At the same time that Monty was talking of a powerful and decisive blow using a 40 division fist, punching through as far as Berlin with a left hook, Whipple began instead to evoke rather a slight stab with a penknife. Far from grouping together forty divisions, only three British corps and two American (18 divisions) would be able to reach the Rhine and cross it. With distances increasing, only three would then be able to carry on to Berlin and it would require the halting of a British corps near Bremen and an American corps near Magdeburg and finally, from the original forty divisions, the number engaged shrank to ten[10]. Sending a handful of divisions, mainly British, under the command of a general who he did not have confidence in, to win a war a thousand kilometres away from their support base made Eisenhower's blood run cold. This was a gamble that he was not willing to take. The days of September were, therefore, marked by Eisenhower's dithering, made worse by Bradley and Patton: 2 September, return to a wide front policy, 12 September, Patton was sacrificed again for the north front, 15 September authorisation given to Patton to continue his offensive. This period of trial and error at the highest level could only slow down the pursuit and hinder the task of the quartermaster services. In his exercise in self-justification, General Lee finally found another reason, Washington had been far too stingy.

THE MIRACLE OF THE WEHRMACHT

Concerning Lee, it is therefore unfair to throw the responsibility of the halting of the pursuit on his services. He did not do wrong considering the fact that the reasons are multiple, beginning with the role played by the Germans. Indeed, during the course of the autumn, the Wehrmacht managed a veritable miracle by re-establishing a coherent frontline. The Third Reich scraped the bottom of the barrel: the ethnic Germans of eastern Europe, civil defense units, boys of 17, older men aged 54. In all, 500,000 extra men were found. The 462. ID tasked with defending Metz thus incorporated a hotch-potch of personnel making a total of 14,000 (cadets from the Wiesbaden school, Waffen SS officer cadets and the Metz signals school, elements of the 1010th Luftwaffe security battal-

---

8. Martin Blumenson paints quite a picture in *La bataille des généraux*, Ed. Charles Corlet, 1995, pp.. 245-256.
This assault has been described, by an expert is such matter, as "the blind leading the blind where an impartial observer can hardly imagine that such a large attack could be launched with such little preparation, with such a lack of knowledge as to the state of the enemy, the terrain and defenses, driving with the help of straight-forward road maps. This is the worst aspect of the American genius of improvisation. Anthony Kemp, *Metz 1944*, Heimdal, 2003, p. 75.
10. Russel Weighley, *Eisenhower's Lieutenants*, Indiana university press, 1981, p. 272 & 281-282.

THE STATISTICAL MIX-UP

Lee denied having failed by producing flattering statistics for his department. It is, however, very difficult today to find reliable data and which also tallies. The archives are incomplete, documents have been lost or were not written. They are also contradictory. There is often a difference between the tonnage delivered by ComZ and the tonnage declared as having been received by the armies (perhaps because some of the supplies were delivered directly to the combatant units without their passing via army depot tasked with general storekeeping. For example, what of the volumes of supplies that the armies went to find in Normandy with their own transportation? In other words, we cannot know exactly what the armies received. We know, however, that there is a clear gap of between 20 and 40% between the armies and ComZ.

Finally, these figures only concern the transport that left the Normandy dumps for the army dumps. It would be useful to make an inventory of the volumes received by each fighting unit at the end of the chain.

	27 August to 2 September		3 to 9 September		10 to 16 September	
	1st Army	3rd Army	1st Army	3rd Army	1st Army	3rd Army
Tonnage requested by the army (including gasoline) (t/day)	5500 (2200)	6000 (1411)	6202 (2200)	6665 (2100)	6500 (+ de 2200)	6800 (+ de 2200)
Minimal allocation attributed by the 12th Army Group (t/day)	5000	2000	3500	3500	5000	3500
Tonnage declared by ADSEC (t/day)	3700	?	4500	2620	5700	3700
Tonnage delivered by aircraft (t/day)	268		502		460	
Tonnage declared received by the army (including gasoline) (t/day)	2225 (1759)	? (644)	3700 (1738)	? (1362)	? (1531)	? (1380)

Sources: 1st US Army G4 Periodic reports, 3rd US Army G4 Periodic Reports, ADSEC operations History, CATOR weekly reports, SHAEF

ion and the Luftwaffe 9. Flak-Division). These inexperienced and poorly-armed soldiers were cut to pieces in the fields of the Beauce and Champagne regions, but they found an area better suited for defense, the marshes of Peel and Holland, the Hürtgen forest and the urban sector around Aachen, and the ywere protected by the fortifications of the Westwall and the Lorraine forts. They also profited from the nomination, at the head of Heeresgruppe B, of Feld-Marshal Model, one of the best German tacticians and who was known as the *'Reich Fireman'* after having turned around desperate situations in the east. This miracle was also made possible by the priority given by Hitler to the Western Front. Several hastily formed Panzerbrigaden and two Panzer-Grenadier Divisionen brought back from Italy thus faced Patton in the Lorraine as early as September. 1,000 panzers were sent to the west in September, 2,229 in November and December, whereas only a thousand were sent to the east. These tanks allowed the Panzerwaffe to get back on its feet after having escaped from numerous allied attempts to encircle it. The German generals had also managed to pull back large amounts of men in impossible conditions: 60% of the strength of Armee-Gruppe G, harried by the Resistance, escaped from the pincer movement made by Patton's armies and those of moving up the Rhone. General Van Zangen, commanding the 15. Armee, managed the exploit of getting 85,000 men, 600 artillery pieces and 600 vehicles over the Scheldt. These veterans, often exhausted and under-equipped, would play a decisive role by integrating and teaching new recruits. The Wehrmacht had become a specialist in amalgamated units. Hitler had at last made the right choice by defending to the utmost each port Festung and depriving the Allies of the precious ports.

At the beginning of September, there was the combination of two things which together, explain the halting of the pursuit. On one side the Allies were stalling. Their manpower was decreasing as they immobilized divisions in order to allow supplies to continue to flow to others (Montgomery could only therefore engage six divisions). Patton was slowed down. The other explanation comes from the fact that the German reinforcements were beginning to arrive and set themselves up along good defensive positions.

Were the few days lost by Patton due to a lack of fuel decisive and delay the end of the war? It is impossible to say with any certitude. Perhaps Metz could have been liberated by a rapid thrust when we look at the desperate reports written by General von Knobelsdorf describing the chaos of early September. The civilian authorities and German citizens fled the city. *"Panic is spread"* and affected the military bases. Stores of munitions and clothing were burnt without any orders being given to do so. However, after Metz, Patton's tanks, suffering from a lack of maintenance, would have come up against the Sarre area of the Westwall. To advance further, Patton would not only have needed several thousand liters of gasoline but also good maintenance, ammunition and extra units as well as experience in attacking fortified positions. What is certain is that it was not only logistics which decided the fate of the battle.

But the fact that ComZ is not solely responsible does not exonerate it in the eyes of Lutes due to its multiple dysfunctions which he saw with his own eyes. This is why, in his self-justification, General Lee had to find someone else to blame, and this fell on Washington which had been much too miserly.

Paris required daily supplies of 1,500 to 2,400 tonnes. After having brought in emergency supplies by plane, the Americans delegated this task to the French authorities. We can see here, the French lieutenants Lucien Briant and Jean Lamy, checking their orders given to them by Lt. Col. Joseph Fleischer. The blackboard indicates the destination of each convoy, where they are to unload, the numbers of the lead vehicles, the men in charge and the bivouac zones. The tent in the background houses the French headquarters staff. Equipped with Dodge Canada D15 General Service vans given by the British Army, the convoys headed for Paris were not allowed to drive on the Red Ball Highway and could only use secondary roads. These trucks with a load capacity of 750 kg were ill-suited for troop supply duties. Paris did not, therefore, take away vital military resources as ComZ stated.
(13-Num 1974, 1977 & 1978, NARA © Archives départementales de la Manche)

Liberty Roads, 1944-1945

CHAPTER 11
A LACK OF HEAVY TRUCKS

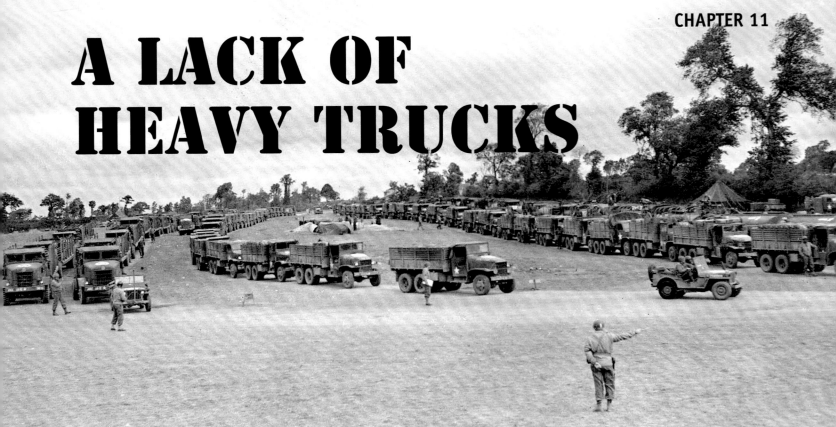

Lee lamented the lack of means attributed by Washington, a delicate affair when one was dealing with the *missi-dominici* of the Army Service Forces, of whom one of the tasks was the supplying of materiel. So, what means exactly did he have at his disposal? It was mostly Light Truck Companies that drove along Red Ball Express Highway. A Light Company comprised of 48 GMC 2½-ton trucks of which 40 were operational and 8 in maintenance.

Above.
In the vicinity of Valognes, a Red Ball prepares to move off. These 40 GMC carry two to three hundred tonnes, an amount which is insufficient for the daily supply needs of a division. On the left, a column of International M425 trailers with a double load capacity wait to set off. They gradually replaced the small GMC as they became more widely available.
(13-Num 1129 NARA © Archives départementales de la Manche)

Next page, below.
An International 4x2 5T M425 tractor belonging to the 3888th QM Co in the process of being loaded directly from a Liberty Ship. Hurriedly designed in 1943, they only became available in Europe in the autumn of 1944. This was too late for the pursuit phase, but in time for the German campaign whey they played a decisive role.
(© Coriello, Bibliothèque municipale de Cherbourg/US NARA)

---

1. Two decks were designed for the AFKWX, one 15 ft (4.6 m), the other 17 ft (5.2 m) compared to the 12 ft (3.7 m) of the standard GMC.
2. There were approximately two trailers per vehicle.

As the mechanics were soon overwhelmed with work, the end of July saw each company strengthened with an additional ten trucks taken from stores in Britain. The company was standardised around a single model of vehicle, the GMC with standard platform (6X6 CCKW 353), or the advanced cabin version (6X6 AFKWX 353) that were popular as they could carry bulkier loads[1], but these were limited to twenty companies. The other truck was the GMC 750-gallon tanker (5 companies). They also towed the Ben Hur 1-Ton (G-518) trailer. Also present were trucks due for use in Burma but which were sent instead to Europe to make up for the lack of tractors, thus, six companies were equipped with Chevrolet G-4113 and G-7113 4X4 1 ½-ton tractors with Stake & Platform 3 ½-ton semi-trailers and two with the Studebaker US6 6X4 2 ½-ton which carried without any problem almost ten tonnes in the G-596 7-Ton semi-trailers which in fact made them Heavy Companies.

The Heavy Companies were a lot less common and were equipped with 48 4X4 Autocar U-7144T, Federal 94X43 or 4X2 IHC M425/426. They pulled all of the semi-trailers in use: the common 6 Ton and 7 Ton, but also the 5 Ton refrigerator, the 2,000 gallon tanker, or (with the exception of the M425) the lower 25 to 40 foot long type C2 initially designed to transport aircraft but which were used to carry very bulky loads. The Americans innovated fantastically by bringing in these articulated vehicles. The idea was born in 1898 and stemmed from the imagination of Alexander Winton. They became popular in the United States in the nineteen-twenties but were not used militarily in Europe. They offered huge advantages: manufacture could be decoupled between a company specialised in tractors and others in semi-trailers that demanded no particular skill. The latter could also be made in all shapes and sizes, from a straightforward dumpster to a photographic laboratory, or a refrigerated unit. Finally, *last but not least*, the tractors could also change their empty trailer for a full one within minutes[2]. Two M2 companies were of precious help. The M2 combined a monstrous tractor, the Diamond T model 980/981 M 19, and a M9 tank-transporter trailer. This was rapidly modified in order to take 16.5 tonnes of various supplies, 36 tonnes of ammunition, or 500 jerrycans. The entire vehicle was not far off 60 tonnes, something that posed a problem crossing bridges and which wore out road surfaces, but it easily did the job of ten GMC trucks.

THE GMC, A STOP-GAP SOLUTION

The MTB offices quite rightly saw the GMC as being a stop-gap solution. The Jimmy was a remarkable and easy to make vehicle, but it was one that was designed for tactical use near the frontline. Designed to last 30,000 km, it struggled in its role as a strategic mule. Even when overloaded, it could only carry half the tonnage of a tractor. Twice as many vehicles were on the road whilst other waited for hours to be unloaded or loaded. The multiplication of vehicles increased the workload of mechanics, especially as the Red Ball had been put together quickly in the hope of ending the war and had not been thought through as a long term mission. Maintenance, therefore, had been deliberately neglected. At the end of November, 15,000 trucks were immobilised.

This situation, however, had been foreseen by the Transportation Corps a year previously. When he took over command of the Motor Transport division (TC), General Ross had asked for an initial report on the requirements for Overlord. For routine operations at D +90 comprising of rotations between the general supply dumps and the advanced dumps, the report came to the conclusion that it would require no less than the equivalent of 240 Light Companies, that is 11,520 GMC. For the G4 at SHAEF, this amount was exaggerated and he brought it down to 160 companies, a number that would remain unchanged whereas the amount of fighting men increased with each passing week.

Ross tried to skirt around the problem by asking for more heavy trucks. What had been learned from operations undertaken in North Africa six months earlier had clearly revealed the need for heavy trucks in order to deal with bulky loads and to ensure long distance road supplies. As early as August 1943, he sent a first report to Washington requesting that 2/3 of the 160 companies that were going to be allocated

to him should be Heavy Companies with the following mix of vehicles[3]:
- 59 equipped with the 4/5 ton range of tractors with lowered type C2 - 25 foot semi-trailers capable of carrying 12.5 tonnes, and 5-tonne refrigerators.
- 9 equivalent but towing 2,000 gallon tankers
- 36 equipped with the advanced cabin GMC capable of carrying a bulkier load than the standard GMC, even if it was just the straightforward 2.5 t.
- 27 equipped with the 750 gallon tanker GMC.
- 2 equipped with the 45 tonne Diamond T M19 tank transporter.

At first, Washington turned a deaf ear to these requests before giving in to them in December 1943, but given the time needed to speed up production, only 66 of the 3,360 hoped for tractors were delivered in time. As we have seen, as a replacement the War Department found other tractors elsewhere, the Chevrolet 1.5 t, Studebaker 6X2 t and tractors that were 4.5 t, but which towed smaller 7 tonne (G-596) trailers made for Burma. Finally, instead of the 11,520 vehicles being large load carriers, the Transportation Corps had to made do with 7,600 trucks, the majority of which were the small 2.5 tonne GMC designed for tactical use and which wore themselves out in an exhausting strategic task that was too much for them. How is it that the largest automobile industry in the world came to find itself with such a shortfall? The answer is simple... because the powers that be left it too late to order them; the responsibility is shared between Roosevelt and the military.

WHY SO FEW HEAVY TRUCKS?

The public announcement of the Victory Program on 6 January 1942 paradoxically affected the war effort in general and the logistical services in particular. Whereas the industrial mobilisation was already well under way as it had begun in 1939, Roosevelt took the initiative of making a declaration that increased all of the projected production rates of planes, tanks, anti-aircraft guns, freight tonnage and so on. In this way, Roosevelt wanted to mobilise all of the population and send a message of hope to his allies. However, his declaration, which went beyond what had been planned by the War Production Board, not only meant that everything had to be recalculated, which would slow down the mobilisation, but set in stone some of the production targets (planes, tanks)[4]. Savings would have to be made elsewhere therefore, on what Roosevelt termed as "accessory": the rear echelon equipment. It became impossible to build a balanced army. On 13 October 1942, the WPB announced to Somervell that half of the "accessory" orders would have to be annulled or postponed. Utility vehicles and their spare parts slipped to the bottom of the list of priorities[5]. This measure did not frighten anyone as, in the General Staff meetings chaired by George Marshall, the Army Ground Force was also hypnotised by the number of divisions, tanks and guns.

The US Army also turned away from heavy trucks because the 1939 doctrine stated again that rail was the only means of transport capable of dealing with the volumes necessary for an army on campaign. The truck would only be used to link the forward dumps at the end of the rail heads with the combatant units. Operating in the combat zone, it had to be taken into account that the road network would be very bad[6] and that the forward dumps set up in fields would turn into muddy bogs. In these conditions, using heavy trucks would be risky and lead to a huge amount of road maintenance for the engineers. It would also result in a diversification of the vehicle park and, therefore, the multiplication of spare parts; the nightmare of mechanics and logistics experts. To top this off, it would mean making the distinction between tactical Trucks Companies and those tasked with using roads.

The disadvantages outweighed the advantages and it was more sensible finally to place the onus on all-terrain trucks that were capable of carrying out a multitude of tasks and which were a lot more operationally flexible, even if at the same dead weight, they carried less, used more gas, and were more expensive and longer to make than a road truck[7]. As big budget cuts had to me made in order to adhere to the Victory Program, the Ordnance Corps suggested concentrating all of the effort on the multi-task 2 ½ ton Light-Heavy rather than heavier vehicles. This truck, which represented 7% of production in 1939, would reach 50% in 1944. The "deuce & a halfs" were officially promoted to the role of being of the US Army's workhorse. In the meetings, it was only the experts of the former Quartermaster Technical Committee who still defended the idea of a "strategic vehicle" heavy road truck, but these were voices in the wilderness.

It was not until the beginning of operations in North Africa and the opening of the road linking Burma and China that it became obvious that Heavy-Heavy vehicles were needed (vehicles with more than a 2.5 ton load capacity). In 1943, the Ordnance Corps validated a monthly production increase of 600 to 6,000 heavy transport vehicles. However, to achieve this, it required the input of 750 million dollars of investment, taking on 200,000 new workers and, in terms of raw materials, taking the equivalent of what was required for 14,000 medium tanks. Indeed, although many companies (Mack, Autocar, White, Federal, Corbitt, International, Ward LaFrance) had the skills necessary to make heavy vehicles, they filled an industrial niche market. Legal restrictions and weight limits for crossing bridges had not encouraged the big vehicle manufacturers. With a dispersed industry, the production lines were not suited to mass production. They had been immediately overwhelmed with orders for specialised engineers' vehicles and tank recovery vehicles for the armoured units. Due to the initial choice in placing the onus on lighter trucks, the administration neglected these smaller manufacturers. Getting mass production going now required a massive effort and the time lost would never be made up.

Below.
In this workshop set up near Isigny, a platform is placed on a GMC in the process of being assembled. A GMC has 9,135 parts and required 260 hours of manpower for the assembly process. An assembly line meant that 100 vehicles per day could be made.
(13- Num 4551, NARA © Archives départementales de la Manche)

3. Joseph Bykovsky & Harold Larson, The *Transportation Corps, Operations Overseas*, CMH, 1957, p. 240.
4. Jim Lacey, *Keep From All Thoughtful Men: How U.S. Economists Won World War II*, Naval Institute Press, 2011, p. 94.
5. Jim Lacey, op. cit, p. 112.
6. It might come as a surprise that the Americans under-estimated the quality of the western European road network. However, it ought to be remembered that at the beginning of the war, they only had, on one hand, the experience of the Great War where the road network near the frontline had simply disappeared, and on the other hand they did not plan only according to the situation in western Europe as they were involved in a world war in the Mediterranean, Asia, and in the Pacific where the road network hardly existed.
7. The construction of an all-terrain vehicle came up against the bottleneck of special components such as the velocity joints which required complex machining that only Bendix Products Division and the Gear Grinding Machine Company mastered. They needed transfer cases full of clutch cogs and rear drive axles made only by Timken-Detroit and Fuller. For the velocity joints alone, it was not until 1942 that Ford, Dodge and Chevrolet developed their own by negotiating, under the impetus of the state, the patents belonging to their competitors, thus multiplying production one-hundred fold. As for Timken, they extended their factory, but it was not until several months that they were able to train qualified personnel, something which led to delays in the delivery of the first GMC trucks.

RAIL: WORSE THAN THE ROAD

Although the railway was the favorite mode of transport for the army, it is obvious that the situation in 1944 was awful. The Anglo-American requirements for operations between the Seine and Loire had been estimated at 2,724 2-8-0 locomotives (of which 1,800 were for the US Army) and 680 0-6-0 locomotives (470 for the US Army) as well as 57,000 rail cars, leaving a deficit of almost 50%. Also, the British government refused to hand back the 450 locomotives lent by the Transportation Corps. General Ross' complaints to the ASF were left unanswered for the straightforward reason that the locomotive factories were producing tanks as a priority. Somervell advised Ross to turn towards the British ally and captured trains. However, the captured trains in August only numbered 50, a drop in the ocean. As for the British, they only progressively freed up trains in exchange for tramp ships and by the end of November not a single locomotive had been handed back! Finally, at the end of the year, only 1,500 locomotives had been brought over to the continent and 800 put back into service by the Franco-American workshops. The Engineers did their best to repair the lines, but the means at their disposal remained meagre. When this is seen in light of the Germans on the eve of Barbarossa in 1941, where the Wehrmacht had one train for 156 soldiers, the US Army only had one for 869 men. The rapid advance had also doubled the workload of the 2nd Military Railway Service as instead of being limited to Normandy and Brittany, its network covered half of northern-France and a large part of Belgium. The situation concerning rail cars was less critical as, although only a third (20,000) had been transferred to the continent by the end of November, almost 200,000 had been found and put into use in Europe.

Above, below and next page.
The US Army hoped to have the time to rebuild the railroad network. If it had had trains at its disposal! Despite the best efforts of the engineers in making the Mielles basin fit for purpose and to allow for unloading directly from the LST (above) or the loan of British train-ferries (below, right), they never managed to fulfill all of the needs.
(NARA)

The production of Heavy-Heavies in 1943-1945, a laborious build-up lasting 18 months

Month	1943	1944	1945 (01-08)
Total	38 314	50 862	32 004
January	2 183	2 788	4 918
February	2 221	2 976	4 189
March	2 927	3 038	5 245
April	3 505	3 404	4 783
May	2 719	4 002	4 574
June	3 974	3 800	4 222
July	3 750	3 980	2 538
August	3 592	4 518	1 545
September	3 154	4 888	
October	2 856	5 566	
November	3 260	5 555	
December	4 353	6 347	

(source: Summary Report of Acceptances Tank-Automotive Matériel 1940-45, by OCO-D, pp. III-IV OHF)

The War Production Board placed the manufacturing of heavy trucks as top-priority. The Ordnance Industry Integration Committee for Heavy Trucks was created in March 1943 in order to ease cooperation. The manufacturers, who in fact more re-assembled parts (apart from Mack), were dependent on their sub-contractors of whom there were not enough. More were required. A company which specialised in armoured plating, Standard Steel Spring, had to, for example, convert itself into a manufacturer of drive axles. However, this reorganisation took a year to accomplish and was too late for the summer of 1944. The lack of powerful engines was such that General Christmas suggested fitting two or three lighter engines together. At the end of the year, the Ordnance Corps remained somewhat pessimistic, *"the lack of manpower and parts (drive axles, gear boxes, engines) make it impossible as things stand to follow the production timetable[8]"*, there was even the risk of seeing production drop in 1944.

This was in fact true as only 2,788 heavy trucks left the factories in January 1944 compared to 4,353 in December 1943. February and March were hardly better. In June, the War Production Board authorised the use of special directives that had been put into place before in order to speed up the manufacturing of invasion barges and heavy artillery. These directives authorised manufacturers to ask for supplies directly from the War Production Board. This was not, however, a miracle solution and the production figures only increased as each factory finished its conversion process. An officer said that, *"you can't modify production like turning a tap"*. In any case, the fact remained that only 50,000 heavy trucks were made in 1944 instead of the planned for 67,000.

The situation was made worse by the wish of some of the military to only use all-terrain vehicles in overseas theatres. They made up two-thirds of the total production. The 50,000 rear-wheel drive heavy trucks were for the most part issued to other arms such as the Marine Corps or allied nations. There were, however, two exceptions. The first of these was the long series of 6X4 Mack NR (NR1 to NR16) from the ten-ton load capacity range developed in 1940 for the British as tank transporters and which were then adopted by the US Army for long distance rear echelon transport (16,500 were made). However, none were issued to the Transportation Corps before the winter of 1944 when 14 companies of NR9 (and its twin the White 1064 of which 2,500 were made) landed at Marseille. The second dates from 1943 when, using whatever it could, the Ordnance resigned itself to developing a 4x2 tractor for the Transportation Corps, the M425 with its 16-foot trailer and 7-tonne load capacity, replaced in 1944 by the M426 capable of pulling the 25-foot trailer. In total, 15,618 trucks left the factories, of which a mere few hundred joined the European western front. The late start to production of heavy trucks and the choice

Trucks	Total	1939-40	1941	1942	1943	1944	1945
Total	3 200 436	46 384	232 545	791 432	983 359	738 643	408 073
Light (ton and less)	988 167	8058	74 514	273 997	256 488	245 201	129 909
Medium (1 ½ ton)	428 196	14 153	37 139	140 375	133 523	80 888	22 118
Light Heavy (2 ½ ton)	812 262	9589	62 123	182 049	193 177	220 012	145 312
Heavy-Heavy (+2 ½ ton)	153 686	804	9838	23 314	38 314	50 862	30 554
Semi-trailers	59 731	236	1603	8661	9436	26 765	13 030
Trailers	499 827	6494	33 311	81 881	241 450	79 188	57 503
Tractors[1]	34 295	993	1675	7433	12 674	8106	3414
Other vehicles	224 272	6057	12 342	73 722	98 297	27 621	6233

1. Except for the 82,099 commercial tractors used by the Corps of Engineers
(Sources: Whiting, Statistics and Summary Report of Acceptation Tank Automotive Matériel 1940-45, by OCO-D, copy in OHF)

8. Memo, Maj Gen Thomas J. Hayes, OCO, for CG, ASF, 16 Dec 43

Below. 15 September, a convoy of 4-5 Ton tractors, each towing two 2,000-gallon tankers (7600 litres) takes a break. Although the tankers bear the markings of the Army Air Force, the fuel they carry could be for Patton's armored forces. The convoy commander is having his papers checked whilst a French policeman is securing the area. This photograph is surprising as the ADSEC avoided halting convoys in towns. (NARA)

Liberty Roads, 1944-1945

Although the Heavy Mack NM *(photo 3)* 6x6 of the 6 t range had been in use since 1940, only 10,000 had left the factory. These were, however, excellent vehicles capable of carrying more than 10 tonnes and towing a further 13. The even better Mack NO only numbered 2,000 and were attached only to heavy artillery units (155 mm and 210 mm). Instead, it was tens of thousands of GMC which were equipped with tankers and light trailers whereas, as we can see in photo 2 taken during exercises in 1942, it was originally designed as a tactical utility vehicle and not as a strategic workhorse.
(NARA)

The official 1941 caption is a reminder of this consumer society's ambitions in the context of war: *"The best dressed army in the world. No matter where the troops may be, there will always be clothing for the men on the ground..."* There was, however, a lack of winter clothing in autumn 1944.
(LC-USW33- 000124-ZC)

TABLE 4—ORDNANCE DEPARTMENT: PROCUREMENT DELIVERIES OF SELECTED MAJOR ITEMS, 1 JULY 1940–31 DECEMBER 1945[a]

Item	Quantity	Item	Quantity
Tank-Automotive Items		*Tank-Automotive Items*—Continued	
Tanks—Total	[b] 88,410	Heavy-Heavy Trucks—Total	[b] 153,686
Light (7 types)	28,919	3½-Ton, 4x2 (2 types)	2,000
Medium (9 types)	57,027	4-Ton, 6x6 (4 types)	29,194
Heavy (5 types)	2,464	4-ton- 4x4 (2 types)	7,317
Motor Carriages for Self-propelled Weapons—Total	[b] 46,706	4-5-Ton, 4x4 tractor	21,974
Antiaircraft guns (10 types)	19,784	5-Ton, 4x2 (7 types)	20,567
Antitank guns (7 types)	17,944	5–6-Ton, 4x4 (3 types)	8,179
Medium field artillery (6 types)	6,969	5–6-Ton, 4x2 (3 types)	3,600
Heavy field artillery (5 types)	727	6-Ton, 6x6 (5 types)	21,084
Mortar carriers (3 types)	1,282	7½-Ton, 6x6, prime mover	2,067
Other Combat Vehicles—Total	[b] 113,967	10-Ton, 6x6, heavy wrecker (2 types)	5,765
Armored cars, wheeled (6 types)	16,438	10-Ton, 6x4 (3 types)	18,088
Cargo carriers—full-track (3 types)	15,889	12-Ton, 6x4, tractor, M20, for trailer tank	5,871
Carriers, half-track (8 types)	39,328	20-Ton, 6x4, tractor	2,143
Scout cars, wheeled	21,963	Tractors, medium, for 50-passenger semi-trailer bus	1,492
Tank recovery vehicles (2 types)	241	Other (28 types)	4,345
Universal carriers—full-track	19,611	Semi-Trailers—Total	[b] 59,731
Special purpose tank, on M4 series chassis	497	Bus, 50-passenger	1,231
Light Trucks—Total	[b] 988,167	2½–4-Ton (4 types)	4,350
¼-Ton, 4x4, command (jeep)	634,569	5-Ton, 2-wheel, stake and platform	8,107
¼-Ton, 4x4, amphibian	12,774	6-Ton, 2-wheel (13 types)	13,085
½-Ton, 4x4 (12 types)	82,454	7-Ton, 2-wheel, cargo	7,752
½-Ton, 4x2 (8 types)	9,415	10-Ton, 2-wheel (3 types)	18,989
¾-Ton, 4x4 (6 types)	248,634	11–20-Ton (5 types)	1,965
Other (8 types)	321	22½-Ton, 4-wheel, low bed	2,201
Medium Trucks—Total	[b] 428,196	40–45-Ton (3 types)	1,408
1½-Ton, 6x6, cargo	43,224	Other (11 types)	643
1½-Ton, 4x4 (12 types)	167,373	Trailers—Total	[b] 499,494
1½-Ton, 4x2 (23 types)	217,012	¼-Ton, 2-wheel, cargo	143,371
Ambulances (3 types)	587	¾-Ton, 2-wheel (3 types)	4,931
Light-Heavy Trucks—Total	[b] 812,262	Truck, bomb lift, M1	20,310
1½–3-Ton, 4x4 (2 types)	2,719	1-Ton, 2-wheel, cargo	259,064
1½–3-Ton, 4x2 (2 types)	3,420	1-Ton, 2-wheel, tank (250-gallon, water)	19,946
2½-Ton, 6x6 (11 types)	676,433	Armored, M8	5,270
2½-Ton, 6x4 (2 types)	117,759	Bomb, M5	16,212
2½-Ton, 4x4 (3 types)	1,279	M20, for carriage, multiple caliber .50, M1, M55	6,471
2½-Ton, 4x2 (14 types)	10,602	Truck, bomb lift, M22	4,037
Buses, 32- and 37-passenger, 4x2 integral	50	4 to 5–6-Ton (5 types)	3,771

for all-terrain trucks, however rational it may have been, impacted heavily in August-October 1944. This is even more obvious when we study the operations of 1945 when the vehicles ordered in 1943 began arriving in huge numbers in Europe.

THE SPARE PARTS NIGHTMARE

Ernie Pyle, the famous war correspondent, wrote that *"It is not only a war of munitions, tanks, guns and trucks.... it is as much a war of spare parts... the seal that leaks, the ventilator belt that snaps, the bolt that is lost.... will hold up GI Joe on the road to Berlin as much as if he did not have any vehicles at all."*

During the Second World War there were hundreds of thousands of referenced spare parts, from a tiny spark plug to a tank engine weighing several tons. *"On the battlefield there are no mechanics available to help you out, it is impossible to travel light and the Ordnance services always need to have the right part at the right time."* In 1943, more than a hundred million spare parts arrived every month for the various fronts[9]. Although experience was of help, it was relatively easy to plan the requirements for spare parts for rifles, machine-guns and artillery pieces that had been used for more than a hundred years, but this was not the case for tanks and vehicles whose use within the army was more recent and which required a more complex maintenance.

On the ground, there was a tendency to over-exaggerate requirements and the administrative services tended to underestimate. Several contradictory reports were published in 1940 to find out who should estimate requirements. As always with the Americans, the answer came from the creation of a Spare Parts Board; an insufficient solution as a year later General Harris warned his superiors of the alarming situation. Instead of planning its purchases, the Quartermaster Corps just purchased from local distributors on a day-to-day basis as if it were an ordinary customer. As

9. See the part concerning spare parts *"Annual, Report Requirements Division"* ASF, ASF file

An anti-aircraft battalion equipped with M4 tracked tractors moves through Cherbourg. Ideally, all of the artillery units should have been equipped with these tracked vehicles, thus freeing up the trucks for the Quartermaster Corps. This was not the case.
(NARA)

Below.
Maintenance of the GMC was very straightforward and breakdowns were rare, as long as the vehicles were looked after.
(NARA)

A 1917 – dated poster which already boasts of the mechanization of the US Army.
(LC-USZC4- 10126)

This impressive view, seen here at Ecausseville, would have made other armies green with envy if it was not for the fact that it was in fact an elephants' graveyard. The Ordnance Corps was snowed under with work and could not cope with the amount of breakdowns which became more widespread in September. The weather which has made the ground soggy here did not help matters.
(NARA)

for the inventory of new strictly military vehicle spare parts, they had simply not been set up. Spare parts could not be ordered, therefore, and even less so manufactured. Finally, a bizarre order forbidding spending more than 10% of purchases on spare parts remained unexplainably in vigour.

In May 1942, the Board was reorganised in order to integrate General Motors. Civilians replaced military personnel who were incapable of planning requirements. However, this experiment failed miserably and after three months of pointless debate, the Board was disbanded. The problem was passed over to the Ordnance Corps. Two years after having become aware of the problem nothing had been solved.

In mid-1942, General Somervell took the bull by the horns and ordered the halting of purchasing spare parts in a piecemeal fashion. Each order now had to be accompanied with a contract for the parts required for the two first years of use financed by a budget that could be as much as 35% of the price of the vehicle. The manufacturers then found themselves submerged with orders and made it known that it was impossible for them to supply both complete vehicles and a sufficient quantity of spare parts. Somervell suggested using small manufacturers, small companies that made and sold discount parts on the civilian market.

The publication of the Victory Program and the announcement of presidential objectives concerning the manufacture of complete items of equipment had made the situation concerning parts even more difficult. It was obvious that it was not seen as being a priority and the attempt made to oblige the manufacturing of a complete vehicle and enough spare parts was a failure. On 1 October 1942, the deficit of spare parts became dramatic to such an extent that a memo published by ASF ordered the Ordnance services to refuse a new vehicle if it was not delivered with its spare parts. Of course this directive was not applicable as even with the best will in the world, it was impossible for the manufacturers to reply favourably to this demand as the War Production Board refused to deliver them with the raw materials essential to the making of the parts as these were not a priority. By mid-1943, the situation was so bad that the Senate opened an inquest. This led to the discovery of numerous incidences of misappropriation of funds concerning the Ordnance Corps' use of the annual half a billion dollars that were allocated to it for the purchasing of parts. The inquest showed the existence of favouritism towards the three big manufacturers of Chrysler, General Motors and Ford. The Corps persisted in dealing with the Big Three when the smaller manufacturers could, most of the time, deliver faster and for a cheaper price. Still favouring the three big manufacturers, the Ordnance purchased big parts such as very expensive drive axles and neglected the purchasing of small parts. It was obvious that something was amiss in the realm of spare parts.

It is sure that the practice consisting of ordering a vehicle with its spare parts from the same manufacturer had the advantage of simplifying administrative work but it did not allow to take advantage of the growing standardisation and prevented putting manufacturers in completion with each other. The practice was costly in terms of money, but also in time as the manufacturer was delayed in honouring its contract. In 1943, the way of calculating was, therefore, once again modified. It was decided to deal in terms of stocks that the orders would complete every four months. Thus, it was no longer a full set of parts that was purchased for each vehicle, but parts (spark plugs, fuel tank, carburettor, tyres) that were used the most in the field, parts which could be purchased from different manufacturers. The Ordnance complained about the increase in administrative work caused by the managing of tens of thousands of specific contracts, arguing that the extra personnel requirements would eat up any money that was saved and that the administrative management of the orders would only lead to an increase in delivery times. Finally, the Ordnance sat on the fence. There was indeed an increase in individual contracts passed with better performing sub-contractors, but others were still negotiated with the Big Three who reserved the right to sub-contract the order. The budget for spare parts grew considerably, going from 700 million dollars in 1942, to 1.3 billion in 1943, absorbing 27% of the total budget for vehicles. Certain manufacturers were not listened to who, naturally with their own interests at heart, recommended simply abandoning the manufacturing of spare parts by putting forward the argument that it was more straightforward and less expensive to replace a damaged vehicle with a new one. In concrete terms, the situation concerning stocks improved somewhat during the course of 1943 and 1944, but did not make good all of the deficits[10].

Added to this manufacturing problem was the difficulty in correctly supplying the fighting units. A spark plug fresh out of the factory was of no use if it remained stored away in the United States or if it was sent to a theatre of operations where there were already thousands in stock. At the front, the situation seems to have been delicate from time to time as seen in a report sent by Colonel Ward E. Becker during operations in Sicily: *"My maintenance chief is pulling his hair out due to the lack of spare parts. Our vehicles have suffered a lot and on average, a 2 and a half ton with 20,000 kilometres on the clock is fit for the scrap heap due to insuf-*

An early production Corbitt 50DS6, these were 6x6 anti-aircraft artillery tractors from the 6 t range. They were reliable and multi-task vehicles and ended up being adopted by numerous services. Three years were lost between the call for tender in 1938 and the signing of the contract in 1941.
(RR)

ficient maintenance. At the same time we have enough rear axles than we know what to do with, but we desperately need bearing kits, carburettor repair kits, seals, spark plugs, oil filters etc. In many units 50 to 75% of trucks need repairing. Excuse this cry for help but if you could see the sorry spectacle of our broken down trucks I really feel that you would find my request is justified.[11]"

Errors in planning, delays in delivery, blocked distribution networks, supplies lost on sunk ships, but also mistreatment, negligence and a lack of knowledge of vehicles by those who used them (such as the North African drivers in the French army who believed that replacing the water in the batteries with wine would increase their performance) all combine in order to explain the lack of spare parts at the front. Needs differed from one theatre to another. In North Africa, the omnipresence of mines meant that many front axles were destroyed, whereas in the Pacific, it was the rear axles which were lacking as the drivers, fearing snipers, reduced the number of return trips by overloading their trucks. Given conditions such as these, it was almost impossible to establish reliable tables to foresee the requirements for spare parts.

However, improvements could be made concerning distribution. To start with, grouped shipments had to be done away with. Indeed, the Ordnance Corps managed its stocks in batches of spare parts. Each batch comprised of all that was necessary to ensure the maintenance of one hundred trucks for a year. When a depot asked for, say, a re-supply of timing belt kits, they were sent a batch of all spare parts, thus finding itself with tons of spare parts that were not required. This overly rigid system meant that transportation services were over burdened and led to an increase in loading and unloading. It also

A nice view of a 4x4 4/5 Ton tractor. Developed in 1941 by Autocar, it was one of the main victims of the low priority given to heavy vehicles. Even by adding a second constructor, White, it only became the workhorse of the Transportation Corps in the winter of 1944. 11,104 Autocar and 2,751 White were made during the war.
(NARA)

meant that huge repair depots had to be opened far from the frontlines.

In spring 1943, the Ordnance Corps decided to overhaul packaging by focussing on what was actually required by the men in the field. The spare parts would be packed separately and easy to handle in a light format (32 kg). They also made maintenance tables listing parts that were interchangeable between the vehicles in service. These bulky publications ended up most of the time being used as paper weights in the depot offices. Finally, despite some improvements, the supply of spare parts remained, until 1945, the main problem

A 76 mm gun being replaced on a TD M10. The maintenance services, which were over-burdened by the GMC breakdowns, could not put to one side their daily work on combat vehicles that were also worn out after three months of intense use.
(13-Num 5667, NARA © Archives départementales de la Manche)

---

10. There is an indispensable source concerning production problems: Harry C. Thomson and Lida Mayo, *The ordnance department: Procurement & Supply*, 1960, pp. 275-320
11. Letter from Col. Becker to Col. William Borden, OCO, 1 August 1943

Liberty Roads, 1944-1945

area in the distribution of supplies. Wastage was high as only 15% of the parts made covered 85% of the repairs carried out on the front.

The problem of the spare parts is a striking example of the Army's failure to draw on experience gained elsewhere. The failings in maintenance that had blighted the AEF in 1917-18, or the Mexican Border War of 1916, was repeated on a much bigger scale during the liberation of Europe in 1944.

Left.
A monstrous Diamond T M20. Designed in 1940 at the behest of the British who need such a vehicle to tow their new Churchill tank. 5,871 were made and adopted by the US Army; it equipped two super-heavy companies on the Highway. *(NARA)*

Above.
A Mack NR, this is the 6x4 of the large 6 t range. A few hundred were deployed in Europe to ease the burden on the Transportation Corps in spring 1945. *(RR)*

Above right and below.
Impressive photos showing an assembly line in the Normandy bocage. Delivering vehicles in kit form was much easier for loading and used up less space, rather than shipping ready to use GMC vehicles across the Atlantic.
(13-Num 4553 & 3506, NARA © Arch. départementales de la Manche)

Next page.
A panorama of some of the Heavy Heavy vehicles encountered on the Red Ball Express. This heavy breakdown Kenworth M1 could winch 21 t *(1)*. An early production Mack NM 6X6 6 Ton recognizable by its metal cabin roof *(2)* and its NR 7 ½ Ton big brother *(5)*. A Diamond-T 968 6X6, 4 Ton belonging to the 5th ID being unloaded *(3)*. A 4x4 4/5 Ton Federal 94x43 tractor *(4)*. The next vehicle was not, of course, part the Red Ball as it is a 6x4 8 Ton White model 64 SW 400 artillery tractor which reveals the situation in which the US Army found itself in the 1930s when it equipped itself with small numbers of civilian vehicles at a time when the decision to use all-terrain vehicles had not been made.
(NARA)

1

2

3

4

5

6

Unloading materiel with the help of civilian personnel from a Rhinoferry into GMC trucks parked up on an Omaha causeway.
(Région Basse Normandie/NARA, p013280)

Liberty Roads, 1944-1945

"LITTLE ARRANGEMENTS AMONGST FRIENDS" CONCERNING THE MARVELLOUS JEEP

"I don't think that we could carry on with the war without the Jeep. It does everything. It goes everywhere. It is as loyal as a dog, solid as a mule and as agile as a goat. It constantly bears double the load for which it was designed to take and still drives along... The Jeep is a heavenly means of military locomotion."

Ernie Pyle,
war correspondent, April 1945

The beginnings of the Jeep reveal the constant quest on the part of the QMC to standardise its vehicle fleet, despite the constraints of the attribution of contracts. Throughout the entire course of its development, the QMC tried to push out the small company that had invented the Jeep, Bentam, and put in its place the huge Ford company. They considered that only Ford was capable of undertaking mass production in wartime and that this prevented the contracts being broken up between various manufacturers and the risk of finding themselves once again with dozens of different vehicles.

The Jeep's origins went back to the First World War when the need for a light multi-task off-road vehicle was felt. In the 1920s, the Ordnance Corps tested caterpillar tracks and a Model T Ford. Marmon Herrington sold the Army sixty-four half-ton 4X4 vehicles (model LD1). Three Roadster Bantams were also loaned to the National Guard. Finally, in June 1940, the Ordnance Technical Committee created a board tasked with the development of a light vehicle. This comprised of representatives from the Army, but also specialist drive system engineers. As stipulated by law, the specifications were very

Top.
The Jeep incarnates America at war: industrial, innovative, practical and uninhibited. *(NARA)*

The Jeep could tow a two-wheeled ¼ Ton trailer which, curiously, could float when loaded.
(NARA)

general: A 4x4 weighing 590 kg when empty, capable of carrying a load of 272 kg, three men and a 0.30 cal. MG, with a road clearance of 16 cm. The manufacturers putting forward a vehicle were asked to deliver 70 vehicles, including eight with four-wheel drive, within 75 days in time to take part in the large military exercises. In this ridiculously short lapse of time it required putting forward a prototype by the 49th day. 135 manufacturers were contacted, including Ford, but only two accepted to take up the challenge!

Bantam called upon a well-known engineer, Karl K. Probst who, in five days, designed the plans. Given the timeframe involved, there was no point in making a totally new design, it was more a case of building a meccano kit using existing parts: the Studebaker Champion drive axle made by the specialist Spicer, the 46hp Continental engine and elements taken from the Bantam catalogue. The vehicle arrived within the allocated timeframe at the Holabird test center. Its weak point was its weight which exceeded the specifications by 250 kg. Willys built a very similar vehicle but not within the timeframe. Although it was cheaper in absolute terms, the Willys project turned out to be more expensive when the delay penalties were taken into account and it was rejected. Bantam, therefore, was chosen for a first batch of 70 vehicles and the trials were successful, with the final report deeming that despite a few faults or mechanical incidents, the *"vehicle is powerful and responds to the requirements of service"*. To the surprise of the Bantam management, the Quartermaster Corps authorised the Willys and Ford representatives to watch the trials, clipboard and pencil in hand. Ideally, the QMC still dreamed of doing business with Ford[1].

Finally, when 1,500 pre-production vehicles were ordered from Bantam under the designation of Model 40 BRC, the QMC recommended the sharing of the contract with Ford and Willys, something which was initially turned down by the Secretary of War, Henry Stimson, who then finally gave in. As it was out of the question for the two manufacturers to be just sub-contractors to the small company, Willys and Ford were exceptionally given the authorisation to put forward their own version. Bantam was disgusted, not only did they risk being pushed aside at the moment of the main contract when they were the only ones to adhere to the timeframe, but also their competitors were going to reap the benefits of the trials. Willys delivered its prototype at the beginning of November 1940 and was followed by Ford three weeks later. Naturally, they both looked exactly like the Bantam version For the Army, the Willys was the best due to its superior power but, and this was a serious drawback, its weight was totally over that stipulated in the specifications with, at 1,099 kg, double the initial specified weight and still 109 kg over the revised specifications of 980 kg. This was a dead-end as legally

speaking, the Army could not choose a vehicle that did not respect the specifications. This obstacle was removed via a dispensation and the Army went ahead anyway and ordered 1,500 from Willys on the understanding that it would revise its design, something that was done by losing as much weigh as possible, even by adding less paint.

Thus, the three manufacturers were still in the race and all made a pre-production run of 1,500 vehicles each (Bantam 40 BRC, Ford GP and Willys M.A.). It was no surprise when, during the final trials for the award of the main contract, the advance gained by Willys was confirmed. Not only was their model better in the field, but it was also cheaper (739$ per vehicle). However, the Quartermaster Corps was still blinkered by the question of production capacities and attempted a final throw of the dice by going ahead anyway and awarding the 16,000 vehicle contract to Ford. But, the Office of Production Management opposed this by arguing the illegality of such a procedure and Willys obtained the contract on 23 July 1941, less than a year after the program was started. This model was immediately modified in order to improve the standardisation with the rest of the vehicle park: new air filter, generator, battery. Known under the designation of MB, 361,349 Jeeps would be made by Willys. In October 1941, the Quartermaster Corps managed to convince Willys to sign a partnership with another manufacturer in order to speed up production. As luck would have it, this just happened to be... Ford. In this way, a manufacturer which had not taken part in the program, and was then pushed out of it, found itself making 277,896 Jeeps.

From a strictly military point of view, the QMC had done the right thing as it had chosen the best model, that made by Willys, largely copied from the Bantam, saw more than 600,000 made, becoming along with the GMC, the symbol of the US Army at war. The procedure may have been morally questionable - it no doubt led to the demise of Bantam in 1956 - but on the eve of war, common sense prevailed. As it was impossible to made Ford become a simple sub-contractor to Bantam, the QMC had no other choice than to push out the smaller company to make way for the big one. We can, however, raise questions concerning the links between the QMC and Ford when we look at the lengths the military went to in order to bring back the big company into the race, almost despite itself. We can also question the obstinate way in which the QMC pushed Bantam out of the production process once the war had started when, in 1942, Bantam put itself forward as a sub-contractor for Willys. Bantam had skills and an industrial capacity and it was a pity that they were not put to better use; in the end they had to made do with making trailers. As for Willys, they did not hesitate in using the popular image of the Jeep and laid claim to being the inventor of it, to such an extent that they were found guilty of false advertising in 1948.

Left.
Colonel HJ Lawes, commander of the Holabird Quartermaster Motor Transport School shows his pupils how to use the Jeep.
(LC-USW33- 027843- ZC)

Top.
The Jeep could also be used as a mobile advanced HQ. PFC James E. Lough of the 67th. Arm. rgt, 2 Arm. div., is seen here requesting by phone a bulldozer to clear the road near Barenton on 11 August.
(13-Num 4097, NARA © Archives départementales de la Manche)

Above and right.
Jeeps were also sent in kit form. They were then assembled, sometimes in hangars, by the Ordnance Corps.
(13-Num 4549, NARA © Archives départementales de la Manche)

1. Jean-Gabriel Jeudy & Marc Touraine, *La jeep, un défi au temps*, EPA, 1981, pp. 18-44 & Paul Gaujac, *La Jeep dans l'armée française*, tome I, Histoire & Collections, 2013, p. 15.

Liberty Roads, 1944-1945

CHAPTER 12

MUDDLED STRUCTURES FAVOURED CONFRONTA

Although Lee's arguments had some effect, Lute was not satisfied. Lutes cannot put the logistical failure of the summer and autumn of 1944 down to a straightforward question of means. It does not explain the frequent arguments between rear echelon officers and commanders, and the inter-service friction which, without doubt, slowed down the distribution chain. How can one explain this structural confusion when the Americans had been at war for two and half years and the invasion had been fine tuned for months on end? To find the answer to this question we have to go back to 1942.

Cherbourg, autumn 1944, despite the best efforts of the port companies, the line of Liberty Ships waiting in the baie de Seine grew longer.
(© Coriello, Bibliothèque municipale de Cherbourg/US NARA)

1. *Field Service Regulations Administration*, 15 November 1943, p. 23.
2. Concerning the matrix organizations and their consequences in the armies, one can consult the work of Michel Goya, *Dans la Matrice*, dated 26 December 2012 in his Blog "La voie de l'épée".
3. JK Ohl, op. cit., p. 210

THE DIFFICULT INTEGRATION OF THE ASF

As early as 1942, Somervell, convinced of the importance of his role, moved heaven and earth in order to become a major player in the allied strategy and its planning phase. However, the beginnings were difficult. Despite his complaints, he came to understand that in the eyes of the General Staff, the Army Services Forces were just a service provider, guaranteeing the fighting men with the provision of adequate equipment in the right place at the right time. This meant that he was not involved the planning process for the landing in North Africa. Worst still, in order to carry out his mission, he was stuck between the Operation Division who decided on the overseas deployment of units, and the War Shipping Administration who had control over shipping. The task of the ASF comprised only of planning movement and loading that fitted best around the decisions made by the OPD and the means allocated by the WSA.

Progressively, Somervell managed to get invited more regularly to the planning table. At the beginning of 1943, he accompanied Marshall to the inter-allied conference at Casablanca, although he never managed to become one of the official decision makers. This situation explains the difficulties encountered by the ASF during the preparation for Overlord. Their incapability of making themselves heard when they rang the alarm bells over the insufficient number of landing vessels or heavy trucks. The ASF were merely there to serve the army. However, the most worrying aspect was their difficulty in finding their place within the General Staff organisational table for the (ETOUSA: European Theatre of Operation, United State Army). This would open up a major quarrel, should the commanders in the field retain the control of logistics or hand it over to an independent organ?

Logistics that ran away from the combatants

Traditionally, the Quartermaster services were controlled by the theatre commander who was free to organise them, as seen in the 1943 regulations:

"A theater of operations is administratively organised to answer the needs of the fighting units and to allow them to carry out their missions. Initially, the organisation can be prescribed by the War Department. The improvement of the administrative organisation is a continual process built on the experience gained in this theater."[1] This had been the case during the Civil War and in France during the First World War.

With the creation of the Army services Forces, Somervell wanted to give as much authority as possible to his subordinates within the overseas theatres of operations. As early as 1942, he convinced Eisenhower that in order to be efficient, the organisation of the ETOUSA theater of operations supply

Liberty Roads, 1944-1945

services ought to follow that of the ASF. A structure named Service of Supply oversaw all of the technical services. On a hierarchical level, it would only come under the administrative authority of Somervell and the operational authority of Eisenhower. Although the authority of the theatre commander appeared safe, it was in fact weakened as he could only choose or sack the service chief named directly by General Marshall upon his own recommendation and that of Somervell. This meant that the theatre commander no longer had control over the internal organisation of the Service of Supply. Within the ETOUSA hierarchy, the SOS chief, General Lee, became equal to the army group commanders and the logistical chain was uncoupled from the combatant activities. The US Army was experimenting with what would be known as matrix management in the world of business a few years later on.

The Americans tried empirically to combine the advantages of two traditional organisational systems, the centralised organisation in Washington (Army Ground Forces, Army Services Forces) and the geographical organisation in operational sectors (the theatres of operation such as ETOUSA). The first type of organisation rationalised the use of resources, but was rigid. As for the second, it was more flexible, with each theatre having its own internal resources in order to adapt, but which demanded more in resources. This experimentation aimed to be both flexible and rational and would become used in the business world during the nineteen-fifties under the name of matrix management. In this way, each person involved found himself at the junction of two chains of command without a formal hierarchical dominating relationship of one over the other [2].

In concrete terms, the Service of Supply autonomously answered the requests of the staffs who planned and carried out operations. To sum up, the commanders no longer had control over operational logistics. The situation became even more complex when, over the course of time and animosities, General Andrews, who had taken over from Eisenhower, tried to sideline

the American armies. He was forced to delegate these roles to his generals in the field, Bradley, Patton and Hodges, that is to say to generals who had no authority over Lee and, worse still, were below him in the chain of command since his nomination as number two of ETOUSA. How could an army group or an army undertake an efficient campaign if they were not in charge of their own logistics? The US Army was pulled between two contrary forces, Lee's centralised service and those of Eisenhower which were decentralised. This reform which made no-one happy was a potential breeding ground for clashes between, on one hand, Lee and Whipple, and on the other, Lee and the

Due to the early arrival of a harsh winter, the fighting men needed more than ever warm clothing. Some units would wait until 1945.
(NARA)

General Lee by increasing his own bureau tasked with supplies (G-4) within the general staff of the European Theatre of Operations which ended up by duplicating the job of the SOS. Somervell advised Lee to do something in order to take control of this G-4[3] and this led to a power struggle. In January 1944, the return of Eisenhower and the creation of SHAEF offered the opportunity to rationalise this can of worms. However, what should have been a spring clean turned out to be just a quick wipe over. A big step was thought to have been taken by integrating - the official term was 'consolidation'- the SOS staff with that of ETOUSA. Not content with retaining his place as SOS chief (a service that would be renamed Communication Zone once in France), Lee was promoted to Lieutenant-General and became the deputy to the theatre commander in charge of supplies. He once again centralised all of the logistics. However, the creation of SHAEF made a new echelon, that of supreme commander with his own staff and its own supply service, creating an echelon above ETOUSA, the same dichotomy that had just been removed. It was no surprise that this led to tensions between Lee and Colonel Whipple, the man in charge of logistics within SHAEF. Both men would send piles of reports, suggestions and contradictory warnings to Eisenhower. To make things even more complicated, Eisenhower held both the position of supreme commander of SHAEF and commander in chief of ETOUSA. He had, therefore, under his command, two staffs that were geographically apart, something that was ripe for confusion and which was time-consuming. In reality, Eisenhower could not coordinate both the action of the Allies (his role within SHAEF) and personally lead the operations of

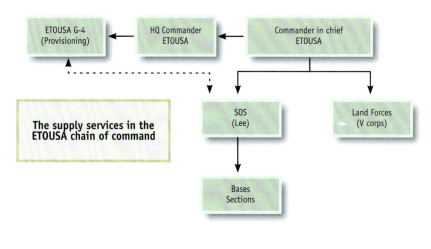

The supply services in the ETOUSA chain of command

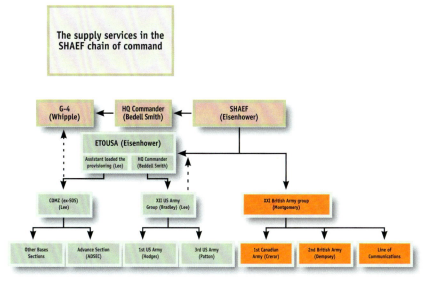

The supply services in the SHAEF chain of command

Liberty Roads, 1944-1945

165

Above.
Despite the lack of equipment being felt, some depots in Normandy were abandoned due to the absence of stock taking.
(NARA)

Above, right.
In Cherbourg, the Americans used the Nardouët powder store with its refrigeration system for the purpose of storing meats and perishable goods.
(NARA)

commanders in the field who would go behind ETOUSA and deal directly with SHAEF.

A comparison with the British logistical chain illustrates the complexity - or even the absurdity - of the American system. The top of the British system was the same; SHAEF. The latter oversaw a sole ground command, Montgomery's XXI Army Group which held authority as much over the fighting units as those of the rear echelon. The man who planned operations - Monty - was also the one who distributed supplies. Finally, the prototype matrix management system of ETOUSA worked in a conflicting way. Each of the two chains of command pursued objectives based on their own logic. This did not lead to an accumulation of quality, but rather one of defects. The system had become confused and, therefore, more rigid than the purely functional organisation, as well as being more expensive than the latter as this confusion imposed a re-bureaucratisation.

Did the administrative calendar of ComZ slow down the pursuit?

The logistical chain could only function in this way in the initial phase of the campaign. Indeed, in the absence of depth, the presence of a Communication Zone behind the 1st Army was impossible. SHAEF, in agreement with Lee, thus established a temporary structure and timeframe detailing the activation dates of each staff/headquarters and the transfer of responsibilities.

• From D-Day to D +20, the command of all logistical units was handed to Bradley, the 1st Army commander. In order to assist him in this task, personnel of the Advance Section were placed under his command.

• From D + 20 to D +41, it was hoped that there would be enough depth to hand over the management of beaches and dumps to the Advance Section. It would remain, however, under First Army authority.

• From D +41 to D + 90, with the entry into Brittany, the Advance Section which accompanied the advance of the Army, would hand over beach and port management to a Normandy Base Section. To coordinate the task of these two logistical echelons, an advance element of ComZ land (Forward Echelon ComZ) and come under control of the XII Army Group that would also be just activated. In concrete terms, Bradley retained control of the quartermaster services as he swapped his role as First Army commander for that of the XII AG.

• It was only on D +90 that Lee and his ComZ headquarters would land in France and officially take command of the rear echelon area s. The situation would at that point return to normal.

Of course, the campaign did not unfold as planned. A period of delay from 6 June to 25 July (D +51) was followed by a period of a considerable acceleration in operations. Therefore,

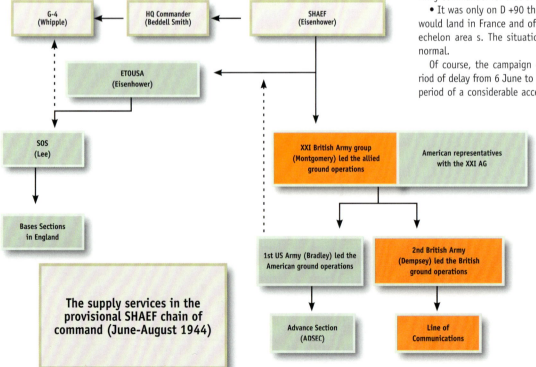

The supply services in the provisional SHAEF chain of command (June-August 1944)

Next page, top left.
Stocktaking in this medical supplies depot, something which was often not undertaken in the heat of the action and which was, nevertheless, indispensable. These supplies were not bulky and were always at the top of the list of priority supplies.
(NARA)

Right.
Colored soldiers clearing a bombed railroad.
(p011889, Région Basse Normandie/NARA)

This is a perfectly made munitions dump with its foliage cover concealing it from possible air attack, its conveyor belt and loading bay.
(13- Num 4587, NARA © Archives départementales de la Manche)

the precious plan had to be revised. However, the only two real departures from the plan were the postponement, then cancellation of the activation of FEComZ and the postponement of the activation of the Normandy Base Section. As planned for D +90, on 2 September, the authority over the rear echelon area moved from Bradley to Lee. One of Lee's first decisions was to transfer his huge headquarters staff (29,000 men) who were camped out from the Cherbourg vicinity to Valognes, to 167 luxurious Parisian hotels. During this time, on 16 August (D +75), the Cherbourg port authorities transformed into the Normandy Base Section and took over all of the dumps and files managed by ADSEC. On the same day, a Brittany Base Section was created, followed on the 24th by the Seine Section and on 5 September, by the Loire Section. Apart from the Normandy section, all were built around a headquarters that had moved from Great Britain. These activations made the supply chain in general complex and the Red Ball Express in particular. Initially, the latter brought into action two structures, ADSEC and the Normandy Base Section but later, the Seine Section then the Oise Section were involved as transit areas. These sections were supposed to immediately become part of the procedures improvised by ADSEC, something that was far from being the case. Between 16 August and 5 September, the logistical chain was, therefore, modified five times, each time causing confusion, fumbling and delays then, during the first fifteen days of Sep-

An operation of the utmost importance: the cleaning of Jerrycans. *(NARA)*

Loading in the Carentan railroad station. The GMC of the 625th Ordnance Ammunition Co. load the contents of a train, no doubt because the station is still the southern terminus. As was the case in many of these units, the bulk of the personnel comprised of African Americans.
(p000788, Région Basse Normandie/NARA)

tember, the central headquarters was in transit and therefore running at a slow pace. Bradley, Patton and even Eisenhower all criticised the fact that Lee seemed to be more preoccupied with finding himself a cosy billet than doing his job, or the fact that he had diverted precious means of transportation and fuel in order to transfer his headquarters. What one should retain is that the operational constraints collided with the planning and that these thirty-one days of great changes took place at the worst time during the height of the pursuit when the Falaise pocket was closed and that the two American armies went in two different directions with one headed towards the Lorraine and the other towards Aachen.

The generals' battle[4]

It was no surprise that an open crisis broke out between Bradley and ComZ when the latter became operational on the continent at the beginning of September. Faced with the lack of supplies that we have seen, Bradley was forced to ration his two armies in both gasoline and ammunition. ComZ had promised to deliver him 66,000 tonnes for the week of 16 to 23 September. But, eight days later, whereas ComZ proudly announced to SHAEF that it had managed to deliver 127,000 tonnes, Bradley's G4, General Moses, only counted 61,000 tonnes, making approximately 400 tonnes per division. He also added that his own services had had to do the job of ComZ and go and fetch an extra 23,000 tonnes of supplies in Normandy.

Also, Moses complained that the supplies delivered did not always correspond to what the army group asked for. This was especially true for spare parts[5]. He ended his report by complaining virulently about Lee: *"The operation would be a success if ComZ had the means and the will to supply our combat forces[6]"*. Bradley headed straight to Ike and after a heated discussion, the supreme commander decided to take matters in hand. He handed over the role of attributing supplies to his own G4 Colonel Whipple, depending on missions fixed by each army group and the capacities of ComZ. A Logistical Plan Branch, a subdivision of the SHAEF G4 was opened to this end. Lee was appalled.

On paper, this decision had the merit of clarifying the chain of command with a decision maker, SHAEF, and executors, ComZ and the XII Army Group. However, SHAEF never managed to establish realistic allocations. Already, its procedure was so heavy that it required fifteen days to gather information, establish arbitration, update them before arbitrarily imposing supplies of 12,500 tonnes per day for an army group and 2,000 tonnes per day for the IX Tactical Air Force. The two allocations for the two halves of November were hardly any better and the procedure was finally suspended at the beginning of December

4. In reference to Blumenson's, *la Bataille des généraux* which evokes the now well-known clash between Monty and Patton.
5. As amazing as it may seem, the cause of the problem was that the depots did not use the same nomenclature as the units tasked with maintenance at the front. Constance McLaughlin Green, Harry C. Thomson and Peler C. Root, The Ordnance Department, CMH vol 3, 1968, p. 296.
6. Quoted by Ruppenthal, op. cit., vol. II, p. 179.

Above left.
Generals Ewart G. Plank, ADSEC commander, Franck S. Ross, head of the Transportation ETOUSA and Raymond G. Moses, G-4 of the 12th US AG.
(NARA)

Left.
Telephone operators at work inside a wooden hut at the Valognes signals center. The panel comprises of a TC-10 telephone exchange (doubled up) made up of a BD-110A switchboard (x3), 1 BD-132A board (relay), 1 Cabinet BE-72, 3 FM FM-19 frames, 2 Power Units PE-75 and 4 Batteries BB-46, that is to say, the standard equipment at the disposal of each army corps.
(p011874, Région Basse Normandie/NARA)

due to the general improvement in the situation. These difficulties are first explained by the tensions existing between the armies and ComZ which led them to send wrong figures to SHAEF, ComZ exaggerating out of pride its capabilities, affirming its ability to deliver up to 30,000 tonnes when it had never been able to reach 20,000 with an average lower than 13,000, the XII Army Group exaggerating its requirements, asking for up 30,00 tonnes when with average deliveries of 12,000 tonnes it had been able to rebuild its stocks during the course of November. Indeed, from 155,000 tonnes on 28 October, its reserves reached 222,000 tonnes on 15 December.

A second example illustrates the power struggles and interservice quarrels.

This was the slow and laborious integration of the SOLOC (Southern Line of Communication) within ComZ. The SOLOC commanded Major-General Thomas B. Larkin was tasked with supplying troops landing in Provence on 15 August. At the beginning of September, when the link-up was achieved on the doorstep of Burgundy, it should have been attached to ComZ in the same way as the combatant units of the 6th US Army Group were to SHAEF. This did not happen. Negotiations concerning rear echelon units lasted for two months and even at that time, the attachment was only theoretical as the compromise allowed Larkin to retain all of his autonomy. It was not until 6 February 1945 that the SOLOC was disbanded and that its two sections - Delta Base Section and CONAD (Continental Advance Section) – were integrated into ComZ. For six months therefore, the SHAEF rear echelon services were dependent on two different services. Larkin and Lee hated each other, their relations led to both services being extremely fussy regarding procedures and attributions. Thus, Marseille remained for the most part, the only port of supply for the 6th US Army Group and finally, there was no downscaling or rationalization.

COMZ, A FAILING ADMINISTRATION?

Aware that things were not functioning properly in Europe, Washington became worried. Several times, Somervell requested reports on

Ike Eisenhower (SHAEF), Omar Bradley (12th US AG)and Major-General Joseph Lawton (Lighting) Collins, commander of the VII Army Corps, on the eve of the breakthrough. They are obviously in good spirits here but the smiles will be more strained in a few days time.
(p011607, Région Basse Normandie/NARA)

the how Lee's services functioned, then starting in 1944, he ordered inquests to be undertaken by men he could trust. As early as April 1944, LeRoy Lutes, the head of operations at ASF, spent a month visiting billets and dining with commanders. He was tasked with separating truth from rumour and finding solutions. He pointed out numerous imperfections to Lee concerning procedures, such as the incapacity at keeping inventories up to date, but also the blurred lines in the definition of spheres of authority of each command. Lee defended himself by insisting on the fact that his newly overhauled headquarters had not been in existence for long. This was something that would be compensated for by thorough planning and thanks to the creation of the future Base Sections by transferring to the continent experienced staffs already active in England. The future would prove him wrong.

The boil was lanced due to a quarrel between ETOUSA who demanded more and more supplies, and the War Department that was not inclined

Almost all of ETOUSA seen here in April 1945: William H. Simpson (9th Army), Georges S. Patton (3rd Army), Carl A. Spaatz (Strategic Air Forces in Europe), Dwight D. Eisenhower (SHAEF & ETOUSA), Omar Bradley (12th US AG), Courtney H. Hodges (1st Army), Leonard T. Gerow (15th Army). Standing: Ralph F. Stearley (IX Tactical Air Command), Hoyt Vandenberg (9th Air Force), Walter Bedell Smith (Chief of Staff, SHAEF), Otto P. Weyland (XIX Tactical Air Command), Richard E. Nugent (XXIX Tactical Air Command). Ground Forces, Air Forces but no Army Service Forces representatives, relegated to the shadow of the "fighting men".
(NARA)

SHAEF ALLOCATIONS, FROM THEORY TO REALITY				
Fortnight	Total asked for by the armies tonnes per day	Estimation of capacities by Lee tonnes per day	Daily tonnage as fixed by SHAEF G4 tonnes per day	Tonnage actually delivered tonnes per day
15-28 October (for the XII AG)	22320	15000	12500 (+2 000 to the IX Tactical Air Force)	11000
5-18 November (for the XII AG)	28333 (+ 55097 for the IX Tactical Air Force)	30000	16700 (+ 3300 to the IX TAF)	12400
19 Nov-2 December (including the XII and VI Army Groups)	30000 (12th AG) 11660 (6th AG) = 41660	24400 via ComZ 12500 via SOLOC = 36900	26300 for the XII AG + 2250 to Build up the ADSEC stocks + 1145 le VII AG = 40 000	12000 for the XII AG, 8000 for ADSEC and 5 000 for the VI AG = 25 000

Liberty Roads, 1944-1945

to accept them. For Washington, Eisenhower and Lee were going too far. There were already hundreds of ships immobilised off the shores of Europe, something that was leading to delays in Pacific operations. On 31 August, Washington reduced the size of each convoy to ten vessels. This did not prevent the situation from worsening and on 28 October, Brigadier-General Franklin, Director of Water Transportation, landed in Paris with the task of *"suggesting solutions in order to speed up unloading, discouraging the theater in using freight ships as floating dumps and to convince those involved to treat this matter with the urgency it required"*. Once he had arrived, he was shocked by what he saw. Out of the 243 ships present, less than sixty were being dealt with. Franklin did not understand why the coordination of navigation around the ports had been placed in the hands of the ComZ G-4 instead of the Transportation Corps chief, General Ross. The latter complained that he was unable to coordinate the arrivals of ships with those of trains or truck convoys tasked with taking away the loads. The G-4 worked with plans that were over optimistic and he did not have any exact knowledge of the berth and departure capacities of each port. However, the situation must have been more complex than that as the measures taken by him led to hardly any improvement in the situation in November. It was obvious that the real source of worry remained the lack of berths and this was something that only the opening of Antwerp could solve.

Lutes returned to Europe in December. He saw that things were organised in a more professional manner than what he had seen in his previous visit, he added that *"numerous procedures are not working as well as we would like them to"*. He pointed out the defiance of men in the field regarding the rear echelon services and that this appeared to him as being a major sticking point. It is true to say that when he arrived, it was in the middle of another crisis. For a month the troops had been complaining about the lack of winter equipment and, worse still, the lack of cigarettes. For Lutes, the time that this situation carried on for saw the front line units tending to over stock and looking for stop-gap solutions in order to acquire supplies directly from the dumps, thus rendering impossible the setting up of an efficient logistical chain. What needed to be re-established was the trust of the "consumers". Lutes, who was no longer prepared to take a diplomatic stance, advised Lee to copy the work of Larkin and SOLOC which had not provoked any anger on the part of the 6th US Army Group.

In order to contribute to this regaining of hearts and minds, Lutes, the highest ranking ASF officer on the continent, promised Eisenhower and Bradley that he would speed up the sending from the USA of more tanks (1,350 for January alone), ammunition and radios. He also promised to improve the time required for these items to reach the front line, something that he estimated at a hundred days, fifty to load in New York and cross the Atlantic and the other fifty for unloading and being sent to the front line. According to Lutes, he could save thirty days[7]. This would be achieved by following procedures as closely as possible, beginning with ComZ sending regular and reliable statistics that would allow the New York port authorities to send items that were really needed in the theatre of operations. For Lutes, it was unacceptable that half of the stocks were still in Normandy or in Brittany.

ComZ hid behind an indisputable lack of means and insisted on the progress already made. Between the end of September and the end of December, the rail network had indeed been doubled (from 3,500 to 7,000 kilometres of single track and 5,000 to 9,500 km of double track, 180 bridges had been repaired and 125 built). However, there still remained a huge gap in the north west and around Paris. The situation was, according to ComZ, also the consequence of the stop-gap measures taken which had diverted personnel since August. The 2nd Military Railway Service complained that it had only been able to count on 15% of its personnel (12,000 men), with the rest being "incompetent".

General Lee, at the wheel, and General Plank, ADSEC commander, delighted here a few minutes after learning of the creation of the Red Ball Express Highway. *(13-Num 0699, NARA © Arch. dép. Manche)*

Cherbourg, an LST has just unloaded at the Mielles mole. In the foreground is a M4A3E2 Jumbo, M32 breakdown tank, in the background are two M-4 "105 mm". Ready to use tanks were rarely unloaded at Cherbourg, the port specialized more in quartermaster supplies and vehicles in kit form. The LST were sent in priority to the beaches.
(p001046, Région Basse-Normandie/NARA)

Deliver 1,350 extra tanks in 60 days, this was the sort of promise that only the USA, at the top of its game in 1945, could make to its generals.
(13-Num 2879, NARA © Archives départementales de la Manche)

General Bradley presents the situation to General Marshall and Admiral King during their visit to the front, under the gaze of Eisenhower. Once more, there are no logistics experts visible in the photo. Perhaps a symbol of the divorce between the *"fighting forces"* and the support units?

Brehon Somervell arrived in France in January 1945 to overhaul the running of ComZ. Lee was on the hot seat.
(Photos NARA)

Lutes pointed out the pipelines. By mid-September they stopped well before Paris (Domfront and Chartres), a month later they had barely got any further with a terminus at Coubert near Paris and no progression was planned for the entire winter! Lutes denounced the lack of planning. On the quaysides at Antwerp, despite having two months in which to prepare for the arrival of the first freight ship, nothing had been thought through for the rapid transportation away or storage of tens of thousands of goods which would be unloaded. The Antwerp-Cologne pipeline was only opened on 8 December. In the space of a few days, the quays were full and goods were stored without any form of cataloguing. The situation was the same at Le Havre and Rouen despite having to deal with far less tonnage. No study had been undertaken in order to measure the turnover capabilities of each depot. To top it all, each ComZ section was responsible for its own convoys, sending them, therefore, without knowing that once they arrived if they could be unloaded correctly. Lutes admitted that he did not understand this strange decentralisation of transportation, the diversity of requisition procedures, but also his worry concerning the lax attitude to the procedures concerning inventories or movement orders that were far removed from reality[8]. This had led to crazy situations where, instead of looking for items of equipment, new ones were ordered from the United States. Finally, Lutes could not find an explanation why in December, there was still no coherent and well-oiled chain open of dumps echeloned in depth. However, on paper, each Base Section had opened one in order to ease the burden on the quays, to sort out and distribute supplies towards the front line. But many only existed on paper or were short-circuited and most of the goods were still sent directly from the ports to the front line. Once the arrived, there was not enough manpower for unloading. Some goods just lay where they were for weeks on end, immobilising precious rail cars and causing jams in the regions of Liege and Verdun, an absurdity given the lack of locomotives. The armies also had an unfortunate tendency to retain the trains as a sort of mobile dump. Precious time was thus lost during the offloading process between rail and road. Delays in turnover sometimes exceeded forty days. Lutes was convinced that this situation was due to a lack of judgement on the part of the

During the course of the autumn the pipelines hardly moved and still had a terminus in the Paris area. A special organisation – the Petroleum Distribution Group – was later created in order to speed up the building of pipelines using personnel who had worked in the oil fields of Texas and California.
(13-Num 1080, NARA © Archives départementales de la Manche)

7. Ruppenthal, *op. cit.*, vol 2, p. 351
8. Ruppenthal *op.cit.*, vol 2, pp. 352-358.

Under Secretary of War Patterson decorates General Somervell for services rendered to the nation in 1945... before dismantling his service, the Army Service Forces, which had, in the eyes of the Army, become too far reaching.

ComZ headquarters who, living in the hope of an imminent end to the war, had not lent their support. The overall picture was such that Somervell himself went to Paris in January 1945 to sort things out and place Lee under his control. Although the US Army never really admitted that things were not really working properly, it is obvious that on the inside there was no doubt that all was not well in the kingdom of "Jesus Christ Himself" Lee. In February 1945, on the eve of the spring offensive, the situation was much improved. There were only 99 ships in European waters compared to the 243 in October and the existence of a chain of dumps was now a reality. ComZ had learned from its mistakes. It was the same for all of the US Army who, in 1944, was still in a learning phase.

Finally, the harmful role of oversized egos like that of Lee and the natural desire for each part of the puzzle to hold onto its own area led to a rickety infrastructure that multiplied interaction and friction, disconnecting logistics from those who needed it and breaking up responsibilities into tiny pieces. However, although this infrastructure looked like a clumsy leviathan, it is also because it had to operate in a context for which it had not been designed, that of a war of movement.

JCH LEE, OR THE FALL OF "CHRIST"

Born in Kansas, the Middle West, in 1887, John C.H. Lee is one of the US Army's most controversial figures. He passed out of West Point in 1909 and chose the Engineer Corps, and was part of the 89th ID during the First World War where he was decorated three times and became a close friend of another young officer, Brehon Somervell. In the inter-war period, he occupied managerial positions and became a distinguished auditor at the Army War College and the Army Industrial College, earning a reputation for being a good organiser despite having an over-sized ego. It was no real surprise, therefore, that in little time he became commander of the 2nd ID before being promoted by Marshall as the chief of logistics for the ETO. At this time he was a popular choice as Marshall had on his desk letters of recommendation from Somervell of course, but also under secretary Stimson and General Clark. On 3 May 1942, Somervell proudly told him the news, proud of having placed a friend in a key position. And what a position it was as Lee was tasked with successfully carrying out BOLERO. This operation took its name from the famous opera by Maurice Ravel and was a reminder of a magnificent crescendo that culminated, as the first notes suggested, in an irresistible force. For the US Army, this comprised of assembling on British soil an irresistible force of one million, four hundred thousand men who, at the given moment, would land in France.

Upon his arrival in Great Britain, the Major-General made himself noticed by asking for a train, a privilege up to that point reserved for the King. Neither Churchill, nor Eisenhower had one. Lee did not care a jot and justified this request by stating that it would allow him to visit each barracks and depot without leaving his headquarters staff and he therefore obtained a train. He lived like a millionaire, liked his etiquette and sometimes spoke about himself in the third person. He liked to rub shoulders with the British aristocracy which he greatly admired. He was so enamoured with his own image that he opened a press service. Due to his initials of JCH, he was nicknamed 'Jesus Christ himself' by his men and John "Court House", by his officers due to his frequent presence in court martials and his authoritarianism. Eisenhower compared him to Cromwell due to his religious fervour. However, Lee had another side to his character and despite his conservatism, he stood out during the course of the war by undertaking a veritable crusade in favour of better recognition for coloured troops and his open criticism of segregation.

General John CH Lee, ComZ commander. *(NARA)*

His tendency to hand out supplies as if granting a favour, his favouritism, quest for power and megalomania made him look like an empire builder and almost cost him his position when General Andrews, Eisenhower's successor at the head of ETOUSA, became so fed up with him that he filled in a dossier requesting his removal; a dossier that never left for Washington due to the accidental death of its author in May 1943. His successor, Jacob Devers, a former West Point comrade, was more inclined to support Lee, declaring that he was the ideal right-hand man and that it was out of the question to replace him. However, in 1944 he obtained his third star, something that was due to a misunderstanding as Marshall later admitted, and his promotion as deputy to Eisenhower was very badly received by other generals and their hostility turned into real hatred. Eisenhower himself became hot under the collar and reproached his autocratic drift and tendency to ignore his orders. In private he admitted that he *"no longer had total trust in Lee and his staff to do the job"*.

In order to unblock the situation, Somervell sent LeRoy Lutes in April 1944 who, in private told Lee of his concerns: his bad relationships and the confused organisation of the Service of Supply were worrying on the eve of Overlord. Lutes reminded him that he *"was there to fulfil the requests of his clients and not to tell them what they required"*. But none of this criticism got through to him. Publicly, Lutes was Lee's advocate. In the presence of Eisenhower he said that the SOS was an efficient organisation that had prepared Overlord well and although *"it was not yet at the top of its game, it was a fast learner and would improve once operations were engaged"*. The thing is Lutes was not totally independent, as seen by a letter addressed to Somervell,

"I have kept in mind that Lee was your protégé and that you could be assured of my loyalty". Upon his departure, nothing was resolved, worse still, Lee had seen this round of visits as an unacceptable and degrading intrusion.

The open crisis in September was a turning point for Lee. For the first time, his grip on power became fragile. Eisenhower stripped him of most of his attributions as deputy. Worse still, Somervell, his best supporter, openly criticised him for his incapacity to unload the Liberty Ships more rapidly. In October, Somervell tasked Lucius Clay to deal with the problem, then placed within Lee's headquarters staff, Brigadier-General John Franklin who arrived in conquered land, undertaking numerous conferences and intervening in order to reform ComZ. This *Missi-Dominici* quite simply took over Lee's authority concerning maritime traffic and port administration.

During this time, Eisenhower's lieutenants did not back down and demanded Lee's head on a plate. Lutes had to come back in December, bearing a cruel letter from Somervell. *"The antagonism between you, Patton, Bradley and Hodges is insupportable. I do not wish to know who is right or wrong, the fact is that we have to keep our customers happy"*. A month later, it was Somervell himself who went to Paris and after an in-depth visit, he left a memo on Lee's desk that was of a rare administrative violence. Apart from a politically correct introduction which recognised the work accomplished, the rest was nothing but criticism and advise. Lee had to get more out of his men, decentralise more, improve his planning and change his procedures. Somervell was telling him what to do and showed the little trust that he placed in Lee. He tasked Clinton Robinson to oversee him and ensure that the reorganisation was undertaken correctly. Lee managed to avoid being sacked but was placed under observation.

9. JK Ohl, *op. cit.*, pp. 227-228.
10. JK Ohl, *op. cit.*, pp. 237-238.

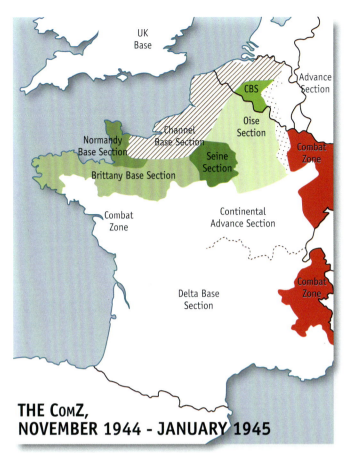

THE COMZ, NOVEMBER 1944 - JANUARY 1945

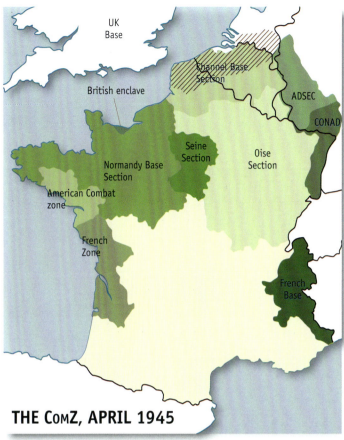

THE COMZ, APRIL 1945

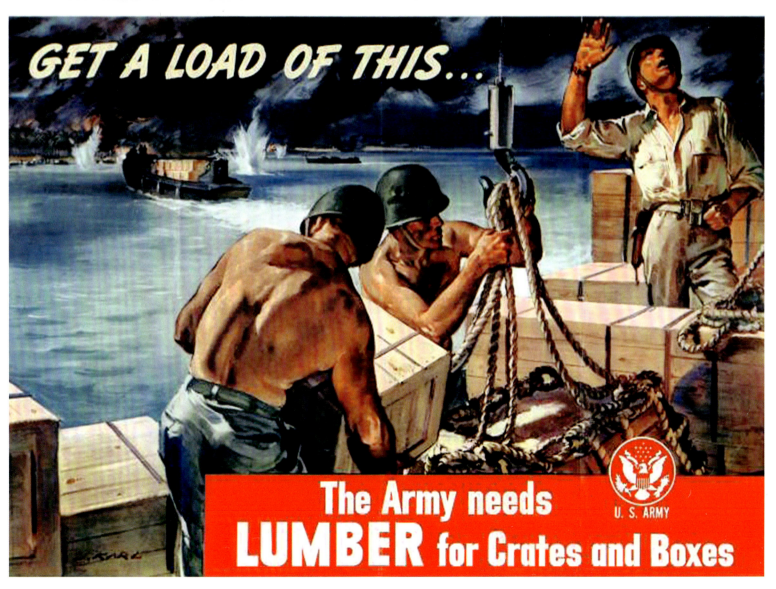

CHAPTER 13

THE FAULT IN THE DOCTRINE

Doctrine is the mother of logistics, the touchstone which unifies planning, determines training, equipment, organization and the use of units. The regulations think that operations will follow a sort of rhythm in depth and that the logistics put into place will be different from those used for operations on a static front. However, it can be seen that in 1944, the American doctrine only foresaw operations in depth[1].

Aggressiveness, firepower and mobility: the entire philosophy concerning the art of war is seen here in this well-constructed photo, taken during manoeuvres in 1942. The tank is an M3, the design of which was already obsolete when it entered into service.
(LC-SC166623)

WHAT WAS THE DOCTRINE OF THE US ARMY?

The American doctrine was impregnated with the works of the Swiss thinker Antoine Henri de Jomini[2]. The experience of the American Civil War also left a deep imprint. Often, the American doctrine can be summed up with what General Ulysses Grant said: *"the key to victory is the destruction of the enemy by the application in one place and at one given time of an overwhelming force supported by a concentration of firepower."* Considered as being a disruptive socioeconomic element in a liberal democracy, war has to be as short as possible, which explains this direct and total approach. In order to achieve it, the general has to respect a few principles:

• Aggressiveness and offensive temperament in order to retain the initiative.
• Concentration of forces,
• Maintaining a solid logistical which constitutes strategic and tactical means,
• Mobility.

The initiative allows for a series of movements and fighting which pin down and destabilize the enemy and allow one to find his weak

---

1. Curiously enough, publications concerning American doctrine are quite rare and quality ones even less so, I mostly used, apart from original sources: Bruno Colson, *La culture stratégique américaine*, Economica, 1993, Walther E Kretchik, *US Army Doctrine*, University Press of Kansas, 2011, Roman Jarymowycz, *Tank Tactics*, Stackpole Books, 2009 (1st ed. 2001), Georges F. Hofman & Donn A. Starry (dir.), *Camp Cold to Desert Storm, a history of US Armored Forces*, University Press of Kentucky, 1999 and Michael D. Doubler, *Closing with the enemy*, University Press of Kansas, 1994.
2. Antoine Henri Jomini was a self-taught military theorist in the first half of the 19th century who served in Napoleonic staffs, then Russian where he became an advisor to the Tsar. He published books which became inescapable within the US Army, such as his *Traité de Grande Tactique* (1805) or the *Précis de l'art de la guerre* (1838).

Above and below
The Union generals Grant and Sherman. They dislocated the economic structure of the South via blockades and raids in depth - using as seen here, scorched earth tactics put into place by Sherman during his march to the sea in 1864-65 – whilst at the same time harassing the enemy with combined operations all along the front. In many ways, their campaigns heralded the Soviet operational art of the 1920s and the American strategy of the Second World War.
(LC- USZ62-116520)

---

3. Michael G. Dana, *"The legacy of Mass Logistics"*, 19 Sept. 2000 article visible at www. Almc.army.mil
4. During the Civil War, the Union Army made up for a lack of tactical inferiority by strategic mobility. This, it was able to move by rail its 23rd Corps from Washington to the southern tip of Tennessee in eleven days, then leave for North Carolina where it launched an offensive against the Confederates at Wilmington, a move of 1,300 km. General Grant at Vicksburg and General Sherman's march of 1864-65 were also models which impregnated the American doctrine.
5. The columns converging to a given point or where a battle decided the fate of a campaign, or even the war. From this stemmed two levels of action: the strategy which covered all of the maneuverer which took place in the theater of operations and which lead to this decisive battle and the tactics which are the way the battle itself plays out.
6. Bruno Colson, *op. cit.*, p. 154.
7. FM 100-5 *Operation*, p. 132.
8. The manual does not at any time mention the economic objectives and concentrates on the destruction of the enemy army. However, in 1864, Grant had undertaken a total war in the aim of destroying the southern military-economic base: the destruction of factories in Atlanta, scorched earth in Georgia and the Shenandoah valley. This global approach to the war was not found eighty years later, apart from with airmen and sailors. Bruno Colson, *op. cit.*, p. 155.
9. Bruno Colson, *op cit.*, p. 205.

---

spot where the decisive pressure will be applied. The concentration of forces and logistics must allow for enough lethal firepower to defeat the enemy along the principles of *"More is better"* and *"Too much is not enough"*[3], inter-arm cooperation is also encouraged as it unleashes the efficiency of firepower.

But movement is also an indispensable virtue in order to manage to arrive at the ideal position. It is tactical in trying to seek envelopment as well as strategic in wide movements inside the enemy's interior lines, and exterior[4] rear. We find here the Napoleonic principle taken up by Jomini of the *"sole point strategy*[5]*"* During the Civil War, the Union generals went even further by combining operations in order to saturate the Confederate defenses and placed the onus on actions in depth in order to destroy its economic base, as seen by Grant's operations at Vicksburg and the 500 km march to the sea by Sherman's 60,000 men.

The gathering, maintenance and mobility of an overwhelming force imply, therefore, massive logistics the management of which is as determining as the tactical skill or strategic sense. On this particular point, Jomini's influence cannot be denied and was deepened by the need to undertake wars over considerable distances. The Civil War affected an immense theatre of operations, from the mouth of the Mississippi to Washington. With Grant, the war became more a question of management and organization of men and materials[6]. It was all about exploiting to the utmost his men and materials and Grant managed his armies like a financial expert or businessman, as well as doing what he could to deprive his enemy of such things. His operations were continually dictated by the constant quest to break up the Confederate economic base.

The American doctrine as laid out in the Field Service Regulations underwent a major change in the 1923 version. Following the experience of the Great War, the Americans no longer really believed in the possibility of in-depth operations, at least as far as ground forces were concerned, on the model of the campaigns of Sherman and Grant. Large industrial armies were capable of deploying along a continuous front and it had become impossible to push through without first having defeated them. However, Pershing had been impressed by the battle led by the French army and in particular with its capacity of employing a mass of reserve that could be moved to a key point in order to push in several devastating offensives that would lead breaking up the enemy front and the new FSR came to the conclusion that *"The decisive victory is the result of a series of offensive engagements undertaken by aggressive and mobile infantry forces that are well supported by the other arms."* The offensive ends with a breakthrough and pursuit. *"The object of the pursuit is the wiping out of hostile forces. This can only be rarely achieved by a frontal push along enemy lines of communications. Direct pressure on the enemy must be combined with an enveloping maneuverer by placing ones mobile forces on the axis of retreat. The encirclement is the conclusion of the maneuverer"*.

The enemy was now crushed in their positions. The strategy no longer consisted of moving one's armies in depth but laterally along the battlefield, either behind the front in order to reposition the reserves, or behind the enemy's back to encircle them. This was a major change to the American doctrine from that of operational maneuver. Operations in depth were no longer envisaged, except for immediate enemy rear echelon areas (100-200 km). Combined operations which sought to break up the enemy military-economic base as Grant had done were now done away with and replaced by a large tactic that was strictly aimed against military forces.[8]

A static front, aggressive attitude, combined operations with a limited objective (attrition, diversion, fixation), a concentration of firepower; this is what sums up in a few words the doctrine of 1923. Nothing was said about what operations would next take place once the enemy army was destroyed. According to Bruno Colson, the American doctrine became one of wiping out the enemy[9].

THE IMPOSSIBLE RETURN OF THE DEPTH OPERATIONAL, THE REGULATION OF 1941

However, the FSR was updated in 1941 using what had been learnt in the fighting that had taken place in Europe since 1936 and the large-scale military exercises which had started in Louisiana in 1940. It took in to account the technical revolution brought about by mechanized forces and reintroduced the notion of operations in depth.

The eighteen new pages concerning the Armored Divisions (versus only two for the Infantry Divisions) insisted on the opportunities presented by in-depth maneuverer. The tank could be used in mass within

Liberty Roads, 1944-1945

Above and below.
During the First World War, each American division had its own direct railroad, a veritable umbilical cord, then narrow-gauge railroads that went right up to the frontlines in order to supply the fighting men. *(LC)*

Next page.
During manoeuvres, these small M2 light tanks, armed with 37 mm guns and derived from the Vickers 6 Ton, were torn to shreds by the artillery, reinforcing the scepticism of the Ground Forces commander, Mc Nair, concerning the future of tanks on the battlefield. The two machine-guns positioned on the chassis each side of the turret were removed.
(LC- USW36-154)

powerful inter-arm and mobile Armored Divisions working closely with the aviation (radio relays, reconnaissance and fire-support). Multi-purpose, the Armored Division had to be *"capable of engaging in any form of combat but its main role is that of undertaking offensive actions within the enemy's rear areas"* [10]. *"Next engaged in a breakthrough, it has to operate at a distance within the enemy's rear areas and block its routes of retreat, engage combat with its strategic reserves and seize strategic objectives. During these missions, the division is integrated in a larger armored corps closely followed by motorized units. As the objective is the total destruction of the enemy by placing a strike force in its rear, the division must advance rapidly at the heart of the breakthrough"* [11]. Mechanized armies were the means to revert back to the wars led by Napoleon, Grant or Sherman[12]. The linear vision of the frontline was outdated.

In concrete terms, this evolution led to the creation of an Armored Force in May 1940, something which was independent of the cavalry and infantry. The tank lobby led by Chaffee, Patton, Andrews or Magruder seemed initially to make the most of the feelings caused by Pearl Harbor and the exploits of Guderian and Rommel as the Victory Program planned for no less than 23 Armored Corps, 61 Arm. Div. and 51 Motorized Div, more than half of the planned for 216 divisions. At the Armored Force headquarters of Fort Knox, the planners began designing a new doctrine and the structure of the future divisions was defined. In March 1942, the Armored Field Force Manual defined the role of the armored troops: *"wage an extremely mobile war with autonomous inter-arm units which are powerful, mobile and specially equipped"*. It saw itself as being a largely independent arm operating deep behind enemy lines in the same was the Air Force did in the air. The first organizational tables generously gave a Supply Battalion to each division so that it could fight autonomously in *"rucksack"* fashion as far as 400 km from its bases, in the same way as the *Panzerdivisionen* as we will see. Following the first unsuccessful maneuverer, the division which was at this time dominated by the tanks, transformed between 1941 and 1943 into a balanced, powerful, mobile and flexible inter-arm tool with the creation of the Combat Commands and Task Forces (staffs to which were attached, depending on requirements to the combatant units allowing for several combats to be undertaken at a distance without overloading the divisional headquarters and without risking breaking communications). What was seen here was not the emergence of a straightforward inter-arm cooperation but that of integration.

However, the opportunities created by the 1941 FM and the theoretical side elaborated at Fort Knox worried some high-ranking officers who did not believe in tanks and who feared that the setting up of such units would be too complex for an army that was in the midst of expanding and comprising, in the majority, of mobilized amateurs. General Lesley J. Mc Nair, an artilleryman, and who would go on to become the first commander of the Army Ground Forces in March 1942, opened a more prudent route.

Mc Nair was convinced that the tank had no future as the key weapon the battlefield. During the military exercises of 1940-41, in particular those held in Carolina and Louisiana, the blind charges led by small light tanks against his anti-tank guns hardly convinced him to change his opinion[13]. For Mc Nair, the rapid concentration of anti-tank artillery at the focal point of the enemy attack was the antidote to the Blitzkrieg. The creation of the Tank Destroyer Force equipped with self-propelled anti-tank weapons was the concrete response[14]. Also, the fighting of 1943 hardly allowed the new Armored Divisions to shine. Each encounter with the Wehrmacht ended up in bitter fighting and ridiculous territorial gains. This was particularly true in Italy where the Allies were halted on the Winter Line and where the 1st Armored Division, landed at Anzio, was used as a tactical reserve in order to break up German counter-attacks, a role which was as far removed as could be from the great advances that its sister divisions would have to undertake in France. The terrible price paid by the Soviets during in-depth operations, such as at Kharkov in 1942 and 1943, did nothing to change Mc Nair's opinion.

---

10. FM 100-5, 1941, p. 263.
11. *Ditto*, p. 275.
12. Bruno Colson, *op. cit.*, p. 211.
13. In six days, two armored divisions lost 844 tanks during trials in the Carolina states.
14. On this subject, consult the articles written by Philippe Naud, *"Seek, Strike & Destroy"*, Tank Zone n° 10, June 2010 and Hugues Wenkin, *"Seek, Strike & Destroy!"*, Batailles & blindés, n° 49, June 2012.

The creation of an armored force in May 1940 created new perspectives to operations in depth. However, the United States were starting from scratch. The handful of M1 tanks that paraded in front of the Capitol in 1939 were totally obsolete. These tanks had been named Combat Cars in order to allow their purchase by the cavalry because, like in France, the tanks were reserved for the infantry.
(LC-DIG-hec-26434)

---

15. The Battle of Normandy would put this doctrine into practice with an American army which was always aggressive and on the attack and which concluded its campaign with an attempt to encircle the enemy at Falaise... except that the war was still not over and had to be pursued.
16." *It is the role of the command to unite tactics, strategy and administration in one harmonious assembly. The total understanding by the commander and his headquarters staff concerning the capabilities and limitations of each service is essential, not only in order to allow for efficient administration but also to guarantee the success of operations. A study of the operations of large units in previous wars shows us that frequently, the failures previously attributed to wrong tactics or strategy was in fact due to a deficient administration"*, FM 100-10 Administration, War Department, 15 Nov. 1943, p. III. The term *"administration"* has been chosen over "logistics" as the manual in fact looked at all aspects of the headquarters, except for combat. It should be noted that in 1917, Colonel Charles C Thorpe assimilated logistics with the administration, creating orders, establishing camps, dumps and the supply chain, the sending forward and supplying of troops, the organization of medical service and communications, see Pure Logistics: the science of war preparation, Franklin Hudson publishing, 1917.
17. See chapter 1.

The FSR was not modified but was more orthodox. Mc Nair rejected the creation of the armored corps, which were deleted as early as 1943, preferring instead a standardized army built around autonomous and multi-function army corps which combined infantry divisions, armored divisions which were also reinforced with colossal support in the form of artillery battalions, anti-aircraft, tank destroyers, tank battalions and transportation. The number of armored divisions went from 61 to 20, allowing for the creation of 65 armored battalions to which we can add a hundred tank destroyer battalions. The Armored Force at Fort Knox which had never obtained the status of an Arm, like the infantry or cavalry, was downgraded and became a straightforward Command in 1943, then a Center in 1944 on the same footing as the Desert Training Center. From this point on, the combination of operations was reduced to a series of attritional combat and the battle in depth was limited to tactical engagements with the final objective of encircling the enemy, the destruction of which remained the ultimate goal. The linear vision of the battlefield was finally retained[15]. In these conditions, the army needed massive and regular logistics, but did not need to be particularly mobile.

LOGISTIC PRINCIPLES IN AGREEMENT WITH THE DOCTRINE

Logistics were theorized and officially integrated as a component of the doctrine for the first time in 1941 via the publication of 187-page addendum to the Field Service Regulations, named FM 100-10 Administration. It was updated in 1943 based on what had been learned from the first battles. A close look at this teaches us a lot as it heralded both the planning of Overlord and the stalling of the pursuit.

After having reminded the reader on the importance of logistics[16], the manual applies the advice of Jomini which states that *"the laws of good logistics indicate the necessity of organizing the line of operations and staging posts which have to form the link between the army and rear base"* and details for the first time the concrete establishment of a supply chain between the United States and the armies[17]. The onus was placed less on the operations than on the organization and the logistics required to ensure the most efficient deployment. We see here the "managerial" American culture, introduced by Ulysse Grant which sought to control those involved whilst at the same time offering enough flexibility to adapt to the circumstances of the moment. The text thus insists at numerous points on the importance of team work.

However, what is striking is that for the most part, this logistical base was a fixed base preparing for the battle, but which did not evolve with it. To use an industrial metaphor, the front became the factory to which the raw materials converged. In the entire 187 pages, there is no mention of supplying an army on the move. The term "pursuit" is never used. We guess that the pursuit of operations is conditioned by the opening of new forward dumps. Three paragraphs cover the subject of moving the railheads, the most forward supply points which have to remain less than fifty kilometres from the frontlines (p. 74). The first of these paragraphs states that it might be necessary to create new railheads, the second that moving them has to be planned with ComZ and the third underlines the fact that an army does not have the material means to move a supply depot by itself. The least that can be said is that this did not preordain very mobile operations.

Due to the static character of logistics, rail logically remained the favoured means of transportation (pages 39 and 44). Its use is seen in detail over 20 pages (half of the chapter dealing with various means of transportation) and the Engineers had to train in laying narrow railways as close as possible to the frontline. On the subject of railways, the North African campaign could have raised eyebrows as railway logistics were disastrous there. Whilst Patton was halted waiting for his ships to be unloaded in Morocco, a race against the clock had been engaged in order to capture the Tunisian ports before the Germans and Italians, a raid of some 900 km from Algiers and 1,600 from Casablanca. The Anglo-American forces suffered notably from the mediocre transport network. To take reinforcements towards the east, Eisenhower had placed all of his hopes in the Algerian rail network. However, only nine trains per day left Casablanca, three of which were loaded with coal and supplies destined for civilians. Even so, they took a week to reach the Tunisian border. The race was lost and the situation bogged-down until the spring. During the winter, 4,500, 5,300, and then 5,400 extra vehicles were successively sent across from the United-States to ease the burden on the rail network. The campaign, therefore, highlighted the limitations of logistics that relied on railways and the need for a huge fleet of trucks to maintain contact with the port dumps and the frontline. But this failure of the rail network did hardly ruffled any feathers in Washington. The War Department estimated that it had been only caused by the modest North African rail network and that the same problem would not be encountered in France. There was also a difference which justified considering North Africa as an exception. The Allies had landed more than a thousand kilometres away from the enemy. In France, the Wehrmacht would be waiting for them on the beaches, would hold on the slightest river, as they were already doing in Italy, the advance would be slowed down and therefore allow for the reconstruction of the rail network. Nobody could foresee that the Germans would collapse at a given time and lead to a strategic withdrawal.

The use of the road would have to be limited, therefore, to rotations between the railheads and the fighting men over a few dozen kilometres. The manual recognized though, that *"The principle of economy and rapidity of service could impose the transportation of supplies or troops by road. In order to deal with these contingencies, the regulating officer in charge of a regulating station will have to have prepared detailed plans for the large-scale use of motorized transport. In such a case, the regulating officer can hold authority over the all road traffic between ComZ and the Combat Zone and directly use the Motor Transport Service units which will be attached to him"*. The use of the term *"contingency"* and the verb *"impose"* highlights well the lack of confidence placed in the road, deemed incapable of dealing with large supply flows. It is not surprising, therefore, that the complaints of Motor Transport Service commander, General Ross, concerning the insufficient road means allocated to his services, were ignored.

The regulations, updated in 1943, followed the recommendations of General Mc Nair that put forward the idea of regiments and battalions

supplying themselves directly with their own means of transportation from the railheads without passing via divisional dumps. Under the pretext of, and rightly so, giving more flexibility and avoiding useless intermediary means, this reform mostly allowed for the economy of means as the divisional supply train was reduced in size without increasing the means of other units. The worst hit was the Armored Division which saw its Supply Battalion simply disappear. Mc Nair who no longer believed in large armored units, made the most of a letter written by Patton to clip their wings. *"Our original idea which was of a division having to autonomously cover 400 km is now wrong. You would be lucky to cover five per day. When a breakthrough takes place, there will always be time to ask the corps or army for temporary extra transportation"* [18]. Despite the opposition from some of his staff officers, Mc Nair made his final decision on 10 August 1943: *"There is no doubt that the division has too much in the way of logistical means. Patton has categorically admitted this. It is also sure that an army can supply an armored division as well as any other unit"* [19]. The divisional supply battalion

was deleted and the various tank battalions, motorized infantry and artillery would be supplied according to same principles as the infantry divisions. This supply depot finally played the role of a leash around a hare's neck. This choice alone shows the modest in-depth actions that the general-staff foresaw for the armored divisions. However, the problem was so obvious that the six paragraphs – a not one more – covering the armored divisions, suggested such a series of solutions to give more freedom of action, such as air supply or the attribution of trucks companies which would carry out enough gasoline, spare parts and rations for the duration of operations. Indeed, as we see in 1944, the 12th US AG brought in as a stop-gap measure two extra QM Trucks Companies (100 trucks) for each division and had to use air supplies and even this was not sufficient. As the doctrine hardly envisaged operations in depth, apart from large-scale tactics of encircling the enemy, logistics were not designed with this in mind.

To the Operative art

This motorized warfare was undertaken at an operational or operative level. Army corps, or whole armies, were engaged for weeks at a time in depth and worked together in a coordinated way but at separated from each other by considerable distances. For example, Patton's army was deployed at the beginning of September from Brest to the gates of the Lorraine. However, having neglected the operational level since the Civil War, an intermediate level was missing from the American logistical chain in Europe between its strategic level (ComZ) and that of tactics (Combat Zone). The gulf between Lee and his generals simply corresponded to this operational void. Lee was a strategic player without any hold on the operational process; the generals had become operational actors without any hold on logistics apart from on a tactical level. Eisenhower tried to fill this void by playing a role of go-between throughout the month of October. But this did not really work as he was himself a strategic player rather than an operational one.

The halting of the pursuit and the four months required to get over it find their deep-rooted cause in this doctrine. It explains the reason why heavy trucks were rejected and the improvisation of rear-echelon services when the breakthrough towards Brittany became a headlong drive through France. The ASF had to, in the same way as the entire army, re-learn at a late stage, war in depth.

By improvisation and an informal apprenticeship, the Americans looked for pragmatic, concrete solutions. Luckily for them, at the school of war they are good learners.

Pvt Robert J. Vance, of the 33rd Arm. Regiment, 3rd AD, is seen here on his Harley Davidson WLA "Liberator". Disappointing in a reconnaissance role, motorbikes revealed themselves to be an indispensable mount for dispatch riders.
(p001046, Région Basse-Normandie/NARA)

At Fort Knox, the home of the Armored Force, it was thought that they would become the equivalent on the ground of the Air Force in the skies, that is to say, an autonomous arm capable of operating beyond the frontline and spreading terror in the enemy's rear.
(LC-USW36-155)

---

18. A personal letter from Patton to General Gillem, 21 May 1943.
19. Greenfield and al., *The Organization of Ground Combat troops*, CMH, 1947, p. 308

Joined together with the M3, the first Sherman M4 tanks were tested out at Fort Knox. Its design had taken into account the industrial constraints – simplicity of manufacture – and logistics – size being dictated by the lack of space on board Liberty Ships, harmonization of spare parts. The Americans had made enormous progress in the space of five years since the small M2 (top, background). The first Half-Tracks (below) were used by the mechanized infantry, indispensable for the new inter-arm units (Combat Command).
(LC- USW361-171, LC-DIG-fsac-1a35208 & LC-DIG-fsac-1a35192)

PART FIVE

REVOLUTION?

ComZ signals center in Valognes. At this time, these cases were just straightforward switchboards (Panel BD-132A), but they foreshadowed the move towards the new forms of communications which would revolutionize the world a half century later. The two men wear the ASF badge.
(p011872, Région Basse-Normandie/NARA)

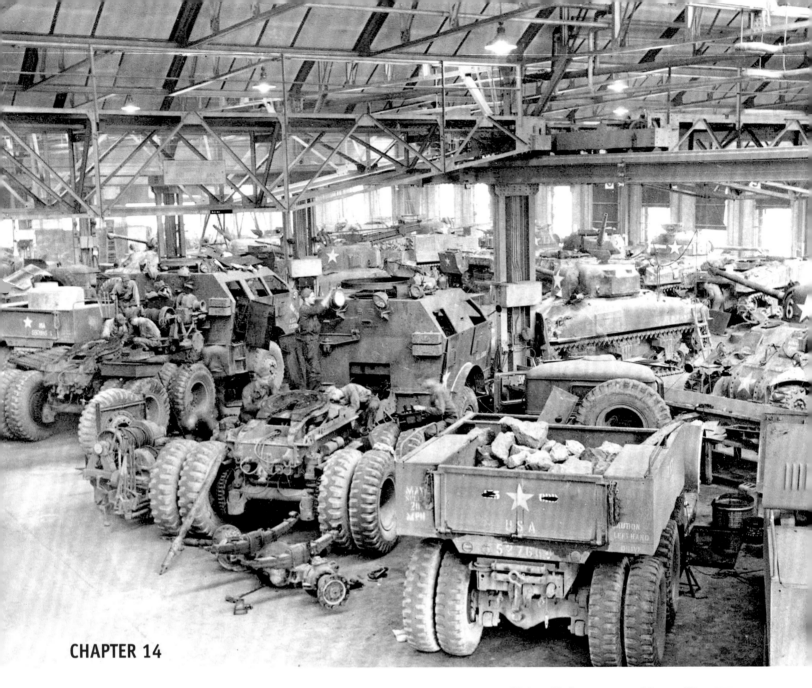

CHAPTER 14

AT THE SCHOOL OF WAR

According to the historian Michael Doubler, the strength of the American army in the Second World War was its flexibility and capacity to learn lessons quickly. *"Contrary to the European armies, the Americans had a permissive vision of the doctrine and considered blind obedience to its regulations more of a vice than a virtue. The commanders believed that a flexible application of its principles would help to overcome any difficulties and encouraged initiative. [...] The process of transformation and adaptation was decentralized and not directive"*[1].

1. M. Doubler, *op. cit.*, p. 279
2. The famous hedgerow cutter placed on the front of tanks to find a way of beating the Normandy bocage was invented by a lowly sergeant, Culin, shown to Bradley and then seeing 500 produced in one week.

Instead of a headquarters collecting, digesting, elaborating new instructions then handing them out, the Americans encouraged men of all ranks to innovate and the good ideas were then spread via informal channels, word of mouth, as well as formal channels such as divisional information bulletins and Battle Experiences and Combat Lessons reports which trickled throughout the entire army. Thanks to this process, American tactics were refined (inter-arm cooperation, combat tactics in the hedgerows and towns), materiel improved[2]... and logistics were much more efficient.

LEARN THE SHORTAGE

At the frontline, the armies learned how to deal with the lack of supplies. In September, the 12th US AG brought in rationing on the same lines as that put into place by the 1st Army in mid-June, that is to say, they imposed a ceiling for the consumption of each type of munition for the four days to come. But this system was not a reasonable one because:

• The 12th US Army Group set the allocations for each army under its command but, as it was not the distributor, it could not guarantee delivery by ComZ

• This system did not offer any visibility for the combatant units which, unable to know what the future allocations would be, could not, therefore, plan their attacks

• It encouraged rivalry between each army in order to receive

Previous page.
Driven by dynamic officers such as Nixon or Medaris, the Ordnance services improved with radio being used to manage stocks, workshops which became veritable factories where the jobs were broken down and where one played... leapfrog.
(13-Num 0844, NARA © Archives départementales de la Manche)

Left.
Several emergency stations, where teams of mechanics worked, were opened along the ABC Road. Each one was equipped with breakdown vehicles.
(NARA)

a higher allocation which led them to cover up the true state of their stores and over-exaggerate what they were really lacking. The rational distribution of available means was therefore distorted.

• The worst is that it led to waste as the unused munitions for a certain period had to be handed back to each army group. Any excess munitions automatically led to a lowering of the next allocations, according to the grotesque principal that of any army did not need something yesterday, it would not, therefore, need it tomorrow. Artillerymen were sometimes put in the situation of firing blindly to use up their ammunition and ensure a decent re-supply.

On 5 November, after functioning for six weeks, the system was improved. The army group allocated a credit every ten days to each army, with the latter being free use it up rapidly, slowly or to store it. It then transmitted its supply forecasts for thirty days. Thus, the decentralized management of stocks made each army responsible and allowed it better visibility with which it could plan its operations.

THE INNOVATION BY THE EXAMPLE, THE *ORDNANCE CORPS*

The technical services also innovated. Take the examples of Colonels Medaris and Nixon, in charge of maintenance with the First and Third Army. Even before the landings, Medaris took the initiative of gathering together radio equipment in order to maintain contact with his teams and allow them to cooperate with each other. In Normandy, where the various companies often operated in fields next to each other, sometimes at shouting distance, Medaris made them use radios in order to become accustomed to their use. The result of this was that at the moment of the pursuit, his teams were much more reactive, passing along supply orders more rapidly, gaining hours and sometimes days and being able to always collaborate, swap spare parts, despite being spread out over hundreds of kilometres. This system was copied by other armies during the course of the autumn and winter. Without this system, Nixon, his Third Army

Below.
The 442nd RCT, a "Nisei" unit comprising of Americans of Japanese descent, head towards the frontline in the Vosges on board Transportation Corps GMC trucks, on loan for this purpose. Knowing how to successfully judge the needs of the frontline units and those of the rear was an art not learnt at the military academies.
(p000825, Région Basse-Normandie/NARA)

Liberty Roads, 1944-1945

The ABC Road, a new one-way Express, was in use between 30 November 1944 and 26 March 1945. 16 Trucks Companies operated on it and were all equipped with the International 4x2 5-Ton M 426 and the 10 tonne trailer. More flexible with its half-trailer and with double the carrying capacity, the M426 proved to be an excellent workhorse. *(NARA/H & C)*

Next page.
A storage area in the shade of an orchard for thousands of jerrycans.
(NARA)

Below.
8,119 Federal 4X4 4/5 ton were made between 1941 and 1945. It was almost the twin vehicle to the Autocar U 7144T, sharing the same Hercules engine and numerous parts such as the gear-box. It is seen here towing a 5-Ton trailer, but it could also carry two 2,000 gallon tankers, refrigerated trailers or low C2 25 or 40 foot trailers and it was not uncommon for the vehicle to pull up to fifteen tonnes.
(NARA/H & C)

counterpart, was unable to coordinate his forward units and was forced to delegate the authority to the corps commanders of the zones they were operating in.

Although Nixon missed the bus concerning radios, he showed his spirit of initiative by improving intake procedures of damaged vehicles. He opened a control point at the entrance where vehicles were sorted according to their problems then sent to various companies who had been specialized. Thus, Nixon transformed his "homespun" workshop into a "factory".

As for ADSEC, it invented the principal of "leap-frogging". Instead of sending back the most damaged equipment, it sent a maintenance company to the army zone to repair it directly in the field at a collecting point. When it moved to follow the advance of the frontline, it left behind its unfinished work which was taken over by another company which itself left any unfinished work to a third rearguard company. This successful practice would go on to be generalized.

With the Ordnance Corps being also tasked with distributing ammunition, Medaris innovated again by creating the first mobile distribution dump for the VII Corps in mid-August. He obtained the five companies of the 102nd QM Truck Battalion (225 trucks) which he attached to the 71st Ordnance Group. The mobile dump was made up of two echelons. A forward echelon distributed munitions directly to the frontline with the help of 125 trucks. The second, 35 km behind, prepared requested supplies for the forward echelon and with its remaining 100 GMC trucks, went to dump 106 which had remained in some 200 km away in Normandy. Within ten days, this dump distributed 6,500 t of munitions on roadsides and even in village streets. Naturally, this hindered traffic circulation but it was of huge help to operations as the trucks could unload directly from the road. They were soon imitated by other services and armies.

ON THE ROAD AGAIN

Of course, the most striking innovations concerned road transport. Making the most of experience gained by the Red Ball Express, other routes were opened during the course of the war: *Green Diamond, White Ball,* but above all the *ABC Road* and *XYZ Roads*.

The ABC Road was a route opened to take goods from Antwerp towards the forward dumps of the 9th and 1st Army. Its name stems from the fact that in order to open it, an agreement had to be negotiated with the British and Canadians to regulate the traffic around Antwerp which was in the British zone. This road constituted a major progress compared with the Red Ball Express:

• In order to avoid any conflicts of authority that had been the case with the Red Ball, the road circulation was centralized by the Channel Base Section commanded by General Jacobs, even if the convoys drove through other sections.

• Circulation was improved and refined. Two companies were tasked with going back and forth between the quaysides and a transit zone, the route's point of departure. At this point, they left behind their trailers which were taken by fourteen transport companies which then took them to three control points, one at Liege, another at Namur and the last at Charleroi where they were dispatched to the dumps corresponding to their load and which were equipped with dealing with them. The coordination between the dumps was guaranteed by an efficient chain of radio communications and the whole arsenal of what had been put in place for the Red Ball was used again (mid-route bivouacs, repair workshops, road patrols).

• To speed up rotations, only the semi-trailers were used (many towed 10 tonnes) and they were thus able to exchange an empty trailer for a full one and there were two drivers per truck.

Thanks to these innovations, although each rotation of 175 km still took twenty hours, the sixteen truck companies managed to transport, without any problems, 245,000 t of goods between 30 November 1944 and 26 March 1945. With 2,000 t transported daily, for only the required number of 768 trucks, it proved that road transport could be a durable mode of transportation and which was reliable, flexible and capable of carrying high tonnage (the road replaced 5 rail convoys per day).

The relative immobility of the front of course makes it difficult to measure the efficiency of these innovations. The real test would come in April 1945 when, once the Rhine was crossed, the American armies would begin a new pursuit.

Liberty Roads, 1944-1945

CHAPTER 15

1945, CONSIDERABLE PROGRESS

Day was just breaking when, on this 4 May 1945, General Wood was going along the banks of the Danube. He had a meeting to attend at Patton's headquarters in order to go over the final details of the offensive in Czechoslovakia a final time. His 4th Armored Division, Patton's best, would be at the forefront.

Men of the 82nd Airborne, arrived in GMC trucks, embark on trains at Duren before heading off towards the frontline of the XV Army, end of April 1945. Three weeks after the beginning of the German campaign, several railroads were already reopened east of the Rhine. (NARA)

Wood's jeep drove passed line after line of GMC trucks but, above all, the large M 426 that towed the ten-tonne trailers. On both sides of the road leading to Deggendorf, the Engineers had set up dumps that were filled with jerry cans, ration boxes and ammunition. Two Bailey bridges had been laid over the Danube, one for vehicles moving up, the other for those returning. Wood smiled as he remembered that the Germans had held this ground two days earlier. He could be reassured by the fact that his men would not go without anything, just as had been the case since they had crossed the Rhine six weeks earlier on 24 March, 400 km away to the west.

It seemed such a long time ago when, on the banks of the Meuse in the summer of 44, a disgusted Patton had ordered him to leave behind his fuel-less Shermans and carry on the advance on foot.

This time the operations were being carried out without any bad surprises and when the Germans capitulated, the Americans found themselves with 130,000 tonnes of ammunition in their forward dumps (ten days of reserves). They also had 168,000 tonnes on the Rhine. Better still, the number of replacement tanks at the end of April was higher than that at the end of March, reaching the ceiling authorized by Washington (7,620 tanks deployed for an authorized total, reserves included, of 7,779).

Empirically, after months of stalling and learning, ComZ had acquired an undeniable savoir-faire and had transformed into a remarkable machine for feeding the war[1].

THE INVENTORS OF THE OPERATIONAL LOGISTICS

This campaign highlights the progress made since August 1944. The Americans were aware that from now on, the set-

In 1945, aerial transport procedures had made great progress. Almost a quarter of Patton's fuel arrived by air.
(13-Num 1183, NARA © Archives départementales de la Manche)

ting up of operations in depth implied logistics of an operational level, that is to say integrated into the operations themselves. With mechanization the units requested too many supplies and went too fast and too far. Operations became too fluid to allow coordinated supply from outside services to function.

These logistics are called operational as opposed to strategic and tactical logistics. Strategic logistics is one of static depots, but which are huge and at a long distance which could only cope with two forms of transport-ships and rail. It supplied theatres of operations. Tactical logistics is one of proximity where flexibility and rapidity are essential. This is the space in which all-terrain vehicles of less than three tonnes thrive unhindered by rutted roads and mud. Between these two, the return to a war of movement created a gap where logistics had to both combine flexibility and volume. Rail no longer had a place, as was also the case for tactical vehicles due to their low load bearing capacities. This was, therefore, the space in which heavy vehicles reigned, capable of carrying loads of ten tonnes, if possible on trailers, organized in convoys and on dedicated roads with a whole arsenal of services (maintenance, bivouac, security, signals...) at their disposition. It demanded a specific operational administration.

However, in 1945, ComZ attributed a designated representative to each army, the Highway Transport Divisions. These HTD allowed those in charge of operations to cooperate efficiently and rapidly with their logistical counterpart who was consulted at each stage of planning and execution. The creation of the HTD decentralized the transport of the strategic echelon to the operational echelon. It also greatly simplified the supply chain with each HTD concentrating all of its powers to the detriment of the territorial players such as the Base Sections.

ComZ also sought to, without always managing, to ensure the supply of the combatants without penalizing the daily work between the dumps situated further down the line. It made the most of much larger means placed at its disposal: 226 Trucks Companies many of which were heavy and which in total were the equivalent of 316 light companies of the summer of 1944 (three times more than at this time). It could, therefore, answer the requirements of the front and rear. The inter-dump flows were considerably rationalized with the setting up of a Monthly Movement Program. This was procedure which centralized the supply flows coordinated by the Transportation Corps. It led to a change of perspective as instead of requisitioning transports to cover needs, the urgency of which was badly prioritized, from now on it was the capacities and localization of transportation means which determined the volumes of supplies to be transported and where. The construction of pipelines was also speeded up and by the end of March, the three biggest army dumps were reached:

---

1. One could of course talk about the collapse of German resistance and the short period of operations of the 9th and 1st Army (24 March-13 April) in order to relativize the performance of ComZ. It should be simply noted that in April 1945, it was not twenty divisions that it had to supply, but 49.

Liberty Roads, 1944-1945

Wesel (North line from Antwerp), Thionville (Major line from Cherbourg) and Sarralbe (South line from the étang de Berre). All this freed up means of transportation and avoided the creation of a blockage further up the supply chain. In the dumps, the often self-propelled cranes were commonplace, storage procedures rationalized and maintenance improved.

Air transportation was also undergoing changes. The improvement of procedures allowed for two to three daily rotations. Thus, with just 329 planes, deliveries increased to 2,150 tonnes per day (more than triple) in the second week of April and to 1,600 tonnes per day for the monthly average. The Third Army coopera-

Repairing a leaky valve on this old German tanker at Melhen west of the Rhine. Although these tankers could not travel any further due to a lack of bridges, their precious fuel was sent via a hastily built pipeline laid across the river bed, thus linking the two banks.
(NARA)

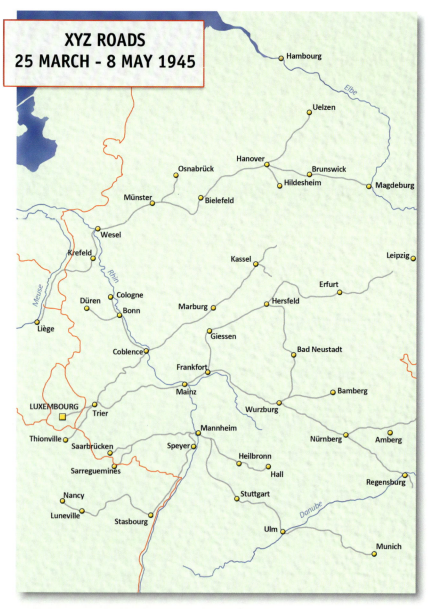

**XYZ ROADS
25 MARCH - 8 MAY 1945**

The winter had provided the time to accumulate building materials near the frontline and it took the 1056th Engineer Group only ten days to build the Robert Gouldin Railway Bridge over the Rhine.
(NARA)

ted in the bringing back into service of 30 airfields with the help of the 2nd Engineer Aviation Brigade. They used, amongst other things, sections of freeways. Thus, the Dakotas and C46 almost kept up with the tanks which received 22 % of their fuel from the air. For the first time, air supply, which up to this point had been used to trickle supplies into areas under siege, was of notable help to operations in depth.

ROADS SUPPLANT RAILROADS

But in order to keep the pursuit supplied, ComZ, along with ADSEC and the Transportation Corps, gave the priority to the road. This was about succeeding in the depth of the front what had worked at the rear with the ABC Road. This was the XYZ Road operation[2]. The principal of these one-way roads remained identical but had been further improved:

• To avoid any friction and provide flexibility, four different itineraries worked in parallel, one for each army. The blockages at the bridges over the Rhine were somewhat limited by the placing of pipelines on the river bed, something which meant that tankers did not need to cross. Thus, whilst wagons and trucks arriving from the rear emptied their tanks on the left bank, other trucks filled theirs on the other side of the river and departed for the frontlines.

• To speed up rotations, only semi-trailers were used (many towed ten tonnes).

• On an administrative level, the management of each road had been centralized and a communications network linked up the various players. To improve the quality of deliveries, supply tables had been calculated according to the units maneuvering or fighting, one giving priority to fuel, the other to ammunition. Depending on its requirements, each army requested to be delivered with one or the other.

• To avoid the wearing out of the vehicle park and the exhaustion of its drivers, each convoy took with it a mechanic and a truck carrying spare parts, workshops were opened along the road as well as canteens where the drivers could change their cold rations for something hot. Rapid 48 to 72-hour rotations allowed for driver turnover. 17,000 men were also used to maintain the roads to which we should add the services of each arm and ad-hoc units such as, for example, 4,000 men of the 7th Armored Division. Bailey Bridges waited to be used as a replacement for destroyed bridges.

Phase X began on the third day of the offensive on 25 March,

Above right.
An indispensable but hard job reserved for African American personnel: cleaning out fuel barrels and jerrycans amongst all the vapors, with their knees soaked in the black mud.
(NARA)

Liberty Roads, 1944-1945

first for the 3rd Army which was already 230 km from its Luxemburg dumps. It grew in strength quickly and went beyond the forecasts as, by the end of April, it was the equivalent of 244 Light Companies who delivered a daily tonnage of 15,000 tonnes. Just at the Rhine, 57 bridges had been built. At the high point of the advance, the rotations covered nearly 800 km but *"only"* took 36 hours. Road, therefore, had taken the place of the railway, in supporting armies. The introduction of the truck into the chain revolutionized logistics in the same way as the tank had done in combat[3]. It was the truck which filled the breach between the railway and the advancing frontline.

Railways did not, however, disappear. It remained the major mode of transport for the inter-supply depot flows and at the outset, the Quartermaster Corps commander at ComZ, hoped to use it to move the forward dumps. More precisely, he dreamed of accompanying the advance of each army with a semi-mobile advanced depot which would be used as an emergency reserve (10 to 15 days of rations and five of gasoline) near the frontline and not as a final intermediary between the rear dumps and those of the army. The logistical chain would therefore save itself a stage whilst retaining a capacity to intervene. The fact that a supply depot was assigned to an army shows once again the operational flexibility. However, Littlejohn's project failed. Due to a lack of means, these advanced dumps were grouped together for two armies which ruined the entire philosophy and none were finally opened during the German campaign.

Consequently, rail, which should have been used to move them, was in fact used in direct support to armies by complementing the road network. Thanks to early planning, it would only require ten days to open the first rail bridges. At the same time, the lines east of the Rhine had been partially repaired. Three weeks after the start of operations, 12,000 tonnes of supplies crossed the Rhine by train.

A REVOLUTION?

But can we really talk of a revolution? Some will see in the enormous means put into play the mechanical explanation for this success. It cannot be denied that the landing of new companies helped ComZ and also allowed to strengthen the army supply units with an extra ten companies. But this would not take into account the most important aspect, that is to say the passage

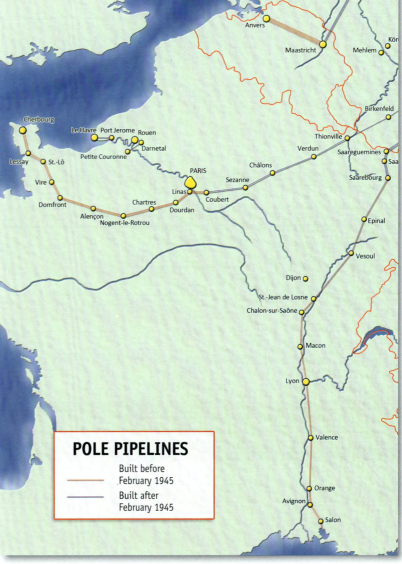

POLE PIPELINES
— Built before February 1945
— Built after February 1945

The XYZ Roads, the rightful heirs of the Red Ball Express

		XYZ ROADS					RED BALL		
Phase	Staff (by trucks)	Staff by coy.*	Implementation	Expected volume	Real volume	Staff (by trucks)	Staff by coy.	Real volume
X	2750	55 (101)	25/03	8000 t/d	8000 t/d	6000 (end of August)	132	7500 t/d
Y	3350	667 (125)	1st/04	10000 t/d	10 000 t/d			
Z	4050	81 (150)	?	12000 t/d	15000 t/d	8500 (End of Sept.)	182	4625 t/d
Gas	816	17	25/03	4100 t/d	4100 t/d			

*(equivalent in type 44 companies)

These engineers of C Co. 202nd Engineer Combat Bn. 3rd US Army are clearing a road with a Caterpillar RD4/D4 and Le Tourneau Angledozer & Power Control Unit Hyster D4 equipment.
(p011770, Région Basse Normandie/NARA)

from a two-stage supply logic (strategic with rail and tactical with the road) to a three-stage logic: strategic with railways which linked the ComZ supply depots together, operational with the establishment of one-way routes used by heavy vehicles to link the depots to the armies and tactical within the army zones with all-terrain Light-Heavy vehicles. This would also not take into account all of the administrative innovations. However, more than a revolution, one can see this stage as being an outcome; the outcome of a great revolution that began at the beginning of the century, that of the internal combustion engine.

After having profoundly modified the war in air, helped get the fighting men out of the trenches in which industrialization had

---

2. Its name comes from the fact that the operation had to gain strength in three phases X, Y and Z.
3. Clayton R Newell, *Logistical Art, Parameters*, March 1989, p. 35.

Liberty Roads, 1944-1945

THE GERMAN CAMPAIGN

The German campaign designates the operations which took place between 15 January and 8 May 1945. Its plans had been validated by SHAEF at the beginning of 1945. They were inspired by the Master Plan and were still anchored in the American doctrine of wearing out.

This campaign is split into three phases.

1. *The destruction of German forces* west of the Rhine. Drawn out and slow with two months of terrible fighting in urban and wooded areas, this attritional phase ended victoriously mid-March. The Wehrmacht had fought with their backs to the wall and ended up worn out, no longer having the means to make the post of the Rhine defensive line.

2. *The combat crossing of the Rhine* using a considerable amount of means, was followed by the encirclement of the Ruhr, wiping out the bulk of the Reich's forces in the west and taking away its industrial heartland. This phase from 22 March to 18 April resulted in the capture of 317,000 men and the destruction of 21 divisions.

3. *At the same time*, 4 April saw the start of a pursuit the objective of which was to bring an end to the war as quickly as possible, with the minimum cost, whilst preserving the alliance with Stalin. This consisted of a penetration in the center by the 12th US Army Group to cut the remaining German forces in two and reach the Elbe accompanied by mopping-up operations on the flanks carried out by the 21st Br. AG and 6th US AG.

Faced with a broken-up enemy, this phase went beyond what was hoped for and as early as 11 April, the Americans were on the Elbe near Magdeburg. At the end of the month, Patton entered into Czechoslovakia.

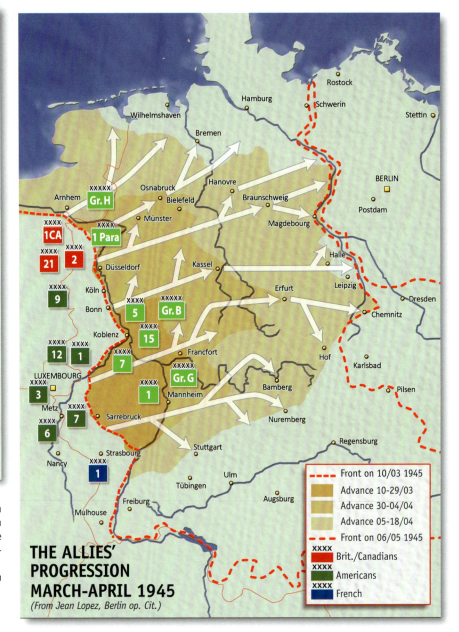

THE ALLIES' PROGRESSION MARCH-APRIL 1945
(From Jean Lopez, Berlin op. Cit.)

put them, the engine at last gave logistics the reach which was indispensable to the acceleration of operations which had begun in 1939. Whereas the Germans put forward the tank-plane duo, the Americans showed the world that another duo was indispensable, that of the tank and the truck.

It was, therefore, not so much a revolution that was seen in 1945, but rather an outcome.

Whilst the engineers are cutting out wooden sections, a steamroller makes a final passage on a road that has just been tarmacked. The US Army had all professions within its ranks. In the background is a Fordson WOT 2B truck.
(p013024, Région Basse Normandie/NARA)

Liberty Roads, 1944-1945

CHAPTER 16

The Wehrmacht was a huge travelling circus of thousands of different types of civilian vehicles that had been requisitioned. The growth of the German army meant that captured vehicles were pressed into service, such as this Citroën. *(RR)*

ALONE IN THE WORLD?

THE BLITZKRIEG, A DENIAL OF LOGISTICS

Affirming that a revolution took place requires a comparison. Could it not be said that the progress made by the Americans can also be seen with the Germans and Soviets? For this reason we are going to briefly look at how two other armies dealt with logistics during three major breakthroughs, these will be the Wehrmacht in May 1940, then in June-July 1941 and the 1st Belorussian Front following the breakthrough on the Vistula in January 1945.

These three choices are explained for reasons of sources, Karl-Heinz Frieser, Martin van Creveld and Klaus Friedrich Schüller who studied the logistics of May 1940, Barbarossa, as well as Antipenko by Jean Lopez which gives an excellent account of the rear echelon chief's experience on the front commanded by Zhukov in 1945[1].

Vernichtungschlacht and logistics

Since 1939 the German army was something of a paradox. On one hand it had at its disposal a powerful tool for breaking up enemy forces with lightning speed, the *Panzerdivision*, an inter-arm unit that was perfectly wielded by master tacticians such as Manstein, Guderian or Hoepner. On the other hand it still relied on a quartermaster service that depended on railways or the horse. However, this paradox was not obvious as the Blitzkrieg had been designed as a tactical solution to the stalemate of trench warfare. It was a doctrine which combined both old recipes such as infiltration by *Stosstruppen* or a command which was decentralised by objectives (*Auftragstaktiks*) and technical innovations, as well as perfect tactical skills. But the Blitzkrieg was not in any way a revolution in the art of carrying out military campaigns as, strategically, the Wehrmacht of 1940 was following in the footsteps of its ancestors of 1870 and 1914. The goal was the destruction of an enemy army via a huge battle aimed at wiping out the latter, or by enveloping the adversary by a huge repetition of the battle of Cannae (*Vernichtungschlacht*). The German army applied on the strategic scale tactical solutions: always surprise the enemy, attack rapidly and in strength where the enemy did not expect it, overwhelm the enemy; these were the keys to success, a decisive success which would guarantee short wars.

Consequently, the German army needed some mobile units capable of encircling the enemy mass. The depth of this encirclement that began at the border, depended on the type of enemy army and terrain, but was not to exceed 300 kilometres. The initial shock guaranteed a rapid breakthrough and in a few days at best, a few weeks at worst, the enemy would be on its knees and forced to capitulate as it had nothing left with which to defend its territory.

In this configuration, logistics occupied a decisive but limited place. It was decisive as it allowed for the deployment of men, materiel and ammunition at a precise area of the front line, a task that was suited for rail transport and planned before war was declared. It was limited in time (short campaign) and in space (border zone), as supplies remained almost solely dependent on tactics with dumps opened BEFORE the start of operations. The very concept of a supply chain was absent from German thinking as supplies were supposed to be sent directly from the economic base at the rear to the forward dumps that were placed as closely as possible to the armies[2]. There was no chain of intermediate dumps, known as *etappe*, as Napoleon had done or the Americans were trying to do. However, the problem of supplying the moving right wing arose; these were the units which would breakthrough

---

1. Karl Heinz Frieser, *Le mythe de la guerre éclair*, Belin, 2003. Martin Van Creveld, Supplying war, *op. cit.* Klaus A. Friedrich Schüller, *Logistik im Russlandfeldzug*, Peter Lang 1987. Antipenko, NA, *In der Hauptrichtung*, Militarverlag der DDR, 1973. Jean Lopez, Berlin. *Les offensives géantes de l'armée rouge*, Economica, 2010. We could add a synthesis, Mickael D. Krause & R Cody Philips (dir.), *Historical perspective of the operationnal art*, CMH, 2005 several chapters of which look at the German and Soviet doctrines.
2. Vladimir Prebilic, "Theorical aspects of military logistics", Defense & Securities analysis, vol 22, n° 2, p. 162 & Clayton R. Newell, "Logistical Art" Parameters, March 1989, p. 35.

in depth and move at a rate of 30 km per day from its logistical base.

During the campaigns of 1870 and 1914, the only solution resided in the use in depth of the rail network, something which was put into action by Moltke the elder in 1870. Such an approach may have had the disadvantage of only making war possible in regions equipped with a good rail network, but this was the case in France. When war was declared, his three armies shared the full use of six railway lines. Five Eisenbahntruppen - a 200-man unit - had been specially trained to repair and maintain the lines captured in enemy territory. Thus, it was possible to advance dumps to situated at the end of the line. From here, each army corps supplied its troops with the help of its horse-drawn supply battalion. However, in 1870, as in 1914, the advance dumps did not follow up. The Eisenbahntruppen struggled to keep up with the timescales and, above all, once a line was opened it was immediately saturated. As there was no central service for coordination, dozens of trains were dispatched but when they arrived there was not enough manpower to unload them and many rail cars became temporary warehouses that immobilised rolling stock and blocked the tracks. In 1870, when the dumps were set up at Pont à Mousson and Mars la Tour in the Lorraine, the III. Armee was already at Sedan and was preparing to pounce on Paris.

As the French refused to recognise their defeat at Sedan, the war carried on and the Prussians were forced to lay siege to Paris. Therefore, it was with no reserve that the III. and I. Armeen marched on the capital. Whereas the siege began at the end of September, no new line was operational. One was blocked by the Belfort forts, the second passed via Mézières which was only conquered at the beginning of January and the third, opened after the capitulation of Toul on 25 September, required two months of extra work in order to rebuild the bridges over the Marne. In the meantime, thousands of men had to be diverted away from the fighting in order to harvest potatoes, corn and vegetables. Markets were opened where French peasants came and sold their produce to the soldiers. It was only at the beginning of December that the forward dumps were opened near Paris and even then, the line came under frequent attacks from *francs-tireurs*. Right to the end, rail traffic remained chaotic and insufficient due to bad maintenance, accidents and sabotage.

The Prussians were lucky that the consumption of ammunition was so low - 56 rounds per man during the first five months, which was less than the personal issue - which meant that it was not necessary to regularly supply the combatants. The Prussian armies were able to live off the land in the manner of the armies of the 17th century. Thus, the logistical fiasco had not prevented the victory of 1871. Its repetition in 1914 played a role in the failure of the Schlieffen Plan.

1940, the "rucksack" *Blitzkrieg*

In 1939, the appearance of the *Panzerdivisionen* rendered the problem much worse as they could move much faster, but they could no longer rely on foraging. If the fuel tanks ran dry, the entire marching wing of the attack would grind to a halt. Not being able to rely on the too slow railways there were only two solutions. The first consisted of leaving in a 'rucksack' fashion, carrying enough reserves in order to remain autonomous until the end of the mission. The mobile units had to be able to fight independently during several days, something which had the advantage of encouraging them to push forward as they had nothing to fear, in the short term, from becoming cut-off from their supply lines. Thus, the divisional supply train had to be a veritable mobile dump which allowed to cover 750 km^3, or at best 300 real kilometres, as the experts considered that it required dividing distances

The Mercedes Benz type LG 2500 dated from 1934. Only 150 had been made for the Greek army as the Wehrmacht had not ordered any following disappointing trials. They ended up in German colors in any case once Greece had been conquered. These trucks were classified as being all-terrain, even if they were 6x4. All of them would disappear in the hell of the Eastern Front as early as the winter of 1941.
(RR)

3. *Truppenführung*, 1934, published in Bruce Condell & David T. Zabecki (ed), On the German Way of war, Stackpole books, 2009, p. 255.

Each Panzer division was accompanied by a motorized supply column. The Wehrmacht's equipment strategy led it to building its vehicle park around 4x2 vehicles that did not perform as well as the American all-terrain vehicles. These 4-tonne Büssing NAG 500 did, however, also exist in a 4x4 version.
(RR)

Liberty Roads, 1944-1945

Except for in the mobile units, the German artillery was still horse-drawn. As early as 1941, the lack of fuel and vehicles forced the Wehrmacht into a first demodernization. *(RR)*

Top left.
This bogged-down truck has to be towed away. Even with light rains, the Russian tracks turned into mud and supplying the armored spearheads, several hundred kilometres away from the railroad terminus, became something of an odyssey which ruined 40% of the vehicles within two weeks.
(RR)

Top right.
A Renault truck on the Eastern Front. We do not realize it but the French vehicle park captured in 1940 and the industrial collaboration of France was indispensable to the Wehrmacht.
(RR)

Below.
A Horch car crosses the Dvina on an engineer-built bridge. Even though the German pontoon bridges were nothing compared to the Anglo-American Baily bridges, they were never the less well-made.
(RR)

---

4. BA-MA, RH 21-1/320, p. 3 Quoted by Karl H. Frieser, *Le mythe de la guerre éclair*, Belin, 2002, p. 121.
5. Comprising of three motorized corps, 5 PzD and 3 ID (mot.), the Kleist group was the armored spearhead which, after having pushed through the Ardennes, broke through the French front on the Meuse, then drove hard to Abbeville and encircled the bulk of the allied armies within ten days.
6. *"By borrowing a few railway expressions, we could say: the troops must no longer 'entrust the sending' of its supplies to the superior authority, but it should hold on to it supplies itself in 'rucksack' fashion or as 'hand luggage"*. Zeitzler, *Panzer-Gruppe von Kleist*, 1st part, p. 184 quoted by KH Frieser, op. cit., p. 122.

at least by two when they were travelled during a fighting phase. The division also had to have its own repair workshop. The second solution was being equipped with a fleet of trucks that would go back and forth between the armoured spearheads and the dumps. But in 1939, once all of the divisions were equipped (900 vehicles for a horse-drawn infantry division and 2 to 3 thousand per motorised unit), the quartermaster services only had 6,600 trucks at their disposal with a capacity of 19,500 tonnes. This was far too little to guarantee a sufficient flow.

However, *"between 10 May 1940 and the capture of Calais, the supplies did not have a single crisis that the Kleist armoured group could not deal with itself without hindering the command[4]"*, stated the group's chief-of-staff Colonel Zeitzler[5]. This is a remarkable statement when we consider that another difficulty arose in 1940 as the marching wing of the attack had to cross through the difficult terrain of the Belgian and Luxemburg Ardennes where roads were scarce and twisting. Following in the wake of the *Panzerdivisionen* were the infantry divisions. How could they place amongst all of these units (40,000 vehicles for the Kleist Group alone) the fleet of supply trucks? The answer is that they did without them. The alternative was to increase the 'rucksack' concept by giving each armoured group a logistical independence for the length of its mission. In concrete terms, as well as its organic elements, the group obtained three extra transport companies tasked loaded to the gills with fuel and ammunition with a total capacity of 4,800 tonnes. This would have to suffice in order the reach the Channel that was 400 km from the border. Also, in order not to dip into these mobile stores, it was planned that once the border was crossed, the fuel tanks would be filled up one last time and that this would be done without stopping to prevent roads from becoming jammed. The solution found came from the.... riders of the *Tour de France* who used feed zones. Placed in strategic areas were stores of jerrycans which were passed to the occupants of vehicles at they moved along. The fuel tanks were then filled up at the next halt and the empty jerry cans were left there and recovered later and re-used by the quartermaster services. Finally, as a last precaution, trains were already prepared in order to open up the most forward dumps as soon as the lines had been secured and repaired. This method was copied by the other mobile corps and finally, almost all of the 6,600 available trucks were attached to other Panzer units. Any failings or insufficient supplies were compensated by the capture of French dumps or even from intact civilian service stations, or by air supply that was almost comparable to the British and Americans as some airfields such as Charleville reached 400 tonnes per day. Thus, the 2. PzD covered more than 400 km without seeing a single supply truck from the rear echelon.

It was a stunning victory and the Wehrmacht had managed to undertake a motorised campaign without using an abundance of motorised materiel. However, when we take a closer look, this victory was that of the negation of logistics as there was no flow between a point A and point B! It demanded a campaign that had to be won quickly otherwise the Panzers would become immobilised. This method was only possible by concentrating all of the motorised means of the marching wing of the advance, and the rest of the army (80% of the total) was reduced to traditional supplying via rail and horse-drawn carts. The success had also masked the luck that the Germans had benefited from, a case of who dares wins. For example, the violence and surprise of the initial attack were such that the Allies were unable to destroy the railway network or the bridges. Thus, German trains were able to

unload a mere five days after the capture of Brussels, something which helped in breaking up the Dunkirk pocket and the establishment of stores for the second phase of the campaign in June. Also, the pursuit was only made possible by the requisition of thousands of Belgian, Dutch and French trucks and vans, meaning that in June, Rommel and Guderian were rolling along in convoys that made it look as if the circus was coming to town. The Wehrmacht reinvented the logistics of Frederick II: live off the land. On the back of this success, the general staff began looking at other prey, although this one would be more difficult to digest: the Russian bear.

Russian roulette, the offensive by *Heeresgruppe Nord* (22 June - 6 September 1941)

The situation in 1941 had hardly changed, contrary to the size of the much more ambitious objectives. We are only going to look at Heeresgruppe Nord. Given that it was the smallest of the army groups, it was the easiest to supply, especially as the road and rail network was of a relatively good quality, particularly in the Baltic states. It was also this group that had the most accessible objective as Leningrad was only 900 km from the border... double the distance covered during the French campaign. The army group was articulated around two armies, the XVI. and XVIII *Armeen* and one *Panzergruppe*, the 4th, making a total of 26 divisions six of which were motorised. The German army was at its peak at this time. Its personnel were experienced, the materiel and procedures tried and tested on the roads of Poland, France and the Balkans. The OKH hoped to encircle and destroy the Red Army by pushing as far and as quickly as possible its tanks into the enemy's rear situated 300 km from the border on the river Dvina. The 'rucksack' system was used again. *Panzergruppe* 4 was, therefore, accompanied by 5,000 trucks for a total capacity of approximately 15,000 tonnes. As the supplies were used up, the trucks went back to the rear to fetch what was required to continue operations and in order to constitute forward dumps. One must, therefore, imagine columns of Panzers followed by columns of trucks driving in front of the horse-drawn infantry divisions and going through unsecured zones. They had considerably more means at their disposal than in May 1940, with almost 15,000 tonnes of supplies carried compared to the previous 4,800 whilst the *Panzergruppe* was less powerful than the Kleist group, 4 PzD and 2 ID (mot.) versus 5 PzD and 3 ID (mot.)[7]. But even with these means, the OKH was aware that in order to go beyond the Dvina, it would be preferable to constitute stocks brought forward by rail. The problem was that the Russian tracks were not the same gauge as those in the west and it would require, either rebuilding the rail network to the western gauge, or using it as it was with captured trains. The Germans hoped to accumulate both solutions. This task

Generalleutnant Rudolf Gercke commanded the Feldtransportwesen, the general railroad and river service. He had to work in collaboration with Major-General Wagner, the OKH quartermaster in charge of road transportation.
(RR)

did not, however, cause the general staff to worry, as they hoped to destroy the Red Army on the borders. Pushing on beyond the Dvina would be a military cake walk requiring modest means and finally, it was less with the following up operations in view than the occupation of a defeated Russia that the Eisenbahntruppen would have to get to work. Once the stocks were reconstituted, the Panzers would continue their drive as far as Leningrad. A leap forward, a halt that was as short as possible, then another leap forward, independent *Panzerdivisionen* and infantry reliant on horse-drawn supplies who occupied the captured ground, this was the plan.

The speed of the advance was spectacular as Manstein's LVI. *Armee Korps* (mot.) reached the Dvina at Dvinsk in five days. However, the Panzers were alone, the trucks which had turned around once empty, were blocked by the columns of troops and horses making their way to the front line. Contrary to what was hoped for, the orders which should have guaranteed the priority passage of the motorised columns were not efficient. The border zone was totally jammed and chaotic. At the front, as early as the 24th, units were asking for supplies to be brought in by air. Above all, the fuel consumption was a third higher than planned. Manstein did not worry one jot about this as he requested permission to push on beyond the Dvina. Hoepner,

---
7. *Das Deutsche Reich und der Zweite Weltkrieg*, Band 4: Der Angriff auf die Sowjetunion, Stuttgart, Deutsche Verlags-Anstalt, 1983, p. 367.

Mud was not the only enemy to contend with, dust was just as bad and got into everything. Given that spare parts were not available, the filters had to be cleaned daily.
(RR)

Above.
A Stug III reconverted into a recovery vehicle. The lack of specialized vehicles meant that others were diverted from their original use and also led to the early wearing out of combat materiel.
(RR)

his superior officer in the *Panzergruppe* tuned him down. In his memoirs, Manstein is insistent that this refusal, dictated according to him by disastrous prudence and not by an objective criteria, the lack of supplies as revealed by the Heeresgruppe archives. Manstein had to wait until 2 July to continue the offensive… for only two days! Finally, three weeks after the beginning of Barbarossa, Manstein had only been able to carry out operations in depth for… seven days (once for five days, the other for two), a third of the time. Yet the restart of the offensive at the beginning of July was only possible by concentrating all of the logistical means for Manstein, immobilising the XVI. Armee. The progression of Reinhardt's XXXXI. AK (mot.) was also spectacular. He many have reached the Dvina two days after Manstein but he was halted for a shorter period - four days - before making a leap of 400 km in ten days and arriving on the outskirts of Louga, 130 km from Leningrad on 12 July. But, stuck in dense forests, without infantry and supplies, the tanks became bogged down. On 19 July, OKH ordered a new halt. On this date, the Eisenbahntruppen had only just about reached Dvinsk, but there were no captured trains to make up for this, for the simple reason that there were not any left! This was because the Russians had had the strategic intelligence to destroy the railway lines, stations, water and coal supply points, signalling equipment and get the bulk of the rolling stock away. The Eisenbahntruppen had to rebuild everything. Already lacking manpower - 40,000 men for the entire Russian front - very badly equipped - one third of the units had no means of transportation - badly trained, they had to deal with an increased workload.

Several thousand retired *Reichbahn* workers or were called up or Organisation Todt men brought in, but above all, labour was supplied by thousands of civilians or POWs. The work was carried out hastily and it was soon noticed that only light trains with less than 30 cars could travel at a speed of less than… 20 km/h. There was an increase in accidents. Finally, at best only 18 trains at best travelled daily on these tracks instead of the indispensable 34. Off-loading could take up to eighty hours instead of the planned for three! Entire trains disappeared as each general had the tendency to kidnap them for his own troops, this was especially true with Luftwaffe officers; the situation was such that machine-guns were placed on trains to put them off. A particular request took eight days to fulfil. In all, less than half of the supplies reached the Dvina. To advance further there was only one railway upon which one train per day travelled! There were still the roads, but 40% of the vehicle park was broken down. With 2,000 trucks of various type, many were French or British, repairs were a total nightmare. Workshops had to adapt German parts on foreign models. Spare parts were also in short supply, the reserves of tyres, 100,000 for the entire Wehrmacht, had melted away within a month. Added to this, the zone had not been secured and the convoys remained under the threat of partisan attack. Within four weeks the situation had become difficult and nothing corresponded to the plan. The forward dumps were almost empty and already 400 km from the front lines. Between them was a no man's land through which travelled an ever dwindling number of trucks over roads that were starting to break up with the arrival of the first rains. A return trip would take a week at best, meaning that daily deliveries reached 1,000 tonnes, half of what was required. At the front line, the vehicle park which was without maintenance, began to dwindle. Divisions fought one step at a time depending on supplies. Un-jamming the situation was only possible at the end of July by using a maritime route to Riga and barges on Lake Peipus[8].

These difficulties highlight a major deficiency in the command structure. Strategically, where the entire rail and river transport network, civilian and military, was centralised by the Chef des *Transportwesen*, General Gercke, road transport was under the authority of Major-General Wagner, the OKH quartermaster, who was also, of course, responsible for all of the supplies which travelled on his trucks and Gercke's trains and barges. This supply chain looks like a pipe with the two ends controlled by Wagner and the centre by Gercke. Tactically, it was no better. Whereas the horse-drawn which columns supplied the infantry divisions were decentralised to make an *Aussenstelle*, an advance quartermaster detachment, the motorised column remained under the direct authority of Wagner. Not only did this create the same dichotomy as seen at the higher level, but the reduced structure like that of the US Army, reduced the commanders in the field to straightforward customers. This led to a conflict between the generals, with Hoepner accusing the *Aussenstelle* laziness and the infantry army commanders of piracy. Wagner accused Gercke of not giving him enough railways; Gercke placed the blame the *Aussenstelle* who took too long to unload. Whatever the case, between 12 July and 8 August, the *Panzerdivisionen* were defending more than they were attacking.

The Soviet counter-attacks were increasing in intensity, wearing down men and materiel and exhausting the reserves of supplies. The re-starting of operations was postponed seven times. On the 26th, Reinhardt was reduced to proposing an attack with one single armoured corps, two *Panzerdivisionen* to conquer a city of 2.5 million inhabitants over wooded and marshy terrain! Wagner said that he was unable to supply him and Leeb refused. After having remained

---

8. *Das Deutsche Reich und der Zweite Weltkrieg*, Band 4: Der Angriff auf die Sowjetunion, Stuttgart, Deutsche Verlags-Anstalt, 1983, p. 367.

Below.
A rail convoy on the Polish line linking Cracow with Przemysl, bringing up troops and equipment to the Soviet border in March 1941. The ideal tool for deployment, rail showed its limitations once combat was underway, if anything because of the difference in gauges between Soviet railroads and those in Europe. Changing the gauges was a huge task that had been underestimated by the general-staff.
(RR)

SOVIET LOGISTICS AND OPERATIONAL ART OF WAR

Above.
The T34 was equipped with huge internal fuel tanks and its operational range could be further increased by external drop-tanks. Thus, it could operate autonomously in depth. As for inter-arm cooperation with infantry, it could do this as long as the latter travelled on it. All of the tanks were equipped with handles allowing the infantry to hold on.
(RR)

A portrait gallery of the men who invented the Soviet operational art: Vladimir Triandafillov, Georgii Isserson and Mikhail Toukhachevsky. The latter did not survive the pre-war purges whereas Isserson spent the war in a goulag. As for Triandafillov, he was killed in a plane crash in 1931. It was, therefore, other officers such as Zhukov and Koniev who put their theory into practice.
(RR)

Soviet "operational art" comes up against a lack of logistical means

Little known in the west, at least up until the nineteen-seventies, *'operational art'* saw the day in the USSR, stemming from the systems of Alexander Svetchin and the work carried out by the Soviet military academy led by Mikhail Frounze and where we also find Triandafillov, Toukhatchevsky, Chapochnikov and Isserson. According to Svetchin, a military system is made up elements that interact, the synergy of which produces a global effect superior to all of its parts. These elements can be combatant units, lines of communications, production centres and are even more numerous if the country is industrialised, something that leads him to conclude that in the industrial era, the military system has a capacity of resilience which renders destruction in one blow an illusion. A battle of destruction is possible as it leaves the enemy system damaged, but still working, with the capacity of mobilising new means. The industrial military system is a hydra.

The only way of defeating it is to disorganise it to such an extent that it becomes paralysed and collapses... it requires hitting the hydra's heart, tendons and lungs and not the part that grows back. In concrete terms, operational art consists of aiming at the parts that ensure the system's interaction: general staffs, political and economical centres, crossroads. These elements are found well to the rear and it requires, therefore, being capable of moving over hundreds of kilometres, hacking off and removing other elements of the enemy system (communication networks, supply chain, units). The synergy of the parts no longer works and the system falls apart. The Soviets, therefore, differ from German and American planners in several ways:

• Not to seek encircling the enemy, except on a tactical level, as all enemy units that are retreating will only worsen the disruption and paralysis of the system[9].

• A single action is not enough to fragment and reach enough of the key elements of the enemy system in order to paralyse it. It requires, therefore, knowing how to combine several operations, the synergy of which will lead to paralysis. To defeat the system, one has to oppose it with another system.: knowing how to co-ordinate several armies moving in different directions, knowing how to operate in depth by mobilising motorised and airborne troops, feeding men and materiel into the battle so that it does not come to a halt before the enemy system is dislocated. It is this capacity to coordinate such a series of operations that is covered by the term, operational art. The decisive battle that the Germans dreamed of was nothing but an illusion.

• Trying to create an attritional battle by a deluge of firepower like the Americans did was, in Soviet eyes, a sterile strategy as it only led to the exhaustion of both sides. It is nothing more than an accumulation of tactical battles with no other goal than to lead mechanically to the strategic destruction of one side or the other. The shortcomings of the Germans and Americans lay in their incapacity to see that industrialisation had created a gaping hole between the strategic and tactical dimensions[10].

• Whereas for the Germans, mechanisation was the antidote to

---

9. One could make a parallel with the civilian exodus which paralyzed armies as much as any bombardment ever did.
10. This awareness in the United States only came about after the Vietnam War, see Jean Lopez, *Berlin, les offensives géantes de l'armée rouge*, Economica, 2010, p. 75. However, although this critcism can be applied to, as we have seen, to the management of land armies, it is less true when we think of the Air Force and its efforts to paralyze the elements of the enemy system via a series of articulated and complementary operations: economic elements (raids on refineries), logistical elements (raids on communication hubs, cutting off the battlefield with the Transportation Plan), trying to break up frontline elements with massive carpet bombing raids, or attacking enemy fighter-bombers.
11. The best book on operational art is by Shimon Naveh, *In pursuit of military excellence*, Cass, 1997, pp. 164-250.

total war, for the Soviets it was the ultimate stage. Operation art demanded colossal means: a mechanised force, airborne army and... logistical support[11].

And this was the great stumbling block that confronted Soviet theorists; how was it possible to support simultaneously several operations in depth? For Triandafillov, only trains could deal with the necessary volumes of supplies. He did not believe in the road given the weather in the eastern Europe which paralysed a basic road network as soon as it rained or snowed. Also, at the end of the nineteen-twenties, the performances of trucks remained very modest. Triandafillov concluded that the success of an offensive depended on a rapid repair of tracks which would allow the second echelon tasked with the exploitation phase to advance faster than the rate of arrival of enemy reserves. Going further still, in order for the offensive to continue one would have to anticipate that the enemy would destroy its infrastructure. The rate of the advance depended on how quickly the railways were rebuilt and, therefore, the speed with which the building materials and manpower was brought up. This logistical effort had to be added, therefore, to that in place in order to propel and maintain the troops. He added that the breakthrough had to be wide enough in order not to become snarled up and that this required the opening of several parallel lines. Even by giving considerable means to the railway engineers, Triandafillov[12] concluded his demonstration with a stark observation, operations deep into enemy lines will exhaust themselves beyond two hundred kilometres[13]. It would require, therefore, successive repeat operations in order to deprive the enemy of his depth, something which confirms the absurdity of imagining that one could destroy the enemy in one go.

Logistics is, therefore, the Achilles heel of operational art. The Soviets tried to get around it as soon as the production line. Thus, the BT and T34 tanks were equipped with larger internal fuel tanks than their adversaries and external fuel tanks that could be dumped were also added, thus doubling their autonomy. However, overall, very little was done and the logistical aspects remained one of a concept rather than a reality when, in 1937, the purges liquidated all of the brainpower. For the Soviets, the history of the *'Great Patriotic War'* is that of the rediscovery of the concepts of operational art and

---

12. His major work is, , Franck Cass, 1994.
13. The fear of logistical paralysis, but also the difficulties in ensuring the initial breakthrough led Svetchine to break away from his comrades and adopt a more orthodox doctrine of attrition.

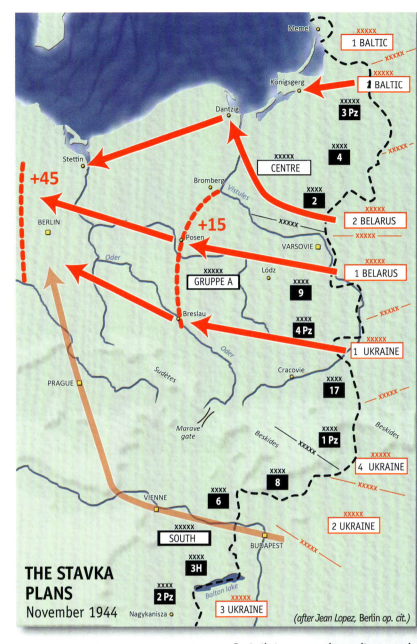

THE STAVKA PLANS
November 1944

(after Jean Lopez, Berlin op. cit.)

Booty that was as precious as it was rare in July 1941, Soviet SO19 locomotives. These allowed the Germans to use the tracks without waiting for the gauges to be brought up to European standards.
(RR)

Although not as numerous as in Europe, large rivers were, however, often much wider. The Soviet bridge builders seen here in Belgorod, are building a passageway alongside the bridge in the background, apparently for infantry and horses.
(RR)

Above and next page.
As was the case with the Wehrmacht, the Red Army did not have the means to possess a homogeneous army. Alongside the mechanized corps was a mass of horse-drawn infantry divisions. This is one of the reasons why, along with the lack of maintenance teams and trucks, why it was difficult for the Soviet marshals to put operational art into practice.
(RR)

their concrete application, something which remained until the end of the war beyond the capacities of the Red Army, as seen by the Vistula-Oder offensive which began on 12 January 1945.

The Vistula Oder (12 January - 2 February 1945)

According to the plans, the battle would take place in two stages and involve six fronts (army groups). The first careful stage would last fifteen days. Whilst the peripheral fronts held down and cut-off the Germans on the flanks (3rd and 2nd Ukrainian Fronts in Hungary, 2nd and 3rd Belorussian Fronts in Eastern Prussia) the two main fronts (1st Belorussian Front and 1st Ukrainian Front) would break through from their Vistula bridgeheads. Once the *Ostheer* was broken up and its meagre reserves stuck in the north and south, operations in the centre would accelerate and push deep into the enemy territory, pushing towards the Silesian industrial area and Berlin, 600 km from the jumping off point. The final objective was to end the war within 45 days. The operation began on 12 January and was successful beyond expectations in its central area. The attack by the 1st Belorussian and Ukrainian Fronts totally dislocated the German front in less than 48 hours instead of the expected fifteen days. Zhukov and Koniev perfectly orchestrated the introduction of four tank armies held in reserve for the exploitation phase. Zhokov's two fronts, 1st tank army and 2nd guards tank army moved off on 15 January and pushed forward 80 km towards the Oder. Logistics had already been used to assemble vast amounts of petrol, rations and ammunition and would now how to prove that it could keep up with the armies.

Up to this point, the Soviet offensives had always run out of steam themselves. By launching its tanks headlong into the attack, they were rapidly cut off from the rear and immobilised due to a lack of fuel or breakdowns. For example, the 580 tanks of the 3rd tank army experienced a break down rate of more than 80% in three weeks of operations in March 1944. The Wehrmacht returning to an offensive role finished off an army incapable of fighting back. Logistical negligence was, therefore, the main enemy of the Red Army.

But in 1945, Red Army logistics had improved a great deal and almost had nothing to envy the US Army. To improve the availability of tanks, it had put into place several reforms. It had taken the combined organic means of maintenance of each army, preventing the army from taking away the resources of the armoured corps that was attached to it. It transformed the maintenance units of mobile corps into a mobile repair base with means that were globally doubled in size and, above all, entirely motorised in order to keep as close a possible to the fighting men.

Finally, in order to be more reactive, each tank brigade had its own repair unit, breakdown tractors and its workshops had enough spare parts to undertake simple repairs in the field. This allowed for half of the tanks to be repaired without being towed away to the rear. The most serious cases were taken away to mobile bases, even though the chronic lack of breakdown tractors still posed problems. The Red Army, therefore, adopted the American repair model of different echelons. Thanks to all this, the armoured corps did not exhaust themselves within a few days as they had previously. Thus, eight days after the attack on the Vistula, the 2nd guards tank army had an availability rate of 86% which was held at 78% on the 12th day of the offensive. The Front's maintenance teams worked hard as in January, they had repaired 3,789 tanks (that is more than 100% of the tanks... meaning that some went to the workshops three times). To feed the battle with supplies in depth, the *Stavka* attributed extra means to each front, put in place emergency aerial supply procedures and attached special transport groups to the tank armies. 80% of the units tasked with repairing lines of communications were placed in the first echelons in order to immediately begin their work. Its last strong point concerned its engineers and, in particular, the railway engineers. In the six months prior to the attack, Antipenko's men, in charge of logistics on Zhukov's front, rebuilt 532 bridges and repaired 626, a rate that is comparable with the American engineers who were better equipped. This allowed for the assembly of 160,000 tonnes of munitions, 60,000 tonnes of fuel and 200,000 tonnes of food which was brought up by 1,400 trains. They had also used the one-way road system, with two leading to the each army and two for the return trip. Once the breakthrough was achieved on the Vistula, the engineers worked like men possessed to rebuild the Warsaw marshalling yards, re-open the railway bridge over the Vistula and repair the 300 km of tracks between Warsaw and Posen, and all this was achieved within fifteen days. Here again, with manpower that was comparable to the 2nd Military Railway Service, Soviet engineers worked equally as well in terms of timeframes and despite a lack of materials (cranes, pre-made bridges) and the fact that they were operating in the middle of the winter with the cold, mud and snow of the Polish steppe, whereas the Americans did so in the middle of the French summer. Thus, from 23 January onwards, eleven days after the breakthrough, the first trains were in action. Without signals, means of communication, qualified personnel and by replacing coal with wood, 8 to 10 trains per day succeeded in bringing up in fifteen

	AMERICANS	SOVIETS
Manpower	23000 men	50000 men
Repairs	125 rebuilt bridges and 180 repaired in three months from September to December.	532 bridges rebuilt and 626 repaired in the last six months of 1944
Ratio (number of men/bridges/months)	226	259
Daily flow	3 300 t/day in August 1944 5 000 t/day in February 1945	3 300 t/day end January

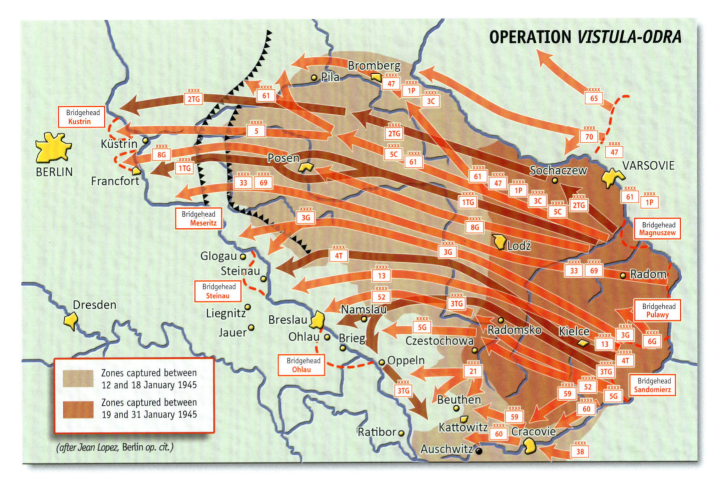

days, 30,000 tonnes of shells and 20,000 tonnes of fuel, for a daily total of 3,300 tonnes per day. Like the Americans, these were locomotives captured from the enemy (380) which ensured the rotations. However, the engineers could not push on any further due to the Germans who, by holding onto fortress zones, cut off the strategic railway lines, in particular the Posen rail hub that was already 100 km behind the armoured spearheads. Thus, rail convoys had to be unloaded where they were halted on the tracks, then put on trucks. The capture of the Kustrin and Frankfurt (Oder) were essential, therefore, to the pursuit of the offensive.

However, just like the Germans and much more than the Americans, the Soviets were incapable of correctly supplying their troops by road. From the very first day of the attack, they were lacking 40,000 tonnes in the forward dumps in order to reach the Oder, quantities available were enough to fill tanks four or five times. In order to be as independent as possible from the rear echelons, the tanks carried extra fuel in drop tanks; 4,200 of the latter were supplied, more than one per tank. For the rest, Zhukov trusted Antipenko to be able to organise fleets of trucks. But here we see the great weakness of the Red Army, its dramatic lack of utility vehicles. An armoured corps, the equivalent of an armoured division, may well have had just as many vehicles, but the real problem lay with the rear echelon units. The ADSEC had 7,000 vehicles at its disposal in August, whereas Antipenko had to make do with a mere 1,400 and these were rarely off-road vehicles. The two special transport groups, each tasked with supplying a tank army only had 600 trucks. But, 600 trucks only brought up half of the allocated ammunition and a third of the fuel allocation on each rotation. The problem was that each trip was over 500 km and on icy roads, meaning that rotations took 20 to 24 days! At that rate, it would require 24,000 trucks for Zhukov's tank armies. Over the great Polish plains were immense columns of GAZ, ZIS and Studebaker trucks, moving at best at 10 km/h when they were not stuck up to their axles in mud. On each return leg, a truck towed another in order to save fuel. The latter was a carefully concocted mixture of petrol and alcohol that had been taken from distilleries. The 1,000 tanker trucks on the front, a considerable number, used a quarter of the fuel they transported and only delivered 10% of what was required., barely a third of what Patton received during the worst week of the pursuit at the end of August, beginning of September.

The situation was hardly any better concerning ammunition and spare parts. Artillery tractors left behind their guns in order to go and find shells in Warsaw, 400 km to the rear, wasting precious fuel! Just

Liberty Roads, 1944-1945

like Ike, Zhukov was deluged with telegrams from his commanders asking for help. All were desperately short of supplies. No truck undertook two rotations as the offensive became bogged down after fifteen days and at this time, the 2nd tank army had been immobilised with empty fuel tanks. It seized bridgeheads on the Oder on 31 January, less than 70 km from Berlin, but did not go any further.

It is obvious that the 1st Belorussian Front, just like the German *Heeresgruppen*, was incapable of keeping up with its armoured spearheads. As soon as the extra fuel carried by the tanks and in the vehicles was used up, the formations had to do what they could in order to find more; using captured stocks or halting. The men had to be resourceful and mixing fuel with vodka was a widespread practice. Even though it soon ruined engines, this stop-gap measure represented 25% of the consumption of the 2nd guards tank army. Rations were not a priority and forced soldiers to forage, meaning that the 'liberated' Polish population suffered. Consequently, what really plagued the Red Army was not so much the black market, but rather pillaging. Each captured enemy dump was immediately sacked, depriving the army of precious items. To top everything off, an early thaw melted the ice of the Vistula and Oder. Bridges built over the Vistula in Koniev's rear echelon area were destroyed by floating ice packs, those of Zhukov were saved by the intervention of Po-2 ground attack aircraft which dropped bombs on the mini icebergs. Traffic was blocked and hundreds of convoys accumulated east of the Vistula. As for the Oder, it became a terrible 500 metre wide obstacle, added to which were dozens of kilometres of marshes traversed by tributaries and canals. Driving through the mud became an ordeal.

On 27 January, Stalin ordered Zhukov, who had reached the Oder, to halt for ten days, something which in fact turned into two and half months. When Zhukov, a few days later at the beginning of February, thought that he had enough supplies for a last push to Berlin, Stalin pretended not to hear and did not believe that this would be possible. He knew that this was the call of a marshal who saw his prey escaping and this was similar to the same proposition made by Reinhardt in 1941 for the capture of Leningrad. The commander was grossly glossing over the supply situation. In any case, Stalin was in no rush, and to pursue an operation which was a considerable success and which had gone far beyond what had been hoped to achieve, would be taking a military risk and was of no use politically as the Anglo-American armies at this time were still 550 km from Berlin. He could allow himself a break. Finally, the Red Army had made a leap of 500 km. It would not be before mid-April and ten weeks later for the attack to resume at the cost of a superhuman logistical effort. 500 km was 350 less than the Americans during the pursuit.

A SPENDTHRIFT GERMANY

The Germans' difficulties in supplying the Blitzkrieg has, for many years, been explained by a lack of means. In the case of Heeresgruppe Nord, although this lack of means existed, it was much less serious than the situation facing Zhukov at the beginning of 1945 who had less than 3,000 trucks with which to supply twice as many tanks. Better still, with 5,000 trucks, HG Nord was on an equal footing with ADSEC at the beginning of operations, especially as it had three times less motorised divisions to supply. It could be said, therefore, that on the day of the breakthrough, it was the Germans who had the largest motorised supply train. Things swung in favour of the Americans in the following days when the Germans lost 40% of their vehicles and ADSEC increased theirs by 60%.

Despite all its experience, the Wehrmacht did not escape from the setting up of a logistical structure that was complex and a breeding ground for confrontation. Each train and its destination were

Next page.
At Brest-Litovsk in 1941 on the border, men move supplies from a German train onto a captured Soviet rail convoy. All of this work is still done by hand. This photo, which is comparable to those taken during the American Civil War, makes the Wehrmacht look archaic. Further north on the frontline, the Germans did not capture a single train, thus making it impossible to supply Reinhardt and Manstein's tanks.
(RR)

HALTING ON THE ODER, FEBRUARY 1945
(after Jean Lopez, Berlin op. cit.)

FIVE OPERATIONS LOOKED AT VIA LOGISTICS

	Fall Gelb (Kleist arm. group)	Barbarossa (Heeresgruppe Nord)	Pursuit (12th AG)	Vistula (1st Belorussian Front)	Germany campaign
INITIAL REQUIREMENTS)					
Manpower	134370	655000	745000	900000	1500000
Tanks	1222	679	2450	3220	5434
Vehicles	41140		200000	80000	400000
Number of horse-drawn divs.	0	20	0	68	0
Number of motorised divs.	8	6	16	7 (corps)	59
DAILY REQUIREMENTS of a horse-drawn div/motorised div. Tonnes per day	-/300	200/300	-/650	150/300	-/450
TOTAL REQUIREMENTS TONNES PER DAY	2400	5800	10400	12300	27000
MEANS					
Motorised park (trucks)	1600	5000	5000 then 8500	1400 approx.	6000
Load capacity (in tonnes)	4800	15000	25000	7000	60000
ratio (load capacity/motorised div)	600	2500	1500	1000	1000
Air supplies	Max 400t/per day	Less than 100 t/per day	600 t/ per day	200-300 t/per day	1 600 t/per day
CONTINGENCIES					
Wear and tear		40% in two weeks	30% after 6 weeks		
Number of days for a rotation	NA	10	4	20	3
Daily volume delivered (actual amount or extrapolated with the formula: vol/mot.div./days)	NA	150	390 (CR)	50	455 (CR)
CONSEQUENCES					
Number of km travelled without stopping	450	300 then 450	850	500	440
Number of days of consecutive operations	A dozen	Less than a dozen (see text)	Forty	A fortnight (see text)	Thirty-five (ordered to halt)
Restoration of rail network	NA	1860 convoys of 450 t on average for the entire Russian Front in October 1941. Estimation: approx. 300 for Hgr. Nord which was not priority = 135 000 t (4 500t/day)	690 000 t in November (23 000 t/day)	650 000 tonnes transported to the Oder in six weeks from March to mid-April = 14 500t/day	18 000 t/day travelled on repaired lines east of the Rhine on 8 May 1945, seven weeks after the start of the offensive

negotiated on a daily basis by Gercke, Wagner and Toppe under the worried gaze of the generals in the field who were totally excluded from the procedure. This is of no real surprise given the fact that this practice was consubstantial with the Nazi regime when we think of the Von Rundstedt-Rommel dual command in the west in 1944, or the four different services tasked with planning the war economy. The Wehrmacht failed despite all of its experience in estimating in a realistic manner its requirements and showed a blinkered approach to logistics. To those disgruntled people who tried to open everybody's eyes, Wagner answered with the magic German propaganda slogan: *"Nothing is impossible for the German soldier!"* It was not due to a lack of means, but rather negligence, that the Eisenbahntruppen remained with a manpower of ten thousand men when the Americans had 20,000 and the Russians 50,000.

The impact of Lend-Lease has been debated since the end of the war. It proved decisive concerning logistics and allowed the national industry to concentrate on the production of weapons. This Studebaker US 6 is a 6x4 variant of the GMC, of which 200,000 were made for China and the USSR. *(RR)*

The Soviet mechanized units were also largely equipped with Anglo-American materiel, the M3 half-track seen here allowed the infantry to accompany more easily the tanks. *(RR)*

With the increasing length and distance of operations, the lack of a supply dump chain became dramatic. The forward dumps were still small and could not answer needs in terms of volume, but also diversity (engineers' material, spare parts, communication equipment). This meant that items had to be sent directly from Germany and equipment which could have been stored in intermediate dumps at strategic road hubs, was instead brought up via a complex system of rotations that was costly in time and subject to errors and unknown factors[14].

Finally, the Germans saw logistics in the same way as their operations; a gamble. They concentrated the maximum amount of means in direct support to the spearhead units ('rucksack') by sacrificing the supplying of infantry units and the creation of a durable supply chain. When operations lasted for more than ten days they were forced to forage from the local population. The Blitzkrieg was the denial of modern logistics and a reinvention of the army supply trains of the modern era.

THE SOVIET DOCTRINE WITHOUT MEANS

As a contrast, the Soviet logistical performance was remarkable given the constraints that they had to deal with. In terrible weather conditions, the Russians had to fight with logistical means that were by far the weakest: few trucks, little water obstacle crossing equipment, few breakdown vehicles, no cranes essential for the dumps, quays and platforms. These were deficits which were partially compensated with sweat and resourcefulness. For example, whereas it took three months to soak up the excesses of the pursuit, Antipenko's men would, in six weeks, following the fall of the Posen, Küstrin and Frankfurt fortresses which blocked the railway lines, managed to change the line linking Warsaw with Frankfurt (Oder) to Russian gauge and repair another. Four roads from Warsaw were also

---
14. Vladimir Prebilic, *"Theorical aspects of military logistics"*, Defense & Securities analysis, vol 22, n° 2, p. 162

These Sherman wait for the end of a raid of fighter-bombers of the 9th Air Force before resuming their running towards Germany the cooperation combined arms integrates from now on the aviation. *(NARA)*

opened and allowed for dumps to be opened on the Oder with 200,000 tonnes of ammunition, 150,000 t of petrol and 300,000 t of various supplies and forage. This performance is also explained by the capacity of the armies to live off the land... not only for food, but also for moving as seen by the vehicles that ran off a mix of fuel and vodka! Similarly, the Soviets foraged more efficiently than the Germans.

Contrary to its counterparts, the Red Army's logistics were remarkably straightforward for the simple reason that the operational commander remained in charge of his logistics: the *Stavka* which coordinated the operations ensured the distribution of supplies between its fronts (the equivalent of an army group) via a central rear echelon service named VGK, whereas the fronts which worked out operations had authority and a free rein over the supplies that they had received. This is a straightforward application of an operational art axiom, *"He who commands is he who supplies"*. Simplicity, austerity and resourcefulness are the words which come to mind when studying Soviet logistics. Well-assisted by the legendary capacity of the Soviet soldier to live with little.

However, although the Soviets invented operational logistics well before the Americans, it has to be admitted that their performance was no way near that of the Americans. In 1945, the Red Army was still incapable of supplying troops deep within the enemy lines as well as being unable to build a mobile logistical chain. It worked by leaps forward. When an offensive ran of steam by itself, a consolidation phase began with the rapid restoration of a rail network allowing to build up stores for the next offensive. The Soviets did not have the logistics corresponding to their doctrine.

Thus, neither doctrine of these two armies was capable of supporting mobile warfare for more than a few days. This allows us to draw several general lessons.

Coutances 29 July, men of the 357th Inf. Rgt., 90th Inf. Div. US, who on this day covered 90 km, march in single file alongside a column of tanks, of which two are Shermans of the 4th Arm. Div., the second is a M4 (105) present in all Assault Platoons, followed by a Half-Track M3, an ambulance Jeep and a M32 ARV recovery vehicle. The US Army was the only army for which every division used the engine to move itself.
(p011790, Région Basse Normandie/NARA)

Liberty Roads, 1944-1945 | 207

GENERAL INFORMATION

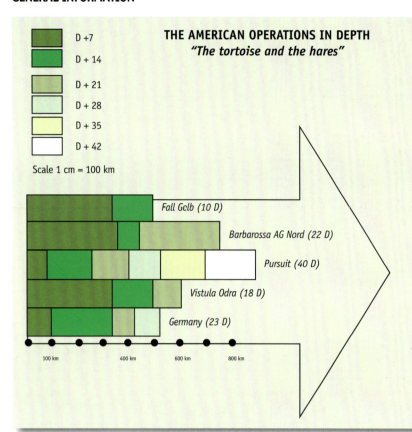

THE AMERICAN OPERATIONS IN DEPTH
"The tortoise and the hares"

This diagram compares the rhythm of the five offensives. Although the pursuit was the one which went the furthest, it was also the slowest.

The Americans struggled more to breakthrough. The Germans and Soviets advanced twice as fast which confirms their greater tactical skill.

However, their offensives ran out of steam more quickly as they were incapable of properly supplying their motorized spearheads. Their advances were, therefore, a straightforward rush forward for the Soviets, and a type of 'stop and go' for the Germans who, during the course of Barbarossa, were capable of moving forward again after a halt of one week. This was the principle of "rucksack" logistics, when the bag was empty the advance stopped by itself.

The Americans though, kept up with their spearheads. Operations could then continue up to six weeks and even progressively accelerate until the link broke and maintenance requirements dictated a halt.

This diagram considerably re-evaluates the American performance. They may have been less spectacular, but their operations in depth were very efficient.

One should not, however, make definitive conclusions as the comparison is based on a limited number of example and excludes, in particular, other operations in the German-Soviet theater as well as the desert.

1. The table of comparison shows that the Soviets achieved un-hoped for results given their derisory vehicle park. The Germans, contrary to a widely held belief, had a large vehicle park in terms of quantity, but not in quality, and the paid a heavy price for turning a blind eye to the constraints of the Russian Front (road network, weather). Once the operations were (badly) engaged, they were incapable of finding alternatives; alternatives which, if they had existed, meant that the rhythm and objectives of the campaign would have to be totally changed. In any case, the German generals were ideologically incapable. Profoundly ingrained with Clausewitz's theories which excluded logistical questions from the art of war[15], the German generals scorned such questions. We have seen this with Manstein and Reinhardt and we see it again with the writings of the chief of staff with *Panzergruppe* 4, Walter Charles de Beaulieu who, in his account of operations, never, even indirectly, mentions the lack of supplies which immobilised his forces. Significantly, his conclusion points out one person responsible for the failure of Hgr. Nord: Hitler[16]. By placing the blame on him, Beaulieu may well saved the reputation of the Wehrmacht, but his account shows that even 25 years after the events, the German military still remained unaware of modern logistical constraints. The same cannot be said of the Americans who, despite not having conceptualised in depth logistics, managed to adapt and keep to forty days, a record at that time that proved wrong the prophets of doom in London.

2. All the armies came up against the "critical distance wall". No army had sufficient means to supply long-term the motorised spearheads which advanced almost a hundred kilometres per day from the dumps. As no army was capable of opening dumps closer to the fighting, at least until the arrival of the railway, the entire weight of the battle rested on the automobile services. The latter, faced with supplying units that were increasingly distant, ended up by hitting full-on this critical distance wall which corresponded to the number of kilometres where the trucks used too much fuel compared to the volume transported and could no longer carry out enough rotations. This critical distance varied depending on the density and state of the roads, the weather, and also the number and load capacities of the vehicles, the vehicle park's quality of maintenance and the fluidity of the administration. For the Soviets, this wall appeared as soon as the first hundred kilometres was covered, the Germans at 300, and the Americans at 400. This difference is explained by the fact that only the Americans manoeuvred during five weeks in the summer of 1944 when such a pursuit had not been foreseen, meaning that the quartermaster services had to improvise before also finally stalling at the end of August. Even by extending the comparison with Hgr. Mitte[17], the Germans only operated in depth for ten days, be it in 1940 or in 1941, it was the same for Zhukov's tank armies that were only on the move for twelve of the offensive's fifteen days.

3. Railways showed their limits during operations in depth. Railways required too much work in terms of repairs and also meant that too many communication hubs had to be controlled. The Germans were aware of this as they had suffered because of it in 1871 and 1914 and they dreamed of being able to do without it via short 'rucksack' campaigns. The Americans reluctantly underwent a similar experience as they had really not planned for operations in depth. Only the Soviets had thought of the in depth battle with the participation of railways. They provided considerable means to the railway engineers, but despite these great efforts, it had not been able to respond present in the required timeframe.

Post war, the Soviets came to the conclusion that the only possible solution was the laying of pipelines by well-trained and superbly equipped special brigades. Whereas the Soviets managed to repair the Polish network within six weeks and deliver almost 15,000 tonnes per day to the Oder, the Eisenbahntruppen managed three times as less after nine weeks working on the railway lines. Only the Americans made the most of the lessons learned in the summer of 1944; they innovated by creating an operational motorised logistical chain which would prove to work well in the spring of 1945.

4. Aircraft had not provided any more of a solution. The load bearing capabilities of aircraft remained insufficient. For example, a C47 Dakota only carried a load of two and half tonnes and a Ju52 one and a half, half of what a standard truck could carry. As this means of transport also meant making landing strips that were soon well behind the front line, the plane was no more than a stop-gap measure that was useful for medivac and the unloading of urgent, but non-bulky supplies, such as medical items.

5. Each army made different doctrinal choices which all showed their limits. The German army tried to get around the problem by

---

15. Contrary to Jomini, for whom mastering the logistics was an art comparable to that of strategy and tactics, Clausewitz, although admitting that a good supply system was indispensable, delegated it to a quartermaster. This was not an art therefore, but a vulgar administrative action.
16. *"But, if the final offensive did not begin in July, it was due to the numerous interventions of the supreme commander: Hitler [...] The lesson to be learned is as follows: the control and command of operations has to be carried out at and from the frontline. Estimating, evaluating and deciding on the ground was, therefore, the necessary condition for a victorious assault on Leningrad"*. W.C. de Beaulieu, *"Objectif Leningrad"*, Historia magazine, 2ᵉ guerre mondiale, n° 26, 1968, pp. 701-708.
17. For example, the 7. PzD. Advanced for three days between 22-25 June, then ten days between 2-16 July.

The motorised pontoon – towed here by tugs – was a much simpler and more rapid to use way of crossing rivers. Two T-34 tanks can be seen here. T< hese pontoons could not, however, cope with the flow necessary for motorized operations. *(RR)*

---

18. French officers, during the re-armament phase of 1943 along American lines, were amazed at the amount of means taken by the quartermaster services and tried their hardest to convince the American authorities to increase, within French units, the proportion of fighting units to the detriment of service units.
19. Vladimir Prebilic, *op. cit.*, pp. 165-166.

reverting to its 'rucksack' doctrine, believing that with the engine, they had found the solution to shorten the duration conflicts. The Soviets thought of a war in depth with the help of railways. They neglected the automobile means and concentrated on the production of weapons, to such an extent that they had to rely almost exclusively on lend-lease for their supply columns. If this is understandable in 1941-42 when they were being strangled, it is obvious that they did not change their methods when they went onto the offensive. The Americans remained loyal to their doctrine which saw ground confrontations on a linear, rather than in depth basis, something which had had the advantage of simplifying the logistical conundrum. And, although they were better equipped, this was thanks to their industrial opulence, the existence back home of modern civilian logistics and the constant quest to give their soldiers a standard of living which was not seen in European armies, rather than an answer to the motorisation of warfare[18]. They may have had the means, but they did not have the doctrine and culture.

Four IHC 4X2 M 426 wait in front of the Napoleon statue in Cherbourg. Their C2 12 ½ Ton trailers were designed for transporting planes but were converted into all-purpose trailers. This is in 1945 and things are less intense. Antwerp had taken over from Cherbourg and only a few crated Jeeps await to be loaded, either onto the trailers, or more likely onto rail wagons.
(13 570_8, NARA © Coriello, Bibliothèque municipale de Cherbourg)

CONCLUSION

At the beginning of 1942, a huge construction site emerged on the banks of the Pontomac. 13,000 workers were busy day and night in order to finish a massive building capable of housing 40,000 Federal employees that were required for the correct functioning of the first army born of globalization. This huge building did not have a name, but given its shape, everyone was already calling it the Pentagon.

Above and next page.
**More than in the air, the limitations of which can be seen here with this modest load of shells on board a C47, it was by sea and land that the United-States won the logistical battle. Dukw, GMC, motor-cranes are seen here in December 1944, the American machine is working flat-out as seen with this mountain of ration stores in front of the Napoleon square in Cherbourg.
The amphibious GMC, or DUKW was naturally nicknamed the duck.
Its single hull structure meant that it could carry a reasonable load for its engine which remained the standard GMC type.**
*(13 Num 1659 & 1217, NARA
© Archives départementales de la Manche & p001094, Région Basse Normandie/NARA)*

A year later, the project became a reality. The construction site was a metaphor for the American logistical effort in the Second World War. In the same way as the workers frequently took liberties with the plans that three-hundred architects hurriedly drew up in a former aircraft hangar, the raising, deployment and deployment of millions of soldiers in seven theatres of operations could not have been possible without proper planning, but also could not have succeeded without a serious dose of adaptation in the field.

In a quirk of history, amongst the men involved in these two projects we find the same man, Brehon Somervell.

The planning is owed to the politicians, military personnel and civilians who succeeded in working together in order to mobilize industry and build a superstructure linking it to the armed forces. The politicians brought their skills acquired during the New Deal in which they had become used to driving a capitalist economy. The military had been able to use what they had learned in 1917-18 as well as possible ideas that they had looked into during the inter-war period within structures such as the Army-Industrial College. However, the capacity of forging a Cyclops of 2.7 million fighting men from a core consisting of an army of 356,000 men without modern equipment, landing 5,000 men daily in Europe between 6 June 1944 and 8 May 1945, engaging 61 divisions whilst at the same time waging a violent war in the Pacific and supporting massively the Allies, would not have been possible with an army cut-off from civilian society.

We have seen how the civilian experience of Brehon Somervell had been of use when leading the Army Service Forces. We have also seen how the Army had had the good idea of allowing civilian skills to trickle into it, by placing in high ranking positions and in key military posts engineers, business leaders, managers and even specialized workers. Made less rigid and functioning well, this globalized and total logistics – and also without an equivalent – abolished the tyranny of distance. One only has to remember the promises made by Lutes to the American generals in the winter of 1944-45. To be capable of gathering together thousands of tanks, thousands of tonnes of munitions, thousands of extra radios in a few weeks at the other side of the world is enough to make every general in the world think.

However, although Washington put into place a remarkable trans-ocean logistics, the same could not be said for theater logistics. ETOUSA fumbled with this a little in 1944, during the terribly perilous D-Day operations, and a lot during the pursuit. The latter, an improvised affair, ran out of steam after 800 km of advance because of:
• Ill-suited means of road transportation.
• A proto-matrix structure which fed confusion, friction, delays and which worsened the void which was growing between strategy and tactics.
• And at the origin of everything, a binary doctrine (strategy-tactics) that was ill-suited for mobile mechanized warfare. The Americans knew how to put massive forces into exterior theatres of operations – strategic logistics – and had an excellent tool for linking forward dumps to regiments – tactical logistics – but they were still missing the operational echelon linking the theater of operations to the army zones. This space which became deeper and deeper with the speeding up of operations revealed a strategic logistics (ComZ) the practices of which had not changed since 1918. It was built around railways and this was incompatible with the battle in depth.
• The crisis continued for several months after the breakup of the logistical chain and the blockages in the liberated ports.

However, running out of steam is not a collapse; with the initiative shown by men such as Sibley, Ayers, Gravelle or Medaris, the supply chain held for forty days, an exploit which has no equivalent in other armies of the Second World War. They made logistics prestigious. Better still, in the same way as the workers used their initiative to make up for any voids left by architects, the men on the ground improved logistics and rethought it to forge an instrument capable of accompanying motorized armies during the German campaign. This instrument innovated by its operational dimension and also the massive use of trucks. Empirically, the Americans put into operation the missing link between strategic logistics and tactical logistics that the Soviets had identified in the 1930s. The strength of Somervell and Lutes was in having speeded up the change at ComZ by stripping General Lee of his powers and giving them to deputies that were more permissive concerning innovation. The success of American logistics was not, therefore, the result of material accumulation, which is of course undeniable and indispensable, but is explained more by skills acquired at the school of war.

It would be interesting to go forward fifty years in the Iraqi desert in 1991. *Desert Storm*, the campaign which liberated Kuwait for Saddam Hussein's occupation, is quite rightly considered as being the undertaking of the new Air-Land Battle which was very much tinted with Soviet procedures, especially in its integrative dimension and in its approach to the battle in depth. However, logistically, this campaign was carried out by giving them a logistical support command for the entire theatre (22nd Support Command) and a logistical support command for each corps engaged (1st Support Command for the XVIIII Airborne Corps & 2nd Support Command for the VII Corps). Each corps had its own logistical base whose mission was to supply in depth by supplying the Corps Supply Points thanks to the fleets of heavy trucks. In concrete terms, this required the opening of dedicated roads in order troops deployed in the middle of the desert and 700 km from the ports of Damman (Dodge, Toyota, Sultan Roads) where rotations could take up to four days, reinventing an administration which centralized movement and opening bivouacs along these roads (Transportation Consolidation Centers). The express sending of priority equipment was used again, this time by air, but the principle remained unchanged from that of 1944[1]. An article written for *Military Review* by those involved concluded that "*SUPCOM had used the doctrine as much as possible, but had always adapted it to conditions on the ground. In general, the usefulness of the doctrine was found in its standardized procedures. However, it did not stifle initiative and innovation by the men on the ground, whatever their rank. As soon as a new technique worked, even if it was unorthodox, it was rapidly adopted*"[2]. A rear base, an operational base, roads and heavy trucks under a centralized command and a trust in the innovation by the men on the ground, the link with 1945 is obvious.

However, these logistics, however innovative they were, are not revolutionary, unless all innovation is a form of revolution. It is part of the revolution brought about by the engine which, after having been adopted by all combatant nations, finally filtered down into the rear echelon units and which owes much to the scientific organization of work and the skills of the great capitalist enterprise which bloomed in American society. These logistics were finally more of an end result than a revolution in itself.

A revolution or transformation, or just a straightforward improvement, one could discuss this forever, what is sure is that in 1945, the United States was the only country capable of undertaking worldwide wars, and also the only one able to operate long-term in deep within enemy territory.

Alone in the world!

---

1. Note that it was in Vietnam that the Americans opened the first regular express air link in order to supply their Cam Ranh base directly from the United States. During the Gulf War, it was limited to one or two daily C141 flights.
2. William G. Pagonis & Harold E. Raugh, *"Good logistics is combat power"*, Military review, 71, n° 9, sept 1991, p. 28-39.

ANNEXE I

A REVEALING CASE STUDY, THE JERRYCAN

In the vicinity of Etreham, tens of thousands of Jerrycans await to be filled. Twelve million were landed in 1944, a huge number but which was, nevertheless insufficient.
(13 Num 0815, NARA © Archives départementales de la Manche)

The American jerrycan did not have a spout, contrary to its German counterpart, and required a spout in order to be emptied. More often, personnel did without this and spilled more than half of the precious fuel. *(NARA)*

Today, the jerrycan is an everyday object. It evokes the allied armies that liberated western Europe but its origins, however, are German, as its name suggests, Jerry being the nickname given to Germans by the British Army.

This fuel can alone sums up the opulence, but also the shortcomings of American logistics and thus forms a sort of significant case study.

A doctrinal immobility

Easy to pile up, handle, quick to empty and to fill, this revolutionary German invention of 1937 simplified, amplified and extended the reach of supplies. Vehicles no longer need the few and far between tankers and could carry these extra fuel cans themselves, something which was ideal for operations in depth such as the Blitzkrieg.

In 1939, the civilian engineer, Paul Pleiss, took one along to the army without raising any interest at all on the part of the Quartermaster Corps. The Corps preferred the bulky 5 or 10 gallon cylindrical cans which required the use of a equipment for pouring the fuel or a pump. In 1940, the QMC went back on its initial judgement, retaining the idea but only retaining the shape and size, but modifying almost everything else and finally ending up with a model that was very inferior to the original. The main error consisted of doing away with a nozzle cap and replacing it with a screw cap[1] as this was standard in American industry[2] and because the tanks of 1941 had a fuel tank orifice which prevented the use of a nozzle. It is obvious that the QMC had not seen the revolutionary character of this can and it was first used as a straightforward reserve can attached to each vehicle. For daily supplying, the QMC still preferred the use of the old cylindrical cans. The laborious beginnings of the jerrycan reveals the Army's doctrinal immobility, capable of adopting new equipment but not seeing the consequences as to its use.

The first jerrycans left the factories in 1941. They were used for the first time during the landings in North Africa and it was here that it became accepted by all that used it. Far from respecting the doctrine, the units on the ground used the jerrycan to such an extent that in Italy, 88% of fuel delivered to the frontline was done so with these cans. The doctrinal innovation stemmed from the men in the field. Much more than one can per vehicle was required. However, the first cans to be used on the frontline took a worrying 13 days to return empty to the dumps, according to the British and those who used the Gasoline Supply Companies[3]. This represented a turnover of twenty million cans for operations in Europe, a staggering quantity. These estimations worried the QMC who then artificially lowered them, the loss rate went from 15 to 5% and the time required for rotation, from 13 to 7 days. Thus, the required quantities were no more than 15.5 million, a number that barely corresponded to their stocks in Britain that were estimated at twelve million[4]. By deliberately underestimating its requirements and refusing to adapt its methods to the reality of the its stocks, the US Army was putting its head in the sand and sowing the seeds of its fiasco.

A negligent industrial management

The jerrycan also reveals of how the trial and error present in the industrial mobilisation. Firstly, it was

---

1. Richard M. Daniel, *"The Little Can That Could"*, Invention & Technology Magazine, 1987
2. This justification must be nuanced as American industry later made models with a spout but which were reserved for transporting.... water.
3. A unit tasked with dealing with gasoline stores by, for example, pouring the contents of barrels and tanks into the jerrycans issued to the combatants.
4. Ruppenthal, *op. cit.* vol 2, p 202
5. This factory made ten out of the twelve million jerrycans in service with ETOUSA on the eve of D-Day.
6. The USAF did not want to re-use jerrycans as it feared this would spoil the high-octane aviation fuel.
7. William F. Ross & Charles F. Romanus, *The Quartermaster Corps, Operation in the war against Germany*, CMH, 1965, p. 665.
8. The contribution of the liberated countries remained insignificant until the end of March 1945, only 10,500 jerrycans were delivered by the Belgians and production in France was barely underway.
9. At the end of the war, the figures had mostly increased as we have estimated that 15 to 19 million jerrycans were in use, to which we can add roughly a third which were lost or destroyed. Ross & Romanus, *op. cit.*, p. 668.

ANNEXE I

Above.
Two American women piling up jerrycans in the United-States. Orders placed with American companies were frozen in July 1944 to the great dismay of the Quartermaster Corps.
(NARA)

with the British were limited to 800,000 per month (300,000 of which were reserved for the USAAF which promised to give them to the Army after having used them once[6]). The low numbers of the requirements deemed necessary reveal an obvious underestimation.

It was no surprise that the situation worsened as early as August when the rapid advance lengthened the time required for rotations and no trace was found of the three and a half million jerrycans that were lost. British deliveries were no longer sufficient, especially as they gave priority to their own army and they could only supply 221,000 per month. They also stated that they might not even be able to supply any at all in the future. Also, the 9th Air Force went back on its agreement to release 310,000 jerry cans. The US Army was in dire straights. Within the QMC, euphoria gave way to panic. In mid-September, Brigadier-General Peckham, in charge of the Fuels and Lubricants branch, imprudently announced to Littlejohn that he could deliver seven million jerrycans that were laying dormant in the United States. The problem was that these only existed in his imagination. Littlejohn, therefore, would have to make do with two million, immediately sent, empty, via Liberty Ships which would store them on their decks as they sailed to Europe, but once again his hopes were dashed[7]. There were not any in the United States and at the beginning of October, the War Department

announced that, with the exception of two factories, all the others had been shut down and their workforces reassigned to priority areas. He would have to make do with 5.4 million, to be delivered within four months at best! In the meantime, the War Department promised to put pressure on the British allies so that they could come to his aid and help find solutions to the problem within the UK. The situation became so critical that an Allied Container Advisory Committee was set up which charged the UK with supplying 55,000 jerrycans per month, but this was at the end of November and the first deliveries would not be before January. In Europe, Littlejohn signed contracts to exchange 64,000 tonnes of steel for the manufacture of jerry cans, with nine million made by French factories and two million by the Belgians. But here too, none would leave the factories before February 1945[8]. To sum up, wherever they might come

Given the lack of fuel supplies, repairing a jerrycan made a lot of sense in the autumn of 1944. As well as requiring high-pressure cleaning, a jerrycan often also required re-welding. Instead of comprising of two welded parts like the German R12, it was made of three parts and four points of welding which increased the risk of rupturing and leakages.
(NARA)

a secondary object that was passed on to a few companies due to the fact that only one was required per vehicle. From 1942 onwards, once operational reports began filtering back to Washington, twenty extra companies were contacted. The Americans worked alongside the British in order to finance the building of a factory in England, Magnatex Ltd.[5], Middlesex, which was opened in 1943. This project was significant as the US Army eventually hoped to acquire their jerrycans solely from the British. This decision is first explained by the desire to rationalise production between the Allies, but also by the decision to finally equip units with a more practical model as the British, later in adopting it, were also more radical as they just went ahead and copied the German model. In July 1944, on the eve of the breakthrough, no more contracts were placed with American manufacturers and those signed

This photo was for many years thought to show one of the departure dumps of the Red Ball Express, but it was in fact taken in southern England. It does, however, show the lack of tanker trucks that meant that the GMC had to be used to transport jerrycans.
(p000394, Région Basse- Normandie/NARA)

Liberty Roads, 1944-1945

APPENDIX I

Since 1939, the British had used 4-gallon petrol cans (18 liters), which could be piled up and were easy to handle, but which presented two major faults: they were fragile and difficult to use without losing some of the precious liquid. The lack of jerrycans, however, forced the British to carry on using them in 1944, as seen here at the Waddesdon depot. *(RR)*

from, the US Army could not hope to receive any more until 1945. From August 44 to February 45, the troops operated with eight to nine million jerry cans, 40% of what was required[9].

Rationing was unavoidable. The attempt to deliver fuel via tanker trucks came up against the lack of means available to the armies to deal with such volumes. In order to concentrate available means for the fighting units, on 1 November, Littlejohn recommended making as many civilian petrol stations operational as possible as these would be useful to the rear echelon units. On 25 November, he ordered that the units attached to the Base Sections would get gasoline directly from a pipeline outlet or via 55 gallon cans (208 litres)[10], the jerrycans would be reserved for ADSEC deliveries and for the combatant units. Finally, Littlejohn crossed swords with ADSEC concerning its tendency to retain all of the jerrycans, despite their being indispensable, in the pipeline terminals. *"Straightforward common sense means that an empty can gets sent back to a pump, but persistent rumours are reaching me that an ADSEC officer has forbidden the sending back of cans. I have, therefore, sent a letter to your G4 in order for him to order that each can is sent back to the rear.[11]"* The final solution, in the short term, was to find the 3.5 million lost jerrycans.

Wastage

With such a number of cans lost in three months, it was obvious that daily management was not satisfactory. During the course of June, the QMC renounced its usual policy. Instead of exchanging an empty can for a full one, units were allowed to leave their jerrycans at collecting points and get their fuel elsewhere. This decision was justified by the unbearable waiting time that the supply units had to endure when they arrived at the dumps. However, in reality most of the cans were dumped. It is understandable that men, fatigued by the fighting in the hedgerows, did not have the time, energy, will or awareness of the usefulness of taking the jerrycans back to a collecting point.

Liberty Roads, 1944-1945

APPENDIX I

The R12, a brilliant invention of simplicity

The opening is situated at the bevelled area and has a short spout to help pouring without disrupting a pile of cans. The opening is secured via screw cap that is easy to open. An ingenious tube inserted in the opening progressively allows air to enter the can as it is emptied, preventing the discharge of fuel.

Three welded tubes act as handles allowing the can to be carried by one man via the middle handle, or by two via the outside handles.

A bulge placed near the handles holds an air bubble which accelerates the poring and allows the jerrycan to float!

The R.12 was simple in design and easy to produce as it was made in two halves of stamped steel that were then welded together, giving a size of 47x34x16 cm. It contained 20 litres.

An embossed cross allows the metal to dilate in very hot weather and reduces the deformation of the metal when the cans are stacked.

When the first Panzer units were formed, the Wehrmacht used a triangular civilian model that was not easy to use. In 1935, several manufacturers were contacted to design a fuel can with very strict specifications: A shape to facilitate transportation and storage, a 20 litre capacity for a weight of 20 kg with handles to help carrying and for passing them along in a human chain. It would appear that its inventor was a certain Vinzenz Grünvogel, an engineer with Muller Maschinen based in Schwelm. Named R.12, it went into production in 1937 and only ceased in 1945.

And its pale imitation, the 5-gallon steel military gasoline can MIL-C-1283D

It has a screw cap, something which considerably affected its performance. It required a tool to unscrew it and was easily lost if the chain retaining it was broken. To avoid the fuel going everywhere when pouring, it required a spout that was stored separately in each vehicle. This spout was nicknamed the 'Donkey dick' and was often lost, meaning no doubt that thousands of litres of the precious liquid soaked into the soil of western Europe.
Ruppenthal, volume 2, *op cit*. P. 201

The body is in one piece made from stamped and folded steel to which the base and upper part are welded. This made manufacture more complicated with four areas requiring welding rather than just one with the R.12. It is lighter, however, as it contains 5 gallons, a little more than 16 litres.

Others preferred to keep them just in case. Some were used to bolster the defences of a position, or used as wheel wedges in workshops; also some were sold along with their precious contents on the black market. As early as July, two companies were tasked with finding abandoned jerrycans. POWs equipped with fishing rods recovered them from rivers and marshes.

Before the pursuit, these bad habits continued to such an extent that the General Staff became acutely worried. How were they to find these lost cans? Appeals made to troops in Stars and Stripes, army cinemas and on the radio remained unanswered. Littlejohn was no more successful with the new Normandy Base Section as no one there appeared concerned with the recovery of the million jerrycans lost in Normandy. Several reports denounce the negligence and lack of initiative which obliged his superiors to intervene[12]. Littlejohn then turned towards the civilians and to the children in particular. In cooperation with the French education ministry, rewards and certificates were handed out to those who found the most cans. Thousands of children would spend their Thursdays picking their way through the countryside and sunken lanes. A million cans were found in this way by the end of the year.

There were still 2.5 million missing, no doubt lost forever in the rivers, or kept by civilians for their own needs.

---

10. The use of these big cans of 190 Kg will cause an inflation of the cases of hernias. Ross & Romanus, *op. cit.*, p. 666.
11. Littlejohn's letter to the ADSEC *Quartermaster*, September 24 1944.
12. Littlejohn's letter to the *Normandy Base section*, September 24 1944.

Liberty Roads, 1944-1945

APPENDIX II

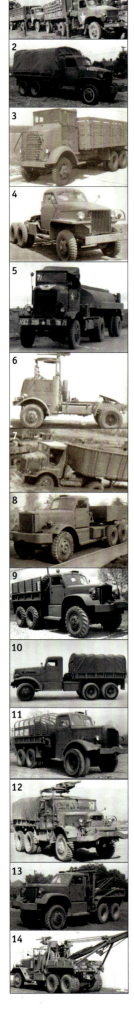

THE WORKHORSES

THE TRANSPORTATION

	Dimension in metres	Wheelbase in metres	Weight empty (kg)	Theoretical load capacity in kg (actual)
1. Chevrolet 4X4 1 ½ Ton (G7113)	A type of chassis much used by manufacturers, these were the first transport vehicles to be ordered in mass by the Army, as well as the French and British. The Fargo division that was responsible within Chrysler for Army sales, supplied as early as 1940, 6,472 chassis of its Dodge T203, a straightforward militarised version of its TE 30. But it was General Motors with its sister companies of			
	5, 7x2,2 x2,7	3,7	3420	2186 trailer (5 500)
2. GMC 6X6 2 ½ Ton CCKW 353 (G508) *(See pp. 111-113)*	6,8x2,2 x2,3	4,2	5103	2427 + 1000 with trailer (up to 7000)
3. GMC 6X6 2 ½-Ton AFKWX 353 (G655)	6,7x2,2 x2,7	4,2	4900	2427 + 1000 with trailer (up to 7000)
4. Studebaker US6 6X4 2 ½ – Ton (G630	Studebaker US6 6X4 2 ½ – Ton (G630 Background: In 1941 it had been planned for Studebaker to make exact copies of the GMC 6x6. However, this idea was abandoned as it would require many modifications to Studebaker's production lines. B developing its own version, the company was able to get the truck off its production lines as early as June 1941. The rate			
	5, 5x2,2x2,2	3,8	3715	7099 with trailer (12 500)
5. Tractor 4X4 4/5 Ton Autocar U-7144T or White 444T (G510)	These tractors were developed in 1941 and were the main victim of the low priority given to heavy trucks. As they wer not designed for use with combatant units, their production was neglected until mid-1943. Even by bringing in a secon manufacture, White, it would be a year before this restructuring bore fruit. It was only from the winter of 1944 onwards tha			
	5,2x2,4 x2,8	3,4	5307	9072 with trailer (15 000)
6. Tractor 4X4 4/5-Ton Federal 94X43 (G513)	Tractor 4X4 4/5-Ton Federal 94X43 (G513) Background: As a complement to the Autocar, the Army adopted in 1941 the			
	5,2x2,4 x2,9	3,4	5420	9 072 with trailer (15 000)
7. Tractor 4X2 5 Ton International M425/426 (G671)	The M425/426 have a special place in the pantheon of army trucks as they were the only ones to be specifically designed fo military use. Faced with the lack of heavy trucks, the Ordnance ordered two 4x2 from the International Harvester Compan a manufacturer that was experienced in making civilian vehicles of this type. IHC also had the advantage of being at a lo production output since it had stopped making its M7 light tank. In order to speed up production, the Ordnance decided			
	5, 1x2,5 x2,7	3	M 425: 5170 M426: 5490	M 425: 5000 with trailer (15 000) M 426: 9 072 with trailer (18 000
8. Tank-transporter tractor, Diamond T Model 980/981, M20 (G159)	Designed in 1940 upon the request of the British who needed a vehicle to transport their new Churchill tank, the Model 98 was the result of a joint project by Diamond-T and the Quartermaster Corps. Its origins explain the diesel engine and it wa no doubt designed as a ballasted tractor (classed M19) towing a Rogers 45 Ton (the M9) tank trailer and not as a semi-traile			
	7,1x2,6x2,6	4,5	12105	45 000 (52 000)

OTHER VEHICLES OCCASIONALLY USED TO TRANSPOR

9. General use truck, 4 ton, 6X6, Diamond-T 968/970, G-509	The 4 tonnes, 6x6 range was only looked at by the Army before the war and the first deliveries date to 1941. Soon, the Mode 968 became the main vehicle produced by the truck specialist Diamond-T. This company's skills allowed it to manufacture			
	6,8x2,4x3	3,8	8 350	3 700 + trailer (12 500)
10. Artillery tractor, 6 Ton, 6X6 (Corbitt 50SD6, White 666, Brockway B-666), G512/514/547	This truck was the result of a tender for contract dating from 1938 to which Corbitt and White had replied. This model wa originally developed for towing anti-aircraft artillery pieces. As was almost always the case, Corbitt proposed a vehicle base on its civilian range and was awarded the contract, but only in 1941, a sign of the red-tape and fumbling that was still			
	C & W: 7, 7x2,5x3 Brockway: 9, 5x5,5x3,4	C&W: 4,7 Brockway: 5,6	C: 10 024 W: 10 397 B: 12 000	5 500 + trailer (15 000)
11. Artillery tractor, 6 Ton, 6X6 Mack NM, G-535	7,2x2,4x2, 9	4,5	10 840	5 500 + trailer (15 000)
12. Artillery tractor, 7 ½ Ton, 6X6 Mack NO, G-532	During manoeuvres in Louisiana in 1940, it was noticed that it took a long time to move heavy 155 mm guns with tracke tractors. The Ordnance Corps looked towards Mack who were developing a heavier version of its NM. The model was adopte			
	7,6x2,6x3,1	4	12 000	7 500 + trailer (25 000)

ACCOMPANYING AN

Harley Davidson model WLA, G523	Military version of the DLD 45 that had been sold since 1929. The US Army purchased 60,000 starting in 1940. Its 10 cm clearance			
	2, 2x0,9x1	1,5	243	120
Ford GPW/Willys MB, ¼ Ton G503 *(See pp. 162-163)*	3, 4x1,6x1, 8	2	1 017	500 + a two-wheeled Bantam ¼ ton trailer, off-road load capacity of 226 k (453 on road)
13. Diamond T Model 969 A, 4 Ton, G509	Derived from the 968 version, this was probably the best breakdown vehicle, at least in terms of flexibility with its Holmes			
	7,4x2,4x3	3,8	9 300	
14. M1A1 (Ward LaFrance, Model 1000 & Kenworth 573), 6 Ton, G116	These models date from the end of the nineteen-thirties when the Ordnance received its first heavy breakdown vehicle, the M1. These wer vehicles designed by Marmon Herrington using the TL 31-6 chassis and a Hercules engine. In 1937 its production was taken over by Corbit then by LaFrance in 1940 and by the tiny Kenworth company in 1941 which, in order to cope with the contract,			
	8,8x2,6x3,2	4,6	12 400	

Liberty Roads, 1944-1945

APPENDIX II

CORPS VEHICLES

Engine	Tyres	Brakes	Theoretical speed (Km/h)	Rampe (%)	Fuel tank (l)	Consummation (litres per 100 km)	Range (km)

...ellow Truck and Chevrolet who got the big contracts. Yellow Truck first made the ACK 353 for France before concentrating on the manufacture of the Jimmy, leaving the 4x4 to Chevrolet. Despite similarities ...ith the GMC, the Chevrolet 4x4 is not the shortened version. It was a 4x4 adaptation of the civilian 4x2 MR. The G-4100 version was replaced by the more basic and militarised G7100. Its all-terrain capabilities ...ere considered as being mediocre but the truck had the reputation of being pleasant to drive on the road. 168,603 were made, 169 of which were semi-trailer versions (G4113 and 7113) which were the only ...hevrolets to drive on the Red Ball by 4/5 Ton range of tractors that were in insufficient numbers.

Engine	Tyres	Brakes	Speed	Rampe	Fuel	Cons.	Range
Chevrolet BV.1001 UP, petrol, 3.85L 83hp at 3100 rpm, 4-speed gearbox	7,5x20 twinned at the rear	Hydraulic	77	65	112	26	430
GMC 270, petrol, 4.4L 104hp at 2750 rpm, 5-speed gearbox	7,5x20 twinned at the rear	Hydrovac	72	65	150	38	480
GMC 270, petrol, 4.4L 104hp at 2750 rpm, 5-speed gearbox	7,5x20 twinned at the rear	Hydrovac	72	65	150	38	480

...f production grew quickly and in the sole month of March 1942, it made 4,000 trucks, as much as the total production of the previous year. Most of the spare parts were not compatible with the GMC and the ...ngine was different, leading the authorities to cede the majority of the 197,678 Studebakers to its allies or to other service branches. It was only the lack of trucks on the eve of D-Day that explains why two ...ompanies equipped with its 6x4 semi-trailer version found themselves on French roads where they rendered great service.

Engine	Tyres	Brakes	Speed	Rampe	Fuel	Cons.	Range
Hercules JXD petrol, 5.3 L 87hp at 2600 rpm, 5-speed gearbox	7,5x20 twinned at the rear	Hydraulic	72	65%	180	50	515

...hey became the workhorse of the Transportation Corps. This was a well-suited vehicle. As with all of the Army trucks, it was progressively stripped of its civilian origins, such as the closed cabin. 11,104 Autocars ...nd 2,751 White were made during the war, an umber that should be compared with that of the 500,000 GMC.

Engine	Tyres	Brakes	Speed	Rampe	Fuel	Cons.	Range
Hercules RXC petrol, 8.7L 131hp at 2400 rpm, 5-speed gearbox	9x20 twinned at the rear	Pneumatic	70	30 (with semi-trailer)	227	73	320

...ederal made tractor. Although similar in appearance, it differed in numerous areas such as the steering box. 8,119 were made.

Engine	Tyres	Brakes	Speed	Rampe	Fuel	Cons.	Range
Hercules RXC petrol, 8.7L 131hp at 2400 rpm, 5-speed gearbox	9x20 twinned at the rear	Pneumatic	66	30 (with semi-trailer)	227	94	250

...ot to opt for an all-terrain vehicle. M425 (H-542-9 for the manufacturer) would have to tow the 16-foot semi-trailer and the 25-foot M426 (H-542-11). IHC used the KR11 as a platform, a civilian model that was ...ill being made for the Allies. All of the parts made by Timken, WC Lipe, Modine and Bendix had already proved their reliability. Production, therefore, was launched just a few months after the contract was placed. ...een to maintain standardisation, the M425 was abandoned in 1944 (4,640 were made) and IHC manufactured 11,000 M426 with help from Marmon-Herrington and Kenworth for the final assembly. The 4x2 was ...ore than a stop-gap solution and rendered immense service in the various theatres of operations.

Engine	Tyres	Brakes	Speed	Rampe	Fuel	Cons.	Range
IHC Red Diamond-450-D essence, 7.4L with 143hp at 2600 rpm, 5-speed gearbox	M425: 9x20 twinned at the rear / M426: 11x20 twinned at the rear	Pneumatic	58	M425: 41 / M426: 25	2X151,5	108	386

...ractor that was more common in the United States. The truck was a straightforward adaptation of the civilian 512 12 Ton which allowed it to go into production as early as the end of 1940. 5,871 were made ...nd adopted by the Army who had, up to that point, neglected the use of tank transporters. Despite its qualities, its trailer tractor design made it unstable and the twelve small wheels of its trailer became easily ...ogged down.

Engine	Tyres	Brakes	Speed	Rampe	Fuel	Cons.	Range
Hercules DFXE diesel, 14.7 L with 178hp at 1800 rpm, 4-speed gearbox	12x20 twinned at the rear	Pneumatic	35	25	570	125	450

FREIGHT AFTER THE IMMOBILISATION OF UNITS (ID, FD ART BN, AA BN)

...ore than 12,000 of these trucks which had dumpster, tanker and bridging variants used by the Engineers. This truck, the manufacturer of which boasted its aesthetic qualities, was also a reliable machine which ...oped well when its load capacities were exceeded.

Engine	Tyres	Brakes	Speed	Rampe	Fuel	Cons.	Range
Hercules RXC petrol, 8.6 L with 119hp at 2200 rpm, 5-speed gearbox	9x16	Pneumatic	65	65	227	78	250

...resent within the Army. The HXC engine was replaced a new, more powerful HXD. Thanks to its flexibility and endurance, its use became generalised within the artillery, Ordnance, Engineers and even the infantry. ...his meant that production rates had to be speeded up and the Ordnance also ordered the White designed truck that had been originally turned down, followed by Brockway who were invited to sub-contract to ...orbitt. Thus, 16,000 trucks left the factories.

Engine	Tyres	Brakes	Speed	Rampe	Fuel	Cons.	Range
...& B: Hercules HXD petrol, 14 L with 202hp at 2200 rpm, 4-speed gearbox / ...W: Hercules HXC petrol, 12.7 L 180hp at 2150 rpm, 4-speed gearbox	C&W: 10 x 22 / B: 12 x 20 Twinned at the rear	Pneumatic	58	50	C&B: 303 / W: 283	Corbitt: 94 / White: 63 / Brockway: 117	Corbitt: 320 / White: 480 / Brockway: 240
Mack EY petrol, 11.6 L with 159hp at 2100 rpm, 5-speed gearbox	10x22 Twinned at the rear	Pneumatic	55	36			

...n November 1942. Its production was delayed and it was at the tail end of priority vehicles. Thus, only 2,000 were made before the end of the war which explains why only the artillery was equipped with this ...ehicle.

Engine	Tyres	Brakes	Speed	Rampe	Fuel	Cons.	Range
Mack EY petrol, 11.6 L with 159hp at 2100 rpm, 5-speed gearbox	12x24	Pneumatic	50	65	605	93	600

MAINTENANCE VEHICLES

...owever, made it ill-suited to off-road use and this was a handicap for reconnaissance missions, but was most certainly not for a police role on roads where its reliability was appreciated.

Engine	Tyres	Brakes	Speed	Rampe	Fuel	Cons.	Range
WLA petrol, 0.74 L with 23hp, 3-speed gearbox	4x18	Cables	95	60	12,5	6,3	190
MB petrol, 2.2L with 60hp at 3820 rpm, three-speed gearbox	6x16	hydraulic	105	60	57	15	380

...win-boom crane that allowed it to be used in any place or on an overturned wreck. 6,420 of these wrecker trucks were made

Engine	Tyres	Brakes	Speed	Rampe	Fuel	Cons.	Range
Hercules RXC petrol, 8.6 L with 119hp at 2200 rpm, 5-speed gearbox	9x20	Pneumatic	65	60	227	78	265

...uilt a production line and expanded by taking over the building of an... attraction park in the Washington State. 1943 saw the appearance of a new version M1A1 (series 5 for LaFrance and 573 for Kenworth), the main difference being in ...s Gar Wood entirely motorised, and not partially, crane. It could lift 9 tonnes and winch 21. A complicated vehicle, it required a well-trained crew. 2,030 M1 were made and 3,735 M1A1, low numbers that can be explained by its high cost ...12,000 dollars) and its manufacturing difficulties.

Engine	Tyres	Brakes	Speed	Rampe	Fuel	Cons.	Range
Continental 22R petrol, 8.2L with 128hp at 2400 rpm, 5-speed gearbox	11x20	Pneumatic	72	60	373	94	320

Liberty Roads, 1944-1945

APPENDIX III

The steering, known as "Recirculating ball" made by Saginaw and which still surprises many collectors, was immediately well received by the military. It allowed for easy driving and was precise and smooth, something that was ideal for novice drivers. This was without doubt one of the GMC's strong points.

The Warner made five-speed Clark 204-VO gear box was developed specifically for the military market. Mounted directly on the clutch housing and coupled with the two-speed transfer case, it provided a greater power range. A traditional four-speed gear box had been mounted on the first ACKWX to be made but did not permit a satisfactory road cruise speed.

The weak point of the GMC was its clutch. It has been blamed on a fragile design and its civilian origins, but in fact the had driving by farm boy drivers was the cause of most of the breakdowns. Most of them had not driven before and did not master correctly a basic single-disk dry clutch. When badly used, its single membrane spring could be easily desynchronised.

The ACKWX 353 was equipped with a civilian 91hp, six-cylinder 256 type engine that had a tendency to overheat. It was, therefore, replaced on the following series by the 6-cylinder 4.41 in-line 270 engine with an output of 104hp that was more powerful and better cooled thanks to an improved water circulation. It was specifically designed in twenty days for the CCKWX. Designed to last 16,000 km, the engine was then totally removed. It was regularly updated. Starting with the second series of CCKW in 1942, the ventilator was modified. In 1943, the 3199 and 3020 variants were introduced, improving the interchangeability with the other engines in service, in particular those of the Jeep and Dodges and preventing the oil from frothing as it had on the previous versions. Update kits were delivered to the Ordnance Corps which makes it almost impossible for a collector to find an original truck today. In 1944, Zenith 28AV11 carburettor was replaced by the 30B11. In 1945, final version of the engine, the 3731, went even further towards standardisation.

GMC AFKWX 353 6x6 2 1/2 ton.

The very effective and innovative Bendix "Hydro-Vac" braking system did not equip the first models and was only introduced in 1942. All of the first series ACKWX, CCKWX and CCKW had to make do with a more basic assisted pedal that required a certain "dexterity".

The 30 gallon fuel tank of the ACKWX was replaced by a 40 gallon version on the following versions. On the 352 version, it was placed across the chassis behind the cabin. Equipped with two caps, it could be filled from either the right or left.

GMC DUKW 353 6x6 2 1/2 ton.

Liberty Roads, 1944-1945

APPENDIX III

The engine hood with two side panels on the ACKWX 353 was replaced on the CCKWX 353 by a simplified single panel that offered easier access to the engine whilst also being cheaper to manufacture.

The spare wheels were designed to be mounted in twos at the front end in order to increase grip on difficult terrain. On the 352 version, they were mounted on the rear of the driver's cabin.

The Budd type metal platform was also the subject of austerity measures and the steel was progressively replaced by wood before being partially reintroduced at the end of 1944.

GMC CCKW 353 6x6 2 1/2 ton.

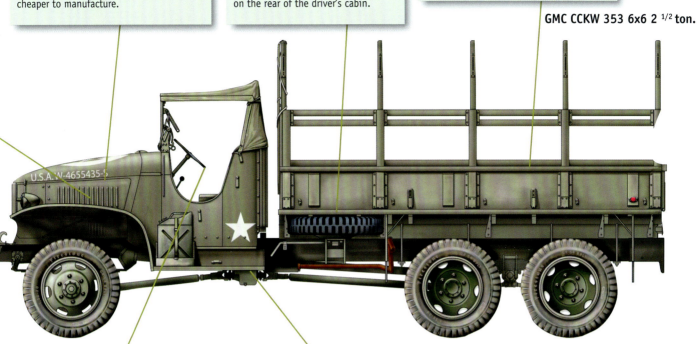

The civilian cabin (984 type) common to all the light trucks made by GMC and Chevrolet were initially simplified starting in 1940 (types 1574 and 1608) with the deleting of the chromed door handles, interior trimming and ashtray before being abandoned starting in 1943 for a more spartan canvas covered cabin (the 1619). The introduction at the end of 1943 of a redesigned version of the hood was a remarkable progress that led Bryce J. Sunderlin to say that it "offered protection from both the rain and the heat whilst providing at the same time good visibility". Also, contrary to the Jeep and Dodge vehicles, it was systematically delivered with its complete winter equipment kit that included side and rear covers... although this did not make up for the lack of a heating system.

Drive was initially ensured by a Timken-made "Split" type drive axle that was mechanically well made but which bent a little under the tonnage, having been designed for lighter 1 ½ ton trucks. Beginning in February 1941, the GMC also received the new GMC "Banjo" type drive axles that were designed with two things in mind: they had to be easy to manufacture and simple to maintain. This axle was oversized to cope with the heavy weights. However, Rubino says that it was "very cheap and did not cope with being driven at high speeds and its transfer case broke". The Split and Banjo axles were made up to the end of the year and worked well alongside each other despite the fact they did not share many parts.

JEEP Willys MB 1/4 ton

Transmission was ensured by two Spicer free floating axles. A lever allowed to engage the forward free floating axle. The chassis was the conventional ladder type with beams and traverses made by Midlands Steel. However, even though they were made by the same manufacturer, the Willys and Ford chassis differed, their attachment points were in the same positions and did not cause any problems concerning maintenance. A dry single plate clutch made by Bock & Beck (model 11123).

The MA model ten-gallon fuel tank was replaced by a 15-gallon version on the following versions, to which was added the famous strap for the 5-gallon jerrycan.
The Jeep was equipped with a 441 or 442 engine from the Willys range, known under the name of "Go Devil". This was a water cooled four-cylinder in line engine with a 60hp output and a 2199cm^3 displacement. On the Ford model, the only differences were found in the connecting rods and the way of fixation that used studs or bolts. Its performance was its strong point when compared with the modest 49hp of the Bantam 40 BRC. It was also more reliable and straightforward.
The Warner T 34J three forward and one reverse gearbox was bolted directly onto the Brown Lipe or Spicer transfer box, offering the possibility of a high range at high speeds or when on difficult terrain with direct drive, and a low range on the road with transmission.

JEEP Willys MB 1/4 ton

Liberty Roads, 1944-1945

APPENDIX III

Chevrolet 4X4 1 ½ ton.

International K7, 2 1/2 ton, 4x2, G-541, used mainly in 1942-44 on New York's docks.

Federal 94x43 4X4 4/5 ton and trailer.

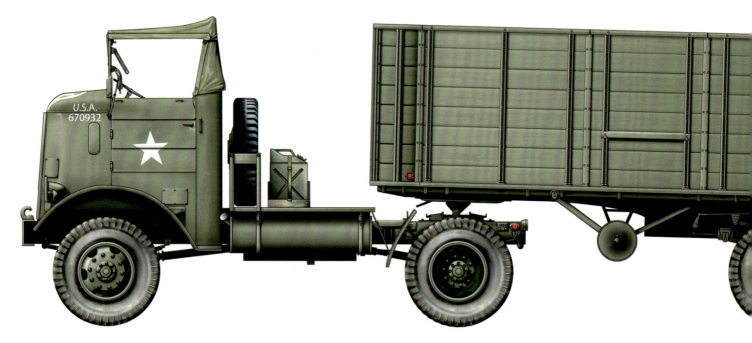

APPENDIX III

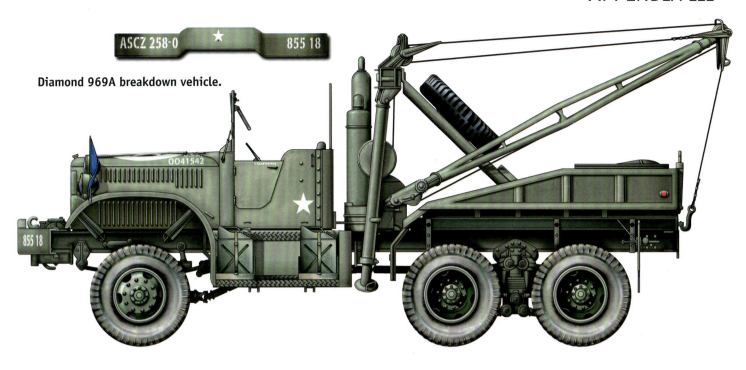

Diamond 969A breakdown vehicle.

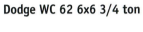

Dodge WC 62 6x6 3/4 ton

Autocar U 7144 T 4x4, 4/5 ton

Liberty Roads, 1944-1945

BIBLIOGRAPHY

PRINTED SOURCES

— *Truppenführung*, 1934, published in Bruce Condell & David T. Zabecki (ed), On the german Way of war, Stackpole books, 2009.

— War Department. *Field Service Regulations*. United State Army, 1923. Government Printing Office, 1924.

— War Department. *Tentative Field Service Regulations*. Field Manual 100-5 Operations. Government Printing Office, 1939.

— War Department. *Field Service Regulations*. Field Manual 100-5 Operations, 1941. Government Printing Office, 1941.

— War Department. *Field Service Regulations*. Field Manual 100-15 Larger units, 1941. Government Printing Office, 1941.

— War Department. *Field Service Regulations*. Field Manual 100-10 Administration, 1941. Government Printing Office, 1941.

— War Department. *Staff Officer's Field Manual*, FM 101-10 Organization, Technical & Logistical Data, 1941. Government Printing Office, 1941

— War Department. *Basic Field Manual, FM 25-10, Motor Transport 1942*. Government Printing Office, 1942.

— War Department. *Field Service Regulations*. Field Manual 100-10 Administration, 1943. Government Printing Office, 1943.

— War Department. *Standart Military Motor Vehicles, Sept.1.1943*. Government Printing Office, 1943, in US Army Vehicles WW2, data and illustrations of all vehicles in US Army service, 1941-45, Booklands Books, sd.

— War Department. *Staff Officer's Field Manual, FM 101-15 Traffic Circulation & Control*, 1944. Government Printing Office, 1944.

— War Department. *Field Manual, FM 10-35, Quartermaster Trucks Companies 1945*. Government Printing Office, 1945.

TESTIMONY AND MEMOIRS

— Antipenko, NA, *In der Hauptrichtung*, Militarverlag der DDR, 1973.

— Martin Blumenson (prés.), *Patton Papers*, Houghton Mifflin and Co, 1972,

— Omar Bradley, A *Soldier's Story*, Henry Holt, 1951.

— Dwight Eisenhower, *Crusade in Europe*, Doubleday, 1948.

— Bernard L. Montgomery, *From Normandy to Baltic*, Hutchinson, 1948.

— Patton, *War as I knew it*, Houghton Mifflin Coy, 1947.

OFFICIAL PUBLICATIONS

The historic services of the US Army went to huge lengths to publish, at the end of the war, the Green Books (the official history of the US Army during the Second World War). These large, difficult to read books, were written by military historians in an often austere prose. Together, they make a mine of information and statistics even if, naturally, certain embarrassing questions for the US Army remain in the background and that they now appear outdated. They nevertheless remain remarkable works which are totally indispensable and the richness of which forces admiration. In this collection there are several books which deal in detail with logistics.

— Army Service Forces, *Logistics in World War Two*, Government Printing Office, 1948.

— Martin Blumenson, *Breakout and Pursuit*, CMH, 1961 trad. fr. La Libération, ed Charles Corlet 1993.

— Joseph Bykovsky & Harold Larson, *The Transportation Corps, Operations Overseas*, CMH, 1957, vol 3.

— Hugh M. Cole, *The Lorraine Campaign*, CMH, 1950.

— Gordon A. Harrison, *Cross Channel Attack*, CMH, 1951.

— Benjamin King, Richard C. Biggs & Eric R. Criner, *Spearhead of logistics, A history ot the US Army Transportation Corps*, CMH, 1994

— Ulysse Lee, *The employment of negro troops*, CMH, 1963.

— Richard M. Leighton and Robert W. Coakley, *Global logistics & Strategy*, 1955 and 1969, 2 vol.

— Maurice Matloff, *Strategic planning for coalition warfare 1943-44*, CMH, 1959

— Charles B. Mc Donald, *The Siegfried line campaign*, CMH, CMH, 1963

— Charles B. Mc Donald, *The last Offensive*, CMH, 1973

— Constance McLaughlin Green, Harry C. Thomson and Peler C. Roots, T*he Ordnance Department*, CMH, 1955, 1960, 1968, 3 vol.

— John D. Millett, *The organization and role of the Army Service Forces*, 1954.

— Erna Risch, *The Quartermaster Corps*, CMH, 1953 and 1955, vol 1 &2.

— William F. Ross & Charles F. Romanus, *The Quartermaster Corps, Operation in the war against Germany*, CMH, 1965

— Roland G Ruppenthal, *Logistical Support of the armies*, CMH, 1953 & 1959, 2 vol.

— Alvin P. Stauffer, *The Quartermaster Corps*, CMH, 1956, vol 3.

— Harry C. Thomson and Lida Mayo, *The Ordnance department: Procurement & Supply*, CMH, 1960

— Chester Wardlow, *The Transportation Corps*, CMH, 1951, 1956 2 vol.

STUDIES

— RO Atkinson, *An army at Dawn*, Henry Holt, 2002

— Philippe Bauduin, *Quand l'or noir coulait à flots*, Heimdal, 2004.

— Emile Becker & Jean Milmeister, *Marquages and organisation*, sl, sd.

— Emile Becker & Guy Dentzer, *GMC*, sl, sd.